Golf Swing Secrets... and Lies

Six Timeless Lessons

Compiled and Written by
Michael Hebron

Contributions by
Bob Bush

Learning Golf Inc.
St. James, New York

Published by Learning Golf Inc.

Production by CyberColor Inc.

PRINTED IN U.S.A.

Library of Congress No. 09620214-3-1

Dedication

The sport, game, and business of golf have two important groups, amateurs and professionals. Amateurs are mentioned first for several reasons. They were the games first players. Amateurs have been the heart and soul of the game from its inception and without amateurs, the sport would not have professionals.

We could say, in some ways, that amateurs own the game. They purchase greens fees, pay membership dues, buy golf equipment, accessories, and golf lessons. Amateurs travel on golf vacations, are members of golf leagues, and are on the committees that govern play. Amateurs also volunteer their time to run many tournaments that raise money for charities.

Amateur golfers all over the world are the game, and this book was written with them in mind. It was also written for professionals who support the amateur's efforts to enjoy their participation in golf at every level, while fostering respect for the game's history and traditions. As the game of golf grows and welcomes new golfers, its values and traditions should not be left behind.

As I became more interested in golf instruction, I was also curious about how I could improve someone's ability to learn the game. After I started my journey in this direction, I soon discovered that there was a difference between trying to help a golf swing and trying to help a golfer. **When you try to help a golf swing, unfortunately, you can win or lose, but when you help a golfer you always win!**

The culture of golf is often divided by **"Low"** and **"High"** handicaps. In this culture there are people who **can** and people who **cannot** play what they themselves believe to be good golf. Unfortunately, in the **can** and **cannot** culture, everything is set up for people to believe that their lack of progress is because of their own shortcomings and they start looking for more "how to" advice. People rarely evaluate how they have been trying to learn. **"How useful is my current approach to learning the game?" "Should I be using a different approach?"**

Only in a few circumstances is someone's "golf IQ" used to recognize what **cannot be taught**, but can clearly be learned through self-discovery. What follows is dedicated to improving self-discovery skills, learning potential, increasing core golf knowledge, and developing workable approaches for long-term progress.

When a learner's self-discovery efforts are **encouraged** and **supported** by advice givers who avoid "How To" advice, our earliest motion patterns can plant the seeds of progress. This book is dedicated to helping reader's discover their possibilities for growth, **through growth oriented choices**. Learning changes behavior. Changing behavior has always happened best through self-discovery and when the opportunity to integrate self-discovery is overlooked, learning will be incomplete or fragmented.

This book is dedicated to helping people discover **they can learn** without "How To" advice or excessive "trying." Hopefully every golfer's self-esteem will soar as they are reminded that learning and growth **through self-discovery are pleasurable and natural experiences.**

In closing, perhaps the instruction industry should be seen as caretakers of swings and games, not teachers of.

MICHAEL AND TRACY HEBRON – 1970

"Michael, what is the secret to this water shot?"

"I'm not sure Tracy, let's read Dad's book"

- **Connecting – Cause and Effect is Learning**
- **Repeating – A Desired Effect is Progress**
- **Second Nature – Is Mastery**

Secret: **The "largest room" is the room for "improvement"**

A Vision

I have an interest in stimulating a change, probably a major change in how things are done when it comes to learning golf (or any skill). What happens now has gone on for a long time. Study after study I refer to in this book have found it's time to move away from "how to" directions and expert models, if people want to experience long-term progress.

What will happen in the future may be more a political question than educational, depending on someone's point of view. But because of what we are now learning about long-term progress, **environments for learning** in all walks of life are changing everyday. Golf instruction should take advantage of these findings and move in the same direction to improve the culture of how people are currently trying to learn golf.

It's been said it takes talent to make progress, but I feel it may also take some courage to move away from "how to" directions and expert models that are always available. (After all, much of the advice is coming from friends and perceived experts). Golfers should trust in their own capacity to learn what is relevant for their swing, and avoid someone else's "how to" advice, when long term progress is their goal.

Golf's First Lie: Believing that someone else has the secret to better golf for our swing and game. Unfortunately it seems everyone we play golf with has some little secret that sooner or later turns out to be a lie. This or any other book (or instructor for that matter) cannot really improve your golf, **only you can.**

Secret: **Instruction information that leads to long-term learning is not telling people how to play or swing. As with an effective approach to learning any skill, golfers must learn to discover and define for themselves what is relevant and what is not about the swing motion they are trying to learn.**

When humans have an **"**internal language**"** that **self-discovery** communicates with , we are learning patterns of motion. Someone else's "how to" directions for learning motion can often be a foreign language, that we do not fully understand. Also, in the past, most sources of golf instruction advice have focused on perceived defects. In **my vision,** becoming aware of "core golf knowledge" is a more valuable insight.

Warning: Much of the information golfers receive and use to improve their golf games with, has historical background, but no rational explanations. This information is justified with "objective" reasons that suggest it will "minimize" or "optimize." These justifications also have no rational foundations. At times, people are rationalizing to justify the historical status quo.

I am aware suggesting a **self-discovery** approach for learning golf that avoids "how to" advice, will run into cultural resistance from some golfers. But everyone learns from self-discovery and we cannot say that about "how to" directions. Some of the information golfers receive is often influenced by what seems to be teachable, while over looking "core golf knowledge". (i.e. Golf's Physical Basics). **In my vision**, the personal knowledge needed for long-term progress is always available from self-discovery skills.

The guiding principles that govern the necessary knowledge for making long-term progress are in Golf's Physical Basics and the Nature of Learning, and have been from the games inspection. (Note the similarities in the pictures of golfers from the 1800's to 2001 throughout this book).

Note: MIT Professor Marvin Minisky said, "**Seymour Papert** is the greatest of all living educational theorist." "A Vision" was based on notes I made while reading Seymour Papert's book, Mindstorms.

Dear Readers,

Welcome to Golf Swing Secrets.....and Lies, and thank you for your interest in this book. Golf has been played in some form for over 500 years, but on the other hand formal or written golf instruction has only been with us for a little more than 100 years. From its inception, the culture of golf instruction has been founded mostly on "how to play" suggestions with little common ground. Its seems everyone we know has some tip or secret. Unfortunately, these tips are all different.

From day one most golf tips have asked golfers to either copy some expert's swing, or to follow a variety of "how to" suggestions, while overlooking the importance of core knowledge about golf's environment. A golf environment that has not changed significantly for over five hundred years..

This book was not written to be the final word on learning golf. In the future, I am sure more information about making progress will come to light. Perhaps, what is presented here will help golfers, who are not happy with their games today, make progress sooner than later. I hope readers will see this work as a book filled with "what if" insights that explore all of the possibilities for learning to make progress, that go beyond "how to" directions. I.e. **"What if you started looking for different ways to make progress?"** The thrill and exhilaration players feel after good shots can be experienced by every golfer, who improves their awareness and learning skills.

Most of this book is non-linear, compiled like a series of short stories so readers can open to almost any page and read on. Golf may be the most non-linear game on earth, and I feel every golfer should be given the freedom to be guided, not led by information. This book is geared to this reality. There are no systems, methods, or "how to" lists that can help golfers develop skills personal in nature that lead to long-term learning. ***"Telling is not teaching, and listening ain't learning.", Bob Barkley PGA MP.*** Golfers who are not happy with their progress need more learning power, not more "how to" lists.

As I've said, when I became more interested in golf instruction, I was also curious about what could improve someone's ability to learn the game. I soon discovered there is a difference between trying to help a golf swing and trying to help a golfer. When you try to help a golf swing, unfortunately you can win or lose, but when you help the golfer you always win.

This book is geared to helping golfers gain more learning power. By finding ways to improve our learning potential, we can improve our performance potential. Unfortunately, progress in golf never follows a straight path that is defined by "how to" advice. To experience long-term learning requires core golf knowledge and unexpected insights.

I would like to thank Bob Bush for his help with this book. Bob is an engineer and technical consultant to many of the golf industries premier companies, including True Temper (a leading shaft manufacturer). Bob worked for True Temper for over 30 years and was a member of the 5-man team that designed and built the 1st Iron Byron for True Temper in 1966. Iron Byron (a mechanical golf swing machine) was built to test equipment within 1/2 % of accuracy. Bob Bush has as much, if not more accurate information about the swing than any other source of which I am aware.

Some insights that Bob and other engineers point out about a golf swing include:

- **Deceleration accounts for up to 13% of a swings force.**
- **Pulling forces (tensile forces) that go down plane start the down swing.**
- **Because of the design angles of the club, efficient impact alignments have not changed in 500 years.**
- **Up to 70% of an efficient swings force is delivered by the right (or trailing) shoulder.**
- **Body mass accounts for less than 1% of initial ball velocity:**
- **Centrifugal force causes the clubhead mass to droop through impact.**
- **Centrifugal force does not cause the shaft to go in-line with the left arm, player generated rotational forces do**
- **The longest drivers of the ball, impact the ball above the center of gravity of their driver, have a high launch angle with little back spin.**
- **Bob and other experts answer many questions in Chapter Four.**

What we may know, is never as useful as what we can learn about what we know. For example, every golfer knows they must strike the ball, but every golfer who wants to improve must learn to apply effective force at impact for the shot at hand. Golfers often and mistakenly attempt to make progress by focusing on a personal flaw and overlook learning the principles that influence every efficient golf swing. The first question is never *"How do I improve my ball flight?"*. **A more relevant first question is *"How does anyone improve ball flight?"*.**

People who make long-term progress in golf, are aware of effective principles before moving onto personal habits that they want to change. Most corporations and small business that succeed are founded on similar principles but individualize their approach to a wide range of clients. Successful golfers also have individual approaches to the game, but at the same time they have all used the same principles for over five-hundred years.

Progress is possible for every golfer. However current studies to which I will refer, suggests that some golfers may have to change how they have been trying to learn before progress arrives. Along with changing their approach to learning, it would help golfers, who are not happy with their games, to realize a basic truth; everything we do to improve is done to improve the alignment and application of force through impact. **The only possible way to improve ball flight is to improve the alignment and application of force through impact! Nature's truths know no other possibilities.**

I.e. For a doctor to improve a surgical incision; for a show horse to improve their ability to jump; for a baseball batter to improve their hitting; the alignment and application of force must improve. Improving the flight of a golf ball is no different. Golfers must learn the application and feel of raw power. Most importantly, they must avoid using effort.

Playing by the rules is important. When golfers hear rules they often think only of the United States Golf Association and their rule book. While the USGA is responsible for the rules of the game, "The Laws and Principles of Motion and Force" (LPMF) are responsible for efficient, repeatable golf swings and any force they create, use and apply. The LPMF are at the foundation of every good golfers game. World-Class golfers play both by the rules of the LPMF and the USGA's rules of golf.

What follows offers straightforward information about golf's environment, the swing, playing the game, and more importantly long-term learning. This book is not based on any guru-like golf advice. In the past, conventionally "how to" suggestions to golfers have focused on symptoms of poor golf – rather than on the prevention of unworkable habits. The ideas presented here come into play everyday, not only when a golfers game is ill.

I have found that golfers do not need to be told what to do. **Golfers who want to improve need to become aware of golf's environment and discover for themselves what creates consistent ball flight for them.** It can help anyone's progress to recognize that only when we experience something different (i.e. a different approach for learning) is something better possible.

In an age that offers "quick fixes" for everything, this book takes its time. I've tried to give readers new and unexpected insights that can help turn information into knowledge. Some may say there is a lot of information here, but you will discover there is a common thread that runs through all of it. **The main message is that self-discovery and problem solving skills are more valuable for learning than someone else's "how to list".** Instruction is normally geared to helping people. **However I have found that instruction becomes more valuable when it is geared to helping people help themselves.**

Today, unfortunately, humans are a species that run mostly on other people's information, whereas at one time we relied on our intuition and natural selection. I am suggesting that golfers who want to improve, go back to using intuition and self-discovery skills, and avoid "how to" advice from well meaning friends. ***"Words can only communicate between people who share the exact same experience"*** **- Alan Watts**

To improve our ability to learn golf (or any body motion) it also helps to know the difference between engineering and reverse engineering. Engineering is used to build and create, but reverse engineering is used to adapt to environments. Golfers who make progress have clearly adapted their swing and style of play to golf's environment.

Golf's environment or "Golf's Physical Basics" are as old as the game itself. Until we change 1) the design angles of the club, 2) ballistic properties of the ball, 3) the field of play, 4) the human form, or 5) the principles of motion and force, these basics are non-negotiable. For over 500 years people who have learned to play good golf have used reverse engineering principles to adapt their swing and style of play to Golf's Physical Basics. Physical basics and reverse engineering will be discussed in more detail later.

Information about playing the game and swinging the club is given here, but this book should not be seen as a thesis on either the swing or the game. Golf Swing Secrets...and Lies, was written to be a **guide** for people who want to learn to improve their golf. There is a difference between a **teacher** and a **guide**. There is also a difference between a **"how to"** list and a book that is a **guide.**

Guides do not stand next to us, they are usually out in front, leading people to unexpected insights that go beyond their current impressions. A guide can empower someone. Some teachers do not (some teachers only ask us to memorize, and give tests). Hopefully Golf Swing Secrets.....and Lies will cause golfers, who are not pleased with their progress, to rethink how they have been trying to improve, and also refine their current perceptions of a golf swing.

Mark McCormick, a successful businessman and sports agent, who wrote What They Don't Teach You at Harvard Business School, said *"In fairness to Harvard, what they don't teach, they cannot teach, and that's the positive use of your insights and perceptions to get where you want to go"*. McCormick referred to this as *"street smarts"*, and he said Harvard does not teach *"street smarts"*. Golfers must use their own insights and perceptions (I.e. "golf smarts"), when long term learning is the goal. "How to" instruction can not teach golf smarts. Golfers must learn what instruction can not teach and what self-discovery can.

Perception of information is where all learning has its start. There are a number of studies referred to in this book that show the quality of a motion is founded on the accuracy of the brain's perception of that motion. As Leonardo Da Vinci said, *"All knowledge (true and false) has its origin in our perceptions."* It may be difficult to learn what works for you, but once you learn, it becomes less difficult to do the right thing.

Today, there are many who believe golf is more of a learned skill than a skill that should be taught. I am one of them. ***"Learning how to learn is at the heart of all education – whether the goal is learning to read, add fractions or throw a ball." – Richard A Magill.***

At times what is written here may seem repetitive. While there are some points made several times, this was done by design. As I feel that some information should be emphasized repeatedly. I also felt this book would be more useful if an idea was presented several ways, realizing that everyone has their own best way of learning to make progress.

The Importance of Core Knowledge

The ideas given here have an audience of golfers who have yet to develop the core golf knowledge and needed insights that lead to long-term learning in mind. *"It takes knowledge to gain knowledge. Some preparation for learning is important. Readiness to learn means already having core knowledge about what you are trying to learn more about"*, E.D. Hirsch Jr. - American Educator, Spring 2000 issue.

Many golfers receive tips not founded on core golf knowledge. Many golfers do not have the core knowledge to integrate instruction information in a workable manner. Without core knowledge, golf instruction in any form is normally not useful for long term learning. The skills of problem solving are prerequisites for progress in all walks of life, (including golf), and are clearly founded on some core knowledge of the domain in which these skills are being applied. Most golfers who are not improving, don't lack the ability to improve, they lack the core knowledge to support future information. **Talent, in my view, is not as important to progress as memory of success founded on core knowledge.**

What follows has been organized into six chapters that could be read as six separate books.

Chapter One — Self-Discovery Yes, "How To" Advice No!

Chapter Two — Golf's Six Awareness Lessons

Chapter Three — Golf's Five Physical Basics

Chapter Four — Questions and Answers, Secrets and Lies

Chapter Five — The Nature of Learning and the Nature of Golf Instruction.

Chapter Six — Extra Credit

I believe readers will find that all Six Lessons in Chapter Two are timeless in their value. Chapter Three discusses Golf Physical Basics that have not changed from the games inception. Classic and timeless hints from 1857 to 2000 are also listed at the end of Chapter Three. In Chapter Four, Bob Bush and other respected industry experts answer questions about the application of force. This chapter also has a section where tour players answer questions about what they "feel" while playing golf. Chapter Five discusses the Nature of Learning motion patterns as well as perception and listening skills. Chapter Six, Extra-Credit, may not be required reading. It contains details that may be of interest to only some readers, but could help every reader. I give my impressions of Homer Kelly's book, The Golfing Machine, in this chapter. Reading Chapter Six would be similar to reading extra credit material in a classroom setting.

Often, information in books is mistakenly compared to what a reader already believes he or she knows. But, long-term learning rarely arrives on the back of comparisons. More often than not, long-term learning comes through the eyes of new or unexpected insights about prior information. When reading what follows, you may want to look at what is given here as an opportunity to change your view of making progress. Breakthroughs in learning often come from discarding past perceptions of information for new ones, and not from new information.

People ,who are not happy with their progress, often listen to the shouts life has to offer and overlook the whispers personal insights provide. It has been said that a little insight can speak volumes. So don't over look the importance of something because it seems small. The information in this book may change as you change your perceptions of what is important.

Should golf instruction be a setting for sharing what someone knows, or a setting for developing the tools for using a golfer's insights in different ways? I would suggest the later, a setting in which the freedom to turn information into personal insights exists. **People, who want to experience long-term learning, must consider using information about learning the game of golf and not only information about the golf swing.**

I no longer suggest using drills or expert models when long-term learning is someone's goal. (Many studies now show they are not as effective as they were once thought to be.) Every golfer is an individual. Drills and expert models are founded on "how to" advice that can fragment self-discovery and personal insights. (The value of drills and expert models are discussed in Chapter 5).

Where Should Learning Start?

Discovering what we must learn first is always the initial stage of progress. This is followed by applying the most useful learning methods for the results you want. Golf Swing Secrets...and Lies is organized with this in mind. This book first presents information golfers should be aware in the form of Six Awareness Lessons, followed by suggestions for learning that information and turning it into knowledge that's personal in nature. Jack Nicklaus said, *"The best thing Mr. Grout did for me was I learned to teach myself."* **(Chapter Five may be the most important chapter in this book).**

"The knack of" anything – can't be taught – but there are environments where the "knack of" comes more easily to people. Golfers, who experience long-term learning have used self-discovery skills to develop "the knack of" good golf, and not someone else's "how to" list. As Paul Runyan said, *"Touch can't be taught, it can only be acquired."*

You will find "quotes" are used through-out this book, they are meant to encourage readers to think a bit. When trying to learn a physical motion, to be informed is not enough. Information must be experienced and personalized, if we are going to learn from it. Hopefully, the quotes and ideas that follow will cause readers to develop new insights that improve pathways to progress. The information here is meant to be embellished and expanded and used to create personal insights to learn from.

Thanks again for reading Golf Swing Secrets...and Lies. Keep in mind people who make and keep making progress are always in the process of growing and becoming. Thomas Jefferson once said, *"The pursuit of – is the genius of America."* Progress in golf is both a physical and intellectual pursuit. Both golfers and their sources of instruction information often pass over the intellectual. Progress intellectually lays the groundwork for any physical progress of which golfers may be capable. Our ideas and perceptions about golf clearly influence what our body can do. **This cannot be overlooked.** At best, progress in golf could be described as an imperfect struggle, often hampered by the misinformation and poor concepts many golfers exchange with each other, and remember, *"Education can inform, but can't create experiences."* – E. Sail.

Secret: **Experiencing efficient motion is the only door to learning efficient motion.**

Paradox: Some things are learnable, but are not teachable.

"If you are tired of always changing your golf tips, try changing your approach to learning golf." – Fred Schumaker. I once heard Dick Harmon say, *"People need three bones to make progress in golf – a wish bone, a funny bone, and a back bone."* How true! Fred and Dick are both respected PGA Professionals whose advice we should take to heart. I have filled this book with over 600 pictures of golfers from the 1800's up to 2001, to demonstrate that Golf Physical Basics and the alignment and application of force have not changed over time. This insight should not be overlooked.

Best of Luck pursuing your goals in golf,

Michael Hebron -

P.S. A "Breakthrough" in learning is a breakout, or breakaway from a past point of view. "How To" directions are trying to **manage** learning, but self-discovery and awareness skills – **lead** learning in the direction of long term progress. Golfers who want to improve should be given the opportunity to be lead, not managed.

Acknowledgments

Before moving on I want to say thank you.

I would like to thank every golfer who has asked for my advice over the years. From beginners to tour professionals, I have learned from all of you. When golfers were pleased with their progress it gave me the encouragement to put my thoughts to paper.

A big thank you to the many experts from both the golf industry and disciplines beyond golf who have always been generous with their time and patient with my questions. A special thanks to Bob Bush and of course the late Sir Isaac Newton. (Newton's Biography is in the glossary)

The PGA Education Department, National Golf Foundation and other organizations have given me many opportunities to share information in clinics, seminars, and workshops for over thirty years. All of these assignments have helped develop my ideas, and I thank everyone.

To the members of the PGA and LPGA, both playing and teaching professionals who have showed an interest in my work. Thank you, your support has always been appreciated.

A special thank you to Jeff Stephens and Jaime Gerson, without their countless hours of help, this book would not have been possible. Also to Harold Snedcof, a new golfer and PhD from Brown University, thanks for your support, guidance, and editing skills. Thank you to Jerry Hogge of Methodist College, his insights and advice about this book were invaluable.

A big thank you to Bob Pellegrino and CyberColor, Inc. for producing a book I am proud to have my name on.

To my family and friends, both in and out of golf, thanks for all of your support and love over the years.

- Michael

I also want to thank Historic Golf Prints #1 of Ft. Walton Beach, FL (1-800-874-0146), Golf Magazine, Golf Digest, and several photographers; Sam Greenwood #2, Stephen Szurlej #3, Tony Roberts #4, Fred Vuick #5, Paul O'Sullivan #6 and John Coppola #7, for the opportunity to obtain some of the pictures I have used in this book. Most of the pictures are from my personal library, but without their pictures, this project would not have been possible. (The number after each source corresponds with their pictures throughout the book). There are over 600 pictures in this book, dating back to the 1800's. While some pictures are very old and in poor condition, I felt it was very important to have these classic images placed next to pictures of todays golfing icons, so readers could note all the similarities.

Table of Contents

Foreword

The Game

We can never overlook the importance of:

- The green grass outdoor experience that the game of golf brings to people's lives.
- The opportunity for companionship and exercise that the game of golf provides.
- The opportunity to learn about trust and believing in ones self that the game of golf gives every player.

We should also keep in mind that some people want to learn to lower their handicaps and play good golf. This cannot happen without learning to repeat efficient impact conditions for the shot at hand. Swings do not have to be ideal, but they should be able to repeat efficient impact conditions more often than not.

The following material was compiled from a variety of sources, in the hope it could be a useful tool for any golfer who is not happy with the results they have received from their current approach for improving their golf. Golf Swing Secrets...and Lies was written to guide readers past the poor concepts and misconceptions many golfers exchange with each other about the swing, playing, and learning the game.

What follows is meant to stimulate the interest of both the experienced and less experienced golfer. To see progress, some readers like some golfers I have worked with in person, will have to set aside some of their current perceptions about learning the game. It is best to see this book as a tool that can be used to combine a golfers creativity and self-discovery skills with their hope of progress and long term learning.

Secret: **Unquestioned assumptions cause poor results that new insights often answer. It helps any golfers progress to always see themselves as a learning golfer.**

Golf Swings Waiting To Be Born

"Growing up I was always good at sports, I do not understand why I am not improving my golf", is a statement that every golf instructor has heard from more than one student. We could say, every golfer who is not happy with their progress, has a Golf Swing Waiting to be Born.

It has always been interesting to me that when most people are throwing a ball, shooting a basketball, swinging a bat, or go bowling, they use body motions that often look more orthodox than when they are swinging a golf club. Why?

Any questions about a lack of progress with golf should not overlook the following; When people play other sports, they receive fewer "how to" directions than many golfers receive when they want to improve. When people are learning other sports they use their self-discovery skills more than "how to" information. This may be one reason why some people are not learning to improve their golf. No one walks on to a basketball court for the first time and shoots the ball at the floor. The basketball net is up. When learning other sports people interact with the environment (the net is up), exploring and constructing skills on their own.

Note: Normally "how to" advice from different sources have little common ground. Several explanations of the same event make "confusion" the master.

"MIND SETS" AND CULTURES

The **culture** of instruction advice is founded mainly on giving golfers "how to" directions and the **"mind-set"** golfers often use when it comes to golf instruction is **"take charge of me, and tell me what to do"**,

I believe that this culture and "mind-set" have undermined a golfer's natural skills of problem solving. Playing good golf is solving problems as we adapt our game and swing for the shot at hand. Someone else's "how to" directions are never as useful as a golfer's own self-discovery skills, when it comes to solving problems for the shot at hand.

Any golfer, who broadens their core knowledge of golf's environment, uses self-discovery and avoids "how to" directions, will improve and find their **"Golf Swing Waiting to be Born". K**eep in mind that it takes some knowledge to gain more knowledge. Unfortunately, many golfers do not have the core golf knowledge needed to make progress.

GOLF'S BEST MENTOR—THE GAME
A GOLFERS BEST TEACHER—SELF-DISCOVERY

It has been said, "learning to play **good** golf can **be** difficult". People often use books and articles as teachers. I would suggest books, articles, and the game itself be seen as **mentors not teachers. Good mentors help people learn very little directly. Mentors are guides that can help to improve insights.** Hopefully, readers will discover what every good golfer has learned, **the best mentor any golfer can have is the course and the game. Their best teacher has always been, their own self-discovery skills.** For over 500 years, golfers who have been open to learning from the shot at hand (not "how to" directions), have been guided in the direction of long-term learning.

The game and shot at hand should be seen as every golfer's primary mentor. Not unlike how the snow, rain, and sun suggests we use snow tires, rain coats, and sun block, **its always golf's environment that suggests the most workable approach for the shot at hand**. Nature knows no other possibilities.

WHAT TYPE OF INSTRUCTION?

In life, school, or golf, what we learn can come in many forms. In golf, instruction can come from our friends, playing partners, books, videos, etc. But perhaps the first decision golfers should make is not **where their instruction should come from, but what type of instruction will lead to long term learning?**

- Is instruction an opportunity to have someone tell you what you must learn, or should it be **an opportunity for someone to help you gain some insights you did not have in the past, so you can see for yourself what must be learned?**
- Is instruction an opportunity for someone to tell you what you must do, **or should it be an opportunity to create a setting in which golfers can discover for themselves what they can do?**
- Is instruction an opportunity for the mind of one person to make suggestions and demands on the body of another, or should it be **an opportunity for the mind of the golfer to gain insight on moving the club and their own body that they did not have in the past?**
- Is instruction an opportunity for someone to tell and show golfers all they know, **or should it be an opportunity for instruction to provide and support a personal learning environment?**
- Should instruction be based on "how to do it" advice, or should it be **support for self-discovery**?

For years, both formal and informal instruction have been geared to helping golfers improve. **But, perhaps, it would be better for golfers who are looking for help – if instruction was geared to helping golfers help themselves.** (There really is a huge difference).

It has been well documented that **self-discovery** is the best road to any long-term learning, where firsthand personal experience and learning go hand in hand. Your goal should be to find ways to develop and improve your perception, awareness, self-discovery and problem solving skills. Improving these skills is the first stage of any long-term progress. If you do not see this logic, I have found that it will be more difficult for you to reach your potential.

Dr. Gordon Shaw, PhD, co-discovered how Mozart's music improved "thinking skills". Dr. Shaw wrote, **Keeping Mozart in the Mind**. This book presented studies that showed if people learned to think (solve problems), and stayed away from learning by route and "how to" directions, learning skills improved. *"We have to learn to think and solve problems for learning to improve"*, Dr. Shaw.

Can't be Separated

Secret: **Many golfers who would like to make progress, seem to be plagued by poor concepts that overlook:** ***How a skill is performed and some conceptual understanding of that skill can't be separated.***

Skill performance is not one side of a coin with conceptual understanding and problem solving skills the other side. True skill acquisition cannot be accomplished without combining concepts and techniques. The ability to repeat a golf swing that is marked by efficient motion patterns conveys a conceptual understanding of that motion.

Many people say they understand what to do to improve their golf, but often cannot execute what they say they understand. No golfer, professional or amateur, gets the same results from their swing every time. But I'm not so sure we can say we "understand" a motion, if we cannot perform that motion more often than not. (let's say, over fifty percent of the time). **Skill performance always starts with decoding (personalizing) information.** Information must first be decoded, then understood to be performed. Unfortunately, most information golfers hear and see comes in the form of "how to" directions that are in conflict with prior "how to" advice leaving golfers confused. Golfers are often fragmenting learning and slowing their progress with unfounded or poor conceptions.

When a golfer improves their core golf knowledge, they soon realize information that will be useful to their progress **is on a very short list**. The ideas and information in this book are geared to helping golfers improve both their core golf–knowledge and their learning potential, with a short check list.

Early Intervention

It is well documented that the best way to learn a skill is through early intervention and prevention, rather than fixing and re-fixing old habits. Golf Swing Secrets...and Lies intends to create a setting in which golfers learn more about cause and effect. Thereby solutions to poor habits become more attainable. By matching workable learning approaches to a golfers problems, long-term learning becomes possible.

Unfortunately, today there is a universal message people hear, read, a view, about "quick fixes" for everything from better health to their golf swing. **Any "quick fix" message that is taken to heart will hijack learning potential.** People are being told to *"just buy some tool, machine, or "how to list", and in no time a variety of skills will be yours"*. The time for early intervention for many golfers reading this book has probably come and gone. But it is never too late to develop new insights about prior information.

Secret: **Golfers who want to improve need to learn what body of information (for them) will lead to progress and what information will not.** ***Knowing the difference is one of the first steps to progress.*** **Information that golfers use often lacks the substance of core golf knowledge that guides golfers in the direction of progress.**

There is a large volume of information (I.e. quick fixes, and "how to" direction) from a variety of sources available today. People certainly have opportunities to learn something about golf, **but not necessarily something useful for improving their golf.** Progress is always founded in the quality of an individual's learning and problem solving skills. Unfortunately, "quick fixes" and "how to" directions are so deeply rooted into the volume of golf advice people hear, read, and view, that any new information a golfer may want to use, can not by itself, overcome the lack of progress quick fixes cause. Golfers must also improve their learning skills.

Hopefully **Golf Swing Secrets...and Lies** will be a tool golfers can use for:

1. Untangling poor concepts from workable knowledge and insights.
2. Recognizing unworkable patterns of motion before they do damage.
3. Learning that poor perceptions can influence any instruction or learning experiences.
4. Recognizing that progress in golf can be more of a mental than physical workout.

The volume of information to which many golfers are exposed before they spend time with me (or any source of instruction advice) will influence their future learning potential. Schools today also understand that they are not as powerful as they may seem to parents. When a child enters school, they have had several years of pre-school experiences that will influence their future learning potential. Both children and golfers repeat patterns established before they arrive at school and golf instruction settings. Past experiences for both are overwhelmingly important to any future progress they may want to make.

Useful golf instruction is often in the business of "trying to break cycles" that have regularly squashed a golfers natural curiosity and learning skills with "quick fixes" and "how to directions". When instruction provides an environment that nourishes awareness and learning skills, golfers gain tools that are not available from "how to advice". As you read on, what follows is my attempt to move golfers who want to improve away from "quick fixes". Paula Bender (learning expert), *"Poor learning patterns are difficult to change through conscious acts of intervention".*

Gullible Sportsman

At times the worlds most gullible sportsman seem to be golfers. We often hear golfer's explaining the reason for their newfound success is the new putter or driver they have just purchased. Or, golfers give some explanation about a new tip or gimmick, as the reason for their improved play.

Why then, the following week do these golfers return to shooting their normal higher scores? If some club, tip, or gimmick were the reasons for improved play, why didn't their improved play continue?

A new club, tip, or gimmick often accomplishes little more than a temporary change in a golfers mental state. Golfers using new gimmicks, new clubs, and different tips, mentally move away from past poor results for the time being. Golfers simply become more relaxed hoping for improved results.

Many golfers (the gadget seekers and tinkers) are consistently trying new products and tips. They seem to be always looking for **"what's out there"** that will improve their golf. But **"what's out there"** never seems to fit or work very long. These gullible golfers continue to look for help in the wrong place, **"out there"**.

Secret: *Improving golf skills starts "internally". "What's out there"* to be purchased does not lead to long-term progress, or even short-term success. *Good golf can't be bought.* But gullible golfers seem to overlook this. Good golf starts internally with improved concepts, and personal feels. As golfers become aware of core golf knowledge and what will improve their learning potential, progress soon follows without gimmicks, tips, or new clubs.

THE EDUCATION OF A GOLFER

The phrase *"The education of,__________"* is used in the title of many books and articles that discuss the learning stages of successful people. These books and articles often start with a sentence similar to the one I found in Sports Illustrated September 25, 2000. *"Perhaps the education of Tim Hudson (Oakland A's baseball pitcher) began last season in Boston, after striking out Nomar Garciaparra."*

These break through moments, when lasting education starts, are difficult to pin point. Progress and education are both a journey. When saying the education of someone started, we must always begin with, **"Perhaps"**.

"Perhaps", my own education in golf (and I feel I'm still learning) started in 1967. That was the year Gene Borek; a fine player with wonderful insights about golf and life hired me to be his assistant. My second week on the job, Gene suggested that I start a journal and write down my thoughts on playing, and giving lessons every week. Thirty years later I'm still making notes.

Gene McMaster suggested that I read **Drawing On the Right Side of the Brain** by Betty Edwards. I also read, **On Learning Golf** by Percy Boomer. Craig Shankland, another fine player and great businessman, (who had more energy than any golf professional 1 had ever met), hired me in 1969. **Any of these events is "Perhaps" where the education of Michael Hebron started.**

It's difficult to say where or when any golfers long-term education starts. But its not difficult to say, "**Long Term Learning"** does not start with "quick fixes" and "how to" directions. Some golfers have learned to play good golf, are you one of them? If not, by reading what follows, **perhaps** the golf education of some readers will start, followed by long-term learning.

The intent of what follows is not to try and teach any specific golf techniques (Secrets). This book was written to offer suggestions and ideas for achieving **long-term learning**. My intent is to present readers with some **guiding principles** that will give them insights about **core golf knowledge and self-discovery skills**. Ideas and suggestions from studies about effective **skill acquisition** will also be discussed.

Knowing **common concepts** (core knowledge) and **what skills** are needed for successful learning, are essential steps for planning any **workable sequence** of information for skill acquisition. The more the sequence of information is matched to individual golfer's skills, the sooner progress and long-term learning arrive.

Some readers may not accept all of what is given here. I am not trying to present ideas with which everyone already agrees. The goal of this work, and perhaps its value, is to stimulate every golfer's desire to explore, use their own self-discovery skills and move away from all the "how to" advice well meaning friends offer. **It is important to note that some studies discussed in this text show "how to" lists, drills, and expert models are not the most efficient tools for learning any body motion, including a golf swing.** What follows suggests that golfers who want to see more progress, should be aware that successful approaches for long-term learning are based on the players ability to adapt to golf's environment, while using self-discovery skills and core golf knowledge.

Note: When the term **Secret** is used, it makes reference to the ideas and the information in this book that are not widely (in my view) used by golfers who are trying to improve.

The term **Lie** in the title, and when used in this book, makes reference to the poor concepts many golfers exchange with each other (I.e. "The hips are the golf swing main source of power". This of course is not true). The term **Lie** also refers to the misconceptions golfers often take away from all of the advice they read, watch, or hear. There are fewer references to **Lies** than **Secrets**, simply because I am not familiar with all the poor concepts and misconceptions of golfers who read this book have. What now follows, are similarities as old as the game.

Alignment and Application of Forces, 1890's to 2000

For as long as THE GAME has been played, good golfers have used similar (if not the same) alignments to apply efficient force through impact. Efficient alignment and application of force has always been based on golf's environment and the shot at hand (Golf's Physical Basics© as they are referred to in this book). Nature knows no other possibilities. Note the similarities over the last 100 years pictured below.

Secret: **If we could look into the future, these efficient alignments of force would not be any different, unless our human form, or the games Physical Basics were to change.** ***"The mechanics of an efficient method, are the same as ever; the fundamentals remain unaltered."*** **- Bobby Jones 1930's.**

1896 | 1900 | 1920's | 2000

1910 | 1920's | 1950's #1 | 1930's

1910 | 1915 | 1980's | 1900's

1920's | 1915 | 1950's #6 | 1950's #6

1920's 1950's #1 1990's 1920's

1920's 1940's 1990's 1920's

1915 1920's 1940's 1950's

1940's 2000 1940's 2000

2000 1900 1930's 1980's

Important Insight's

A golf club does not move until the golfers body parts move first. Some approaches for helping golfers improve are telling golfers "how to" move their bodies. But I have found that giving golfers body thoughts can slow progress. On the other hand, after golfers become aware of where a golf club should be aligned through impact, learning is always accelerated.

While it is true that a golf club does react to the bodies moving parts, when it comes to **long term learning**, a stronger case can be made for golfers **learning where** the club should be aligned through impact for the shot at hand. **I have found that it is more useful to know what to do with the club, than trying to focus on "how to" move body parts.**

Note: Information in this book is based on the following observation. Every golfer is an individual, with different body types, coordination abilities, and strength levels. Also, a golfers body rarely feels or reacts the same way every day. On the other hand, during the swing, the length and weight of the club and ball location are constants that never change. **I have found that golfers make faster progress by learning about efficient golf club alignments, than when they focus on "how to" move body parts.**

It helps progress to recognize that golf clubs are built and designed for impact alignments, not address alignments. Clubs are built with (1) their handle end **angled forward** of the clubface, and (2) their shaft coming up from the ground on a roof like **inclined angle**, Golfers who want to improve can use these two shaft angles as a blueprint for the alignment and application of force through impact for most shots in a game of golf.

A golfers body parts will normally make the appropriate motions after the golfer learns that golf clubs should be returning through impact with (1) the clubface behind the handle end of the shaft, (2) on an angle that is parallel to the original lie angle that the club occupied at address.

Normally, instruction advice does not have to talk very much about how golfers should move their bodies **after golfers know efficient impact alignments for the club and the shot at hand.**

Riddle's that can't be solved

Riddle's that can't be solved, is how some golfers describe their swing or playing golf when they are trying to improve. These golfers are often people who look to someone else for answers that only self-discovery can answer. **Golfers who want to improve and experience long-term learning should look for guidance, not answers from advice.**

There are many golfers who want to simplify golf's curriculum, as they look for ways to stop their struggle to make progress. Golf's curriculum is non-negotiable, (it's founded on Natural Law's and the principles of motion and force). **But what can always be made more effective, is our approach for learning golf's curriculum.**

It has been said that we can learn from everything we do, but often this is not the case. On the other hand, by seeing "advice" and "suggestions" as **guides and mentors** and ourselves as the **teacher**, we can indeed learn from everything we do.

What follows was written to expose readers to principles that can guide golfers in the direction of long-term progress and core golf knowledge. It is information that can be used to develop the tools for learning efficient **golf techniques that are personal in nature**. By seeing the word **lesson** as a noun, rather than a verb, we can improve our learning potential. People take golf lessons and people are given golf lessons, but often do not learn the **lesson** that people need to learn.

WHAT MAKES A GOOD EDUCATION?

On January 14, 2001, the New York Times ran an editorial by Randle C. Archibold that discussed, "What makes a good education?" In this column there were several points made by experts and the writer about learning, that golfers who are trying to improve should consider. As you read, it may help your insights about learning golf to replace "a good education" with "useful instruction advice" (uia).

Dr. Botstein, *"a good education (uia) develops the skills of critical thinking (I.e. problem solving)."*

Robert Silvirs, *"a good education (uia) develops some intellectual curiosity about learning and exploring possibilities for understanding".*

Leon Botstine, *"A good education (uia) helps you learn to ask useful questions".*

The column points out that a good education (uia) should include gaining the tools to form judgments and options independently, with critical reasoning.

Webster's Dictionary defines "education" as:

1. Training by which people learn to develop and use their mental and physical process.
2. Gaining experience, or a stage of instruction
3. The fruit of training or instruction.

It also defines "learn" as:

1. To acquire knowledge by study or experience.
2. To come to know or become aware.

Note: That the word "teach" is not used in the definitions of education or learn. To educate according to Webster's definition and experts from the field of skill acquisition, is **to train for a particular end**.

"Teaching is really the art of ***assisting discovery****."* - Mark Van Doren

"Trust only the ***moment****, not words. Trust the* ***event****, not words."* - Alfred Adler.

"When we interact with ***nature****, we are dealing with things* ***first hand****, and we get rules and standards that service us for life."* - John Burroughs

The information that follows hopefully will give readers unexpected insights about learning golf and some tools for progress. Learning golf should be a **celebration of imagination** for both players and their sources of instruction. Learning to improve ones golf should be a series of **"what ifs"**, in the pursuit of progress that the lure of good golf creates.

Note: Progress is an "awakening" that is always **personal in nature**. The more we look for the most useful information for making progress, the more our search will narrow to **Golf's Physical Basics© and self-discovery skills.**

DO WE LEARN TO PLAY OR PLAY TO LEARN?

Secret: **If you have been trying to improve, and have not, the answer is, we must play to learn! This answer holds the reason for long-term progress.**

Studies have found when we are engaged in **"True Play"** the genes in our nervous system are totally involved with gathering the kind of information that long-term learning if founded on. Webster's Dictionary defines **Play** as – **movement giving full play to ones imagination.** During **True Play**, we are playing full out with our imagination, interacting with the environment. The greater the variations, the more opportunities there are to learn.

During **True Play**, children run and fall, jump and skip, catch and miss, throw long and short, kick high and low, swing and miss, or hit, as they interact with the environment. During **True Play**, infants crawl and fall, touch, taste, look around, pull themselves up, as they interact with the environment. **True Play** has no rules or "How To" directions from advice givers.

Studies show we do not really learn motor skills, like typing, swinging, throwing, etc... However, the body can be **conditioned** to perform these and other motion patterns. Almost magically motion patterns can go from being uncoordinated one day, to being acceptable motions the next day. "We get it!" But what is often overlooked is how "we got it", and why some people take so long to make progress.

During **True Play**, the genes in our nervous system are encoded with and are learning information about dynamic balance, timing, sequencing, touch, sight, the environment, eye-hand coordination, etc. Because our genes have the genius of being both learners and teachers, they can take all the information they have learned during **True Play** that is personal in nature and condition the body to perform motion patterns.

During **True Play**, all actions, workable and unworkable, and the reactions to these actions are being encoded into our genes. (Unworkable motions are very valuable for learning). During **True Play**, our genes have the opportunity to adapt to a variety of problem solving opportunities, which in turn improves ones ability to condition the body to perform different motion patterns. **The skills and tools of adapting, not "How To" directions, promote long-term learning.**

When golfers use self-discovery (True Play), with total freedom to investigate and interact with 1.) golf's environment, 2.) golf's physical basics, and 3.) the shot at hand, our genes are encoded with information that is personal in nature about timing, sequencing, dynamic balance, etc. for future use and long-term learning.

Secret: In the end, we must play (True Play) to learn.

How many times in our lives have we said or heard, "I just played a round with it, and I came to figure out how it worked." Studies have found **True Play** to be the only place to start long-term progress. It can help anyone's progress to recognize learning and conditioning are not the same. We all can be conditioned to perform efficient motion patterns when we use the information that is gathered during **True Play**.

As I've said, the culture that many golfers learn and play golf in is divided by high and low handicap golfers. This culture has golfers who have "got it", and golfers who "don't have it." In this culture of "got it" and "don't have it" golfers often attribute their unsuccessful learning experiences to their own perceived disabilities. Poor shots are tied to their belief that they are not "getting it". Within this culture, golfers define themselves in terms of their perceived limitations and this is unfortunate.

Rarely do golfers relate their lack of progress to "how" they have been trying to learn and assume that they are just not "getting it". **I have found approaches to learning the game that use True Play and self-discovery skills, while avoiding "how to" directions, always promote long-term progress. Keep in mind that we play golf not "golf swing", and when we are learning by experiencing True Play, we can gain long-term progress**.

Chapter One

Self-Discovery Yes, "How To" Advice No!

Isaac Stern (premier violinist)

About himself,
"I was enormously lucky to have a teacher who let me learn how to learn. He did not make me play the way he did."

About his students,
"I am not here to teach you how to play. Learn to think for yourself, to have "wow" moments. Join the art with the mind to move from a possibility to a certainty."

Note:

This book or any other book about the game cannot possibly give a "working knowledge" of good golf. The ideas and suggestions given in this book are geared to helping readers gain insights for long-term learning that "how to" advice does not offer. As Henry Cotton (winner of 1934, 37, 48, British Open) said, *"You must develop your own style, as you follow general principals. Discover what is useful to you and what is not. Tips from others work for only a few days."*

For years some golfers, who have tried to improve with "How to" advice, overlooked the value of learning core golf knowledge and using self-discovery skills. Today individuals who have studied learning, have observed that golfers who are aware of core golf knowledge and use self-discovery, improve faster than golfers who use "how to" advice. I realize it may be difficult for golfers who have used and believe in "how to" suggestions to put their trust in self-discovery, but again anyone who does, will be rewarded.

Secret: **For any golfer—The most valuable lesson is becoming aware of and learning what can not be taught by someone else.**

Malcolm Thompson (Educational innovator for over thirty-five years) found that students improved learning by 35% when encouraged to explore on their own. These results were documented by Columbia University in 1995. Task Streams, Founded by Thompson in 1991 transformed learning environments into student centered environments where teachers act as mentors, providing pathways to progress that encourage students to "explore", "construct", and "discover" skills on their own.

Early History of Improving

The genesis of the game is really unknown, but the first written evidence of people playing golf appeared in records of the 1457 Scottish Parliament. At that time playing golf was said to be "interfering with the practice of archery", and laws were passed to stop this perceived threat to Scotland's national defense. Since the very existence's of these laws gives evidence golf was so well established in Scotland by 1457, the game must have had its start years before. Records indicate golf came to America late in the 1700's (1779 in New York, 1786 in Charleston, South Carolina) with the game taking hold by 1887. There was one club in America in 1888, five years latter there were 16, and by 1900 there were 1,040 golf clubs in America.

Today, the professional game is being played at levels thought unthinkable a hundred years ago. Some **early progress** in golf's level of play was noted in a book written in 1912, today considered one of golf's important classics, The Royal and Ancient Game of Golf edited by Harold H Hilton and Gordon G. Smith. This beautiful, leather bound book published in London contains a complete history of the game up to 1912. In this classic, Hilton (who won The Open as amateur in 1892) points out, while the Scott's took to the game before the English, the level of play improved when the people from the south (as he called the English) started to play. The English played differently than the Scot's, who had been playing long before the English. Hilton noted the English played **without the burden of traditional information and with a free mind**. (I will also be asking readers to use an approach to learning without traditional information and a free mind.)

"Hilton" believed John Ball (who at the age of 14 finished 6th in The 1887 Open and the only player at that time to win the British Amateur and the Open in the same year 1890) was the best example of the new and improved approach to the game. John Ball was so good, he was looked upon as a phenomenon who could only be admired, not imitated (sounds like Nicklaus and Tiger). In 1893, John Taylor's play in The Open marked the next era in the history of the game when its standards of play **improve**. Scientifically what Taylor started, Harry Vardon carried on, and James Braid consummated. In Hilton's view, Vardon was the best with the "guttie ball", and Braid the best with the new American rubber core ball. Let us now move away from early history of improvements and on to information people today can use to improve their golf, while keeping in mind useful instruction normally improves insights by changing poor concepts.

Improving Learning and Performance

As I have said, when any golfer wants to make progress, **the first question should never be " how can I improve my ball flight?** There is a more fundamental question all golfers must answer first – **"how does anyone improve their ball flight?"** There is only one way, and it's discussed here. Many people believe that a sign of wisdom is **asking the right question**. I have found that golfers who are not making progress often ask the wrong questions. It's how we form questions, that sets the tone for progress.

Secret: Useful instruction is not about giving people the right answers, it is more about helping people learn to ask the right questions. Useful instruction changes insights. *"Learn the means to education, not things."* - R. Emerson

By improving our learning potential we can improve our performance potential. Hopefully Golf Swing Secrets...and Lies will be a useful tool for improving learning potential, and when it does, learning to play the game and long-term progress become less difficult. Some of the information here will encourage golfers to become aware and learn from their own actions. *"I do not think one person can tell another person how to move various parts of their body to produce a powerful golf stroke."*, Theodore P. Jorgensen of the University of Nebraska.

Golf instruction can be written for many reasons. This book was written to give people who are not happy with their golf, some reasons to **rethink** how they currently perceive a golf swing, and **refine** how they have been trying to improve. It was written with the hope that it could make a difference. Some of the information in the book is based on studies and research done at a variety of locations including;

True Temper, Titleist, Harvard, University of Chicago, Yale University, University of Southern California, UCLA, and New York University. I have also learned from other's in the field of golf instruction, Greg McHatton, Hank Haney, Jim Petralia, Mac O'Grady, Dr. Jim Suttie, Chuck Cook, Jeff Gschwind, Chuck Hogan, Bob Rotella, Dr Richard Coop, Fran Pirozzolo, Ben Doyle, Paul Runyan, Homer Kelly, Fred Shoemaker, Dave Pelz, Gene Borek, Carl Lohren, and my son Michael, to name a few. No one grows and makes progress on their own, we need the support and knowledge others can provide. I thank everyone who has helped me.

For over thirty years I have been very fortunate. I've enjoyed what I have been able to do in golf, and during this time golf has been very kind to me. Kinder in some ways, than anyone could possibly expect: Receiving National PGA awards in 1990 and 1991, writing other books golfers have enjoyed, and being asked to give workshops and clinics to other PGA instructors over the years in places such as: France, Italy, Spain, Switzerland, Canada, Japan, Sweden, Finland, British Colombia, and throughout the US. But one of my most fulfilling experiences has always been the opportunity to work one on one with club golfers. It has also been rewarding to work with playing professionals, some of whom have won the US Open, Masters, PGA, World Series of Golf, PGA Club Pro Championship, European Open, LPGA and PGA Tour tournaments. Please note that I said work with them, I did not teach them. There is a big difference and I believe that is one of golf's **secrets**. By the way, there is also a good chance I learned more from them than they learned from me.

It is accurate to say there are many golfers unhappy with the progress they make when they try to improve. I have also heard, "One man can make a difference." A book is not a man, but my hope is that the information offered here can make a difference in the games of people who read it. **Golf instruction books are normally written to help people. This one was written to help people help themselves, and there is a huge difference.** *"Schools that fail have not given students the skills of acquisition for learning."* – Richard Riley U.S. Secretary of Education

As an instructor, I moved away from using "how to" suggestions in the late 1980's, and started using **awareness and self-discovery approaches in my lessons**. The feeling I have at the start of a lesson today is very different than I had years ago. Today, I feel like Tiger Woods playing in a mini tour event. I know golfers will make progress, when they use awareness and self-discovery skills. There really is no comparison between a golfer who develops insights that are personal in nature and a golfer who walks away from a lesson with a "how to list". The difference in learning potential is huge.

Secret: **Using a "how to list" is looking outside ourselves for answers, where self-discovery looks inward to where long-term learning is born.**

I began reading studies about self-discovery approaches for learning over fifteen years ago. I soon realized that any "how to" approach is just a reflection, and like reflections in a mirror, they are not authentic or real. Using "how to" lists can give the illusion of progress. Current studies by Dr. Eleanor Langer of Harvard and others discussed in this book indicate why. Golfers who want to improve need to be aware of what Golf's Physical Basics require for the shot at hand, and avoid all the conflicting "how to" advice friends offer. It's **the shot at hand that clearly defines what to do , not "how to lists."**

A lot of my reading and questions about golf were done because of my interest in improving my approach for helping people learn golf. Also, because of my feelings for a sport more and more people have come to believe is the greatest game of all. You could say, most of what I have done in golf was for self-improvement. I am not looking for followers, but if you like what is being said, please come aboard.

What is presented here can help people learn to play a game that is easy to care for in ways that words often cannot describe. But by seeing the look on someone's face after they flight a ball for the first time; or by seeing the joy of companionship a child and parent experience during a round of golf; or by seeing the excitement of reaching one's goals in golf soon replaced by deeper feelings of accomplishment; you may come to understand what words cannot describe about the game of golf and why I enjoy working in the profession I do.

Each of the six lessons that follow were written to give readers the opportunity to see learning golf through the eyes of—what if?

• **What if** I developed a more complete picture of what to do, without someone telling me "how to do it?

• **What if** I gained new insights about swinging, playing, and learning golf, without someone else's how to suggestions?

Because nature knows no other possibilities, golf has five physical basics that have not changed in over five hundred years. I am suggesting learning to use these basics is best done by combining the nature of learning with information about golf's enviroment.

Paradox: Some things are learned better when we don't try to teach them.

"Bobby Jones realized that if he was going to play at a championship level, he would have to work out his own problems." - Cary Middlecoff

Instruction Should be an Anchor – Not Just a Life Preserver!

In all of sport – there are very few motions that can look as simple and easy as a effective golf swing. The club swings back, in, and up over the one shoulder, then down, out, and around over the other shoulder as the ball flies off. People are attracted to golf for many reasons. One, at first golf really does not appear to be too difficult to play. After all, the young and not so young play, the tall and short play, and people with and without much sports experience play. The game seems to say, "COME ONE – COME ALL".

"Why from day one has golf been so difficult for many, if not most people?" One answer is that golf is an imperfect game, played by imperfect people. Often such a response does not meet the needs of most that ask why is golf so hard to learn? There are many answers, but there is one that may be over looked: The Volume of Golf Instruction Information. **Golf looks so simple everyone tells us what to do – so simple everyone believes they know what to tell us to do. Golfers often overlook instruction information (from any source) should be an anchor, not just a life preserver used in emergencies.**

There have always been golf books to read along with golfing friends who feel they can help each other. People have said, "why not listen and read" – believing they cannot hurt what they are currently doing. **But this is not true!**. In fact, lots of damage can be done, especially to new golfers who often use misconceptions and poor concepts. There is a saying, "Well begun is half done" and all golfers should start with accurate information– something many golfers who are playing today did not.

Secret: **Is there a best way to learn and play? Yes, and that best way will always be – the easiest way for that one player to learn and apply golf's few essential elements.**

Colotaine Rapaille, the French born Medical Anthropologist points out the lasting effect of **well begun**, *"There is always a first time we imprint something, and (we) create mental highways. We make use of these highways all of the time and they soon become unconscious. There is a little window of time, when we first imprint ideas."* (May 7, 2000—N.Y. Times Magazine)

Original impressions of how easy learning the game and swing will be, soon change after people start to play or try to improve. "What's wrong?" "It looks so easy." "Good players make such smooth swings, I should be able to do that." "Anybody should be able to play a reasonable game." Sooner or later people discover that it's a bit of a journey from where one starts to where one would like to be in golf. Everyone also discovers their journey is filled with secrets and lies. **Perhaps if golfers would change the approach they are now using to learn with, more people would experience long term learning.** I suggest, FIRST STAY AWARE, THEN DISCOVER, THEN CREATE.

The more things change, the more they stay the same, seems to be an accurate description of what happens to many golfers, who go from golf tip to golf tip. The more frequently golfers make changes, using this or that tip from their friends – the more their games seem to stay the same. These golfers often see little or no progress from the time and effort they put into their golf. The approach to instructional information here in **Golf Swing...Secrets and Lies** tries to combine the nature of learning with the nature of golf. **Some long-held beliefs about the golf swing, and how people have been trying to learn golf that are based on poor concepts and misconceptions are going to be discussed here.**

Several times a year I am asked, *"So Michael, what is the latest idea or newest theory in golf instruction?"* It helps long-term learning to know a new system or method could be developed by anyone (and it seems a new one comes along every year or two for golf). But there is a big difference between a new system based on someone's opinions and having the action itself (the swing) reveal what is true about it. **One problem with traditional approaches to instruction: it's often trying to transform a not knowing state into a knowing one, by using someone else's "How To Do It list".** Using someone else's "how to" advice can cause players to lose any personal understanding of and feel for what actually causes the results they see after impact. It always helps progress if we don't chase knowledge, and let knowledge come to us. *"There is more wisdom in things as they are, than in all the words we use."* - A. Watts

Bobby Jones said, *"Any number of players have devoted enough thought, time, and practice to become reasonably good, if they had only started out with an accurate conception of what to do. Often there is a confusion of ideas making intelligent progress impossible."*

Mr. Jones does not need me or any other golf instructor to say we agree with his assessment of why many golfers are not making progress. But I agree with him and will tell you why. When a golfer, professional or amateur, is not playing at the level he or she believe they are capable of, more often than not they are using poor concepts or a less than useful perception of what must be done to execute the shot at hand. These poor concepts and perceptions are often based on misinformation or incomplete information. As Bobby Jones pointed out, intelligent progress without accurate information is difficult if not impossible.

W.R. Chambers in 1862 said, *"When observing others play, golfers often acquire false ideas and erroneous styles, difficult to shake off, and acquire a right style afterwards."*.

Golf, like life, has some **secrets**. Golf has also taken on some misconceptions that have slowed the progress of some golfers who want to improve. When a player who is not making progress, becomes aware of what was once overlooked, he or she can move on. But often **this is not the case with misconceptions. When a player is misled and a misconception is being used over and over, the damage to their game becomes difficult to discard.**

What this book can do is help you change your perception of the information which you now use to play or improve your golf with. For anyone who has been sitting on a plateau without seeing progress for awhile, a new perception of information is often where long-term learning starts.. **By uniting the nature of learning with the nature of golf, hopefully golfers can move forward into long-term learning and fulfillment.**

"For long-term learning, students need skills to analyze information and when best to use it, not only information."– Richard Riley U.S. Secretary of Education.. **Long-term learning comes from an incubating silence that leads to an outward expression of what is going on in ones head.**

Secret: One reason it is hard to build an effective golf swing and develop what would be called a "good game" is because there are so many different ways to swing and play. Most good golfers look somewhat different from each other with highly individual swings. But **Jack Nicklaus** one said, *"I believe all good players have a swing and game that was built on elements that were demanded by the laws of physics, even though I recognize their styles and points of emphasis may have been different."*

Good golfers have found **their own ways** of satisfying the basic principles of motion and force, which, by the way, have **balance and timing** as their first consideration. **Balance and timing are not the same old story, they are the only story and must be our first consideration, when trying to improve our golf game.**

It helps to recognize that what we do in one segment of the swing, or with one segment of the body, has an immediate and direct effect on the whole. **This cannot be overlooked**. Many golfers play a game called "hit and hope golf." They hit and hope the ball will go where they want it to go. Like all other body actions, a golf swing is a sequence of many small movements, each of which is a reaction to previous movement. A swing can be a chain reaction where one segment of a system transfers its energy to the next segment of the system. This chain reaction leads up to the most important principal of the swing's power (according to research done by True Temper Shaft Co.) **a transfer of momentum through impact.**

An **efficient golf swing** happens in a specific **space**, goes through a specific **sequence**, and over a specific period of **time**. **The time period of a swing is a form of information that is every bit as important as swing mechanics**. Golfers, at times, are like the contemporary physicist, and are still looking for their version on the unfound theory – the unfound secret. Maybe by bringing the element of swing time (tempo – rhythm) together with swing mechanics we may arrive at some previously unfound paths to progress.

Secret: **Balancing in three-dimensional space (left to right, up to down, and front to back) and swing-timing are anchors of the game, they are not just life preservers to be used in emergencies.**

FRAGMENTED INSTRUCTION AND A LACK OF PROGRESS

Today it is not an understatement to say that we have more opinions (secrets and lies) about the golf swing and playing the game than anyone could use. **When it comes to playing and swinging there really is no shortage of ideas.** This volume of information in and of itself is not necessarily bad. There are many ways to deliver a message, but when it comes to information about golf, most of it is filled with **disagreements and little common ground**. Of course this presents problems for people who are trying to improve their golf.

Who or what should golfers believe in? The instructor who charges the most? The best golfer in their foursome? The tip on TV? The latest book? The hottest new teacher? Their home professional? What they were told in a golf school? Their spouse? Everyone has advice, and all of it is different. Who or what should golfers believe?

"The Golfers Manual", a small unimpressive looking book *(3"X5")*, with only 96 pages published in 1857, is believed to be golf's first instruction book. Chapter four of this earliest written attempt to help golfers improve their play starts with; ***"Regarding golf, in no other sport on the face of the earth is there so much difference of opinion as there is in golf, each no doubt thinking their style not only more correct but by far the superior way,"* .** This quote was in golf's first instructional book written in the late 1850's and not in a book from the 1990's!

There is no limit to the amount of information available today when it comes to golf instruction. For the most part there is little agreement or common ground to be found in most advice leaving golfers asking, *"Who or what should I believe in?"* For me the question is, "what caused golf instruction to be so fragmented?" To understand one reason why I feel there has been little common ground in golf information from day one, let us take a short look into the age of some other disciplines.

Human Science: In 3300 BC writing is developed in Mesopotamia. 2900 BC the first known map is produced in Egypt. 1500 BC a book for farmers was written.

Art: In 3000 BC Egyptians use wax to set colors. In 2700 BC the Chinese make bronze artifacts.

Science: In 2800 BC Egyptian priests calculate a solar year of 365 days. In 2500 BC math books are written in Mesopotamia. In 2000 BC medical books are written in UR.

Philosophy: In 2650 BC the Egyptian books of wisdom are written. 2400 BC the first known book of philosophy is written by Piah-hotep.

Politics: In 2371 BC the worlds first empire is formed by King Sargon I in Mesopotamia.

Technology is now over one million years old and has always dealt with things people use.

Advances in scientific thinking speed up about 600 BC with the ancient Greeks in the Ionian town of Miletus, on the West coast of what today is modern Turkey. **Today science is still asking why, what, and how? These are the same questions that all golfers who want to improve ask.**

One obvious difference between golf instruction and these other disciplines is that they all have had more time to share ideas, and learn from mistakes. Formal golf instruction is only a little more than 100 years old. Science and technology and other disciplines therefore have a big advantage over golf information when it comes to common ground. **Thousands of years ago, during the early stages of math, music, writing, science, and technology etc., the world's population was not very large and people lived relatively close to one another.** As ideas came forward in these fields, people could talk to each other. Over time ideas would be refined, with information more or less coming off the same page.

Unfortunately golf instruction information did not have this same advantage. By the time golf's first instruction books were being published in the late 1800's, golf was already being played in India, America, England, Scotland, Canada, Hong Kong, Bangkok, South Africa, New Zealand, Australia, etc. However, golfers had no means to quickly communicate their ideas about golf to each other. Golfers in one part of the world had no knowledge of what golfers in other parts of the world believed about the swing and playing the game. The world of golf had little opportunity for a common ground, when it came to ideas about playing the game.

Without and common ground in swing theories, many different styles were used. The **St. Andrews** swing was very long with the grip end of the club moving in the right hand at the top of the swing. Other swings included the **Pigtail**, the **Headsman**, the **Pendulum**, the **Recoil**, the **Hammer Hurling**, the **Double Jointed**, the **Surprise**, and one even had the name of the **Disappointment**. During the 1800's players took pride in where they learned the game. There was the St. Andrews School, North Benick School, Hoy Lake School, Westward Ho! School etc. Every school had its own ideas about the game. Today, we still have one book, one friend, one instruction tape, one TV tip, in disagreement with the previous or next piece of golf instruction we may read, hear, or see.

As we can see golf information did not have the advantage of originally coming out of an approach that was built on common ground. Unfortunately most ideas golfers share with each other today are still **founded on information and tips with little common ground**. At times it seems golfers are saying, *"I know this may not be the best idea, but at least it is something to work on."*

Secret: **Ladies and gentleman, boys and girls going from tip to tip is the foundation of frustration, not long-term progress.**

R.C. Robertson 1870's, ***"In no other game is a player provided with such a staggering amount of instruction. This state of affairs is horrifying. This occurs in no other pastime."***

Golf instruction, while available in several high tech forms today, is really an infant when compared to the other disciples that influence our lives on a daily basis. Listing the age of these disciplines was done with the hope readers would recognize how young golf instruction is, and possibly why it's fragmented. **Hopefully, the ideas about Golf's Physical Basics (i.e. golf's environment) and learning golf given here will be a step in the direction of giving golfers some common ground they can use when exchanging suggestions for improving their golf.** *"There has been so much said about golf in so many books from diverse sources, and there is no end to golf books. We have had enough of them, maybe too many."* – 1899 Horace Hutchinson

LITTLE PROGRESS

The cover story of the 1998 August issue of Senior Golfer, was **"Why aren't we getting any better?"**. This well-written article by Nick Mastroni started with *"Something is wrong! Despite all the new technology for balls and clubs; 24 hour golf on television, more instruction videos; more books; more golf schools; more lessons, and in many cases, more practice: handicaps are not any lower than they were 17 years ago."* The USGA director of handicaps, Kevin O'Connor says, *"The average handicap of 16.2 for men, and 26.5 for women, has been the same for 17 years."*

The article also points out, these averages do not take into account all the golfers who do not have U.S.G.A. handicaps. Only 5.3 million of the 24.7 million U.S. golfers carry a handicap. If all golfers were included, the U.S.G.A. believes the average handicaps would be much higher. I know golf can be a hard game, but no so hard that most who play today can not break 100. For example, I know a 28 year old woman who had never played golf before 1997, shooting scores in the 130's –140's that summer. Within 9 months she shot in the low 90's, after 12 months in the mid 80's (and after 2 ½ years passed her LPGA Playing Ability Test and her PGA the following year). During this time she was made aware of Golf's Physical Basics, and did not receive "how to swing" advice.

The article quotes well known instructor, PGA Master Professional Dr. Gary Wiren, *"**there is information overkill today**. Many golfers try everything they read, hear, and see. They know 120 ways to swing. The proliferation of information can be determined."*

Another well-known instructor Shelby Futch, owner and director of John Jacobs Golf Schools said, *"**Players are not to blame** – golf instruction methods and the demands they place on students must share in the criticism. Being compared to Greg Norman's swing, when you are a 17 handicap, can be overwhelming sending any student home discouraged."*

The story also included several quotes from Dr. Ned Armstrong, a well known orthopedic surgeon from Atlanta Georgia, whose ideas and suggestions have helped many golf instructors over the years. Armstrong said, *"Golf instruction truly needs a reference point or blueprint, one that is consistent with the human anatomy and mother nature's laws. **As it is now, there is no set of standards for golf instruction.** Today's teaching methods are like branches or leaves on a tree – but what is missing is a trunk. There is no foundation from which golf instruction is based."* (Golf's environment or **Golf's Physical Basics**, presented here, could be used as anyone's blueprint for their swing and game.)

Dr. Armstrong is in favor of "what to", not "how to" instruction. He points out, if golfers knew and understood causes – they would not constantly be trying something new when they play badly. *"You don't want to get into the unfortunate cycle of always developing compensatory solutions, grasping for some better way,"* said Armstrong. *"Golfers would be much better at coaching themselves if they understood causes of ball flight. They could "troubleshoot" effectively when their swing gets out of kilter. To me, personal troubleshooting is the paramount and essence of being a good player. But concepts of swinging have become so cluttered, few amateurs can help themselves"* said Dr. Armstrong.

Secret: **When several PGA Tour players were asked what they believed the biggest differences between top amateurs and tour professionals they answered, *"Amateurs don't adapt their swings and games to current conditions as well as professionals".***

"You can teach a lesson for that day, but if you can help someone learn by creating curiosity, they will continue to learn as long as they live." - C.P. Bedford

Ballet has always been Different

Ballet dancers and golfers have both learned to move their bodies through acceptable motion patterns. Some believe ballet is more difficult to learn than golf, with performers from these two disciplines spending years of training to reach their levels of competence.

Several years ago I asked my daughter-in-law Eileen, who at the time was a professional ballet dancer with the American Ballet Theater (she was picked by Mikel Barishnakof from a junior class) to tell me about ballet classes.

It has already been said, there has been little common ground and lots of conflicting information in golf instruction from day one, **but ballet is different and always had its instruction information, you could say, coming off the same page.**

Ballet is classified into three distinct techniques, the **classic**, the **graceful**, and the **strong**. The classic had its origin in Italy, the graceful in France, and the strong in Russia. Today we have ballet schools in almost every large and small town in the world where young children are being introduced to ballet. There are well known professional dance companies like American Ballet Theater, New York City Ballet, and the Bolshoi Ballet from Russia. There are also any number of dancers, young and not so young, at every skill level taking classes every day somewhere in the world. We can certainly say ballet has broad-based participation at every age and skill level, and probably in every country in the world. **What you cannot say, is that basic instruction information for ballet is broad based or filled with disagreements.**

Note: Eileen told me that in every ballet class, school, or company in the world, the instruction information has as its foundation **the exact same fundamental principles.** There are five basic ballet positions or alignments that all dancers, (tall, short, strong, weak, young, and old) use in every class, school, or company in the world uses as the foundation for learning and improving their ballet skills. **There are also common words and language used by every ballet class in the world. Unfortunately golf instruction has never had a common vocabulary. Perhaps when you read more about Golf's Physical Basics later in this book, you will start to see some common ground for all golfers and their swings that you were not aware of.** As Dr. Harold L Kalaway, Director of Neurology at Rush Medical College in Chicago, and author of "Why Michael Can't Hit" points out, *"Neurologically, all skill acquisition is the same"* When the tips and advice golfers exchange with each other do not take this into consideration, long-term learning is fragmented. Learning golf can also be difficult because the terms in golf can mean different things to different people.

In the 1940's Percy Boomer said, *"It is impossible to build a sound game by accepting tips from everyone who is willing to offer them."*

Self-Discovery and Learning

While it is best to see this book as a work in progress, much of what is said here comes from current studies and research in a variety of disciplines. Golf can be an activity somewhere between easy and impossible, and as we commit to improving, we must discover where we should start. Exactly what should I learn first? (and this can be different from one golfer to the next) It's my hope that you will find what follows a useful **tool** for learning where you should start.

To grow, expand, and make progress often depends on questioning old or traditional beliefs. *"I am growing, expanding, and making progress."* Is there anyone reading this book who would not want to use those seven words as their answer to the question, *"How's your golf doing these days?" (I am growing, expanding and making progress).* I am going to suggest golfers who are not happy with their progress make a step forward, or maybe sideways, into self-discovery. I believe this approach will make people aware of **what will be personally relevant for improving their golf.**

Secret: **There is a law of motion upon which every efficient golf swing is founded. It states: once you create force, if you can influence the direction of that force, you can influence the direction of what the force is applied to.**

This law cannot be overlooked, it's the core principal of good golf. Perhaps readers will discover the core principal of learning good golf is self-discovery and not "how to lists".

One of the goals of what I call **self-discovery instruction**, is to make playing good golf a real possibility for any golfer. Good golf is predicting outcomes! Someone reading this book can predict the outcome of his or her swing better than the rest of us. But, results don't just happen, **there are always causes and reasons (not secrets) for the outcome (both workable and unworkable) players receive for their efforts in golf.** For example, the misalignment and misapplication of force causes unworkable shots. *"My counsel to all who love the game and want to excel – think out the connection between cause and effect."* – 1907 Harry Vardon

To say we know something, and to know the difference between **what works** and **what does not**, is not the same!

- What we know and believe may be based on a misconception.
- What we know and believe may not even be true.
- What we know and believe may not even work
- What we know and believe, we may misapply.

"To learn what we do not know is the beginning of wisdom." – Maha Stavira Sangarakshita.

Secret: **Golfers who want to improve must decide if they want to be a knower or a learner.**

Learning at times, requires putting aside what we already believe we know. The principles of motion and force are founded on **external** natural laws. Keep in mind that their application is influenced by our **internal** emotions, insights, and intuition (our beliefs).

The title of this book may give the impression that I feel golfers are always receiving information that is not true. This is not the case. But I do think some people believe that the tips they receive will be "the secrets" to better golf. Unfortunately these tips are often misinformation. Golfers can also misinterpret and misapply what they read, hear, and watch to improve their golf with.

The ideas in this book are based on the feeling that it is time for some golfers to change the way they have been trying to learn and improve their golf. As has already been noted, very little has changed in the way many golfers have tried to improve, since 1857, the year golf's first instruction book, "The Golfers Manual", was published. *"In the 1990's the average PhD thesis is nothing but a transfer of bones from one grave yard to another." J.F. Dobie* –This process is similar to the tips one golfer with a high handicap is passing on to another golfer, who wants to see progress.

When it comes to learning golf, **it's time for a change**. Current studies about skill acquisition and long-term learning support this view. It is time for a paradigm shift when it comes to learning golf and the culture of instruction. Evidence that questions the value of conventional "how to" approaches to learning should be taken into consideration. **These studies should no longer be viewed as unconventional advice from non-golf experts**. It's my view now, it was foolish to view them as unconventional in the first place. This book is my shot at moving golfers away from "how to" advice, into hints about self-discovery and awareness instruction. *"Mr. Grout taught; me how to take responsibility for my own game, so I did not have to run back to him when my game was in trouble."* - Jack Nicklaus

Golfers who want to improve must learn there is a huge difference in being ready to play and being prepared to play. Everyone is ready, but not everyone is prepared. Many golfers are hampered by tips from everyone with whom they play golf with. When looking up the definition of tip, you find: **Tip; a piece of confidential information; a secret revealed**. Look up the meaning of hint, you find: **Hint; an indication; an indirect suggestion**. This book is more about hints and guidance, than tips and how to lists. What is given here hopefully can give readers insights they have not had in the past into learning golf. In the nineteen-forties Percy Boomer said, *"Much on the science of golf has been written, little on learning golf."*

There is a real possibility that because of the current explosion in the volume of information available today about everything; (more TV channels; more books; more magazines; the World Wide Web; etc.), people could easily be turned off by more golf information. With this in mind, I have tried to make the information here **entertaining**, then **educational**, and finally, **empowering**. *"Golf instructors are vice presidents in charge of fun."* – Dick Harmon By finding **ways you can** improve through self-discovery, studies show (and I guarantee) people can have the kind of progress they have not seen in the past, and more fun playing the game. When you read ahead, you may be surprised by what Ben Hogan and Tiger Woods had to say about self-discovery.

Notice I did not say "ways to," I said **"ways you can."** "Ways to," suggests someone else is telling you how to do something; while **"ways you can"** suggests you are discovering ways you can accomplish your goals. No one else can play golf for you. Hopefully you will find the information here a useful guide. *"The object of education is to prepare people to educate themselves throughout their lives." – R.M Hutchins.* **When golfers go from tip to tip, book to book, video to video, it could be said they are fishing for ideas in an ocean of "how to information" that can make anyone feel the Golf Gods have gone crazy.**

Some learning experts believe many golfers, who after years of reading, watching, or receiving "how to" instruction information without seeing much progress, have developed an instinctive resistance to instruction. Golf Swing Secrets.....and Lies offers a different kind of golf medicine, perhaps one that will not cause any allergic reactions. Hopefully the following will be interesting reading. Some people suggest that learning should be fun, I suggest that playing should be fun, but our approach to learning should be interesting. **Golfers at every age and ability should be given ideas and suggestions that promotes interest in self-discovery.**

No golfer can reach their potential unless they use a swing that is repeatable. This makes the universal goal of every golfer who wants to make progress simply **eliminate any movements or concepts that tend to keep efficient swings from repeating. Progress in golf is normally founded on subtracting not adding motions.** What is presented here was written to point readers in a direction that gives them the tools to develop a swing that is repeatable, powerful, and uses the fewest moving parts for the shot at hand. A basic swing technique that is **athletically** and **scientifically** sound, based on Golf's Physical Basics©.

Secret: Every golfer is an individual, therefore what can lead to progress can change from one golfer to the next. **But every golfer must learn to apply effective force down into the ball before their club makes contact with the ground** (the exception is green-side bunkers). Also, keep in mind golf is a game of force and power and force are liabilities when misapplied

The principles that govern the motions of an effective golf swing are not exclusive to golf. The very same principles that govern any and all motion on earth, also govern effective golf swings. Any efforts to develop an effective swing without taking into consideration principles of motion and force normally go un-rewarded. It seems, when it comes to learning or improving one's golf, any shortcut often becomes the longest road to progress. Homer Kelly once said, *"The only useful shortcut comes from more know how – and careless beginnings can be disastrous."*

While golfers must always find ways to personalize the feel or art of effective motions, the principles of force are also needed to insure precision during the swing. Almost everything we build is some combination of art and engineering. **Any world-class golfer is an artist applying engineering principles**. David Forgan 1880's, *"Golf is a science, a study of a lifetime, in which you can exhaust yourself, but never the subject."*. The definition of science is **learning through experience.**

Learning the principles of efficient swings and their application is a step by step process. High handicaps begin growing into low handicaps by building more precision into a golfers games, and **often by simply reducing the number of tips being used, and becoming aware of**

golf's environment (i.e. "Golf's Physical Basics"). As John L. Low said in 1897, *"Golf is a game of beginnings. Each step becomes the beginning of a new series."* I.e. grip, alignment, posture, start of the swing, etc.

Secret: A blueprint for predicting outcome can start with enhancing the player's ability to influence the three elements of a golf club: its shaft, clubhead, and clubface through impact. When learning to drive a car, people are really learning to influence a steering wheel, break pedal, and gas pedal. Golf is no different, we must learn to influence a club's three elements; shaft, clubhead, and clubface. But the first step to improving how people play and swing is to combine the Nature of Learning with the Nature of Golf and Golf Instruction. **How could any approach to learning be effective if its nature was not taken into consideration first?** *"There is a difference between learning and performance." – R. A. Magill*

Cooperative Learning

Much of what is offered here is based on **Cooperative Learning**, a proven and heavily researched learning strategy. **It is an approach that is instructor oriented, not instructor centered.** I have found, and studies mentioned here, show by getting "how to" instruction off center stage, and letting golfers share the responsibility for learning it accelerates long-term learning. With Cooperative Learning, golfers are expected to carry out some tasks without direct supervision, clearly promoting personal insights and higher achievements. **Golfers, who want to improve, do better, when experts structure learning experiences with guidance and support, and do not tell people what to do.**

Cooperative Learning strategies recognize that the initial stage of effective learning is for people to realize for themselves what must be learned (golfers who want to improve, must learn an efficient alignment and application of force). Personal insights into what produces the end result you want is always the foundation of long-term learning. I once read **real art** is not only the result and fulfillment of someone's dreams, **real art** also inspire new insights and rethinking. What is given here, hopefully will cause golfers to rethink their ideas about improving their golf. Where people create personal insights, improved play is not far behind. **Note**: **Personal insights are normally the foundation of anyone's progress with golf or the arts.**

Secret: **There is a big difference between an efficient swing, and an efficient swing you develop for yourself.**

Self Modeling

Self modeling was discussed in a research paper published in the September 1999 issue of The Sports Psychologist. This paper was authored by Joanna Starek (Department of Kinesiology and Applied Physiology at the University of Colorado at Boulder) and Penny McCullagh (Department of Kinesiology and Physical Education at California State University, Hayward California).

One study (Hosford 1980) in this paper found some positive results of self-observation included increased self-acceptance, increased interest, and more openness to feedback. Another study (Bandura 1986) also found reviving past performances was the strongest mediator of skill efficiency.

Secret: **All learning requires feedback. These and other studies have shown people are more open to feedback, when the feedback comes from self-observation, than when the information is coming from other sources.**

According to Bandura (1997), one's capabilities to perform a skill are enhanced by self modeling. Starek and McCullogh's research indicated participants in self-modeling environment's performed better than the participants that took part in the study that used other modeling conditions.

Golfers who want to make progress and experience long-term learning may want to consider learning from their own swing and style of play, and avoid "how to" advice from well meaning friends. Its been demonstrated that people exposed to self-modeling exhibit higher achievement than people in controlled conditions (Schunk and Hanson 1989).

This study extended its findings to demonstrate that self-modeling is not just an effective technique for learning new skills, but that it also may be more effective then any other forms of modeling.

"After the initial shock of seeing myself flounder around, it helped. I paid more attention and focused on what I needed to do. It helped to watch myself. I really tried to remember what I was actually doing.", said one participant. (I suggest using mirrors, not "how to" directions.)

It was found that other forms of modeling most likely engaged in some form of social comparison, forming self-judgments that do not increase performance. Starek and McCullagh's research says, ***"The most important findings from this study were that there was a significant performance difference between people in the self-modeling group and people in other modeling conditions".***

Percy Boomer 1940, *"One fault in teaching golf, the teacher tries to change specific faults by using specific instructions"*. Golfers should be given the tools to make their own choices, that's what makes learning an authentic experience.

Ben Hogan and Self-discovery

Ben Hogan's name and style of play have always brought to mind a technical excellence that other golfers have measured themselves by. In 1957 after years of playing outstanding golf he wrote, "Ben Hogan's Five Lessons." This book was thought to be a classic from day one. Over the last 40 years many successful golfers, both professional and amateurs have given credit to the technical information in Five Lessons for their progress. But I find it interesting that Ben Hogan himself did not believe his success was based on some technical advantage or any "how to list".

Ben Hogan stated to me (when I visited with him in 1988) that he believed his success was based on his ability to manage the course and his game. Mr. Hogan said if he was caddying for someone who won a tournament, they would have won by 6 – 8 strokes more than they did, because of how he would have helped them manage their games in the tournament. Unfortunately the next time I was with him was when I attended his funeral in Fort Worth, Texas, in 1998.

Mr. Hogan clearly states in Five Lessons that the only way any golfer could make progress was through self-discovery and awareness. ***"If you were teaching a child how to open a door, you would teach him about the doorknob, so he could open the door himself. You would not open the door for him and then describe at length how the door was opened. I am an advocate of the kind of teaching that stresses the exact feel of movement to the player"***. Sounds like self-discovery to me.

Ben Hogan said, *"I don't deal in theory. I see no reason why the average golfer, if they go about it intelligently, can't play the type of shots a fine golfer does.* ***Like anything, it takes some learning, but learning correctly is 10 times less difficult and takes a lot less effort than the wrong way does."*** Ben Hogan talks about learning correctly, and there are many stories Mr. Hogan tells about how he experimented overtime with different grips, swings, and ways of standing to the ball. Sounds a lot like learning by self-discovery to me.

In the mid 1950's after years of what Mr. Hogan called *"digging for it in the dirt"* he said, *"As I see it, some measures, long esteemed to be of paramount importance in the swing, are really not important at all."* Ben Hogan went on to say, *"On the other hand, some other measures considered only to be of secondary importance – seem to me as invaluable.* ***Actions that cause the results you are after, are the only true fundamentals of golf."***

As we can see, Ben Hogan based his approach on finding the causes of results, and clearly believed every individual needed to discover more or less on their own what was going to work best for them.

In my view Ben Hogan discovered that 1) the club should be on plane with the clubhead behind the hands through and after impact, 2) the importance of balance and swing timing, and 3) how one stands to the ball.

Throughout his two books, Power Golf, and Five Lessons Ben Hogan talked about his discoveries for his swing and game. Hogan said when he hit shots he was proud of, he expected good results because he had been working on that shot since he was 12. "I've arrived at a set of fundamentals that accomplish a very definite purpose," said Hogan. As I see it, Ben Hogan's purpose was to have the club on plane, and his hands forward of the club head through impact and where the clubface was pointing at impact corresponded with the shot at hand.

In 1970 Nick Seitz wrote a story for Golf Digest – "Ben Hogan Today" in which he noted; early every afternoon, his leg and whether permitting, Ben Hogan will empty his shag bag and hit balls for 40 – 90 minutes, He starts with a 9 iron and works through the set, hitting basic shots, then before changing clubs will hit two different types of shots. Left or right, low or high. Ben Hogan said, *"The basic swing stays the same, but I am always experimenting, looking for better ways. I never hit a shot in competition I have not practiced. I am a curious person and enjoy experimenting."* It sounds like self-discovery to me.

The following are excerpts from six of Don Wades books: And then Jack said to Arnie, And Seve told Freddie, And Arnie told Chi Chi, And Freddie told Tiger, And Chi Chi told Fuzzy, And Fuzzy told Seve – Don calls his books a collection of the greatest true golf stories of all time.

PGA champion Dave Mark said, *"Everyone talks about how Hogan likes to practice, but he loved to experiment. He would hit all kinds of weird shots in practice rounds."*

U.S. Open champion Ken Venturi said, *"Ben Hogan was always helpful to me during practice rounds, but he wouldn't teach, he expected you to learn through observing."*

When playing with a talented assistant in Dallas, the assistant asked Hogan how he would play a shot from 150 yards. Hogan answered by hitting every club in his bag (except his putter) on to the green from 150 yards.

During a practice round on tour, Hogan noticed a young pro was always watching him and taking note of what club he would hit – Hogan finally said to him, *"It is too easy to get fooled – don't go by someone else's club selection."* Then Hogan hit a 6 iron long, short, and finally pin high.

When Nick Faldo asked Hogan for advice he replied, *"Well Nick, you are a fine player, I might only confuse you. I have always believed we are better off working it out for ourselves."*

"Hogan's secret, was that he was just more observant." – Ken Venturi

"Hogan never stopped experimenting and never stopped learning. That is what made him the consummate master of the game for twenty years." - Bryon Nelson

Tiger Woods and Self-Discovery

Tiger Woods talked freely about self-discovery and awareness during a clinic he gave at the Johnny Walker Classic in Bangkok, Thailand in November of 2000.

Self Discovery

Tiger, *"As a junior golfer I always practiced with my pop. We always played games on the range that were creative and competitive. We did all sorts of things to learn different shots".*

- *"Who could hit the highest shot"*
- *"Who could hit the biggest hook"*
- *"Who could hit it closest to a tree"*
- *"Who could make the ball jump left or right after it hit the ground"*
- *"Who could back the ball up the most on the range"*

- *"Who could make the most five foot putts"*

Tiger, *"We always tried to make the ball do different things from different situations. Today I still like to play games when I practice. In fact when I am off the tour, I prefer to practice and experiment more than play. I am always trying to do different things, just like I did when I was young with my pop. I like the challenge".*

Awareness

"On the course, ***the lie I have****, dictates the shot I will play"*

"I always listen to my body. Some days when I warm up the shots fly low, other days it flies higher. Some days the ball is drawing on other days it is fading. ***I just play with what I am doing that day".***

"I try to hit the ***inside*** *part of the ball".*

"To hit the ball longer, I take a wider stance with my right foot. This keeps my head behind the ball longer, making the swing ***release its angles later****."*

"I like to hit the ball low or flat. When I want to do this I feel like my left arm is staying ahead of my right arm through impact. This releases the club later for me and the ball flies lower."

Self-Discovery

"I was told that Hogan hit low three-woods and four-woods by trying to squeeze the ball into the ground or trapping it (hitting flyers), making it go longer and lower. I tried to learn this shot for the 1998 British Open, by turning my left hand more to the left, putting the ball back in my stance, and lowering my bodies center of gravity at address with a wider stance. When I first learned the shot, I was chicken to play it in a tournament".

Self-Discovery

"I learned to make my normal swings at 75% of my power and use 90% for longer shots. I learned when I swing all out I don't make solid contact. Which is the most important element of ball striking."

Self-Discovery

"For higher shots, I learned to put the ball more forward in my stance, and keep the back of my left hand facing the sky, as I release early."

Self-Discovery

During the 2000 PGA Championship Clinic, Tiger Woods said, *"I learned the game from the green back. My Pop said it was going to take time for my full swing to mature, but I could learn to develop a good short game right from the start."*

Tiger, *"To hit it longer, I start my head back more, then keep it back".*

During this same Champions Clinic, Jack Nicklaus said, *"Its important to keep a steady head back of the ball. Also I let my head turn under, right cheek to the ground".*

What We Don't Know

At the risk of sounding obvious, one difference between high and low handicap golfers is the swings they use, and the impact conditions they create for the shot at hand. A good golfer can also predicting the outcome of his or her swing more accurately than a less experienced golfer can. People who play good golf know where the ball should go and more often than not what must be done to produce that result.

Secret: We have all heard "What we don't know can't hurt us," but when it comes to golf, this of course is not true. What we are **not aware of** in golf can and does hurt our game and swing, preventing and slowing down any progress a golfer is trying to make.

Golf is a game that clearly rewards precision. Any willy-nilly approach, (one where the player is not aware of effective concepts or one without a effective plan) will not give golfers, gifted or not, the results of which they are capable. Golf would not be the game it is without the continual hope of doing better the next time we play. Golfers should have more than hope, but without some insights into effective golf concepts and learning strategies, people will only have hope of better play with no real plan for achieving it.

Secret: **It's more useful to your progress to hit shots, which you do not care for, and understand the cause, than to be hitting greens and fairways and not know what causes those results.**

Both our workable and unworkable shots have the exact same moment of truth...impact. **The ball blindly follows the information it receives at impact from the swing and club**. See the ball as a **computer**, the swing as a **program**, and ball flight as its **print out**. Everything players do to improve their swings should be done to have effective impact alignments for the shot at hand, (be it putts, irons, or tee shots). Its not unfair to say, that all golfers would like to make swings that can influence the flight of the ball and understand what they did while swinging the club. Keep in mind, the quantity and quality of the shots your swing will produce is founded on how you adapt to Golf's Physical Basics (golf's environment), and your awareness of what you are doing.

"Hogan realized that the only person who was going to get him to the top was himself." - Jack Nicklaus

"What we have to learn, we learn by doing." - Aristotle

Defined Information

Secret: The foundation for much of what we learn is defined and somewhat non-negotiable information. I.e. The alphabet; numbers, rules of grammar; math and science formulas; etc. When information about a subject is clearly defined, there is a good chance both the instructor's responsibilities and learner's expectations are more easily met. **Unfortunately the culture of golf instruction does not have a history of defined information.**

Good results in golf are not a moving target that any old swing can achieve. Results are specific in nature, with the outcome of the swing either what the player wanted to achieve or not. Golfers at every level of the game want the same kind of results. Everyone would like to learn how to hit more fairways, greens, make more putts, and in competition, make fewer swings than their opponents.

While defined information is clearly the foundation for much of what people have learned, the lack of a common ground in golf instruction may have slowed the progress of many golfers. If golf instruction can take some of the credit when a world-class player is winning tournaments, the instruction industry must also take a look at itself when other golfers experience a lack of progress and are not learning to improve. **We can't have it both ways.**

When people are not improving some of the reasons given in the past have been:

- Some golfers do not practice enough.
- Some golfers have unrealistic expectations.
- Some golfers do not understand it takes time to improve.

While these reasons have some truth to them, the instruction industry rarely, if ever points to its lack of common ground as one of the possible reasons for golfers slow or lack of progress.

I have done a fair amount of reading and talking to accepted authorities about a wide range of subjects over the years. This is done with the hope of improving myself as both a player and instructor. While some of what I read and talk about is golf related, much more of it is not. Human movement, motor learning, human performance, physics, and geometry are a few of the areas about which I have gathered information.

With help from George and Susan Lewis* and others, I have been able to gather a number of golf books and information on many interesting subjects and disciplines for my library. Almost every author or research team from other disciplines from whom I have learned talk freely about how they have moved away from old information they once believed and used in their work on to new discoveries and insights. One author from the field of education said *"My own metamorphosis from one end of the continuum to the other, reminds me of how important it is to accept the reality of different ways of thinking."*

Sigmund Freud said, *"The rules by which we first attempt to understand the world lead to a false views."*

Golf has always been a game where the players skills are mixed with some chance (good and bad breaks), with chance playing a role in their level of play. Perhaps this is why defined information (i.e. Golf's Physical Basics) has not been the focus for many golfers who see the results they receive from their swing and game often founded on chance, or the "rub of the green.".

George and Susan Lewis run Golfinia which is a rare golf book business in Westchester NY (914)-835-5100

Golf's Hell

The Country Where Golf is King, by Ed Laskody is a book filled with wonderfully dry humor and insights into human nature. The story's main character, Jim Blake, is obsessed with improving his golf, and with his wife's blessing he takes an extended trip to the country where "golf is king". Shortly after arriving Jim learns there is a **golf hell** that houses an instruction merry-go-round on which the golf swing is divided into parts and tips. Jim is also warned once most golfers get on this merry-go-round of tips they stay on for the rest of their golfing lives trying to improve.

Each stall on this instruction merry-go-round is labeled with a different tip, i.e. pause at the top, finish high, etc. At first Jim thinks these tips are good and overlooks the fact that they are coming from a merry-go-round in **golf hell**. These tips will only let golfers approximate a swing, and serve the hellish purpose of stopping any golfer from learning their swing.

Jim Blake sounds like many golfers who want to improve, but they are in **golf hell** hearing a lot of "how to tips" from well meaning friends. The Country Where Golf is King, comes to the conclusion that golf is a problem to be solved, not a mystery to be lived, with science as our guide.

Secret: **Science is defined as knowledge gained through experience, and golfers who gain long term progress do not use science, they do science, learning through self-discovery.**

My approach to Giving Advice

My efforts to help someone improve their approach to learning golf, is based on the following:

- Learning starts with **perception of information**
- **When it comes to progress, golfers** are more important than instructors
- **Awareness** and **self-discovery** skills are more useful than following someone's "how to do it" list
- **There is no right or wrong way**. Some ways are just more effective
- **Learning** environments are more useful than "how to" environments
- **Efficient alignment and application of force** are key principles of golf.
- Different ball flight **is only possible** when we align and apply force differently.
- **Golf's Physical Basics**, (non-negotiable for over 500 years).
- **Principles of Reverse Engineering.**
- **Balancing** is more useful than balance
- **Swing Time** (tempo – rhythm) that is steady, is more useful than over acceleration or effort

- **Structure** is more useful than softness
- **A blueprint** for the swing and shot at hand can be based on the design angles of the club
- **On-plane force** is more useful than effort
- Golf clubs have **3 elements** – shaft, club head, and clubface. All 3 (independently or together) influence ball flight
- Ball flight has **2 elements** – distance and direction
- Golf swings have **2 elements** – shape and source of power
- **Learning the cause** is always more useful than asking **why**
- There is a **most efficient** impact alignment of the shaft, clubface, and club head for a desired ball flight.
- **Sequencing**, from the most stable segment to the least stable, from a large mass to a small mass.
- Information is not as important as **innovation**
- At times **forgetting** may be a higher art then learning
- Physics, Science, and Geometry principles

Secret: *"To discover the laws of nature, there must be on assumption that rules exist. The very assumption there are rules is perhaps the most important first step. By their very nature, rules place limits on what is allowed and what is not. The view that some things are impossible is not a popular one, yet it is perhaps the most important message of natural law."* - Tony Rothman Ph.D.

- **Physics**—natural things (from the Greek word "physika"). A science dealing with nature at its most fundamental level; the search for laws that govern behavior. *"With laws of motion and force as our shepherd we will see the errors of our ways."* – Tony Rothman Ph.D. author of "Instant Physics."

Golf Use: Any old swing, or any old approach to making progress in golf does not give the results which we are normally looking for. **The individuality that runs throughout every world-class golf swing must comply with the laws of nature.** Following the rules allows efficient motion patterns, breaking the rules guarantees failure. **To know physics is to do physics**.

Secret: Knowledge of physics resides not so much in concepts, as it does in the connections between concepts. No concept may violate any other concept. I.e. your grip must match your posture, your alignment must match your ball location, etc.

- **Science** – learning , knowing (from the Latin word "scientia").
  1. Knowledge, especially knowledge gained through **experience**.
  2. Observation, identification, description, **experimental investigation** and exploration of phenomena.
  3. Knowledge of principles and the causes, especially as they relate to the physical world and forces of nature.
  4. Ability to produce solutions for problems with an **efficient system of rules**.

Golf use: A golfer should **experiment** to gain knowledge of causes that produce solutions with a system of rules, for the shot at hand.

- **Geometry** – to measure land (From the Greek word "geometrein").
  1. Measurement and relationship of points, lines, angles, surfaces and solids.
  2. The branch of mathematics which investigates relationships of space and solids.

Golf use: A golfer should evaluate the alignments and relationships of force lines (vectors).

- **Descriptive Geometry –**
  1. The graphic solution of problems involving **three-dimensions**.
  2. The geometry of properties that **remain** invariant (constant) under projection.

3. Remain **unchanged** by physical operations.

Golf use: A golfer should evaluate how **constant** the alignments and relationships of force remains through impact.

Hopefully this book will gives readers the tools to know the difference between workable and unworkable information for them. As I have said, there will be more than enough information about the swing and playing the game given here. However, don't overlook the value of information about learning and skill acquisition that is also given here. I can assure you by moving away from "how to play golf" suggestions onto becoming aware of golf's environments (i.e. Golf's Physical Basics), long-term learning not only becomes possible, it becomes easier.

Lessons one through six follow. These are not "how to" lessons, but contain information which any golfer (professional or amateur) who would like to improve their alignment and application of force, should be aware. These awareness lessons are followed by suggestions for learning to make progress, in Chapter Five. Now lets move on to lessons one through six, and keep in mind they are not "how to" lessons. Hopefully these awareness lessons will turn empirical information into unexpected insights and knowledge that leads to long term progress.

Sir Walter Simpson 1870's,
"Let's keep in mind there are good golfers with one leg, or one eye, or one arm".

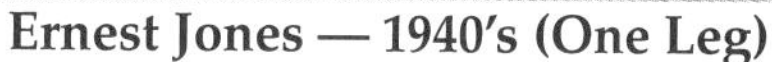

Ernest Jones — 1940's (One Leg)

1930's — One Arm

Note: Both players have on-plane shoulders, and their spine is angled both over the ball and away from the target. (Nature knows no other possibilities)

Ben Hogan—*"Golfers should school themselves to think in terms of the cause and not the result"*

Secret: **Instruction does not have to be a "reaction" to poor habits. (A "reaction" that is normally trying to fix swings with "how to" directions). Instruction in any form can be actions that guide golfers in the direction of unexpected insights. Insights that are often overlooked when golfers are processing "how to" advice. Instruction that reveals core golf knowledge, is proactive not reactive.**

Golfers who want to improve can be penchants for "fads" and different "how to" suggestions from a variety of sources that often provide little or no progress. Hopefully the upcoming awareness lessons will cause some unexpected insights that will open doors to long-term progress and improved play. "**Thinking skills must be integrated in physical actions.**" - Larry Debel

Chapter Two

Golf's
Six Awareness Lessons

Golf's Six Awareness Lessons

Lesson One .... It's A Game of Force

Lesson Two .... Form Follows Function

Lesson Three .... Golf's Physical Basics

Lesson Four .... Visualizations: 1920's to 2000

Lesson Five .... Playing and Swinging

Lesson Six .... What Makes it Work

LESSON ONE

Be Aware, It's A Game of Force

Law: Once you create a force, if you can influence the direction of that force, you can influence the direction of what that force is applied to.

Secret: **For over 500 years,** the only possible way to improve ball flight has been to improve the alignment and application of force through impact. Nature knows no other possibilities.

WHERE SHOULD WE START?

I will not know most of the people who read this book, or any of their ideas about the golf swing or playing the game. Therefore before introducing my ideas I am going to ask readers first to take a look at the golf swing and playing the game from a new point of view. I ask you to rename the game of golf, **a game of force**. While I have been asking golfers who are not happy with their progress, to move away from "how to play" suggestions, and onto self-discovery, some readers may ask, "What should I discover?" **My suggestion is that readers should start by seeing good golf as a game of force, and only then move on.**

If looking at golf as a "game of force" does not add more understanding to both the swing and the game, I may have failed in my upcoming attempt to help readers improve their golf. There is a good chance people will not make the kind of progress they are capable of without some understanding that **good golf is creating, aligning, and applying on-plane force.**

Let's imagine people no longer say, *"I'm going to play golf,"* or *"I'm going to practice my golf,"* or *"I'm going to take a golf lesson"* – in the future people now say, *"I'm going to practice creating forces," "I am going to play a game of applying on-plane forces through impact," or "I am going to take a force lesson."*

Secret: Describing golf as a game of creating, aligning, and applying forces, is a much more accurate way to explain what really happens (for better or worse) on a golf course.

Aligning and applying on plane force.

While it takes only a few seconds (less than two) from the start of the swing until impact, in that short time the swing can get into a lot of trouble.

The game that is played on a golf course from this new point of view is not one which tries to control the ball; **it is trying to influence the direction and application of force through impact**, which in turn influences ball flight. (It is not golf swing then ball flight.) Its golf swing, application of force, then ball flight. Where force must be aligned and applied is solely defined by the shot at hand and Golf's Physical Basics, not "how to" lists.

Note: The sole purpose (end result) of golf motion is to produce, use and sustain force. The sole purpose (end result) of this force is to influence ball flight. Many golfers approach the game and swing by focusing on ball flight, overlooking on or off-plane forces which are the cause of ball flight. Keep in mind, at times the forces a golf motion produces are efficient and at other times there is a misapplication of forces through impact.

I'm not sure how many golfers have ever looked at playing the game and swinging the club from a **force point of view**, but every time ball flight improves, it is because the application and alignment of force has improved! Golfers who now say – oh no! I just sliced the ball out of bounds," when playing a game of force will now realize, *"force came to the ball from outside the target line or the force from my rights shoulder was too high or the force from the clubhead was traveling across the target line from out to in.,"*

Secret: The game of golf is really a game of creating and influencing lines of force which influence ball flight.

Isaac Newton (Biography in Chapter Six) was the first person to formally describe the relationship between force and motion. I often tell students we have to "keep Isaac happy" during lessons. Forces are interactions between two or more objects. Forces can be either a **push or a pull.**

Whenever a force acts and causes motion, the change in motion (acceleration) will always be in the direction of the applied force. To fully describe a force, three characteristics need to be defined. 1) The **magnitude** of the force, 2) The **line** (direction) of the force, and 3) The **point of application** of the force.

"The forward swing should allow the club to follow. To manage this type of stroke is not easy, but it is deadly in the whole game."
- 1881 R. Forgan

To understand the motion of any ball (including a golf ball), we need to know the direction and point of application of the force applied to the ball, and what influences the magnitude of the force. If several forces act at the same time, (as in efficient golf swings), the net force is a **load** that causes objects to move or be deformed. **In the case of a golf ball, it is deformed, then moves.**

"Let the weight of the club head do it", is an old saying. Yes, let the weight of the club head do the work, but how? The answer—by pulling it through impact.

When golfers want to improve, the first decision they should make is: **What must I learn**? Playing partners, friends, TV tips, etc. are all sources of advice, but often there is **little common ground** in the suggestions available to players who want to improve. Of course what can lead to progress can vary from one golfer to the next, but every golfer must learn to **apply effective force down into the ball before their club makes contact with the ground**. Some in golf refer to this as impacting a small ball before a big ball (Earth). (Exception: Green side bunkers where the club hits the sand before the ball.)

Pulling Forces – 1960's

Every golf swing produces results that have the elements of **distance** and **direction.** The quality of any golfer's game is measured by their **accuracy** in moving a ball from one point on the course to another. **Note: Improving distance and direction can only be accomplished by improving the application and alignment of force through impact. Nature knows no other possibilities!**

Two of the primary elements of effective golf swings are **1.** Stable on-plane swing motion, and **2.** Club face stability through impact. Both are the bi-product of effective **application and alignment of force through impact**. Improving ones grip, posture, balance, timing, etc. is done **solely** to influence application of efficient force through impact. All golfers need efficient swing mechanics that can produce efficient force dynamics, i.e. a transfer of energy throughout the swing that leads up to a transfer of momentum through impact.

Pulling Forces – 1900's

Pull vs Push

There are principles of physics that tell us all forces do not produce the same results. For example, **pulling** forces and **pushing** forces give different results, as do rotational and linear forces. Efficient golf swings are founded more on **pulling** than **pushing forces** and for good reasons. Nature knows no other possibilities. **Note: 1.** When mass (a club) is **pulled**, it will align itself with and **automatically** follow the direction of a **pulling** force; **2.** A **pulling** force will also **stabilize** a mass and keep that mass on a **constant** path.

On the other hand, when **pushing forces** are being applied to a mass, these forces must be **applied exactly through the center of the mass** to produce the same results a **pulling** force will automatically provide (stable mass – constant path). A **push** applied off center causes mass to rotate off-line. (Natures truths knows no other possibilities). Mass rotates left when a **pushing** force is right of center, and rotates right when the **pushing** force is left of center. **Note:** Mass will not rotate on its own, mass must be caused to rotate by a force.

Pulling Forces – 1940's

Golfers who are trying to improve, should keep in mind the following. When the mass of a golf club is being influenced more by rotational **pulling** forces than pushing forces, several important results are accomplished more or less automatically. **Pulling** the club will guard against **1.** Deceleration through impact, **2.** Loss of a stable clubface, **3.** An unstable swing motion. **Note:** an unstable clubface is one, if not the main cause of shots with uncontrolled side spin.

Secret: The basic element of an effective golf swing is a stable, on-plane force through impact. (i.e. Rotational pulling forces)

Mass x Velocity = Force

Yes, but the mass must be effective mass. When the weight of the club is being pulled behind the golfers hands through impact, it is more efficient than if it is pushed past their hands.

WARNING – While it is true that the mass of a golfers arms, hands, and club will all automatically fall in line with **pulling** forces, at times these forces may not be on-plane or parallel to each other causing off-line ball flight. While golfers should apply **pulling** forces through impact, these forces must also be efficiently aligned and applied on-plane for the shot at hand.

Every segment of a golfers system (shoulders, chest, back, mid-section, thighs, arms, hands, etc.) can be trained to **pull** the club separately or all together. **What pulls the club is the player's choice, and it normally depends on the shot at hand.** Ben Hogan said, *"The left side pulls the club down"*.

The effective mass of a club head can be vaired by:

- Change in rate of motion
- Size of swing radius
- Where the release point is located in the downswing.

Many golfers with efficient putting styles feel they **pull** a putter (not push or flip it) through impact only with the arms. Other golfers with efficient styles feel they **pull** a putter with the shoulders or a combination of shoulders and arms. When **chipping**, some golfers feel they **pull** a club with both the shoulders and mid-section of their body, while other chipping styles only use the shoulders and arms to **pull** a club. Some players feel they **pull** the club through impact with their back muscles.

"It's easy to start with a wrong idea, and difficult to acquire the right style, all because of erroneous deductions."

- 1863 W.R. Chambers

When pitching, many players will add some **pulling** force from their mid-section to the motion of the shoulders and arms. As the shot at hand requires golfers to make longer swings, more segments of a golfer's body will start to make contributions in applying **pulling** forces. Like falling dominos, the bodies larger segments (or links) **pull** smaller segments through impact by transferring their energy on to the smaller segment.

"By going about it intelligently, learning a small number of movements, and eliminate a lot of movements, progress is possible."

- Ben Hogan

During the **downswing** of long swings some world-class golfers feel they will **pull** a club with the bodies mid-section going out in the direction of the ball (not the target) first, then around to the left. Other golfers **pull** a club down-plane first with the right shoulder, then with the mid-section of the body. Some other players **pull** a club down-plane with the back muscles turning away from the target (not to the target), the same direction the back goes when we throw a ball. In other styles the **pull** back down-plane is allowed to be a reaction to what could be called the loading actions of the back swing, an action many in golf believe automatically release the **pulling** forces of down-swing.

Secret: What pulls the club is always the players choice but some ways are more efficient.

Note: When a club is passing the player's hands its is no longer being **pulled** and it loses some stability through impact. When rotational **pulling** forces are replaced unconsciously with **pushing** forces from the hands through impact (right wrist is no longer bent back and left wrist is not flat), ball flights become less accurate with a loss of distance. (Nature knows no other possibility.)

Suggestion: Golfers who want to improve, should consider more **pulling forces** through impact than **pushing** forces. **Pulling** forces transport the angles a golf swing created during the backswing (bent right elbow, bent right wrist, cocked left wrist, upper left arm on chest.) down to impact. Unlike **pulling** forces, some **pushing forces** often expand or release these angles prematurely.

1950's #6

Note: Bio-mechanics, (the study of movement) clearly state, when muscles contract or **shorten**, this creates a **pull** on the bone to which the muscles tendon is attached, producing movement or **velocity**. These muscle actions are called concentric control. On the other hand, **deceleration** of motion is typically controlled by the lengthening of muscles or eccentric control. This is why effective golf swings have pulling forces (shortening of muscles) through impact applying and aligning force down into the ball. Nature knows no other possibility.

Secret: Muscles work in pairs, called "agonist" and "antagonist". When one muscle shortens or pulls, it causes its pair to relax and lengthen. The shortening or pull happens first causing the antagonist muscle to relax and lengthen. When the mass of the golf club is pulled effectively, the bio-mechanics of the body's muscle system is both shortening and lengthening of pairs of muscles. But keep in mind the shortening or **pull happens first.**

1930's

What do I have to learn? Golfers should learn to apply forces down into the ball before their club makes contact with the ground. (Exception: green side bunkers.) World-class player and instructor Henry Cotton said in 1936, ***"You can't mix in a push with the whip of the swing and get anywhere."*** Golfers must also recognize effective force through impact does not come from motions that are forced. (The alignment and application of force will be discussed in more detail later.)

1920's

What is an Efficient Swing?

We could say that in efficient swings: The body (hips, shoulders and spine) all turn. The arms swing, and the left wrist and the right elbow both hinge and unhinge. Over time, golf instruction has talked about the basics of turning, swinging, hinging and unhinging in a wide variety of ways.

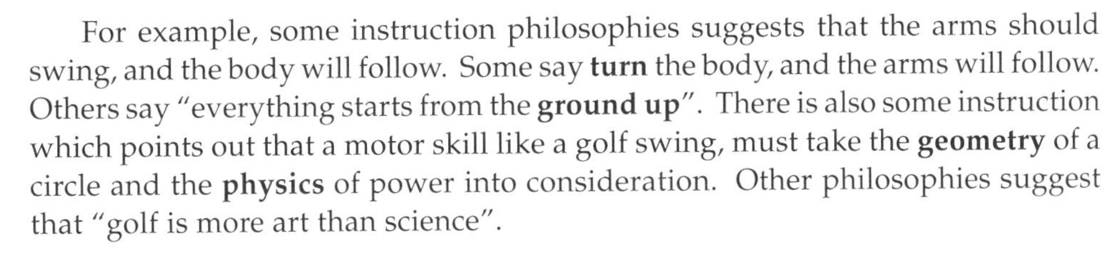

For example, some instruction philosophies suggests that the arms should swing, and the body will follow. Some say **turn** the body, and the arms will follow. Others say "everything starts from the **ground up**". There is also some instruction which points out that a motor skill like a golf swing, must take the **geometry** of a circle and the **physics** of power into consideration. Other philosophies suggest that "golf is more art than science".

There are also some approaches to golf instruction that say "the four main **learning styles** must be our first consideration" These learning styles can be described as: visual (eyes) pictures; Kinesthetic (feel) touch; action (doer) drills; analytical (thinkers) words-details. Some teachers suggest *85%* of a full swing can be learned in a **chip shot**. What is your description of a effective swing? **What do you believe in?** (You may want to write down your ideas about your swing now, and notice if they change as you read on, or in the future.)

2000 #2

1920's

"What is Good Golf?" Is A Much Easier Question!

Good golf is simply predicting the flight of the ball, with the player predicting the distance and direction of their shots before they swing. Period end of sentence! On the other hand, most people play "Hit and Hope" golf - they swing and hope it goes to the target. Good golf is normally produced by a swing that has the fewest moving parts for the shot at hand and takes place in the smallest possible space.

Secret: Some golfers can predict the outcome of their swing better than the rest of us. If they want the ball to go 50 yards, 100 yards, or 185 yards; high or low; with or without spin; **THEY CAN DO IT!**, creating the desired results.

Walter Hagen—1930's

It seems like there are many ways to swing and arrive at effective impact conditions. Just look around, there are as many ways as there are good golfers. So if there is no one way, what is a golfer to do when looking for information to learn from? Thousands of books and articles have been written since golf's first instruction book The Golfers Manual was published in 1857. There is some good ideas in every one of them, but if read by the wrong person these ideas would either be of little use, or even bad for their game. Well-known and respected instructor John Jacobs said, *"When it comes to golf instruction what is one man's meat, is the next man's poison."*

Secret: Information, ideas and suggestions any golfer uses must fit that person's physical and mental make up, practice and training time available, current information base, and the type of swing they are trying to use. **But most of all, when training and practicing, use an approach that let's you become more aware of your present swing and style of play. Then use that information, and Golf's Physical Basics, not the next tip from a well-meaning friend.**

Ben Hogan—1940's

Common Impact Alignments 1900-2000

It could be said *"everything a golfer does to improve their play is done to improve golf's moment of truth:* ***the alignment and application of force at and through impact"***.

Over time when we watch the world's best golfers, they have used swings that have all looked different from each other. It is useful to realize that these swings are being made by different body styles and swing tempos. The swings that do not appear to be similar when in motion, have more than a few common impact alignments when still pictures of them are analyzed. Nature simply knows no other possibilities.

These common impact alignments should not be seen as common to world-class golfers, but common to any efficient swings founded on golf's environment. These alignments have always been similar through impact due to the design of a golf club.

John Daly—1990's #5

IMPACT ALIGNMENTS

Common Alignments	Effect
The **spine** is angled both over to the ball and away from the target.	Without these two spine angles the right shoulder and other elements of the swing could not travel down-plane to impact.
The **ears** and **eyes** are more or less level.	When they are not level, the players balance can be effected.
The **neck** is over and out, more or less parallel to the ground.	With this neck alignment, the requirements of balancing and on-plane right shoulder are more easily met.
The players **face** is more down than up, looking at the ball with the chin off the chest.	This alignment helps keep both eyes fully focused on the ball and level to the ground.
The player's **head** is behind the ball, more or less over the right leg.	This alignment improves spine and right shoulder alignments, and application of force through impact.
The **right shoulder** is lower than the left, and moving down-plane. If a line was placed just outside the players shoes, (vertical to the ground), the right shoulder joint more or less goes through that line at impact.	This alignment is the result of an on-plane right shoulder turn, and spine angle that is angled away from the target (up to 70% of the swing force is delivered by the right shoulder).
The **right elbow** is down in front of the right hip bone.	This alignment allows the body and hips to support and keep force on the right arm and shaft through impact.
The **right arm** is still bent at the elbow.	A bent right arm keeps force on the bent right hand and shaft through impact.
The **right wrist** is still bent back.	This alignment supports and keeps force on the left hand and shaft through impact, and keeps the clubhead behind the hands.
The **right forearm** is on-plane.	This alignment supports alignment of force at impact.
The **upper left arm** is still on the upper chest.	This alignment allows the body to support and apply pressure to the left arm through impact.
The **left wrist** is flat and uncocked.	This alignment allows the club to be in-line with the left arm through impact.

James Braid—1910

Tiger Woods—2000 #2

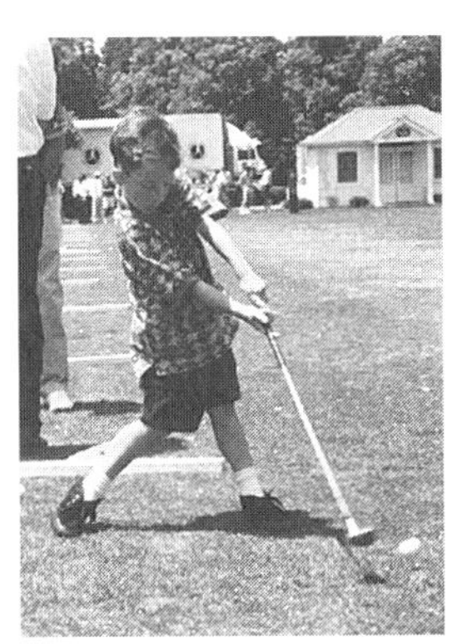
A 7 Year Old—1997

Sam Snead—1950 #1

Arnold Palmer—1990's #4

The **club shaft** looking down the target line is in-line with the right forearm.	This alignment (right forearm on-plane) allows the right arm and shoulder to support and keep force on the shaft through impact.
The **left hip joint** is higher than right, and turning inside the left knee joint.	This alignment keeps the application of rotational force on-plane.
The **right foot** more or less on the ground or rolling into an on-plane angle.	This alignment keeps the application of rotational force on-plane.
The **shoulders** are on-plane, and not as open as hips.	This alignment supports and aligns on-plane force.

Henry Cotton—1940's

The principles of motion and force know no other alignments. From day one, the world's best golfers all had common impact alignments, and at the same time when they were winning, probably the best short game in the tournament. **Bob Bush an engineer and one of the golf industries leading consultants said, *"Over time good golfers have always had similar impact alignments, simply because the design angles of a golf club have never changed."***

Secret: **World-class golf swings may look different in motion, but they have always had common alignments at impact, because Golf's Physical Basics have not changed over time. Charles Coody (PGA Tour), "Through the ball, we all look the same, we just have different ways of getting there".**

David Duval—2000 #2

Our Goal: A swing that works in the simplest and most powerful form. There is no one perfect swing. Rather, there are a variety of possibilities that could be workable. As long as they do not violate any physical laws of motion and force.

The elevation of ball flight is a result of the 1.) design characteristics of the golf ball **(it's compressible)**, 2.) the loft angle designed into the clubface, and 3.) the alignments and application of on-plane forces.

While there are common impact alignments effective swings use for the shot at hand, these alignments feel different to individual golfers. Individual golfers may also use different approaches to achieve common impact alignments. Become aware of what impact alignments are required by Golf's Physical Basics and the shot at hand, not "how to" suggestions.

Secret: **Many golfers thoughts go directly from the golf swing to ball flight, overlooking the application and alignment of force. How the golf swing aligns and applies force is what produces the ball flight for the shot at hand. Nature knows no other possibilities.**

Hal Sutton—2000

The pictures of impact in this lesson include golfers dating back over the last 100 years. Golfers both past and present, have similar impact alignments. Again ,this is because the basic design angles of a golf club have never changed. Efficient alignment and application of force has always been founded on the shot at hand and the design of the club being used (i.e. golf's environment).

Principles (or rules) of motion and force have always required efficient alignment and application of force through impact to be parallel to the angle of the clubs shaft at address (inclined). If the basic design angles a golf club (you could say) "are born with", ever changed, efficient impact alignment of force would also change. Currently, for example, putting swings and driver swings have dissimilar on-plane impact alignments because these two clubs are designed with dissimilar shaft angles.

Efficient golf swing motion and the alignment and application of force through impact are based on golf's environment (Golf's Physical Basics), and the design angles of the golf club being used. I suggest seeing golf as a game of force, and improving your golf starts by improving the alignment and application of force through impact. *"Things do not just happen, they are brought about."* - W.H. Hays

As I said, these common alignments **should not be seen** as common to world-class golfers, but common to any efficient swings that are founded on Golf's Physical Basics.

TIMELESS AND CLASSIC IMPACT ALIGNMENTS

Jack Nicklaus #4

Gary Player #2

Arnold Palmer #4

Lee Trevino #4

Zone's

There is an expression golfers sometimes use after a very good round or tournament: "I was In the Zone". This expression – "in the zone" – is normally associated with a mental state golfers say they somehow experience when they are playing well. Any number of mental game teachers (i.e., Rotella, Cook, Graham) make mention of this zone as a place where players seem to think better, see more, and swing with their best tempo.

The following ideas focus on being "in the zone". But not the mental zone we have been referring to. We will be talking about what I call physical zones. Your golf swing takes place in three dimensions:

1. Over a certain amount of time.
2. In a certain sequence.
3. Through a certain space or "zone".

When working on their swings, I feel some players have **slowed their progress down** by trying to make the club and body move perfectly through exact checkpoints. Perhaps, if instead of using exact checkpoints, these players were to use a "zone", or a general area to evaluate their swing, they would see more initial progress. (Learning Research supports using "in the ball park" models).

I am not suggesting that anyone lower their standards, or stop trying to do the best they can. But it may give most golfers a much freer swing if they see and feel "zones" instead of exact checkpoints which they believe the club and body must move through. Keep in mind, freedom and trust are the first steps to any golfer's progress.

The following pictures have the different "physical zones" identified on them, along with a description of workable and unworkable golf swings. These "zones" are suggested guidelines that golfers can use to improve their swing.

SOUND SWINGS—HAND ZONE:

The player's hands go down slightly at first or stay level, as they move in from the target line during the first 12 inches to 18 inches of the swing. The reason the hands can stay level is they move around with the turn of the body, and may go down a little because the left shoulder goes down plane.

UNSOUND SWINGS—HAND ZONE:

The player's hands move straight back from the ball or out and away from the body, as they go up too early in the swing.

Hand Zone

RIGHT LEG ZONE—SOUND SWINGS

At address the upper right leg is leaning to the target and stays flexed in its zone (at this angle) from the start of the swing through impact.

UNSOUND SWINGS—RIGHT LEG ZONE

The right leg often moves in several different directions: up, down, in, and out, throughout the swing.

Right Leg Zone **Right Leg Zone #1**

SHOULDER ZONE—SOUND SWINGS

The zone of the shoulder turn to the top of the swing is the same zone it turns down plane on through impact. In sound swings, the left shoulder goes back on plane 6 to 8 inches. The space the left shoulder passes through on its way to the top of the back swing is the same space the right shoulder passes through during the downswing when it is on plane.

UNSOUND SWINGS—SHOULDER ZONE

The angle the shoulder turns on is either too flat (too low) or too up and down, causing pulled and pushed shots.

Shoulder Zone #5

Shoulder Zone #5

Shoulder Zone #5

Patty Berg—1940's

Byron Nelson—1940's

Ben Hogan—1950's #6

Arnold Palmer—1960's

GOLF'S STRIKE ZONE©

The Strike Zone is normally a term associated with baseball, and has been at the foundation of that game from its inception. Every effective pitcher has learned to **align forces** from their body's motion to throw a ball through the **strike zone** accurately.

Golf also has a **strike zone** at its foundation. Every good golfer has learned to **align force** from their swing to transport golf clubs accurately through **Golf's Strike Zone**© (I.e. before, during and after impact). Many golfers overlook **Golf's Strike Zone** and only focus on impact.

While home plate helps define baseball's **strike zone**, it's the golf club's shaft (or lie angle) that helps define the strike zone for golfers. The **strike zone** in both games should be seen **as a guideline for the location of where forces should be aligned**. Golf's most consistent players have swings that create efficient force. These swings also **align their force** parallel to the lie angle the shaft occupied at address through **Golf's Strike Zone**©.

Golf swings have several sources of force including:

A. Right Shoulder

B. Right forearm

C. Hands

D. The Club Shaft (transfers swing forces down-plane through the **strike zone** into the ball.)

E. Clubhead

When baseball fans see the ball go through the **strike zone**, they may overlook the pitchers hand, arm, shoulder, and the **forces** the body parts create have also been aligned to move the ball through the **strike zone**. In golf, efficient alignment and application of force has had similar requirements for over 500 years. i.e. A golf swings source of force must also be aligned to, and travel through **Golf's Strike Zone**.

Looking over pictures of past and present world-class golfers notice the a) right shoulder, b) right forearm, c) hands, d) club shaft and e) clubhead all travel on parallel planes in **Golf's Strike Zone** before, during, and after impact.

Today's golfers who are looking for ways to improve their swing (or alignment and application of force) can use the same guidelines every efficient swing has used over time. By focusing on where the a) right shoulder or b) right forearm, or c) hands, or d) shaft, or e), clubhead are aligned through **Golf's Strike Zone** we can improve ball flight. **Note:** The pictures are on pages 60, 61 and 62.

It helps progress to focus on only one source (not all 5) at a time. Find the one that works best for you. They are listed in their order of importance for force application and learning sequence. **Studies by Bob Bush and True Temper show up to 70% of the swings force is delivered by the right shoulder when it's on plane throughout the strike zone.** On the other hand, the clubhead moves so fast, it's more difficult to focus on, and it should be our last choice. Note: Right shoulder alignment influences the right forearm alignment. Then right forearm influences hand alignment, finally hand alignment influences club alignment.

In general, when the ball is pulled left, the right shoulder and right forearm (and the force they create) are normally traveling through **Golf's Strike Zone** too high, over the plane, into the body. When the ball is pushed right, the right shoulder and right forearm (and the force they create) are normally traveling through **Golf's Strike Zone** too low, under the plane, and too much from inside the target line.

Mickey Wright—1950's #1

The only possible way to improve ball flight is to improve the alignment and application of force through Golf's Strike Zone. Natures truths knows no other possibilities. *"Once you create force, if you can influence the direction of force, you can influence the direction of what force is applied to."* Learn to be aware of **Golf's Strike Zone**, then swing your right shoulder, right forearm, hands, club shaft, and clubhead parallel to the angle the club shaft occupied at address through impact to keep the forces your swing creates in **Golf's Strike Zone**.

Secret: By keeping swing motions in **Golf's Strike Zone,** players have fewer moving parts, less compensations, and a more efficient alignment and application of force. We could say, from address to finish the longer swing motions stay in **Golf's Strike Zone** the better. This is an ambitious goal, but one that will and has paid many dividends from the games inception.

Tiger Woods—1999 #2

Lee Trevino

"Every good golfer has their left hand leading through impact" #4

Ian Baker Finch—1990's #5

John Daly—1990's #5

Lesson One—Summary

Golf's Strike Zone

Summary: Spine angled both over to ball and away from target, level eyes and ears, face looking down, right shoulder and forearm on plane, bent right elbow and wrist, club in line with left arm (front view), in line with right forearm (back view), head back over right knee, right foot rolling on plane, right knee turning inside left foot, right hip lower than left hip, right shoulder lower than left. Goal: Alignment and application of force in Golf's Strike Zone.

A. Right Shoulder **B.** Right Forearm **C.** Hands **D.** Club Shaft **E.** Club Head

All of these are in Golf's Strike Zone

Sam Snead—1950's #6

Jack Nicklaus—1960's #1

LESSON TWO

Be Aware,
Form Follows Function

Everything is connected,
and interacts with the environment.

It seems, everything works for the same reasons.

FORM SHOULD FOLLOW FUNCTION

Secret: As you start to work on your game, I suggest that you do not try to improve your golf swing per se. Start with the age-old concept of **form follows function.** Always start by asking what do I want the golf ball to do? i.e. fly high, low, left, right, straight. The answer to that question is the starting point for any ideas about grip, posture, alignment, etc., for the shot at hand.

Right Forearm On-Plane

Ben Hogan #6

Sam Snead #6

Cary Middlecoff #6

The form of any action is based on what function that action is meant to accomplish. Every golfer, who wants to improve, should keep this in mind. Progress in golf is clearly influenced by how closely a player can apply the principles of **Form Follows Function**. Where and how a player applies swing force is based on what function they expect their swing to accomplish (i.e. chip, pitch, high or low iron short, hooking or slicing wood shots). The ball responds blindly to the form of the swing. **Every ball flight in golf is a direct result of the form of the swing through impact**.

After you decide where you want the ball to go (function) you now must become familiar with the most workable impact alignments (form) for that shot's distance and direction. Impact alignments will be discussed later, and when golfers are aware of the effective impact alignments of the shaft, clubhead and face for the shot at hand, progress becomes possible.

Secret: **It is more useful to focus on what you want to do, then how to do it.** (especially if your ideas of how to do something are coming from someone else.) As you make progress with your understanding of **Form Follows Function**, you will discover there is very little latitude for the form of the swing through impact for the shot (function) at hand. Understanding **this lack of latitude in form through impact, in my mind, can make learning and progress less difficult.**

THE SWING'S TWO ELEMENTS

Golf swings do not just happen, they are made to happen by golfers. Like everything else we make, golf swings are founded on the golfer's concepts, hopefully concepts based on Golf's Physical Basics, and form follows function.

When working on your game in the past, have you ever thought about how many elements there are to learn about a golf swing? Some of the answers I have heard to this question are "5, 10, maybe 15 elements to learn".

Secret: **Fortunately we can say that there are only two.** After a golf ball is impacted by a clubface, the ball does only two things; it goes in some **Direction**, and it goes for a **Distance. It then follows, what a player needs to learn is:** 1. What influences **Direction?** 2. What influences **Distance?** These two main elements of ball flight (Distance and Direction) are influenced by the swings two main elements, its **shape** (plane) and it's **source of power** (efficient on-plane force at impact).

Within the elements of distance and direction of ball flight there are two sub-elements: **Elevation** (high or low) and **Side Spins** (going left to right or right to left). Of course the ball can also be made to go straight. **As was said earlier, good golf is simply predicting the outcome of ball flight.** There are good golfers reading this book that can predict the outcome of his or her swing better than the rest of us. If they want the ball to go 50 yards, or 100 yards, or 185 yards; high or low; with or without spin; **THEY CAN DO IT!** Of course this is what we admire in and aspire to learn, the ability to influence the **Distance** and **Direction** of the flight of the ball. **Perhaps, you have never looked at playing good golf as predicting outcomes, but that's what it is, (with form following function).**

From a side hill 15 foot putt, to a 190 yard shot into a par 3, to a fairway wood shot to the top of a hill, people are playing good golf when they use the club and swing (form) that will produce the required outcome for the shot they want to make (function). At times a player may want to improve their grip, posture, alignment, mental game, they also may wish to improve what one body part is doing during his/her swing. **But all that players are ultimately trying to improve is their influence over the Distance or Direction of the flight of the ball.** It helps everyone's progress to be aware that ball flight is always influenced by how their swing aligns the clubface, clubhead, and shaft through impact.

Right Wrist and Elbow Still Bent

Babe Zaharias #6

I would like to suggest that readers base any approach they are using to make progress with, on the principles of "form follows function". The shape (or plane) of the swing should be constant and repeatable (for direction control), and its sources of force or pressure, efficient (for distance control). I do not mean to bore readers by repeating myself, but everything a player does to improve their swing and playing the game is done to improve how they influence **Distance** and **Direction, realizing that "form should follow function"**.

Secret: How many elements are there to learn about a golf swing? Only two, its **shape** and its **sources** of power (not several).

Ben Hogan #6

Many golfers I have met, believe the reason they are not making progress is because of the amount of information they feel must be learned. While making progress in golf will take some time and effort, I suggest any and all relevant information could be put on a very short list. This short list has a foundation that is based on the swing's two elements, its shape, source of power, and the two elements of ball flight, distance and direction. (If the ball flight had four or five elements, there would be four or five swing elements to learn).

Two Elements

The Shape of the Swing

Referred to as its swing plane, and when the club is said to be on plane, the swing will take place with few if any compensating motions as the club stays parallel to the angle the shaft occupied address through impact

The Swing's Source of Power

When the clubhead is staying behind the player's hands through impact, efficient force not effort becomes the swings source of power. Everything you or any golfer does to improve their golf is really done to improve the shape and source of power of the swing.

Jack Nicklaus #1

Influencing Distance and Direction

Gary Wiren's Laws, Principles and Preferences is a useful tool for gaining insights about Form Follows Function and the Distance and Direction of ball flight. The following is based on the presentation Gary made at the First World's Scientific Congress of Golf. In July 1990 St. Andrews, Scotland.

Gary Wiren *"It's time to eliminate unnecessary confusion among golfers."* In an effort to help golfers navigate through all the conflicting information that's available about playing the game of golf, Gary wrote Laws, Principals and Preferences.

Laws

When "Laws" are mentioned, Gary is referring to the physical forces that are ABSOLUTES for influencing the flight of the ball. Five (5) factors that absolutely influence the Distance and Direction of the ball flight are:

1. **Speed**; The velocity of the club head through impact.
2. **Centeredness of Impact**; The contact point which could either be on the center of the clubface, toe, heel, or above or below the "Sweet Spot."
3. **Path**; The direction of the arc of the clubhead, (i.e. the path in which clubhead is traveling away from or back to the ball).
4. **Club face**; The direction the club face is facing at and through impact.
5. **Angle of Approach**; The angle of the descending and ascending arc of the clubhead through Impact.

Useful Questions

I would suggest that the following are useful questions for any golfer who will like to improve.

1. Where on the clubface was the ball impacted?
2. On what path was the clubhead traveling?
3. Where was the clubface facing through impact?
4. What was the angle of approach for the clubhead?

These are the kinds of questions which give golfers information that leads to long-term learning. Asking "how to" move a particular body part would not be as useful for any golfer's progress.

Principles

Gary Wiren also listed Principles that influenced how the Laws influence the distance and direction of ball flight.

Principles	*Primary Influence*
Grip (Style of grip)	Direction (clubface)
Aim (Alignment to target).	Direction
Set up (Posture) (influences all 5 laws).	Distance and Direction
Swing plane (Through impact).	Direction
Width of Arc (Entire Swing)	Distance
Length of Arc (Size of backswing).	Distance
Alignments at End of Backswing (clubface, left wrist, back of left hand, shaft, left arm).	Direction

Lever System (Angles formed by left wrist, right wrist, right elbow, left arm).	Distance
Timing (Swings rhythm)	Distance - Direction
Release (Expanding angles)	Distance - Direction
Dynamic Balance (Movement of body's center of gravity).	Distance - Direction
Swing Centers (Rotation forces).	Distance - Direction
Connection (Arms to body).	Distance - Direction

Preference

Preference is the third and final element of Gary Wiren's **Laws, Principals, and Preferences**. (I.e. What preference works best for the individual golfer).

Golfers must stay within the Laws. However, there can be individual preferences for how the Laws are used. For example, the grip (a principle) influences clubface alignment (a law) through impact. It's always the player's choice, (preference) for the grip style which they use to apply the Law (i.e. over lap, interlock, one-knuckle or two, left hand low, etc).

Keep in mind, the swing's Form should Follow the Function which the player wants their swing to accomplish (influencing the **distance** and **direction** of ball flight).

LESSON TWO—SUMMARY

How many elements are there to learn about a golf swing? 5, 10, 15?

Fortunately there are only two.

After a golf ball is impacted by the clubhead, the ball does 2 things:

1. The ball goes forward in some DIRECTION.
2. The ball goes forward for a DISTANCE.

It then follows what we need to learn is:

1. What causes the ball go in a certain direction?

   Answer: The shape of the golf swing. (its plane) – where was the plane of the shaft, clubface, and clubhead through impact?

2. What causes the ball go for a certain distance?

   Answer: A source of efficient force –was the shaft, clubface, and clubhead behind the hands through impact?

<u>**Shape**</u>	<u>**Source of Force**</u>
Responsible for Direction	**Responsible for Distance**
Swing Plane	Force from lagging components
Shaft and face Angles	Hands Forward of Clubhead
Alignment of force through impact	Bent right elbow and hand at impact
	Application of on-plane forces

Goal: A swing shape that is repeatable, and a source of force that is efficient.

Note: Keep in mind, everything starts with the players concept.

*The lessons that follow are founded on the belief that golf is a game of force, and form follows function.

LESSON THREE

Be Aware of
Golf's Physical Basics©
(Golf's Environment)

For over 500 years —
efficient, repeatable golf swings have been
founded on Golf's Physical Basics.

Nature knows no other possibilities.

INTRODUCTION TO GOLF'S PHYSICAL BASICS ©

Along with the nature of learning, Golf Swing Secrets...and Lies we will discuss the golf swing. Information about the swing is based on what I call Golf's Physical Basics. These basics are non-negotiable, and have been the same for every golfer dating back hundreds of years to when people first started to swing a club and play golf, (long before any formal instruction was available). Golf's Physical Basics are presented here to help readers who are not happy with their progress develop new insights and perceptions, they are not intended to tell anyone how they must swing and play.

"We seek to impress upon the novice that golf is a science. In fact, one of the most exact sciences that mere physical force can not achieve. Lay aside all private whims."
- R. Forgan, 1881
- The Golfers Handbook

Secret: **Guidelines for swinging and playing really become self-evident when they are founded on Golf's Physical Basics.**

It's always a good idea to use a list of basics when learning to improve ones golf, but whose list of basics is going to be used? Some people go from tip to tip where there is little common ground and where there are disagreements over what should be on a list of basics. My suggestion, use Golf's Physical Basics, a list that always had common ground and avoids disagreements.

As has already been said, there was no formal golf instruction information available hundreds of years ago, but from day one:

Some learners can't make progress with new information because they are still listening to past information

- The purpose of the game has always been to enjoy ourselves, as we learn to influence both the distance and direction of ball flight.
- Golf has always been played with a stick, a ball, and on an ever changing field of play.
- The club golfers use has always had a head, clubface, and shaft, with all three determining ball flight.
- The club has always been designed with its handle end angled forward of the clubface, and with the shaft angled up from the ground on a roof like, inclined angle.
- Golfers have always stood inside the ball and target line.
- The motion of the swing has always had some source of power. Its motion has always had some level of balance and timing.
- Golfers have always had hands, arms, and bodies.

"Golf's basics are the same for everyone— If this was recognized golf would be easier to learn,"
- Paul Runyon
March 2000

I do not believe anything has been overlooked. These elements have all been the same from day one. When looking to improve influence over the flight of the ball, any effective approach can be founded on elements listed above, as are Golf's Physical Basics listed below.

Golf's Five Physical Basics:

1. The design of the club, i.e. the angles of a shaft, clubface, and head.
2. Golfers stand inside the target line and ball.
3. The ballistic properties of the compressible ball.
4. The elements of balance and time.
5. The field of play and ever changing playing conditions.

This may seem like a short list, especially when compared to all the information that is available to golfers today. But all basic requirements of a effective swing and playing the game are based on Golf's Physical Basics.

Through impact:

- The club is on-plane, or it is not (Physical Basic #1)
- The clubhead mass is behind the grip or it is not. (Physical Basic #1)
- The ball has been compressed or it was not. (Physical Basic #3)
- The swing has efficient timing and balance or it does not. (Physical Basic #4)
- The player has adapted his stance and swing motion to the shot at hand, or he has not. (Physical Basic #2 ,5)

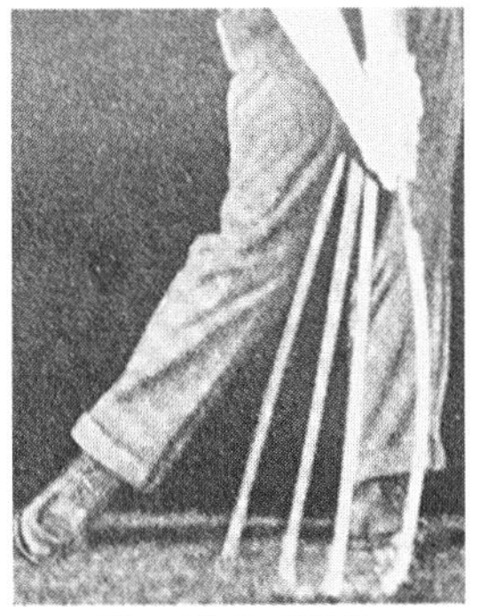

The Club PB#1

Let me say that again – all the basic elements of an effective swing and playing the game are be based on **Golf's Physical Basics**. The origin of these basics is not someone's opinion, natures truths simply knows no other possibilities. Unless the design angles of the club, ballistic properties of the ball, the human form, field of play, or principles of motion and force change, these physical basics are non-negotiable and are the foundation of good golf.

Address PB#2

"The search for solutions leads to finding the tools for solutions." **Golf's Physical Basics** are the tools and blueprints for a effective swing and playing the game. (They are discussed in more detail in Chapter Four)

Golfers who make progress and experience long-term learning, **adapt** their swing to Golf's Physical Basics (golf's environment) with a process called **reverse engineering**. Engineering builds to create, on the other hand **reverse engineering adapt to environments**. In 1993 I wrote and compiled, Building and Improving your Golf Mind, Golf Body, Golf Swing. In hindsight I would title that book, Adapting to Improve your Golf Mind, Golf Body, Golf Swing. People, who make progress in golf, have learned the value of **adapting** to Golf's Physical Basics with reverse engineering principles. The body humans occupy today was developed over millions of years using reverse engineering and natural selection to **adapt** every gene in our body to ever changing environments (good golfers also **adapt**). Reverse engineering is discussed in more detail in Chapter Five.

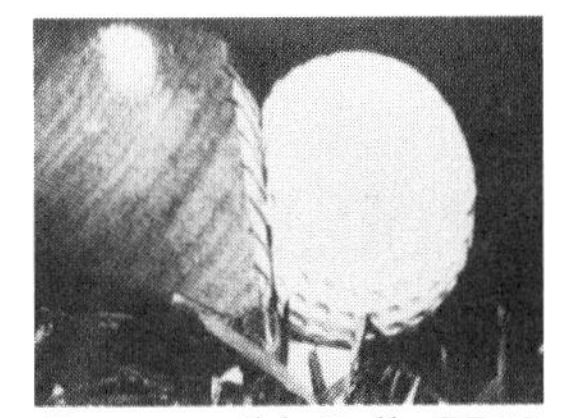

Compressible Balls PB#3

There Is No One Way.....But!

Secret: How players want to respond to **Golf's Physical Basics**, is really up to each individual, there is no one way.

Balance and Timing PB#4

Golf's Physical Basics have not changed for over 500 years, but there is no one way to play or swing. There is always some latitude when it comes to learning golf, every golfer is an individual and information should be personalized, but an effective swing must meet the requirements of the physical basics of the game, and the field of play. **Just any old swing or any old advice will not lead to improved control of ball flight.**

Golf is a game that rewards precision, therefore the more precision you can build into your game and swing, the sooner you will be predicting the **distance** and **direction** of your ball flight. Players and coaches from every sport have always looked for ways to communicate information that would develop better learning skills, and improve performances. **In golf, that information must take the games environment (Physical Basics) into consideration.**

Field of Play PB#5

Communication is always better than no communication, and faster is better than slower. Today, we have instant communication from country to country, city to city, office to office, even from home to home. But all of this instant communication may not be better, if there is **misinformation** being exchanged and then used.

Secret: Often it is not a lack of talent, effort, or time that prevents progress. Over the years many golfers have not made the kind of progress of which they were capable, because of **miscommunication** and **misinformation**.

What moves the ball? Good physics and geometry.

What repeats a swing? Appropriate learning.

How do we learn? Through awareness.

- 1998 D. Chattem

We could call **Golf's Physical Basics** a generalization. At times, generalizations can be described as less than complete descriptions, but **Golf's Physical Basics** are really a higher generalization containing principles that lead to insights about the game and swing. These insights often lift players to new skill levels.

Note: Albert Einstein's **Theory of Relativity** was published in 1905. It stated that all observers, **regardless of their location,** would discover the same laws of nature. His theory seemed to start with the intrinsic uncertainty as to what is truth. Then realized **nature does not contain any other possibilities. Golf's Physical Basics like nature do not contain any other possibilities.**

Golf's Physical Basics (a ball, a club, a field of play, balance, timing and standing inside the ball and target line) contains no misinformation. These elements are all physical in nature and have little chance for misinterpretation. Taking into consideration **Golf's Physical Basics** will help all observers, **regardless of their location**, to see similar **impact alignments** for the shot at hand.

"Swing the same for all clubs. I always believed, and tried to play each club differently. But I see from pictures there is only an infinite variation."

1903 Harold Hilton

1892-98 Open Champion

When a golf club leaves the factory, we can say it has been "born" with some measurable elements: it's length, lie angle, face angle, face loft, roll, and bulge, shaft flex, and overall weight. Because of these consistent elements you could say there is one best way for that club to move throughout the swing and impact for the shot at hand. **Although there may be one best way, I am not sure any player has ever made that perfect swing**.

Players come in different sizes, strengths, abilities, and backgrounds. Every world-class player has made some personal adjustments in their swing which would not be found in a description of that one best way. My point, simply put, while no one has ever made the perfect swing, **Golf's Physical Basics** have not changed over time. They are the foundation for any effective approach to impact conditions for the shot at hand, and I have found that "How to play" lists from well meaning friends do not produce consistent results.

"Its impossible to play good golf with a swing that will not repeat."

- Ben Hogan

When getting a tip for your game and swing, (when someone is telling us what to do), we are putting our trust in that person and in the information that is being shared. In the future, you may want to consider using **Golf's Physical Basics** as your blueprint for building a effective swing and game, rather than tips from your golfing friends. Learn to become more aware of the golf club's three elements. its head, face, shaft, and what you want them to do during impact for the shot at hand.

Secret: The requirements of **Golf's Physical Basics** are really non-negotiable. By trusting in your own capacity to learn through self discovery you will soon be able to predict ball flight and understand what you and your swing did to produce that outcome.

For all golfers, one of the many challenges will always be, that sometimes inefficient swings do hit fairways, greens and even make holes-in-one. But golf is a game of consistency, and "once in awhile" is not the goal of most golfers. As I said earlier, golf is a game that can reward precision. The more precision that's built into ones game, the more consistent the results will be. For any golfer to hit more fairways, greens, and make more putts, requires a repeatable effective swing. For hundreds of years, **Golf's Physical Basics** have been the true foundation for efficient swings, and not "how to" tips from our golfing friends. These basics will be discussed in detail in the upcoming Lessons. **However before moving on lets first look back to 1687,1857,1897, 1922, and 1932.**

"The Game of Golf"
Willie Park—1897

Thought to be golf's first instruction book by a professional

1687, Thomas Kincaid—Golf's First Analyst

The First World Scientific Congress of Golf was held in St. Andrews, Scotland, July 9th—13th, 1990. Over fifty presentations were given. **The following is based on D. Linning's presentation on how golf's fundamentals have not changed over time.**

Thomas Kincaid was born in 1661, in Edinburgh, Scotland. Kincaid studied to be a physician, never practiced, but had means. He devoted his time to golf, archery, and ligature. He became a champion archer, composed Latin verse, and was thought to be "learned above the common man, well versed in the humanities", by his contemporaries. Kincaid kept several diaries on various topics including; music, archery, ligature, and golf. Some of his diaries have survived and are in the National Library in Scotland.

The more you have been involved with the history of ideas, and where those ideas have been before, the more current your ideas are today.

Thomas Kincaid's thoughts on golf were recorded in January of 1687. Three hundred years ago Kincaid identified the following features of golf.

- The ball must be straight before your chest a little towards the left foot (Physical Basic #2)
- The clubs swing path should lie within a swing plane (Physical Basic #1)
- There should be a swing center. (Physical Basic #2)
- The ball should be struck with precision. (Physical Basic #3)

Diary Entries:

Jan 20th— *"The motion must be performed with the turning of your body".*

Jan 20th— *"You must not raise your body in bringing back the club, or incline it further in bringing down the club".* (Physical Basic #2)

Jan 25th— *"I found that the club must always move in a circle making a forty-five degree angle with the horizon". (Physical Basic #1)*

Jan 20th— *"Turn yourself, without moving your body out of place".*

Jan 20th— *"You must never bring the club about with the motion of the arm first, but only towards the end of the stroke".* (Physical Basic #3)

Mr. Linning closed his presentation with, *"The golf swing itself is a product of skill, optimized to make effective use of a human physique which has not changed significantly in the last three hundred years".*

1700's

1857 — GOLF'S FIRST INSTRUCTION BOOK

The Golfers Manual
H.B. Farnie 1857

The Golfers Manual, written by A Keen Hand (H.B. Farnie) in 1857 and was filled with information based on the same physical basics presented here. Farnie wrote some the following in what is believed to be golf's first instruction book.

"The club lies with its natural slant on the ground (Physical Basic #1), *returning to the ball in the same position, when it was grasped. The club in returning to the ground does not alter its position. Keep the club from variation during the swing."*

"It is our desire to impress upon people, science not effort gives the weakest arm nerved with knowledge of the act, the knack of golf that sends the ball on its flight. Just watch the gentle craft, the ease, skill, and grace of the movement. Golf is an art."

"As far as the path smoothed for the scientific swing – the club is permitted full latitude of sweep without any strain on the wrists." (Physical Basic #4)

"The perfection of the swing lies in its approximation of its circumference, (Physical Basic #1) *the circle being performed by the club. This is an advantage easily appreciated. It is obvious when the swing motion is a continuous sweep moving naturally on-plane, and when it is not, raised in abrupt diagonal or other irregular manner."*

"The club must be returned with increasing velocity, with the ball receiving the greatest momentum, with ease to the players." (Physical Basic #3)

Note: Farnie's choice of words such as "velocity" and "momentum" clearly show his insight into how physics influenced an efficient golf swing. **Velocity is speed with direction, and momentum is the by product of a transferred of energy at impact.**

Farnie then went on, *"When less distance is required from the same club, swing either of two ways – 1. Diminish swing velocity with full swing, or 2. Use half swing.* (Physical Basic #3 and #4)

"Skill in golf is far more avail than strength. The accomplished golfer depends as much on the flexibility of his wrists as the sweep of the club. Free play of the wrists without effort, free sweep without effort. (Physical Basic #4) *"The distance one stands from the ball* (Physical Basic #2), *is proportionate to the length of the club. Eyes on the ball, as the club yields gently to motion of the swing without the slightest check in the swing."*

PHYSICAL BASICS IN 1897

One summer weekend several years ago I walked into a used book store in Sag Harbor, a little village on the eastern end of Long Island and found a copy of the "1897 Encyclopedia of Sports," published in England. This two-volume encyclopedia must have been a massive undertaking at the time. Of 1,287 pages containing information about 150 sports, 18 pages were devoted to golf. The following is a short outline of what the Earl of Suffolk, Hedley Peek and F.G. Aflalo, editors of this wonderful encyclopedia, compiled on golf.

"Golf at first would become a calling, and then a science, using various clubs (Physical Basic #1) *suited to the nature of the stroke."* It is interesting that the concept of the design of the club and the nature of the stroke were recognized in print in 1897. It is also interesting as time moved on, most

golf instruction overlooked these important physical basics of golf (as suggestions about the game and swing were being put forward). I have been fortunate to be able to compile an extensive golf library over the years. It contains more than 1,000 books and magazines dating back to the 1850's. In most of them there is little mention of the connection between the nature of the stroke and the design of the club.

The Encyclopedia of Sports said, *"Matters that make a successful stroke in golf most difficult to accomplish include: the length of the shaft; the short clubhead; the restricted hitting surface;* (Physical Basic #1) *the small ball;* (Physical Basic #2) *the inadequacies of the ground* (Physical Basic #5), *and the state of the weather. Two small points must be brought into contact, the center of the clubface and a spot at the back of the ball* (Physical Basic #3). *All this is what a golfer's stroke should be built on."* The Encyclopedia went on to say," *Individual differences in, stature* (Physical Basic #2), *and temperament are sufficient to account for the different styles among good players. Beginners will be well advised to pay no attention to the unimportant details when they differ, and look to where the styles agree (at impact)."* **I believe this last sentence should be listed as one of the secrets to playing good golf.**

Other suggestions in the Encyclopedia include, *"As far as possible different shots should be played in the same way* (Physical Basic #4). *I.e. half shots should be a part segment of the full swing; quarter shots are like part of a half swing; and putting just a small stroke in the same manner."* The text also pointed out, *"when the club is truly swung, it contacts the ball before it has commenced upwards."* (Physical Basic #3) This, in my view, is a very important insight. Many golfers believe they lift the ball with their swing, causing ineffective alignments through impact, however efficient swings apply force down into the ball.

It is interesting to me that over one hundred years ago in a publication, which had over one thousand pages with only eighteen pages devoted to golf, so many fundamental insights into the games non-negotiable Physical Basics could be found, now lets move on to 1922.

Golf's Fundamentals
Seymore Dunn 1922

Dunn Said — 1922

There has been a book or two written about almost every subject known to man. Some books stand the test of time, and today they are considered classics in their field. In 1922, almost eighty years ago, a golf professional with Scotch heritage, Seymour Dunn wrote Golf Fundamentals. Today this book is considered a classic by serious students of the game of golf.

"Learning Does not stem from do this and don't do that— it stems from what happens when you do this and don't do that."

- D. McCluggage

History tells us "Old Willie Dunn" and his brother Jamie Dunn played in the great golf match of 1849 against Tom Morris and Allen Robinson for the sum of 400 pounds sterling – a side. Old Willie Dunn's son, Tom Dunn, became more famous than his father, he was universally acknowledged as the leading authority on golf from age 20 until he died at age 52. Seymour Dunn, born, 1882, was the youngest son of Tom Dunn. Seymour said the information in Golf Fundamentals was a life study handed down by many generations of Dunn's. The Dunn family was from Musselborough, known then as the center of golf in Scotland because it was older than St. Andrews. By the way, Seymour Dunn's mother was the greatest woman golfer of her day, and her father, John Gourlay, was the famous leather and feather golf ball maker. You could say this family had a few golfing genes.

Dunn's Golf Fundamentals contains some ideas and information that had never been presented before in such a clear and concise manner. The Preface for this classic book could have easily served as a preface for this or any of my books. Dunn's Preface reads:

"This book is intended **as a reminder of the principal points** to study in the science of golf. In order that this book be accurate, technical terms are used. The sciences of Geometry, Anatomy, Mechanics and Dynamics, and Psychology are used to show reasons for my thoughts."

It's interesting, that the subtitle Dunn used for Golf Fundamentals was "Orthodoxy of Style". He said his book was a **reminder of the principles** in science that can be applied to anyone's game and swing. It seems to me Seymour Dunn was not telling readers that he was going to teach them some method that guaranteed better golf. In his book, Dunn simply said, an orthodox style was possible by applying a few principles from **Geometry** (swing shape) (Physical Basic #1), **Anatomy** (body motion) (Physical Basic #4), **Mechanics and Dynamics** (source of power) (Physical Basic #3), and **Psychology** (playing) (Physical Basic #5). His approach to instruction was to remind golfers that the true principles are always available to any player, who would like to use them to improve. He was not giving tips.

Dunn's book has over 280 pages filled with wonderful pictures and diagrams – some of his thoughts include:

- Dunn felt there are many styles that work.
- Dunn suggested to always learn the principles first, then they could be adapted to any individuals style.
- He pointed out short swings, long swings, and those in-between are all based on the same exact principles.
- Dunn said, "While the principles themselves are invariable, their application can be widely varied, but the underlying principles should not be violated in the slightest degree."
- Dunn told golfers to develop their own style, but always work on the principles all efficient swings are based.

It was very interesting to me that Dunn wanted golfers to read lots of books on golf, and take all the lessons they could. He felt a broad knowledge of the game was important. Dunn said, *"Even though there are many books written by men who have never studied, or know anything of the true principles, with many instructors also in the same position, still read and take lessons."* But when taking lessons from instructors, who do not base their work on true principles of efficient swings, Dunn suggested. *"Never overlook the principles, whether your instructor understands them or not. Begin right, learn and study principles first. Do not do what some ardent golfers do, and pursue the details of some famous golfers style (and not true principles), and never play better."*

"Another common mistake is buying a set of clubs off the wall. There are no two players alike, in physique or strength. The best way to buy clubs is to have your measurements properly taken, and have clubs made especially for you."

For me, Seymour Dunn and his book were in some ways both ahead of their time in 1922. Many golfers still base their approach to learning and playing golf today on poor concepts – Dunn and his book are all still ahead of their time today. The principles that Dunn wrote about were:

- A swing center. (Physical Basic #2)
- A swing radius. (Physical Basic #2)
- A swing plane. (Physical Basic #1)
- Impact alignments. (Physical Basic #3)

Dunn referred to these principles as essentials (Homer Kelly also talked about essentials in his book, The Golfing Machine published in 1969). Dunn said *"Golfers should imagine that the ball is to be flattened out like a pancake at impact (just as the blacksmith flattens out a piece of iron on his anvil) and then it goes off like a bullet"* (Physical Basic #3). He went on to say, *"the golf swing is the proper blending of round about, and up and down* (Physical Basic #1)*, and since the swing requires exactness, we must all go very deeply in the matter in order to understand (exactness) completely."*

Dunn pointed out, *"to dispatch the ball in a given direction we must simply:*

1. Strike with the center of the clubface. (Physical Basic #3)
2. Have the clubhead traveling in the direction of play during impact. (Physical Basic #1)
3. Have the clubface at right angles to the direction of play during impact (I would respectively suggest the clubface be square to the target when the ball leaves the clubface, not impact). (Physical Basic #3)

Secret: Dunn used the term, "during impact", not "at impact." Of course there is a huge difference, and this was an important choice of words. Dunn realized impact was taking place on an arc, and that the ball was in contact with the clubface for both some time and for some distance. **Golf balls do not go into flight instantly.** Dunn had this very important insight.

Any failure to strike the ball with the center of the clubface Dunn traced to a violation of one or more of these essentials:

- Maintaining a steady swing center through impact. (Physical Basic #2)
- Maintaining a proper swing radius. (Physical Basic #1)
- Maintaining a proper swing plane. (Physical Basic #1)

These essential principles (not tips) are at the foundation of all Dunn's lessons. He said, *"They should all be mastered. By mastered I meant not merely understood, but practices till physical application has become second nature – an unconscious habit."* Dunn called his book and his work **a reminder of principles points** upon which anyone could build and orthodox style of golf with, as are **Golf's Physical Basics** presented here. Now lets move on to 1932.

* Research by Bob Bush at True Temper showed that the ball stays on the club face for three-quarters of an inch, and five-thousandths of a second.

A NEW WAY — 1932

Alex Morrison, one of the most celebrated golf instructor of his time wrote in 1932, A New Way to Better Golf. At the time, his ideas were considered by many to be unorthodox. He said, *"The game is surrounded by more misstatements, misconceptions, superstitions, and fetishes* ***than any other form of human activity.*** *The average golfer has little knowledge of the principles of executing a golf shot. No more then the meaningless maxims posted on the fences at public driving ranges."*

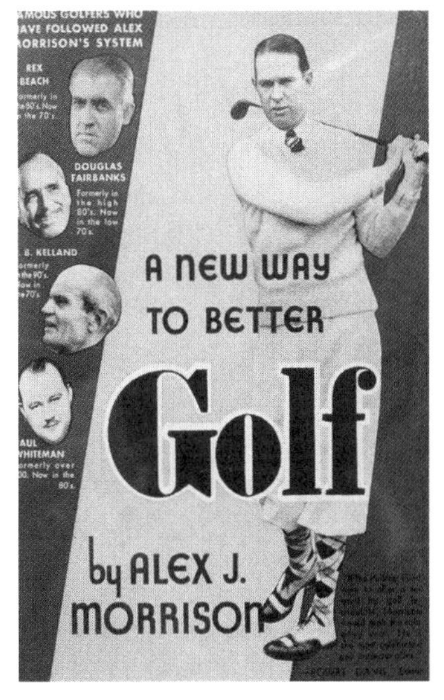

A New Way
Alex Morrison 1932

Morrison said – ***"The obvious and logical first point in analyzing the swing must be the required actions of the club and the ball. The club and ball is the only intelligent place to start*** (Physical Basics #1 and #3). ***Even a casual observation of the game must recognize the club, ball, and playing conditions*** (Physical Basic #5) ***are the only true foundation for information about efficient swings, and not some list of do's and don'ts about the swing and body."*** This is the same starting point for **Golf's Physical Basics** that some sixty years later I make reference to here in **"Golf Swing Secrets...and Lies".**

"The trials and tribulations that the average golfer undergoes are simply the result of an erroneous approach to the game" -Alex Morrison. Alex felt the correct swing could be learned by anyone. But he also felt it was important to realize that learning the correct swing does not mean that the player will always execute it under all playing conditions. *"The excellence of anyone's game depends entirely on self-control. That is, the extent to which the mind takes charge and the body responds to its commands".*

"I'm a curious person, experimenting is my enjoyment. The basics of the swing remain the same, but I look for different ways to hit shots."
- Ben Hogan

1920's

1920's

1930's

Morrison recognized that golf was a game which was a direct challenge to self-control, the kind of self-control from which inner peace arises. Self-control based on confidence in ones ability. Morrison also recognized that golf instruction should be based on **the scientific principles of force** (Physical Basic #3), and not on some meaningless misstatements and poor concepts.

While A New Way to Better Golf was the title of Morrison's book, the information upon which his ideas were based, were not new or unorthodox. The disciplines of Science, Geometry, Physics, and Human Anatomy existed long before Morrison's book and also before golf's first instruction book, The Golfers Manual published in 1857. **Morrison felt that the average golfer was getting the kind of golf lesson they wanted but not the kind they needed**. Most golfers were trying to learn (unsuccessfully) by popular not scientific methods. He said, *"What is being overlooked is that the clubface must strike the ball exactly with correct angles, and with the required force."* (All of **Golf's Physical Basics**)

Morrison said, *"The average player lives in fear of doing the wrong things. If the word concentration had been erased early from the golfer's dictionary, and replaced by relaxation, fewer players would be struggling. The average golfer silently rehearses a list of don'ts before they swing, then get results that bear little if any relation to their intentions. These golfers who have a sincere desire to better their game, all get bewildered concentrating on all the "don'ts" of golf, with one "don't" as false as the next. All these "don'ts" have no place in good golf"*.

Alex Morrison's goal for the swing was simply; ***"a full flowing motion, without mental or physical interpretation*** (Physical Basic #4). ***A swing that is an example of a scientific principal correctly applied.*** *Not Bobby Jones swing or any other champion's swing – but a swing motion that had underlying principles that were the same for any action the body could make."* (It's called Biomechanics)

Back in 1932 Morrison's ideas based on scientific principles seemed too technical for many golfers. He would often hear, *"That's the trouble with the game today – I am not a scientist, I do not know anything about the principles of force and I could care less. I just want to play better"*. Today, 70 years latter it is no different, many people just want results and when they are not happy with their game, they go from one tip to the next tip, from one book to the next book, etc.

Secret: **When a player has any doubts about what the outcome of their swing will be, results are more varied then when they have confidence in their swing and its outcome.**

Players who go from here to there and back again with ideas about their swing and game, are clearly showing a lack of confidence that an understanding of the underlying principles of motion and force can bring to their game. With insights into a few principles of motion and force, golfers may hit some shots for which they don't care for, but will understand the cause and not jump ship looking for new answers.

Morrison also points out how freedom of motion (Physical Basic #4) is important to the golf swing and playing the game. **Motion without tension** that is free to generate and correctly apply force. *"Power and force are easily obtained by efficient employment of the bones, joints, tendons, and muscles of the body, propelling the club with maximum leverage."*

Morrison said, *"I know I will be considered erratic by those who have expressed their own opinions (not of science) on the subject. But when people are unconvinced, the fault lies in my explanation, or in faulty application of the principles – not in the underlying principles of force and motion. My explanation is founded on no one's personal opinions, or their idiosyncrasies, but on the anatomical structure of the human body."* Even back in the late 1920's and early 1930's Alex Morrison tried to guide golfers through the misinformation and poor concepts that were available then. Today, the variety of golf information, (most of it with little or no common ground) has increased at least ten-fold and maybe more, making progress even more difficult.

Golf's Physical Basics, have been at the foundation of the game from day one. They are all as useful today as they were over 500 years ago. **These Physical Basics are discussed in detail after lesson six in Chapter Three.** (p. 139)

LESSON THREE—SUMMARY

Secret: Unless the design angles of the club, ballistic properties of the ball, the human form, the field of play, or the principals of motion and force are changed, these are the Physical Basics of golf.

- Physical Basic #1—The Design of the club
- Physical Basic #2—Standing inside or to the side of the ball and target line
- Physical Basic #3—Balls are compressionable
- Physical Basic #4—Timing and Balance
- Physical Basic #5—The field of play and ever changing playing conditions.

"The mechanics of the efficient golfing method are the same as ever. The fundamentals have remained the same."

- Bobby Jones 1930's

LESSON FOUR

Visualizations

1920's to 2000

Note:

There is little text in lesson four.

The following pictures are the common alignments
that have always been used to apply
on plane force through impact.

Be mindful of lessons one through three
as you view lesson four.

Be Aware

Here in Lesson Four there are pictures of world class golfers dating back over one hundred years. Note the similarities. The two design angles of the clubs shaft and the shot at hand, (i.e. Golf's Environment) have required the alignment and application of force to be similar for over five hundred years. Nature knows no other possibilities. Hopefully readers will see the similarities and use them as guidelines for making progress.

ADDRESS

Spine bent over to (above) the ball and angled away from the target

1890's

1930's

1900

1920

2000 #7

1950's

1950's

1930's

1900

TOP OF BACKSWING

Elbow joints in front of body, pointing down to the ground

1950's

1910

1915

1950's

1990's

1990's

1900's

1910

1999

Elbows Point Down

2000

1990's

2000

2000

1990's #5

1990's

1990's

1990's

1990's

DOWN PLANE

Spine angled away from target, right shoulder going down plane

1930's

1940's

1999

1999 #5

1990's

1998

1920's

1950's

1905

Right Forearm on Shaft Plane

1920's

2000 #7

1915

1990's

1990's #4

2000

1999

1940's

1910

Impact

Spine angled away from target. Right shoulder, right forearm, hands, shaft, club head, all parallel to the shaft plane. Ears and eyes level.

1920's

1950's #6

1950's #6

2000 #2

1990's #5

1990's

1960's #1

1960's #1

1950's #1

Right Shoulder Down Plane

1940's

1999

1999

1999 #2

1999 #7

1930's

1950's

1999 #7

1950's #6

SPINE ANGLED OVER TO THE BALL AND BACK FROM TARGET

1930

1940

1950

1999 #5

1999 #2

1915

1999 #7

1999 #2

1999 #2

Shoulders on Plane

1920's

1930's

1920's

1990's #2

1990's #2

1990's #5

1999 #5

2000 #7

1940's

Follow Through

Right Forearm on Plane

1910

1999

1930's

1999

1910

1999 #2

1999 #2

1915

1930's

Long Arms at Follow Through

1920's

1930's

1940's

1990's #2

1990's #5

1990's #2

1990's #2

2000 #5

1990's #5

EYES ON PLANE

1920's

1930's

1950's

1990's #2

1990's #2

1990's #2

1990's #4

2000 #5

1990's #5

FINISH

1920's

1930's

1920's

2000 #5

1990's #7

1990's #5

1900

1930

1920's

FACE DOWN, EYES AND EARS LEVEL, NECK PARALLEL TO THE GROUND, RIGHT FOREARM ON PLANE

1920's

1930's

1920's

1990's #5

1990's #4

1990's #2

1990's #4

1990's #5

1990's #4

RIGHT FOREARM ON PLANE

1920's

1940's

1920's

1990's #2

1990's #4

1990's #4

1990's #5

2000 #5

1990's #5

EYES AND EARS LEVEL

1960's

1930's

1920's

2000 #2

1990's #2

1990's #2

1930's

1990's #2

1990's #4

EYES, SHOULDERS, AND SHAFT ALL PARALLEL TO SHAFT PLANE

1990's #4

1990's #2

1990's #5

1990's #5

1990's #2

1990's #5

1990's #5

1990's #5

1990's #5

SHOULDERS PARALLEL TO THE SHAFT PLANE

1920's

1920's

1920's

1990's #2

1930's

1990's #2

1990's #2

2000 #5

1990's #2

VISUALIZATIONS—PART II

The value of using **visualizations** has always been recognized by good golfers and experts from the field of learning motor skills. What follows are some suggestions for **visualizations** based on golf equipment and a golfers body parts.

THE GOLF BALL

Practice balls normally have a line or stripe on them that can be used for several **visualizations**. (The name on the golf ball can also be used).

Ⓐ #4

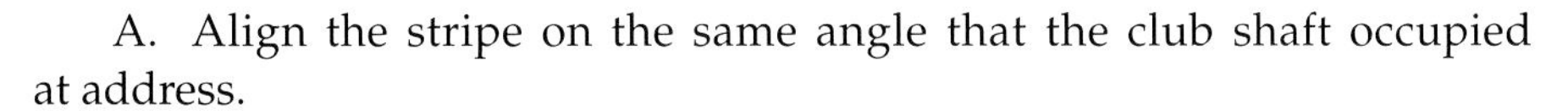

A. Align the stripe on the same angle that the club shaft occupied at address.

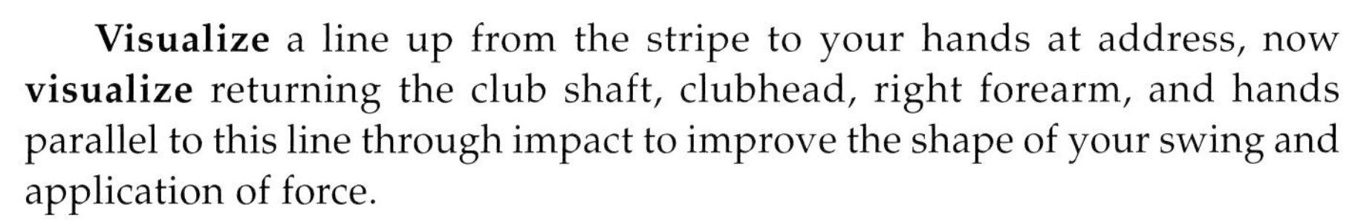

Visualize a line up from the stripe to your hands at address, now **visualize** returning the club shaft, clubhead, right forearm, and hands parallel to this line through impact to improve the shape of your swing and application of force.

B. Point the stripe on a range ball down the target line, then **visualize** this line extending on each side of the ball. This line can be used several ways.

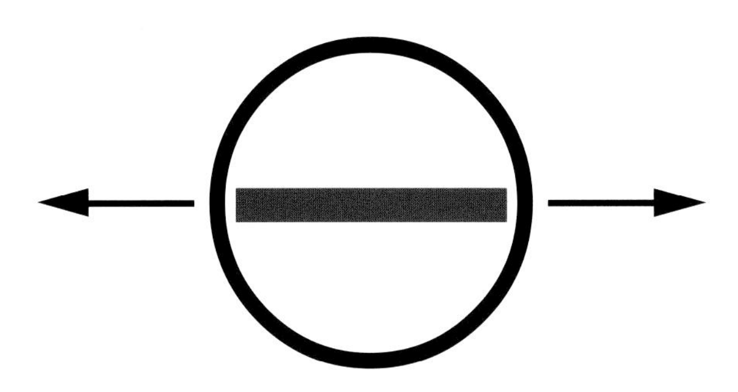

Ⓑ

1. To improve alignment at address, golfers can align themselves parallel to the stripe on the ball.

2. To improve the shape of their swing, golfers should **visualize** their swing keeping the clubhead inside this line during both the backswing and downswing.

3. To improve the swings application of force at impact, **visualize** the swing path back to impact is form inside this line.

① #5

C. Add two more short stripes to a range ball, then point the three stripes away from the player.

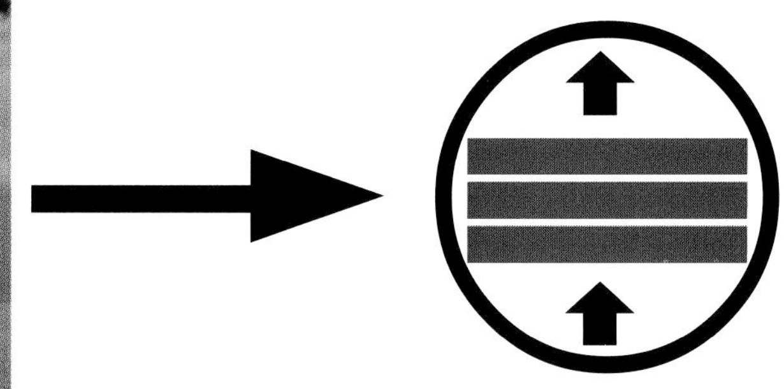

1. When practicing your putting, **visualize** these three stripes rotating one over the other before you putt. Then after stroking the ball, your good strokes will indeed roll the ball with the three stripes rotating one over the other.

2. Point the stripes down the target line. The ball now has an inside, middle, and outside line.

② #6

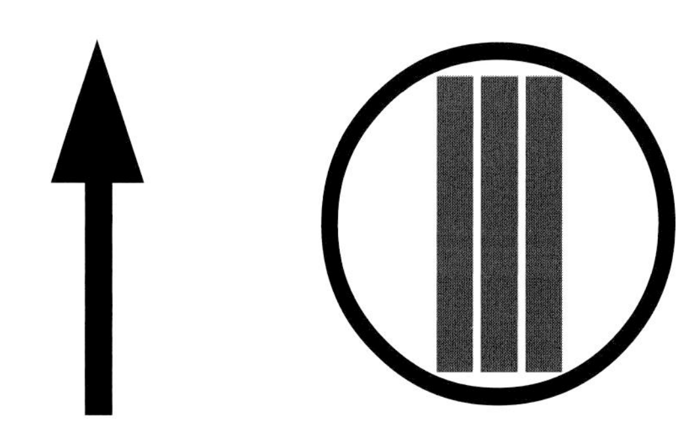

To improve swing shape, **visualize** your swing returning your hands, then the clubhead down a path (or plane) to the inside line.

Hole in the Butt End of the Grip

Most golf clubs have a small hole in the butt end of the grip that can be used for several visualizations.

Ⓐ #5

A. When putting, **visualize** this hole being somewhat forward of the clubface at address and impact.

B. To improve the application of force for most long and short game shots, **visualize** the hole in the grip passing through impact before the shaft or clubhead.

Ⓑ **Short**

Ⓑ **Long** #4

C. For most green side bunker shots, visualize the hole in the grip behind the ball at address. This alignment of the grip will turn the bounce on the sand wedge down. Now **visualize** the bounce acting as a plow displacing sand under the ball.

Ⓒ

The Shaft

For more power, **visualize** returning the **whole shaft** to the ball, not just the clubhead.

#4

#1

2. For more power, **visualize** retuning the right-forearm on the same angle that the **shaft** occupied at address through impact.

#7

#4

SHOULDER PATH

To improve direction and power, **visualize** the shoulders turning on the same angle that the club's (lie) shaft angle occupied at address. **Visualize** the right shoulder rotating through the same space that the left shoulder passes through during the backswing.

#2

#2

EYES - EARS

A. To improve balancing, **visualize** your **eyes and ears** level at address and through impact.

Ⓐ #2

Ⓐ #5

B. To improve your balance and swing plane, **visualize** your **eyes** on plane after impact.

Ⓑ #2 Ⓑ #7

ARMS

A. To improve your swing plane, **visualize** your **left arm** swinging parallel to the lie angle of the shaft at address.

Ⓐ #4 Ⓐ

B. To improve your swing plane, **visualize** your **right arm** swinging parallel to the lie angle that the shaft occupied at address.

Ⓑ #5 Ⓑ #7

C. For more power, **visualize** the right **forearm** returning below the angle that it occupied at address, or on the angle the shaft occupied at address.

Ⓒ #6 Ⓒ

D. For more power, **visualize** long **arms** after impact, with right shoulder on plane.

Ⓓ #2 Ⓓ #4

Right Elbow

A. To improve your swing plane, **visualize** a line up from the inside corner of the ball at address going through your right elbow and beyond. Now **visualize** the right elbow staying on this line through out the swing.

Ⓐ #4 Ⓐ #4

B. To improve your swing plane, **visualize** the right elbow always staying inside your shirt seam during the backswing and pointing down.

Ⓑ

#5

Ⓑ

#5

C. For more power, **visualize** the right elbow staying forward of the clubhead for most of the downswing .

Ⓒ

Ⓒ

SWING

A. To prevent a reverse pivot and a loss of balance, **visualize** the left shoulder turning more than the left knee during the backswing.

Ⓐ

Ⓐ

B. To improve the plane of your shoulder turn, **visualize** during the downswing the spines still angled away from the ball.

Ⓑ #4

Ⓑ #5

C. To improve tempo, **visualize** the arms never swinging faster than your bodies rate of rotation.

D. **Visualize** the tempo of your swing by saying a long "one" to yourself throughout the entire swing, instead of "one—two". I have found that saying "one—two", causes golfers to over-accelerate.

E. For better rhythm during the downswing, **visualize** the hands and the right shoulder traveling down plane together. With the hands never jumping to out race the right shoulder.

F. **Visualize** that the backswing is only six to eight inches long. Note: When the left shoulder turns its only traveling six to eight inches, but the clubhead travels many feet. Also, **visualize** when the body turns slow, the clubhead swings faster. Nature knows no other possibilities.

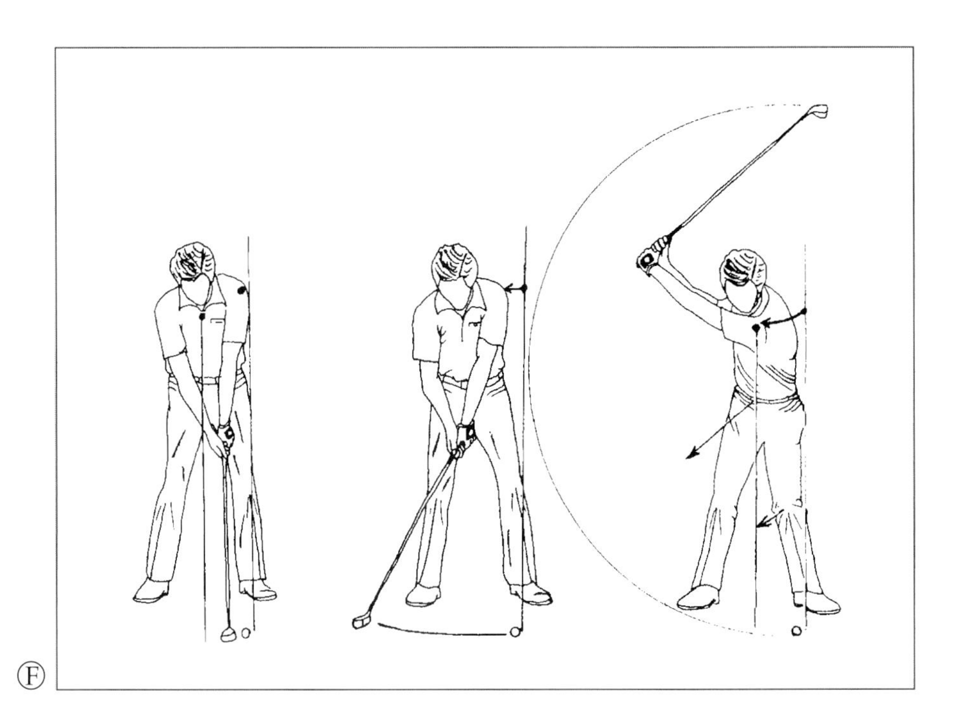

Ⓕ

G. **Visualize** the hands only traveling chest high in the backswing, but because of momentum the club keeps traveling. This **visualization** can help prevent over swinging.

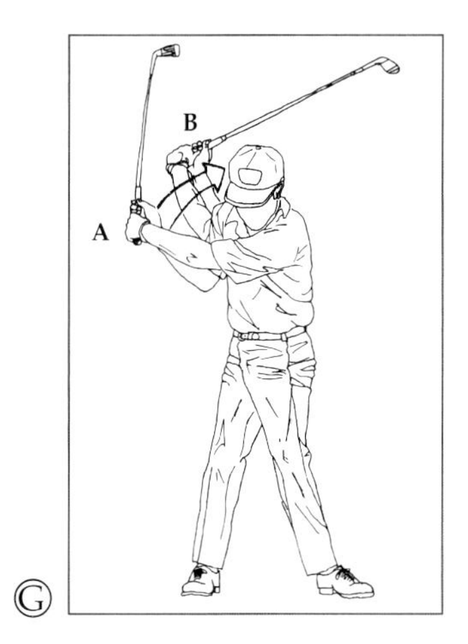

H. To improve timing, rhythm, and sequencing of body parts, **visualize** leaving the club behind as you start your downswing.

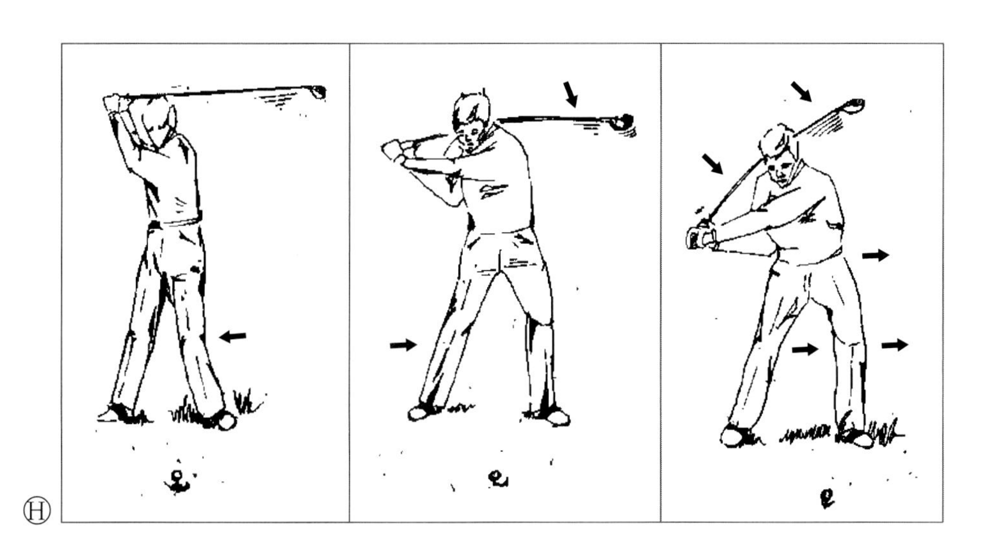

I. To improve rhythm and application of force, **visualize** the hands and chest staying together.

#2

J. To improve the shoulder plane, **visualize** the right ear facing the ground after impact.

#4   #5

K. To improve balance, **visualize** your mid-section facing the target at finish.

#7

L. To improve swing path, **visualize** the shaft of the club at address is a roof of a house. Now swing the club and shoulders parallel to the angle of the roof.

LESSON FIVE

Playing And Swinging

Be Aware

- **The purpose of the game, enjoyment**
- **The object of the game, to influence ball flight**
- **The object of the swing, to influence the alignment and application of force through impact, for the shot at hand**

PLAYING AND SWINGING

We could say that at the very foundation of the game of golf is **motion** (i.e., a player's body moves, the golf club moves, and so does the golf ball). **Learning to improve a golf swing simply starts with learning and improving motion.** The motion of the body, club, and ball are different for the expert golfer than the non-expert. If the foundation of golf is motion, *influencing* and *predicting* motion then becomes the foundation of *good* golf.

"Rhythm is the connecting thread that enhances the development of skills and abilities"
- Kowalski 2000

Note: Everyone reading this book who is not happy with their swing and game, either has too much or too little motion with their body, club, or in their ball flight.

Secret: At the foundation of motion are the elements of Balancing and Timing. **Before** using any information about the golf swing and playing the game, please realize it is not possible to reach your potential, or even make much progress, without improving your timing and balancing. I.e. tempo - rhythm.

A golfer could have useful information and concepts about the swing and playing the game, but if their approach overlooks effective **balancing** and **timing**, progress will be very difficult if not impossible. There are many world-class golfers who **do not** have a model swing, but their **balancing** and **timing** are both effective or you could say, world-class. *"The mechanical movements in golf, are not the whole secret."* - Percy Boomer 1940's.

With efficient body motion the player is **balancing** in three-dimensional space (up to down, front to back, and side to side). Efficient swing motion also has **swing timing** that keeps the club in front of the body, as the arms, club and body all move, with no one body part out racing any other. Efficient motion has **timing** that produces a flat left wrist and a bent right wrist through impact, with the club shaft staying in line with the left arm.

Achieving a more consistent game is something everyone who plays golf would like to experience. After learning more about the game of golf we come to realize playing up to ones potential **everyday** just does not happen. Both the experienced professional and everyone else who plays will have some off days. This may be one of the reasons why so many people love to play golf and can be heard saying, *"Just wait until the next swing, or the next hole, or the back nine, or the next time I play, I will do better!"* (They enjoy the challenge.)

While we recognized the course and conditions the game is played under are always changing, and players games can come and go, **some golfers are "more consistent" than others are**. Its not unfair to say players with consistent games use swings that are more consistent, giving more consistent results.

Secret: **Repeatable golf swings normally have the fewest moving parts for the shot at hand. Take place in the smallest possible space, giving players the balancing and timing that repeatable results are built on.**

Swing tips are not what efficient swings are built on. Without the core elements of **balancing and timing,** consistent swings are not possible. **Balancing and timing** are prerequisites of efficient swings. Improving them should be the player's first goal.

Time! A Core Element

When we are trying to gain some insights for our own game, it's never a bad idea to watch world-class golfers play. There seems to be many different ways to get good results in golf and most world-class golfers have very individual swings, **so what should we look for?**

"If one swings within himself, and does not attempt to over accelerate any movements there will be rhythmical harmony which all good golfers use in getting distance."

– 1902 C.S. Hanks

Tom Lehman, Jim Furyk, Nancy Lopez, Lee Trevino, Laura Davies, Tiger Woods, Jack Nicklaus, and Bob Murphy are all examples and proof positive there are many ways to play world-class golf. With what appears to be little common ground in the swings and games of top golfers, what can be learned?

Secret: **Fortunately, there is a core element that every world-class player has, and it's the element of time. In fact, the element of time is one of the main reason efficient swings have repeatable impact conditions.**

Again, what is this all-important element of **time**? For some useful insights, start with music. Music has notes that not only have to be played correctly; these notes also have to be played in the correct **time**. If they are not played in correct **time**, we hear noise, and not a flowing in-time sound called music - music that has a "beat" to it. It's this beat that represents the element of time all music has. Music can either be **in or out of time,** with a loss of its beat. Golf swings can also be in or out of **time**.

Secret: **Every world-class golfer has blended his or her swing mechanics (notes) into a flowing motion (music), a motion that swings the club away from address then back down to impact within a time frame many non-expert players do not have. When hitting shots they do not care for, expert golfers often have not lost their swing mechanics, they have lost the beat of their swing and are out of time.**

In music, tempo is a reference to time (i.e. slow, medium, fast). Rhythm is a reference to the synchronization of all time elements in a piece of music (i.e. timing). Note the difference.

A golf swing could be moving the club through a very acceptable space, similar to all notes in music being played correctly, but if either the swing or notes were not in time, the results of both efforts would be less than satisfactory.

Time (tempo) is one of the most important **swing motion considerations**. Some very unorthodox swings (highly individual styles) have won golf tournaments because the player was swinging in time and rarely lost the beat of his or her swing motion. I was told that Arnold Palmer, some years ago, was once picked up at the airport by a young assistant, and as they drove to the tournament, Arnold asked to stop at a local sport shop so he could buy a stopwatch. **Palmer wanted the assistant to time his swing as he practiced.**

Secret: **When we are swinging at our best, all our swings (from putter to driver) have the same beat to them. Studies show that all efficient swings more or less take the same amount of time from startup back to impact.**

When Tom Lehman made that unfortunate swing on the 17th hole in the 1997 U.S. Open, and Tiger Woods was hitting iron shots over greens during the last round of the 1997 Colonial, they probably were not so much out of swing, as they had lost the beat of their swing and control of the flight of the ball.

It has been said that many amateur golfers never hit the same shot twice, rarely making the same swing twice. If golfers would start to make the element of **time** or the beat of their swing, their **main in-swing concern**, progress and better ball striking would soon follow.

TIME AND LEARNING

Recent neuroscience research has demonstrated that a person's genetic make-up provides only a broad blueprint for body motion. **It's the past experiences in our lives that appear to account for many of our specific capacities to move.** Studies show timing and sequencing of the body's actions are essential components of coordination in all athletic skills.

Secret: Our basic thinking, planning, and organization capacities are influenced by our ability to sequence ideas, with timing information.

Studies show that one's ability to feel and express a steady beat of time is fundamental to movement affecting sport skills. The High Scope Educational Research Foundation found that a person's timing abilities affect self-control and gross motor skills. (Kiger, 1994, Mitchell 1994, Petrlin 1991).

"There is an individual tempo of the personality. There with which is a natural tempo we all perform any deliberately will action."

- M. Peterlin

In 1996 Melk, one of the many researchers who demonstrated that the brain's motor control center also keeps track of time, expressed the belief that **timing is the foundation of all learning and memory.** The key challenge for long-term learning is to develop ways to create the most relevant types of experience from which to learn from, and **time seems to be very relevant to learning.**

In 1991 Peterlin did studies in Michigan that indicated when a persons "**beat**" or "**time**" competence is enhanced, inner control improves. **Studies found that people with poor perceptions of time (tempo) are more clumsy then people with good perceptions of time.** Improving ones perception of time imparts information and feedback that leads to enhancing human motion. This is especially true, when sensory processing must be rapidly integrated with motor skill planning and coordination to isolate and move particular muscle groups. i.e. A golf swing.

Secret: Basic timing, one's ability to feel and express a steady beat of time, involves both rhythmic perception and rhythmic performance. In 1987 Welkart concurred that rhythmic skill involves one's perception of time and then synchronizing one's body motion with that perception. As one's ability to match movement to a steady beat improved, so did motor performance.

It seems that time is a "core element" in both learning and performing an effective golf swing. Unfortunately time or beat is personal in nature and each player is the only one, who is familiar with what his or her time feels like (workable and unworkable). Any improvements in this area can only be guided by instruction. **Good timing must be learned and acquired by the players own ability to be aware of both "in time", or "out of time" swings they make.**

Secret: From start to finish the time or beat of an effective swing is a pattern of information which each golfer must learn. It is as important to progress as swing plane or impact alignments. Time or beat and sequencing of motion are pieces of information that are often over looking in learning golf.

It helps to recognize that **time** (tempo - rhythm) is information in its own right. **Time is an element that must be understood by any sources of instruction, if our knowledge of learning the golf swing is to move beyond our present day levels.** Mechanical reasons are often given as the cause of ball flight (good or bad). Maybe golfers could gain some insights from dancers and musicians that could improve their swing and game. In dance and music, the quality of time can be the difference between the expert and the non-expert. **In golf the element of time and not poor alignments is often the cause of poor ball flight.**

Note: Golfers must learn: the blending of alignments into a flowing well timed motion is the foundation of effective mechanics.

Secret: The highly skilled golfer has learned a feel for the time or beat of their swing. The less skilled golfer will start to make progress once they do.

Finding Your Beat

To find the beat of your swing, have a friend time your swing as you hit some 5-foot and then 10-foot putts, by counting 1,001, 1,002, 1,003. Begin counting at the start of the swing and stop at impact. Then move on to a few chips, pitches, half swings, and then finish with full swing. When the beat of the swing is efficient, every swing from putt to drive should more or less get back to impact on the same count. While every player's beat or time frame may be different from that of other players, the overall individual time for each player when the swing is in time, or on its beat is the same. (My beat is just short of 1,002.)

A noted music teacher said her main goal with a new student was to train their ear to hear different sounds – and the difference between in time sounds, and out of time sounds.

*Golfers must learn to feel tempo and rhythm that is both in or out of time.

Secret: Not only should the shape of a swing match the individual player's body style, the beat or time element of the swing should also match.

Warning: Whenever something causes a shift in the beat or speed of the player's swing (i.e. being nervous on the first tee or during an important shot), this change can cause the player to lose his "effort-free" actions, and a motion filled with "effort" takes over. A swing that has effort has probably lost its beat, its balancing capabilities, and any ball control it was once capable of.

Secret: The core element of highly skilled golfers is not the shape of their swing (they are all different), it's their ability to blend swing mechanics into a flowing, in-time motion with a beat.

When observing players on any practice range at PGA, LPGA or Senior Tour tournaments, you can see these gifted golfers swinging in time. There are no jumping actions at any time in their swings, just a flowing, graceful motion. Some styles have faster beats than others, but all have the required time element found in all efficient swings.

Studies by the University of Chicago found professional golfers use 12 to 15 seconds to plan their actions, and the average amatures pre-shot return is only 3 to 5 seconds, leaving them less prepared.

Effective time elements are not only found in world-class player's swings, but they can also be seen in their **pre-shot actions**. There is a pace or beat to all the motions of a world-class golfer's body language. Every lesson given at our golf schools or in our private instruction has the element of **time** at its foundation. When golfers discover a feel for the beat of their swing (as must any player looking for some success must), the learning necessary to improve swing mechanics becomes possible.

Secret: When swings have no repeatable beat to them, it is not possible to have any long-term improvement in swing mechanics, period end of sentence!

FEEL THE BEAT

Unfortunately, the individual player is the only one, who knows what his or her own beat feels like. The player is the only one, who can recognize the feel of "in" or "out" of time swings. Instructors can make you aware of the element of time and help you discover your most effective beat, but they cannot feel your beat.

When working to improve the element of time in your swing, keep your mind free of all swing thoughts. **Keep the mind clear and open to an awareness of the element of time.** Feel the beat and repeat the beat, without regard for where the ball goes. As the beat improves and you can repeat it time and again, your swing mechanics can also improve. But if the element of time is not effective, any knowledge of swing mechanics (both physical and mental) is less valuable. **World class swings are appealing to our eye because of how world class golfer apply and use the core elements of time and balance. i.e. tempo – rhythm.**

"It's not enough to study action under a microscope, you need to know what it feels like."

- Roger Fisher

Secret: All actions and motions happen in **three dimensions**. They take place in the right amount of **space**, in the proper **sequence**, and in the right **time**. An effective golf swing keeps the club on plane or in the proper **space**. It keeps the club behind the hands or in proper **sequence**, and it has the correct beat or is in the correct **time**. Of the three - space, sequence, and time - **time is the most influential**. When motion and actions are out of time, space and sequence normally are lost.

"By remembering a feel, the words think and thought don't have to be used."

- Percy Boomer 1940's

BALANCING – A CORE ELEMENT

Mark O'Meara, Tom Weiskopf, Ben Hogan, Steve Elkington, Mac O'Grady, Nancy Lopez and Patty Sheehan are a few examples of golfers, who have swings with the kind of balancing we have always enjoyed watching.

By definition, **balancing** is the body's ability to perform purposeful movement while resisting the force of gravity, a natural law that pulls everything to the center of the earth.

The information about "balancing" given here parallels studies done by Dr. Tony Toole of Florida State

When golfers are trying to improve, they are often and correctly told to work on only one segment of their game or swing at a time. This is certainly good advice, and progress can come from this suggestion. But the **main** consideration, when using any suggestion to improve (posture, swing, ball position, etc.), a golfer needs to keep in mind is: **how will balancing in three-dimensional space be affected?** Every adjustment we make, or suggestion we use, must take the balanced state of the golfer into consideration.

Secret: The greater the precision golfers can build into their swing, the more success they can expect. One of the main reasons precision is lost, or cannot be attained, is the lack of, or loss of **the balance state**.

The first system to fully develop (5 months after conception) in humans is the vestibular. The system controls our sense of motion and balance.

Humans are born with internal balance centers located in the eyes, ears and neck. We automatically make adjustments, when our body moves off center and out of balance. This system is really a subconscious protection mechanism that prevents physical injuries. Without the compensating movements that our central nervous system provides, the body would constantly fall over.

Most unnecessary and unorthodox movements which can be observed in golf swings, are often nothing more than compensations for a swing that has moved off center and out of balance. These unwanted actions are being introduced automatically by the central nervous system as a reaction to the body and swing being out of balance. Consequently the only way to stop unwanted actions is to improve balancing.

The player's body is their most important piece of equipment.

Secret: Many swing movements golfers would like to improve or eliminate, can only be helped by improved balancing.

One of the most recognizable examples of the CNS's (central nervous system) balance correction capabilities can be observed when a young child waddles. The side-to-side motions of the child's body are not conscious efforts. Rather, these movements are caused or introduced by the internal balance centers located in the eyes, ears and neck. The child's center of gravity is being relocated automatically to re-establish a balanced state with every step or waddle.

Structure before and during motion governs the quality of function and force.

The human body is a living, moving machine that always tries to stay on center and in balance. The CNS is constantly making the necessary subconscious adjustments to achieve balance. Golfers will always develop "some way" to deliver the clubhead to the ball, but often have what could be called a **misapplication of force**. One of the reasons effective swings **do not** misapply force, is because they perform in conditions where the center of gravity **is not constantly** being required to move around to re-establish balance.

The body has a **natural circle of balance**. This natural balance or on-centered condition is influenced by the width of the stance, the position of the eyes, ears, and neck at address, and throughout the swing. Before moving on to some suggestions to improve balancing, please let me give you some information on why our bodies move, information which you may not be aware of.

Goal: Optimum performance, with the least wear and tear on the body.

It may help your understanding of balancing to imagine when the body is on center and in balance it is not moving. When you are standing still, you are on center and balanced. For one of your body segments (links) to move in an orderly fashion, another body segment (link) must move off center or, you could even say move "out of balance". During an effective swing the player is not balanced, **per se**, golfers are balancing their body's thirteen major joints in three-dimensional space, (side to side, up to down, and front to back).

Try taking a step in an orderly fashion without moving your chest. You will find that it is difficult to do. But, when your upper body segments (links) move forward or off center, the lower body segments (links) reacting to the off balanced condition of the upper body, move forward in an orderly coordinated fashion to recapture balance.

Secret: What should be understood, before moving on, is that both coordinated and uncoordinated movements are caused by an off-centered or out-of-balance condition.

Note: Two useful ways of looking at movement during the golf swing are: **how long (length of time)** the body or a segment is off center; and is the motion the body is going through it **taking into consideration the next stage of the movement that follows.**

When we observe a smooth, coordinated golf swing, we see a motion that has taken into consideration the next stage of motion, and body links that are only off balance for a short period of time. When golfers overlook the next orderly stage of the swing, or when a body segment is off balance too long, motion becomes uncoordinated.

A low center of gravity adds stability to motion.

When I described the walking motion earlier, it was a smooth coordinated reaction to the off-balanced condition of upper body links that lasted for a very short period of time. Now picture the upper body staying off balance for a much longer period of time: i.e. when we trip. You can see how the leg stride would lose its smooth, coordinated pattern of motion, therefore becoming a quick, jerky, out-of-control reaction to body links being off center for too long – It would also be a motion that did not take into consideration the next stage of orderly movement of body links.

Perhaps, when observing a golf swing which you feel is unpleasant to the eye, or one you feel is out of control, you can now recognize a swing that has **body links** that are off balance too long. **You will also be able to see that it is a swing that overlooks the next stage of orderly motion that it should pass through.**

"What I can do to improve my balance before, during and after my swing?" A question golfers must ask and answer, when they are looking to improve and get more enjoyment from their golf. When your efforts to improve take into consideration how the golf swing information you are about to use is going to affect balancing, real progress is possible. Most movements golfers would like to remove from their swing are often just compensations and reactions to an off-balanced state that lasted too long.

Suggestions for Balancing

Centers of the **Eyes** both looking at the ball.

Ears as level as possible through the swing.

Note: The hair (silia) in the inner ear reads the fluids of the ear. When the eyes and ears are not level, a message is sent to the brain causing compensating movements. When both eyes are not fully on the ball, the brain may not receive enough information about ball location for a golfer to reach his or her true potential. If we were to cover the left eye of many golfers who turn their head off the ball at the start of their swing, they would not be able to see the ball at the top of the backswing.

Knee joints work in tandem. Many golfers over-use their left leg in the backswing causing the right knee to break down. **The left shoulder should always turn more than the left knee.** In many swings, the reverse is true, causing balancing problems in the backswing.

The spine *(lumbar segment)* bends over to the ball at address approximately 15-20 degrees from the top of the lowest segment (sacral). The next segment (thoracic) bends over another 15-20 degrees from the top of the lumbar. During an effective swing, these spine angles are constant as possible. Any quick change would cause some balancing problems.

Face Down, Eyes and Ears Level #2

The neck (cervical segment) of a golfers spine, who retains a balancing state is also over to the ball approximately 15-20 degrees. The neck is not straight up. Most world-class golfers have their face down looking at the ball, chin off their chest. **They do not have their head up, neck straight, with eyes turned down. This position can cause balancing problems.**

Golfers who are balancing to promote effective motion, have their **buttocks** placed more under the upper body than out at address. When the buttocks are placed out several inches beyond the heels, the hips must make several unnecessary compensating movements during the swing, especially in the downswing. To improve your balancing, your hips should feel more under your trunk than pushed out at address.

On-balance golfers also keep their **upper arms and elbows** close to their body during the back and downswing. It may help your balancing to picture that your arms are in front of your body throughout the swing.

On-balance golfers have their **13 major joints** balanced at address. A side view shows that their knee joints are over the balls of their feet, and kneecaps are over the center of their toes. Their ankle joints are placed under their hip joints, and the elbows are nine to ten inches apart, while the shoulder joints are over kneecaps.

Ⓐ Ben Hogan

Ⓐ Bryon Nelson

Note: three spine angles, and how the hips are under the upper body, not way out past the heels of the feet.

Some Principles of Balancing

- ***THE WIDER THE BASE OF SUPPORT, THE MORE STABLE THE BODY.*** (Not so wide that an over use of the legs is required to swing.)
- ***THE LOWER THE CENTER OF GRAVITY, THE GREATER THE STABILITY.*** (Not so low as to limit the body's ability to rotate. When the knee joint is over flexed, it limits rotation.)
- ***THE CLOSER THE CENTER OF GRAVITY STAYS TO THE MIDDLE OF THE BASE OF SUPPORT, THE GREATER THE STABILITY.*** The center of gravity should never move outside the base of support. (Swing in the smallest possible space, staying inside your feet from start to finish.)
- ***TO APPLY A FORCE, WIDEN THE BASE OF SUPPORT IN LINE WITH THE DIRECTION OF FORCE.*** (Not so wide as to cause off-balance movement.)
- ***KEEP OBJECTS TO BE MOVED CLOSE TO THE BODY OR CENTER OF GRAVITY.*** (Efficient swings that are balancing correctly have the upper arms close to the player's chest throughout most of the swing.)
- ***TO STAY IN BALANCE, LEAN AWAY FROM THE DIRECTION YOU ARE MOVING.*** (On-balance golfers finish with their, spine leaning slightly away from the target.)

These are general balance and balancing suggestions. Please keep in mind that there are always some exceptions to any rule.

No One Way

Over time there have been trillions of swings made by millions of golfers. Believe it or not, no two swings have ever been exactly alike. No two! It helps to realize **there is no one way to swing or play**. Believing in such an approach would only slow down progress. There are as many ways to play and swing, as there are world-class golfers. Similarly there are many combinations of food that could make up what would be considered a healthy meal or balanced diet. Efficient swings are simply athletically and scientifically balanced.

Secret: There are a few basics in all efficient swings that are non-negotiable, (i.e. **Golf's Physical Basics**) but what must be understood is there are different ways these basics can be produced.

Throughout the history of golf most world-class players have had highly individual golf swings. To learn from these different styles we must learn to recognize the core elements common to all, and **overlook personal swing habits.**

"In a golf swing certain things are caused to happen, and others are allowed to happen. Faults arise, when what should be allowed is caused to happen."

- D. McCluggage

To repeat, Jack Nicklaus made a profound statement when talking about good players. *"I believe all good players have achieved certain goals in their swing and game that were demanded by the* ***laws of physics.*** *This even though their styles and points of emphasis may have been different."*

In efficient swings, most forces are working parallel through impact (this is an important core element). Another core element is that efficient swings use a transfer of energy to develop force. They don't rely on effort. At the start of the downswing you have a large mass (the body) moving at a low rate of motion. At the end of the downswing you have a small mass (clubhead) moving at a high rate of velocity. Fortunately, behind every successful system or technique is a fundamental natural law to guide and influence our concepts of **What To Do**.

It helps progress to recognize that the human body is a system of links and levers. All motions in the body is subject to every ordinary principles of physics, and **so is the golf swing**. Good golfers have found their way of satisfying basic principles of motion and force.

Secret: The motion needed to make a golf swing is not encoded into our original human motion system. Since we can't change the design of our skeleton or muscle systems, people have to learn how to adapt the body to the requirements of **Golf's Physical Basics**, and the game.

It may help progress to never try to consciously influence more than one element of your swing at a time. **Maybe one of the keys to building a effective swing is to leave alone the things that cannot be controlled**. Then you can become aware of things you can influence. Develop a swing that becomes a chain reaction. A swing that can efficiently repeat itself. A swing where one body link can cause others to follow. Similar to other body actions we perform everyday, a golf swing can be a sequence of many small "invisible movements". Each of which is a reaction to the movement that preceded it, **producing one visible golf swing**.

Warning: One of the human brain's most powerful instincts is to maintain the body's center of gravity in a state of balance. When the body even comes close to losing it's balanced state, the brain's natural need to maintain balance takes over, and introduces a compensating motion into the swing. These extra motions will kill the opportunity for most players to perform a effective swing.

Any approach to instruction that gives golfers the impression they can improve without making changes to their present style is misleading. **But this is an approach that many players have bought into**. Any golfer who wants to improve can. However, if they believe they will improve without changing some present habits, they are probably wasting time, money, and effort they are now spending to make progress.

Secret: First, set goal that are realistic. Next match your physical condition and athletic talent to your goals. If you then feel the time and effort you now spend on your game is enough to see improvement **(and you have not)**, it is time to either change the sources of information you are using or change the way you have been using the information.

LESSON SIX

Be Aware of What Makes It Work

Secret: Motion, Balancing, Timing, and Force are

"Rooted in the Ground
Driven by the Core
Reflected in the Arms
Manifested in the Hands"

– Tai Chi

WHAT MAKES IT ALL WORK?

When someone starts to play golf, most individuals will start gathering information (from books, lessons, friends, etc.) about the golf swing and playing the game. For some, that is years of gathering, for others the time may be shorter. I'm sure many people from both groups have enough information about the swing to write a few articles that would be considered worth while reading, even by the harshest critics.

If there is some truth to what I have just written, why then are so many golfers not reaching their potential? Perhaps many golfers do indeed know something about the swing, but probably have little knowledge of **what makes it work**. Have you ever asked, "**what makes a golf swing work?**" Or have you just gathered information about the swing? There is a huge difference.

Perhaps the first element that makes a golf swing work is **freedom**. World-class golfers have developed a style and swing that move freely. If and when there is tension in their bodies, it is never at the cost of a free moving swing and club.

Secret: At the foundation of good golf is freedom of motion.

Another element that makes a golf swing work is **effective posture, alignment, and grip** for the shot at hand. These elements are not the same old story, they are really the only story.

The next element that makes a golf swing work is **optimum ball location** for the shot at hand. The ball must be located properly between the feet, and the proper distance from the body at address. Both of these permit or prevents **workable ball flight, and can be learned through self-discovery.**

Next, the elements of **effective balance and swing timing** make a golf swing work. Just watch players on the LPGA, PGA and Senior PGA Tours. You will notice that all swings are somewhat individual, but there is common ground when it comes to their balance and swing timing (i.e. tempo – rhythm).

Of course, **a set of clubs that fits** a player's swing and body style also help make a golf swing work.

At times both players and instruction information have focused on just the golf swing at the cost of what **makes the golf swing work**. There is a good chance that if the grip, posture, alignment, ball location, balance, swing timing, are all effective, and the player is using clubs that fit his or her swing and body style, **there will be less to talk and think about when it comes to the swing** (and that is our goal).

TRUST FREEDOM, AND LET GO!

Secret: When a golfer does not have the ability to let it go...let it happen....or swing without being judgmental, all the golf ideas in the world will not help.

I am not sure why, but probably more books and articles have been written about how to play golf than any other sport. Someone once said, *"Golf is the only game that has more teachers than players."*

While I do not believe that there is only one way to swing or play, there is one principle that every golfer must accomplish before they have any possibility of making progress at a reasonable rate. Without this one principle – the ideal student...using ideal information...presented in an ideal way... in the ideal setting...with the ideal amount of time...using ideal clubs and balls...in ideal weather...under the eye of the ideal instructor, could not reach his or her potential or make progress at a reasonable rate. **This one principle is that important! Freedom, is the principle.**

Secret: When a golfer does not have the ability to let it go, to swing without fear, to let it happen, to trust it, or swing without being judgmental, any and all swing ideas become less useful.

True and lasting progress is not possible without the principle of freedom. **It seems freedom makes everything else possible**. Example: Let's say forcing is effort, and power is the ability to get things done. Excess forcing negates power. The more we try, the less we get. True power comes from freedom.

Every book or instructor has their own approach to helping golfers learn to improve. However, a golfer's ability to use a suggestion has its foundation, in his or her ability to trust and to "let it happen". As I have said, good golf is predicting ball flight before the swing. When the best players in the world want the ball to move high or low, left or right, 10 feet, 10 yards, or 150 yards, it does. This ability is founded on trusting, a **"let-it-go"** swing.

On the other hand, many club golfers can **"only hope"** their shots hit fairways and greens. They don't have insights into where their ball will go before they swing. This lack of insight creates a lack of trust and a controlled approach with little or no freedom.

Secret: **Players with efficient swings probably did not start out playing golf with controlled ball flight. They first discovered what a free, lack of control swing felt like. Then they moved on to influencing ball flight with a let it happen approach.**

It is the old question of what comes first, the chicken or the egg. **My suggestion would be a freedom of motion will beget ball control.** Many club golfers use an approach that is exactly opposite. They try to control what the ball will do with a swing that lacks freedom.

Fred Shoemaker is a PGA instructor who is based in Carmel, California. I've held both Fred and his work in high esteem for years and use some of his ideas about "**letting go**" in every lesson I give.

Some of what follows in this chapter is based on what Fred and his staff talk about in their **Schools for Extraordinary Golf**:

- Thinking about how you look on the first tee.
- Being concerned about what people will think about your score before you play.
- Being concerned what people will think about you, after they know what you shot.
- Letting the score you shot lead you to how you feel about yourself.
- Judging results as good or bad, rather than accepting what you get.
- Practicing as though something is wrong with your swing.

I could go on, but all of the above are traits of a golfer who have the "skill of *self-interference*". This golfer lacks the ability to trust and let go!

Secret: **Humans are the only species on earth with the ability to interfere with their own performance. Self-interference is a learned skill; we are not born with it.**

"The thinking or knowing mind, does not understand hand-eye coordination; it knows how to play, but it's the feeling-awareness mind that plays golf. The job of the thinking/knowing mind is to be very clear about the goal (not swing tips) and not get in the way of the feeling/awareness mind's execution of motion." – Tim Galloway

"Thinking should be replaced by feel (when playing). Thinking is always at the mercy of your mental state, i.e. excitement, depression, self-image, or any other emotion that can destroy us." *

"Control by remembered feel is invaluable in learning golf. Give up thinking about controlling your shots and remember the feel of a comfortable, reliable motion." *

Golf's number one bogey is the urge to act in the obvious way to achieve a desired result. Example: swinging hard for distance instead of letting the clubhead velocity be a result of freedom.

"The end-gainer concentrates on results rather than the means whereby the result can be best gained." *

"With a properly felt swing, the swing's feel becomes our aim, and the ball reacts and takes care of itself." *

The best way, and maybe the only way, to avoid self-interference is to stay in the present, focused on the task at hand. Thinking about past mistakes or future results that you wish to avoid creates self-interference and lack of effective alignments and freedom.

* On Learning Golf, by Percy Boomer (If I owned only one golf book it would be On Learning Golf.)

LEARNING TO LET GO

A good first step for learning how to stay in the present and let go, would be to feel that the swing you are using is okay for now.

Next, go to your range and start hitting balls with your favorite club. Just swing, do not make any adjustments from swing to swing. None! Where the ball goes is not important at this time. What is important is what you are feeling. Do your best and pay attention to the feel of your swing without adjustments or evaluations. Now start to become aware of either the clubface, head or shaft and where you would like them to be during your swing.

Secret: The absolute first step to a "free let-it-go swing" is to become aware of your present swing, even if it's producing unworkable shots. i.e. where is the clubhead etc.?

The only way you can change a swing habit is to learn what that habit feels like. Practice with your current swing without changing anything for a substantial period of time and pay attention to the feel of its motion and where either the clubhead, face or shaft is. **Do not try to fix anything**. If you keep manipulating something, it will be hard to feel what is happening. By leaving your swing alone you can learn the feel of what you want to change or repeat. When golfers aren't really aware of what their swing is actually doing, they have no starting point for change. One way to learn the feel of your swing is to hit some balls with your eyes closed and focus on a total body feel. Or you could pick either the clubhead, clubface, or shaft to focus on during the swing.

The average club golfer rarely hits two shots in a round of golf that look alike, causing a lack of freedom in style of play. Self-interference will now take over, decreasing a golfer's ability to gather any feel information about past swings. Without this past information, there is no valid starting point for change.

The suggestion to hit balls without adjustments or evaluations may sound like strange advice. But if you can focus on your present swing and learn what that swing feels like, I believe you will be on your way to improving your game and swing with a "let it go approach".

Secret: It is much better to hit a poor shot and be able to accurately tell what you did, than to hit a good one and have no idea what happened in your swing.

"Those who fail to study history, are doomed to repeat it."

– Author Unkown

CONSISTENCY

Your interpretation of your feel will vary at first. But soon you will recognize the feel of swings both workable and unworkable. This can lead to consistency. Stay aware and just observe what you do without giving yourself and swing tips to follow – just swing.

Being consistent means being able to repeat anything. If you could repeat the same slice every time, you would be better off than many golfers, who do not know where their ball will go. Becoming more aware of your present swing is not from the Quick Fix School. *"A quick fix is like the date on a milk carton, (Stays fresh until...), they do not last very long."* – F. Schoemaker

Everyone knows that a quick fix does not last, but we keep looking for them. They are tempting because everyone has had a few days where everything went their way and the game seemed easy with their level of play going up. But, in truth, we do not sustain the level of play we experienced on one of those breakthrough days because our swing lacks consistency.

The path to consistency is built on a commitment to learning how to "let it go". This is built on trust, which is built on being aware of what your swing feels like now.

"Once the relationship between mental (thinking-knowing) and physical (feeling-doing) is correctly recognized, the blanks seem to fill in." *- Tim Gallwey

- Trust is rare because golfers always feel something is wrong, and that they have to "fix it".
- Learning is natural; we have to block ourselves to keep from learning.
- Take away self-interference first and then expand awareness.
- From a calm place you can see, feel, learn and do more.
- Awareness of the reality of your present swing is the first step to progress. Where is the clubhead, face and shaft?
- Get absorbed in the feel of the clubhead, face, or shaft.
- Stay in the present where there is no room for fear, doubt or anxiety.
- The way we learn golf has almost nothing in common with how we learned school subjects.
- In school, it's the mental memory of words and numbers that leads to progress. In golf, it is the feel of motion that must be recognized.

For more of Fred Shoemakers ideas, I suggest reading his book, Extraordinary Golf.

Pictures and Feels

Note: As I said earlier, instruction, that does not improve the ways in which students play or at least give them a better understanding of their current swing, is instruction that is being misunderstood or instruction that is going in the wrong direction.

Every human gathers information with an internal system that extends throughout the body, which is responsible for movement. The brain, spinal cord, cells and other fibers make up this system. The information is then communicated to the appropriate muscle group to create the desired movements. When we learn to trust and use information from our eyes and sense of touch, our game can improve. (Stay away from **"how to"** lists and become aware of where the shaft, clubhead and clubface are through impact.)

Problems arise when the body's natural and reliable system of gathering information is interrupted by fears, doubts and self-talk, such as, *"This is a hard putt,"* or *"I never par this hole."* The brain cannot tell the body anything by using words. Muscles do not understand the language of words. Only an image-rich language that invokes a personal picture or feel (which is already familiar to the student's body) can be used to communicate effectively. We should learn to trust the automatic system we all have to gather information.

Secret: **Motor skill actions are either conscious or unconscious imitations of the sum total of all the information about the motion which the brain has at that time. It is our own personal perception (picture or feel) of the golf swing that creates movement in our bodies.**

Learning and playing golf is a creative process. All golf shots have brain work, then body action, followed by club path, clubface angle and ball flight. **The brain controls the body. The body controls the club, and the club controls the ball.**

When trying to improve your golf, my suggestion is to use mental pictures and feel, and stay away from words, such as "up-down", "inside-out", "fast-slow". We all used pictures and feels as children to learn many motor skills. Golfers should be encouraged to trust in their own capacities to learn from their own experiences – to have faith in what they see, hear, and feel. **As I have said, in its most workable form the role of instruction is to help students understand and focus on the most relevant parts of that personal experience.**

For example, if you were to go to a Pro-Am tournament, you would certainly recognize the differences in the swings of the amateurs and the professionals. **Without being told anything, the average golfer already has the ability to distinguish the effective swing from the ineffective swing.** They look very different. Any instruction advice should help students understand the differences, so student's don't develop misconceptions.

Learning is also a function of awareness, Without being aware, there is no learning. Whenever awareness is increased, the quality of performance, enjoyment and learning improved. For example; the best golfers understand the shot at hand because they have stayed aware and in tune with the course, the conditions and themselves. **They have stayed in the present**. Their minds are not simply on results. **Awareness makes understanding possible**. Awareness happens when or if we allow it to occur. Golfers often have misconceptions interfering with their own abilities to perform and to learn. For this reason, we often do not reach our potential.

When playing badly, your mind is filled with a checklist of "do's and don'ts", self-judgment, doubt and fear of failure. When playing your best, your mind is relaxed, absorbed in the present, quiet and free of tension. Athletes often call this experience, "playing out of one's mind." A state free of mental interference should be every golfer's goal. Golf is both mental and physical.

Secret: **The body does what the brain commands. Eyes do not see, ears do not hear, hands do not feel, and the nose does not smell. Everything the human does, happens in the brain first.**

My suggestion to golfers is that they should play and learn golf more with pictures and feels. When learning any motor skill (golf included) they are more useful. Consider when the Olympic diver is about to perform, or the tennis star is about to serve, or the fisherman is about to cast his line. They all had a clear picture or feel of what they were about to do before the body went into action.

All golf shots have brainwork, body action, club path, face angle and ball flight. The brain controls the body, the body controls the club and the club controls the ball. When a clubface impacts the ball, they are joined and stay together **for five-hundredths of a second, and three-quarters of an inch before the ball separates.**

During the time and space of impact, the ball is being programmed. It's told to go up, down, left, right, long or short. The golf shot you produced was created in your brain. It did not happen by chance. The process started in the brain, moved to the body, then to the club and finally to the ball. Your brain provides a very reliable and accurate system of telling the body what to do.

So why (if the brain is always accurately telling the body what to do) are golfers not playing up to their potential? Because at times the gofer's perception of the swing is inaccurate, and the brain is using information based on misconceptions.

Secret: **When learning or improving a motor skill, you must first improve the information the brain receives. Studies show communication is only five percent words. That 85 % of the information your brain receives has come form the eyes, and 50 % of what we hear is forgotten immediately. Golfers must try to see and feel the swing beforehand (I.e. On-Plane forces). Recalling the last successful shot, even if it was a chip or putt, is still very useful.**

Vision - Golf's Missing Link?

Once vision is understood, its application can improve any golfer's performance. **Vision is more than just looking**, it's a **basic sports ingredient that every golfer must understand.** *"A champion is one who understands vision and how it's used. Vision is a learned and developed skill."* - Dr. Martin

"Of all the movements required in sports, visual concentration is the last to be achieved. Its also the most difficult to develop and hold on to. But to succeed, visual concentration that must be mastered." - Dr. Martin

Dr. Wayne F. Martin is a graduate of University of Washington and Illinois College of Ophthalmology in Chicago. Dr. Martin pioneered research to determine if top athletes had different visual skills than those of the general public. He has received many awards from his professional peers including the Silver Certificate for his contributions to the field of sports vision. What follows is based on his and other expert findings found in his book An Insight To Sports.

"Any flinching, choking, or loss of concentration can be any athlete's greatest fear. The most significant reason for target rejection, flinching, or head movement, is faulty eye movement (i.e. poor visual perception , centering, or reaction time)." - Dr. Martin.

Like other skills, vision can be trained and improved. But much will depend on how we learn to use vision. Many mistakes and missed shots in golf are triggered through faulty visual movements. As with computers, *"garbage in - garbage out."* - Dr. Martin.

Vision

Our body and its muscle movements are centered around signals from our vision. **Once we become aware of what workable vision is, (for any skill), learning begins.** Vision is simply the process of reacting to what we see. Golfers often see poor concepts and misconceptions. This faulty way of looking at things leads to poor results.

Understanding vision (and golf swings) requires learning about a few technical components. To be accurate this cannot be avoided. Every effort will be made to make information about these components readable. Do we need to talk in a technical manner? Yes, to a degree.

Accurate terms and concepts can seem technical at first, especially, when readers are not familiar with them. But the more these terms and concepts are used and explained, the less technical these terms normally seem. Accurate terms and concepts reveal accurate insights about what must be learned. When information seems to technical at first glance, this impression often shifts quickly into a deeper understanding. This shift causes people to say: *"yes, why didn't I see that sooner."*

"See vision as the hub of a wheel whose spokes are the components that make up a top athlete. Vision tells the athlete's components the "what, the where, the why, and when" to act." Dr. Martin

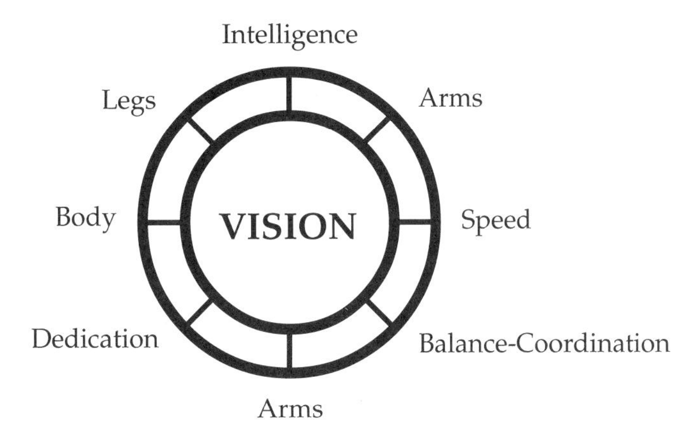

Vision is a "motor - muscular movement" that responds to the stimulus of light. **While we are quick to recognize faulty body motions in sports, we rarely recognize the faulty eye movements that have caused unwanted body motions.**

"Vision is the net sum of many components needed to provide efficient body motion. The primary concern of most athletes seems to be 20/20 vision. While 20/20 vision is a component of vision, it is only a small part of the visual process, and secondary to performance" - Dr. Martin.

Maximum light must be permitted to enter the eyes of an athlete. But every effort must be made to eliminate squinting. *"Some people are light sensitive, so there may be a need for outdoor sun wear. But only with the amount of tint that will provide comfort, without preventing maximum light stimulus from entering"* - Dr. Martin.

Top athletes, few as they are, have put forth the effort required to master visual concentration. Robert Rigor one of the sports worlds great photographers said *"I've found the greatest athletes have the greatest eyes. I'm always fascinated and taking pictures of their eyes."*

Ted Williams - *"In the game you are not concerned with mechanics, its now time to apply visual concentration."*

Chris Evert - *"The eyes manage the mechanics of the game."*

Bob Charles - After success on the PGA Tour, said when playing poorly on the Sr. PGA Tour, *"It wasn't the greens it was my eyes. The eyes are the game, and mine are gone."*

The eyes could be seen as a quarterback, that tells the body what to do. Its often assumed eyes that no longer have 20/20 vision are a problem for athletes. But its the lack of **visual centering** (not less than 20/20 vision) that is the main problem, according to Dr. Martin and other experts.

Components of Vision

ACCOMMODATION, the changing of focus to maintain clear vision is classified into three primary areas - 1. Myopia, inability to see distance clearly. 2. Hyperopia, the ability to see distance clearly (20/20) through stress and effort. 3. Astigmatism, (distortions) may be in combination with either myopia or hyperopia.

HYPEROPIA - is what Dr. Martin calls, "the fool hen of vision". This condition may be unknown to its victim. This person is often unaware of the degrees of tension and hyper vision activity they undergo to obtain 20/20 vision.

This tension and stress causes nervousness and fatigue, (among other symptoms) that lower the performance capabilities of any athlete. These athletes often blame anyone or anything for their poor performance, (while at times showing flashes of excellent ability). Its the hyper activity of their vision that causes the stress and poor performances. (Its not vision that is no longer 20/20).

"It is my feeling the Willie May's, the Joe DiMaggio's, and the Arnold Palmer's of the world did not slow down at first because of their bodies or minds. What happened? Their visual centering, visual concentration, and visual control, began to slow. Even though many athletes still have 20/20 vision, their eye reflexes which tell them the what, why, where, and when began to stutter." - Dr. Martin

Yes 20/20 vision is nice to have, but if hyperpsia stress is needed to maintain good vision, it will interfere with the efficiency of the athletes performance.

CONVERGENCE is directing two eyes by voluntary muscles to maintain visual focus a single image **(point of impact).**

One way of explaining convergence of our two eyes on a single image is to say there is a **primary** zone of vision, and a **secondary** zone. The **primary** zone is where your vergence must be centered, and the **secondary** zone is the surrounding non-specific area around any sports point of impact.

Any stress, lack of concentration, or insecurity of performance can cause a shift back to our **secondary** zone, causing confusing, indecisions, and misses.

"Zeroing in on the ***point of impact*** *of any target in sport is important, and is referred to as the primary zone. Yes, we are aware of the total field of vision (secondary zones), but, at the same time we must be centered exactly on our* ***point of impact****".* - Dr. Martin

When stress is present, (in an effort to maintain clear vision), convergence and divergence (vengeance) are affected. Vision now pays more attention to the total field of vision (secondary zone) than to the exact **point of impact** (primary zone). Whenever our vision is allowed (mostly through stress) to **expand beyond** impact point, (paying attention to background information) skill performance is lowered.

Example: Look at the word "convergence". We see a group of letters. Now switch your total attention to just a letter. The other letters now become background information. Under stress both the single letter and letters that were once in the background start to be equally important in our visual field. This loss of total focus on **point of impact** (primary zone) affects our ability to perform at our highest level. When golfers are distracted (by nerves, noise, swing thoughts, weather) they loss their focus of the primary zone! (i.e. **point of impact**).

Visualization

"Visualization is a visual - mental plan - It's an inner approach to successfully completing any body motions. Most top athletes visualize before performing. Vision is our trigger mechanism. It directs the muscles of the body. The eyes lead the muscles." - Dr. Martin

Visualization is a tool best used with our eyes closed. Visualize the entire procedure with your eyes closed. There have been several studies done that point to the value of visualization. In one study three groups of basketball players practiced their free-throw shots. Group A practiced every day for 20 days and improved 24%. Group B practiced only the first and last day and showed no improvement. Group C practiced on the first and last day, but spent 20 minutes a day visualizing sinking baskets, and correcting their alignment when they missed a shot. They improved 23%. Visualization is one method of practicing and learning visual concentration.

It will help your golf to visualize unworkable alignments and the poor body motions which they cause. It's useful to go back and forth between workable and unworkable visualizations. Seeing and feeling the differences tells your eyes what to see, and our bodies what to do. The eyes are learning what visualizations are useful. Vision isn't automatic, it must be learned. We must act to see. **Learn to center your vision on the primary zone**, (point of impact). *"The hands will follow the eyes to impact point."* - Dr. Martin

Golf and Vision

"Concentration on visual skills is often neglected. Swing and stroke only when visually ready." - Dr. Martin

The transition from the secondary zone to the primary zone is a thin line. **Many golfers never cross over from secondary to the primary zone, swinging before they complete of the act of visual readiness.**

Once the ball is addressed and you are ready to swing, the thought process should be restricted to striking the ball through the precise point of impact (with no "how to direction" or quick fix ideas in the mind). Eyes of course on the primary zone - (**impact point, inside corner of the ball**), with no drifting to the secondary zone.

"Any variation in centering will cause inconsistency in striking" Dr. Martin, **After impact our eyes should turn on-plane and be looking at the target.** *"The body will perform to the point of its visual attention."* - Fil Le Anderson, University of Washington.

"Once we address the ball, vision is the priority. See the precise ***point of impact*** *as the club returns through the ball. We normally make contact where our vision is focused."* - Dr. Martin

Experiment: As we look down as the ball, let's visualize numbers on a clock with 3 o'clock on the back center of the ball.

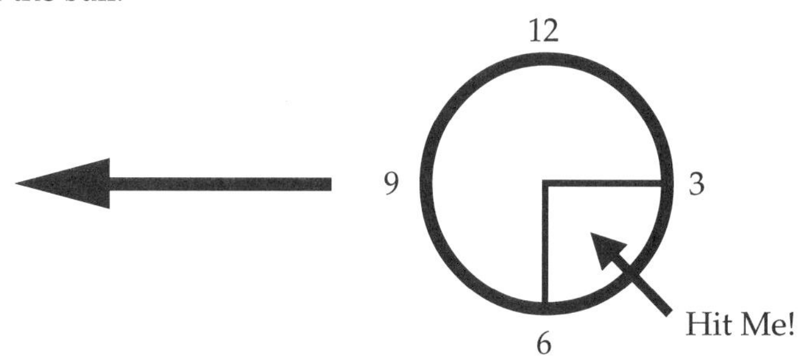

Now with no swing thoughts, using an 8 iron to make little chip shots, focus on 4 o'clock as your primary zone, or point of impact. Do this several times. Each time, only focusing on 4 o'clock as your primary visual zone, or point of impact.

Next do the same exercise, using 1 o'clock as your primary zone or point of impact. Note the difference.

I have done the exercise with many golfers and they soon learn, they need few if any swing thoughts when they focus on the point of impact, 4 o'clock. When 4 o'clock is the primary zone for vision, the club returns to the impact point from inside the target line. When 4 o'clock is the primary visual zone (impact point), the club returns to the ball on-plane.

"Inconsistencies are the result of responding and acting within the secondary zone of generalities" - Dr. Martin. When the brain is confused, almost anything can happen. Never start motion until you are visually ready, and in position to act. You must be centering your vision with precision. *"The information the eyes gather must stay ahead of the body movement. The eye will never catch up with any premature body movement"* - Dr. Martin.

The golf swing wants to return the clubhead to the player's point of visual attention. Any thoughts in the direction of "how to advice" lowers a golfers success rate. Being overly involved with mechanical thoughts moves golfers in the direction of secondary zones and away from visual attention on the point of impact.

Secret: **Any visual generalities about point of impact will not help long-term learning. Practice centering on primary zones or points of impact. It will make a difference.**

HEAD: The head holds the optical system and aids in controlling balance movement. When the head is off balance, interference with vergence and alignment takes place. This can cause switching from primary to secondary zones. When we have control over head motion, it results in a smooth fluent motion with the body.

"The visual act must be completed before the rest of the body makes any movement to hit the ball. *Golfers must be visually committed to the point of impact. Completion of this visual act is the minute difference between average performers and top performers."* Dr. Martin.

The eyes must work as a team. Any focus strain or hyper effort to maintain clear 20/20 vision, even if minor, should be corrected by a competent doctor.

"For most acts of looking our eyes have been trained to look eye level and below eyelevel in a convergence pattern. Due to our work habits, the converging muscles of the eyes have been developed to take abuse and withstand fatigue as they work efficiently to look eye level and lower. The divergence muscles, used to look up and away, are used sparingly and are not as strong." - Dr. Martin

Experiment: Look across the room at the **bottom** of the wall, now look from side to side, corner to corner. Note the speed and easy of your vision. Now look up to the **top** of the wall. Look from side to side across the **top** of the wall. Note: Your eyes work more slowly and may feel uncomfortable. They require more effort to track the edge of the ceiling than the edge of the floor. Golfers, who may be comfortable looking down at the ball, may have difficulty looking up at targets further down the fairway (have your eyes checked).

Training Suggestion: *"Looking across a room, now let your eyes work from one corner of the ceiling to the other corner for several minutes a day. This will use and strengthen eye muscles that are normally not used very often, (except when playing golf). You can also look across the room and focus on the face of the clock. Now focus on just one number. Now go back to focusing on the whole clock, then look at just one number. Going back and forth from big to small focus will improve your ability to focus on your primary zone, or impact point"* - Dr. Martin. Any golfer who wants to improve should not overlook the importance of **Visual Concentration and Primary Zones of Vision.**

Ben Hogan's Twelve Fundamentals

Noted neuro-psychologist, Dr. Fran Pirozzolo, known for his work with professional athletes, including the New York Yankees, and several of the worlds leading golfers, believes that Ben Hogan's real secret was rooted in twelve fundamentals. This is seven more than readers of "Hogan's Five Lessons" may have assumed he used.

Dr. Pirozzolo said, *"An athletes mind must conquer matter. An athlete could work to hone their technique until the end of time, and still miss the mark.* ***The secret to outstanding athletic performances is ones mental approach****. No modern sports psychologist with fancy degrees and letters next to their name could improve on the advice Ben Hogan provided on the mental side of the game. His explicit instruction stands today as a model for any golfer"*. With Fran's permission, Hogan's twelve fundamentals follows.

1. **Loving the Challenge:** Ben Hogan was motivated by his enjoyment and the challenge of the game itself, not the rewards of fame or fortune. He finished his book with these words: *"I have loved playing the game and practicing it. Whether my schedule for the following day called for a tournament round or merely a trip to the practice tee, the prospect that there was going to be golf in it made me feel privileged and extremely happy, and I couldn't wait for the sun to come up the next morning so that I could get out on the course again."*

   Two mental characteristics most great athletes share are their **intrinsic motivation** and their **ego commitment**, neither of which is seen any better than in Hogan. He loved everything about playing golf (except perhaps putting in his later years). He was completely assured in golf, and because his ego was so heavily invested in it, he was never able to tolerate not doing well. Above all, he had to find a way to win.

2. **Mental Toughness:** A widely held **misconception** in contemporary society is that struggles against adversity wears you down and makes you weak. Nonsense!!! The best forms or training give you more than you can handle. And the greatest champions have usually battled adversity successfully.

   Ben Hogan overcame obstacles as much as anyone from his era. He experienced an unusual amount of stress in his childhood and his early career in golf. His father's suicide, when Ben was only 12, would have been enough adversity for a lifetime. Because of dreadful bouts with the hooks and career disruptions, he was penniless twice and had to return to Fort Worth. In mid-career he took a hiatus for military service, not to mention the catastrophic car wreck that nearly ended his life at the peak of his career. Hogan overcame these obstacles, as well as the minor ones that he confronted on the golf course. He urged golfers to feel challenged by difficult situations.

   When people have experienced real catastrophes, they can downplay the little difficulties they encounter. They tend not to think that a missed three-footer is the worst thing that could ever happen. We've seen the bad examples on television. A whiny tour pro misses a short putt and then stomps off the green like a two-year-old having a temper tantrum. If he can't handle a little adversity, I say he should learn how to make piecrust' instead of trying to compete with some of the world's greatest athletes.

3. **Acceptance of Mistakes:** Hogan had a much-deserved reputation for being a sourpuss and a perfectionist. He was always "striving to do better". **Nevertheless he stressed that mistakes were human**. He himself never expected to hit more than one or two shots in a round the way he intended. Not having the genius of Hogan, how can we expect to play more shots perfectly?

   "No golfer", Hogan said, *"can always be at the peak of his game"*. The key element is not to expect perfection but to expect to make mistakes. Don't be self-satisfied, arrogant or smug. Everyone has played with the golfer who hits a long straight drive and, when his group admires the shot, instead of saying thanks, feels compelled to let us know how really inferior we are by telling us that his shot wasn't really very good for him. He thinks he's got Hogan's perfectionism, **but he really hasn't got a clue.**

4. **Self Control:** Most golfers unfortunately, assume that if a negative thought intrudes upon the mental movie being shown in the mind's eye, that they should play it out to the fullest. They add emotional tones that they feel should be associated with a drive into the woods. The negative thought is no longer a brief commercial interruption that can be ignored - or confronted or disputed - but a whole miniseries with highly charged action and violent emotions.

   Truly extraordinary players are so well prepared that they have a plan for handling all situations. **They exercise self-control**. Some golfers are on a thrill-a-minute roller coaster ride because situation influence their behavior and there is no skill they can call on to guide their next response. Hogan, on the other hand, had an answer for every challenge he might confront? **Self-control**. He was legendary for his consistent attitude on the course, and he did not display negative physical responses that other players showed.

   While still a cub reporter, Dan Jenkins was once assigned to cover Hogan's preparation for the U.S. Open at Oakland Hills. He watched in amazement as Hogan hit scores of low left-to-right, three-iron shots about 150 yards. Jenkins asked Hogan what in the world he was doing, to which Hogan replied, *"I might need that shot at Oakland Hills."*

5. **Self-Trust:** Because Hogan believed so strong in his system of playing golf, **he was able to trust himself** when the pressure was on. He honestly believed that the more pressure he was under, the better he would perform. This self-trust, the deep-seated belief that you will have it all together at crunch time, is a characteristic of all clutch performers in any sport and in all walks of life.

   Hogan had no self-doubt when it came down to the final holes at a major championship. He took his habit of peaking under pressure as natural and expected. There is even a famous picture of him hitting a one iron shot to the final green at Merion, which enabled him to win the U.S. Open Championship. He says in his book that it wasn't really unusual for him to hit that shot, he had done it many times. Like Michael Jordan in basketball and Joe Montana in football, he knew he could rise to meet the challenge when the game was on the line.

6. **Process Goals:** One of Hogan's great mental assets was his ability to set process goals rather than result goals. Hogan had the attitude that it was more important to play the way you wanted to than to shoot a specific score. He was the only one who knew what he was trying to accomplish with each shot, each round and each tournament.

   Hogan maintained that a golfer should *"school himself to think in terms of the cause and not the result."* Further, he felt that the greatest pleasure for average golfers would come from incremental improvement.

7. **Learning From Experience:** I urge most of the athletes I work with to use a journal in order to keep track of what they're working on and how it's going. These journals log information about practice, fitness, diet, family, spiritual and mental goals. In his book Hogan is actually pictured jotting down what he is working on.

   Hogan knew that human learning was a trail-and-error experiment. But only by keeping a diary of his experiences could he determine **what was right for him**. Many of us have less efficient methods of training. We might be hitting it well, and for no obvious reason (and perhaps against the advice of our pro) we decide that a weaker grip might be just the thing to get to the next level. After a month-long slump, we have a vision: maybe we should go back to our normal grip!

8. **Use of Mental Imagery:** Hogan did three things that showed his appreciation for the role of mental rehearsal in golf. **He recommended the use of a mirror to rehearse the swing**. He is shown in the book using the mental image of pane of glass running across his shoulders and through the ball. He also played each tournament course in his mind's eye while he was driving to the event.

   Neuroscientists have now given their blessing to visualization, or mental rehearsal because their studies have shown what great athletes have always known: Visualization accelerates learning and enhances performance. By practicing mentally, we are rehearsing our "plan of action." We are warming up parts of the brain that are active in carrying out our swings.

   Jack Nicklaus once observed that he never hit a shot in practice or in competition without first seeing it in his mind's eye. Every golfer benefits from visualization. Why is it that only Nicklaus and Hogan stay committed to this mental performance enhancer?

9. **Single-Minded Attention:** Hogan was famous for his ability to stay, focused in spite of what was happening around him. Claude Harmon once related to me the story of his hole-in-one in the Masters that went unnoticed by his playing partner, Ben Hogan. Ben had made a birdie and remarked to Claude as they walked off the green that he thought it was the first time he had ever birdied 12 in competition. One could fault Hogan for not cheering his pal, but the fact was, Hogan was so absorbed in what he was doing that he scarcely noticed what happened around him.

   When Hogan won the British Open at Carnoustie, the British people, who were seeing him in action for the first time, labeled him the "wee iceman", because he seemed unaffected by what went on around him. This in stark contrast to mentally weak golfers who get flustered *"by the uproar of butterflies in the adjoining fairway."*

10. **Staying Loose:** Hogan recognized the importance of maintaining the proper level of intensity. He urged reader's to understand the significance and connection between how we feel and how we swing, and he advised that we should keep unwanted muscle tension out of our swings. He observed that feeling a little keyed up before competing is a good thing, but that we shouldn't expect to feel as relaxed as we feel when we are "loafing at home in the evening watching a TV show."

    Hogan, as much as anyone seemed to appreciate that his ideal performance state was to be **physically relaxed yet mentally aggressive**. Most golfers get it reversed. They get all worked up and physically tense, yet they don't have the mental trust and belief and are set-up to fail time and again.

11. **Heeding Both Mind and Body:** Hogan gives an eloquent account of an attitude change in the winter of 1946 that enabled him to perform more consistently. Essentially, he debated whether the chicken or egg came first. Did his change in attitude (to have greater self-confidence and self trust) enable him to believe in his swing and therefore perform well? Or did all of the physical training provide the results that gave him increased confidence? Even Hogan claimed not to know which change made the biggest difference to him. **My feeling is that golf is 100 percent mental and 100 percent physical!** Why not work on both mental and physical excellence?

    Many athletes have the kind of "aha experience" that makes the difference between a great career and a merely average one. They access what they have achieved and realize that what has stood in the way of getting the most out of their physical talent has been their mental game. **They discover that they have met the enemy and that *"the enemy is us!"*** By giving themselves a better mental approach, they can clear the way for physical excellence and performances that are truly extraordinary.

12. **Vivid Appreciation:** Surprising as it may seem, Hogan saw achievement in golf as an almost spiritual exercise, as was reflected in his televised interviews in 1990. He maintained that when he played the way he wanted to, *"it was like touching the feet of God"*. Further, Hogan said, *"the greatest thing about golf is that it trains the mind and the body!"*

We live in an age when everyone is a critic. **Too bad everyone isn't a good student? And too bad we can't have the clean mind of a child.** Host of us are cynical, we think we've seen it all but Hogan was different. He marveled at Demaret's supination of the left wrist. He admired the staccato waggle of Johnny Revolta. And he truly appreciated the beautiful grips of Walter Hagen and Jackie Burke. In a recent article by Jaime Diaz, **Hogan said he tried to learn something new about the game of golf every day.**

"I agree with Hogan's contemporaries - Hogan really did possess some secrets that enabled him to outperform everyone. But, contrary to popular opinion, he did share them with us. We just didn't understand", Fran Pirozzolo.

Secret: It seems that people who play good golf, "Think out of the box". These golfers do not use a narrow approach to the game and the shot at hand. They see all of their options.

Nutrition and Conditioning Suggestions

We all play golf with our bodies. **Our body is our most important piece of equipment.** Any steps taken to improve your physical conditioning and diet will also be steps that can help improve your performance on the golf course.

What follows are some suggestions for both your **diet** and **physical conditioning programs.** I have always recommended yoga classes and stretching to many of the people who I meet on my lesson tee.

Bob Anderson's stretching suggestions are included in this section. I would also like to mention a product called Stretch Mate©, developed by Fred Doland of Boston Massachusetts (508-429-0707). Stretch Mate© fits comfortably in most dens. I own two.

Nutrition—The Three "W's" of Nutrition

What — we should eat?

1. Complex Carbohydrates

Fruits	Vegetables	Pastas
Beans	Lentils	Rice
Whole Grain Breads		

2. Diet Consists of: 55-60% complex carbohydrates
   15-20% protein (fish—lean meat)
   25-30% fat

When — Meals should be on a regular schedule and should reflect need or projected output mentally and physically.

Why — Lack of sufficient fuel in the body will cause fatigue, muscle tightness, loss of ability to concentrate, and overall inability to maintain top performance levels.

Hydration

- Drink a minimum of 1 1/2 to 2 1/2 quarts of water per day
- Things to Drink—Water and all types of fruit juices (diluted juices)
- Dehydration causes the same symptoms as the WHY in nutrition.

Nutrition Information

• One double cheeseburger contains approximately	3/4 cup of fat
• One order of fries contains approximately	1/2 to 3/4 cup of fat
• One candy bar contains	2-3 tsp. of sugar
• One soda contains	10-12 tsp. of sugar

One meal of a double cheeseburger, fries, soda, and a candy bar equals one and a half cups of fat, twelve to fifteen teaspoons of sugar and over one thousand five hundred calories!

Nutrition Point Value

Eat foods with a high point value

Cereals

Oatmeal
Nutrigrain
Grape Nuts
Shredded Wheat
Zero (O) Fat Cereals — 5 Pts

French Toast
White Bread Toast
Bran Muffins
Blueberry Muffins — 1 Pts.

Raisin Bran
Wheaties
Total
Bran Flakes
Cheerios — 2 Pts

Sugar Smacks
Frosted Flakes
Frosted Mini Wheat
Honey Nut Cheerios — 0 Pts.

Pork Products

Ham
Bacon
Sausage — 0 Pts.

Complex Carbohydrates

Fruits
Vegetables
Grain
Bread
Rice
Pasta
Lentils — 5 Pts.

Sandwiches on Wheat

Chicken (Not Fried)
Tuna
Turkey — 5 Pts.

Hot Dogs
Hamburgers — 0 Pts.

Desserts

Fruits
Non Fat Yogurt — 5 Pts.

All Sugar Items

Cookies
Cake
Doughnuts
Pastries
Candy — 0 Pts.

Dairy Products

Milk
Eggs
Cheese — 2 Pts.

Dinners

Spaghetti
Chicken
Fish
Turkey
Broiled Steak — 5 Pts.

Salads

Green Salad
Pasta
Spinach
Fruit-No Dressing or Cream — 5 Pts.

Hydrators

Water—More than 3 Quarts — 5 Pts.

Apple Juice
Orange Juice
Grapefruit Juice
Grape Juice — 3 Pts.

BOB ANDERSON'S STRETCHING SUGGESTIONS

Chapter Three

Golf's
Physical Basics©
(Golf's Environment)

For over 500 years —
efficient, repeatable golf swings
have been founded on Golf's Physical Basics.

Nature knows no other possibilities.

This Chapter gives a detailed explanation of each Physical Basic.

For readers who want fewer details, they are given below.

Golf's Five Physical Basics

• **Physical Basic #1—The Design of the Club** — At address, golf clubs are angled up from the ground on a roof-like inclined angle, with the grip angled forward of the clubhead. Golfers should do their best to return the shaft through impact parallel to the lie angle that it occupied at address with the clubhead behind the grip end. Note: Clubs are designed for impact alignments, not address alignments.

• **Physical Basic #2—Standing Inside the Target Line** — Because golfers stand inside the ball and are holding a club that comes up from the ground on a roof-like inclined angle, normally the most efficient motion a golfer can make with the club, moves its shaft, head, and face on an arc (not straight line) that does not travel outside the target line in the backswing or downswing.

• **Physical Basic #3—Golf Balls are Compressible** — It is useful for golfers to realize that golf balls are compressible, and the alignment and application of on-plane force should be compressing the ball, not moving it, with a swing that keeps the clubface behind their hands through impact.

• **Physical Basic #4—Timing and Balance** — These are core elements of efficient swings. It is useful to feel that the swing does not make any sudden jumps or over accelerates the club at any time during the swing. There should be a feeling that the hands and the right shoulder are traveling at the same rate of rotation during the downswing.

• **Physical Basics #5—The Field of Play, and Ever Changing Playing Conditions** — The conditions of the shot at hand (uphill, downhill, wind, etc.) determines the appropriate ball flight, the alignment and application of force, and swing motion that will produce predictable outcomes. Form follows function.

PHYSICAL BASIC #1

The Club

(The Club's Two Shaft Angles)

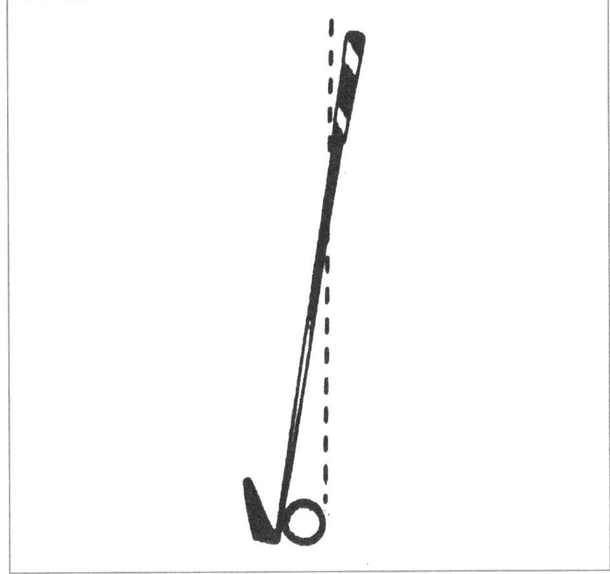

"The best advice I can give—
you must obey the club and what the club wants you to do—
letting results be natural."

- Harry Vardon 1910

Secret: Golf clubs are designed for impact alignments, not address. The heart and soul of the golf swing is its lie angle (plane), especially through impact.

"Golfers should first and most importantly learn how the
clubface and ball interact at impact. No one can play good golf until they
know the many ways a ball can be expected to react when struck in different ways."

- Bobby Jones 1930's

A Blueprint

"So much depends upon the golfers clubs – we will give some ideas of their form."
– W. R. Chambers 1862

Millions of men and women all over the world (professional and amateur) have played the game of golf for hundreds of years and maybe longer. Some people are new to the game, others have played for years, and some fall somewhere in between. But from day one, anyone playing golf has had a common goal: **To improve the next time they play!**

Some reasons golfers fail to build effective consistent swings include:

- People often try to work on their game and swing without a plan.
- When a plan is used it is often based on:
  - Misinformation.
  - Misapplication of information.
  - Misinterpreting information.
  - Incomplete knowledge.

Checking Plane
1920's

Secret: Fortunately when the plans for building a consistent swing and game use a blueprint for the alignment and application of force based on the design of the golf club (physical basic #1) all these reasons can be avoided.

Some may feel the design of the club is an unusual starting point for any blueprint for building effective forces for in golf swing **motion**, but consider what other sports use as their foundation for **motions** that are considered effective.

- The **motion** used by a world-class pool player is based on **design** of the pool table, pool cue, and balls.
- The **motion** the best tennis players learned to use is based on the **design** of the tennis racket, ball, and court.
- The **motion** of a successful croquet swing is based on the **design** of the croquet stick and playing field.
- The **motion** of a hockey player's shot is based on the **design** of the hockey stick.

On Plane Shoulders
Seymore Dunn 1930's

From putter to driver **every** golf club is born with a specific and measurable design to them. Golfers with an effective alignment and application of force either use the original **design** angles built into the club at the factory **(i.e. shaft lie angle, face loft angle, and the angle the handle is forward of the clubface),** or they intentionally alter one or more of these design angles through impact for the shot at hand. It will help your progress to see that every club has **three elements**: clubhead, clubface, and shaft. (Do not see it as one piece of equipment.)

From day one every shot in golf has had some type of ball flight (i.e. straight, high, low, long, short, hooks, slices, pushes, and pulls), The alignment and application of force for all these ball flights were influenced by one or more of the following at impact:

- Player's perceptions of impact alignments.
- Player's grip, posture, or alignment, at address and impact.
- At impact, the lie angle of the shaft to the ground and ball.
- At impact, the loft angle of the clubface to the ground and ball.
- At impact, the amount that the grip end of the club is forward or behind the clubface.
- At impact, the direction the clubface is facing.

On Plane Shoulders
2000 #2

- The path the clubhead is traveling on, before, during and after impact.
- At impact, what area of the clubface touches the ball.
- What area of the golf ball is hit by the clubface.
- Clubhead velocity when contact is made (impact) and clubhead velocity when the ball is leaving the clubface (separation).

"Golf begins and ends with the player hitting a ball with a club."

– *from* "Search for the Perfect Swing"

As golfers become aware of the design angles of the club and how these design angles can influence both the direction and distance of ball flight, it becomes **self-evident** why these angles can be used as a non-negotiable blueprint for any plans to develop an efficient swing.

Note: Tennis and pool players can influence the direction, distance, and side spin that balls have with the face of the racket or tip of the pool cue at impact. Also, both the path of the swinging racket and of the pool stroke at impact influence where their respective balls go. The distance and direction of a hockey puck and croquet ball are also influenced by the path and face angle of the sticks used in these games at impact. (Golf balls are influenced by the same principals).

PHYSICAL BASIC #1

The design angles a golf club has had for over five hundred years. Golf clubs are designed for impact alignments, not address alignments. It is useful to see the club as three elements; 1. Shaft, 2. Face and 3. Head

Shaft

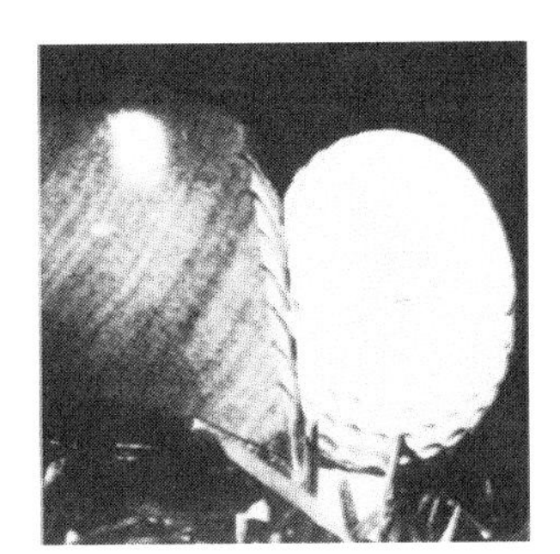

Face

Head

Now let's discuss these three elements of the club that have had the same design elements for over five-hundred years.

1700's

1900

1960's #1

2000 #2

SHAFT

1. Shaft: The Shaft has two design angles: **A**. The **Handle** end of the shaft is designed to be angled forward of the clubface. **B**. The **Shaft** is designed to be angled up from the ground on a roof like inclined angle

1950's #1 | 1920's | 1960's #1 | 1930's

Note: These two shaft angles (up from the ground and forward of the face) define the required alignment and angle that clubs should have as they swing through golf's moment of truth – Impact. I.e. The clubface is behind the grip end of the shaft, as the shaft and swing forces stay parallel to the original shaft angle present at address through impact. **(This is referred to as swinging the club on its plane.)**

Every shot in golf has had some type of ball flight, and that flight is influenced by how the swing intentionally or unintentionally angles and aligns the clubface, head, and shaft through impact.

2000 #2 | 1950's | 1980's

1950's #6 | 1950's #6 | 1950's

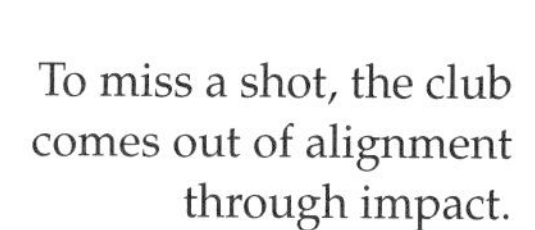

To miss a shot, the club comes out of alignment through impact.

CLUBFACE

2. Clubface: The clubface should point to the line the player wants the ball to start on as it leaves the clubface at separation (not impact).

1960's #1

1990's #7

2000

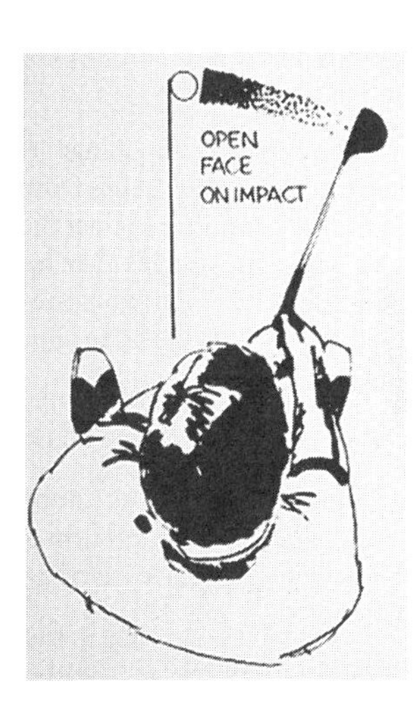

SHOULD THE CLUBFACE IMPACT THE BACK OF THE BALL? – NO!

Lie: Golfers should impact the back of the ball, with a clubface that is square to the target at impact. Not So! – a misconception.

Secret: As the club returns to the ball, it is traveling on its arc, (not a straight line). It is returning to the inside back corner of the ball with a slightly open clubface at impact. Any attempt to hit the back of the ball with a square clubface can cause the left wrist to bend back away from the ball and loss of force and pressure through impact.

If the golf clubs shafts were traveling on a vertical plane (as it does in croquet), the face could hit the back of the ball looking square to the target. But because golfers stand inside the ball, the efficient swing is returning the club from inside the target line to the inside back corner of the ball with a slightly open **clubface** at impact. After impact and ball separation, the arc of the swing moves back inside the target line. Tiger Woods, "I try to hit the inside part of the ball".

Baseball bats and tennis rackets are also moving in an arc and return to impact with a forward leaning shaft (Physical Basic #1), an open face, to the inside back corner of baseballs and tennis balls. (Not the back of the balls.)

In golf, players stand inside the ball and target line (physical basic #2). This requires the swing to move the club in an arc (not a straight line to the back of the ball). The club in efficient swings moves away form the ball and returns to the ball without ever going outside the target line when it is on plane. (The great Sam Snead's downswing started a little outside the plane line, but Snead aimed a little to the right of his target, and was back on plane through impact.)

On plane club, dovit, and force, all moving on an arc, not straight line.

"Too many golfers think of the swing as straight back, and straight through the ball, like a pendulum. See clubhead path following the rim of a tilted wheel, and yourself as the hub of that wheel."

– Gary Middlecoff 1969

"The line taken by the clubhead is a curved arc through impact, not a straight line."

– Douglas Edgar 1920

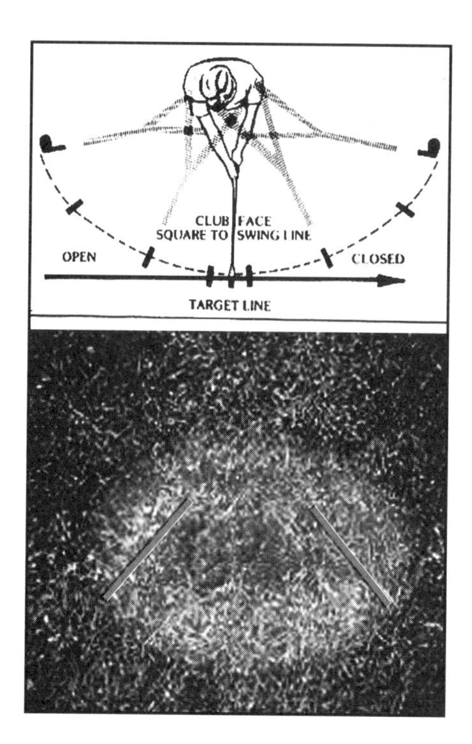

Note: The **clubface** is square to the arc. Open at impact, square to the target at separation.

* These pictures of divots by Tiger Woods were taken by me at the 1999 Ryder Cup during practice round he played with Steve Pate.

Note: There was a television infomercial aired during the late summer of 1998 – that suggested the secret of hitting the ball straight was keep the club on a straight line 20 inches before and 20 inches after impact. This suggestion flies in the face every physical law that influences efficient golf swings. It is a poor concept, and due to the design angle of the shaft, I am not sure it is physically possible (I believe Bob Bush once said it was not).

Note: Shoulders parallel to the shaft plane, club head traveling inside target line.

Jack Nicklaus #1

Ben Hogan

Sam Snead

Clubhead

3. Clubhead: A efficient golf swing has the clubhead traveling on an arc that stays parallel to the original design angle of the shaft (on plane) through impact. The clubhead also normally approaches the ball from inside the target line, and stays behind the player's hands (flat left wrist joint, and a bent right wrist) through impact.

1999

1930's

1940's

2000 #2

Seymore Dunn's
Off Plane
Demonstration
1930's

"The club's lie angle becomes the swing plane angle through impact."
Mike Hebron Jr.

Seymore Dunn
On Plane Force

THE CLUB'S "THREE ELEMENTS"
A BLUEPRINT FOR TRAINING

Golfers can work on their swing and game in a variety of ways, but I would suggest no longer just thinking about improving the swing, be more specific. Use your training and practice time to discover what motions you can use to produce efficient alignments of a golf club's 3 elements (clubface, head, and shaft) for the shot you want to make. **Develop a swing using a blueprint based on the elements a golf club, not tips from your friends.**

"The best advice I can give – you must obey the club and what the club wants you to do, letting results be natural."– 1919 Harry Vardon

When working on your game and swing, pick one (face, head or shaft) at a time to be aware of. Becoming aware of the club's 3 elements is a much easier skill to learn than learning how to type reasonably well, **much easier**! There are only three elements (face, head, and shaft to be aware of) not the 100+ keys that are on most modern computer keyboards to learn. I know many 6 year olds who are aware of what their clubface, clubhead, and shaft are doing at impact more often than not.

Note: When schools offer driver education classes, a general description of what people intend to do is learn to drive. When driver education is looked at from a different point of view, people are really learning to influence, a **steering wheel, a gas and break pedals**. When students learn to influence these three elements of a car, they are developing a foundation for learning to drive a car.

Driving a car is really the end result of learning to influence a **steering wheel, a gas, and break pedal**. Just as a effective golf swing is clearly the end product of learning to influence the shaft, face, and head of a golf club. My suggestion: do not try to learn the golf swing per se, but become aware of, and learn the required alignments of **shaft, clubface, and clubhead** at impact for the shot at hand. Where do you want the shaft, the clubhead, and clubface for the shot at hand?

By focusing on what you want at impact, not "how to" advice, progress arrives. See efficient impact alignments before you swing, and the end product can become an effective alignment and application of swing force. Just as learning to influence a steering wheel, gas and break pedal is the foundation for improving driving skills, learning to influence a club's three elements are the foundation for improving golf skills.

Seymore Dunn On Plane Force

- *"Was the clubface open or closed at impact?"* – Did the ball start right or left?
- *"Was the clubface behind my hands or ahead of them?"* – Was impact weak or solid?
- *"Was the shaft above, below, or on the same lie angle it occupied at address through impact?"* – Did the ball fly left, right or straight?
- *"Where was the shaft pointing at the top of the swing?"* Did the ball have any side spin in flight?

Keep in mind – ball flight is the result of how the club's three elements are aligned through impact. Natures truths knows no other possibilities.

Note: By knowing **what** you did, you see **what** you can do!

Some general observations about the design of a club are:

- In general: when the shaft and swing forces are not parallel to the angle the shaft occupied at address through impact, it causes a ball flight the player does not want.

- When the face of the club is either open or closed to the clubhead path side spin is increased. An open clubface, with the clubhead coming to the ball from outside the target line increases left to right side spin. A closed face with the clubhead coming from inside the target line increases right to left side spin (in both examples there is a misalignment of force.)

- When the face of the club is looking in the same direction the clubhead is traveling into impact on, an out to in path it pulls the ball left. With an in to out path, the ball is pushed off line to the right. (Both flights without side spin.)

- When the players' swing shape lets the club go through impact without any changes to its original angles, the shaft, clubhead, and clubface are all said to be on plane (with the clubface behind the grip end), the player has an efficient application and alignment of force, and straight **boring** ball flight.

- When players with consistent swings **intentionally** alters one or more of the original design angles through impact, they can **intentionally** alter the application of force and the flight of the ball, making it go high or low, or give the ball a left to right or right to left side spin for the shot at hand.

- When the original design angles are changing **unintentionally** through impact, it produces thin and fat shots. Shots can also go higher or lower than we want, hooking and slicing out of control unintentionally. All caused by the original design angles going through impact unintentionally out of control, producing a misapplication of force.

I would like to believe any suggestions I may make, allows golfers to use any force they create without adding effort.

Muscles are either at rest or they are not. When free, they are available to fire, when tight they are not.

*"The ideal waggle consists in a gentle to and fro, once or twice in **the same plane** as the arc which the clubhead sets out to describe in actual stroke."*

Spalding Athletic Library 1897

Secret: **Any efforts and plans to create effective swing force that can be repeated on a constant basis, will be less productive than they could be, if the design angles of the golf club are not taken into consideration.**

Keep in mind every desired ball flight has a corresponding alignment and path of clubface, head, and shaft for the shot at hand. This alignment must be taken into consideration before the player swings. **It's only after players are aware of impact alignments for the club's 3 elements is it possible to build a effective repeatable swing**. Train so you learn to be aware of where the clubface, head, and shaft are at impact. (I.e. A sand shot requires different alignments than the driver swing. Players should be previewing seeing and feeling impact alignments before they start their swing.)

1910
On-plane "waggle"

Secret: It's quite possible no one has ever asked you to become aware of the clubface, head, and shaft before. But this **is the only real key to a consistent swing!** Let me ask, *"If we do not become aware of where the clubface, head and shaft are, how can we either repeat or change our current swing and ball flight?"* **Becoming aware of our current alignments is the first step to progress.**

IMMEDIATE FEEDBACK

When taking foul shots in basketball, and the ball misses to the left, our next attempt would be adjusted more to the right. Our ability to make that adjustment exists because all the information needed to make the adjustment was immediately available and recognized by the player. (I.e. the height of the basket, our distance from the basket, along with seeing past results.) When golfers know the impact alignments for a particular ball flight, their feel system can become aware of what these alignments feel like. When the mind is not filled with swing tips and "how to advice", golfers now have the opportunity (several seconds) after each swing to absorb and evaluate the feel of motion as they observe ball flight. **A mind filled with swing tips, is similar to a basketball player taking foul shots with a blind fold on – and someone else telling them what adjustments to make.**

Secret: **Always train within your own comfort zone and your own limitations. Use a club that you know can control ball flight and stay aware after impact to what you feel. After every swing golfers have several seconds to compare the feel of the swing to the corresponding ball flight, and that is where long-term learning starts.**

Like basketball players, golfers also need accurate and immediate feedback (about golf's environment). I.e. ball flight and the **feel** of impact **alignments** of the club shaft, head and clubface. The player's ability to recognize the feel of both workable and unworkable impact alignments is where long-term learning and the ability to repeat efficient swings have their start.

Secret: Golfers should be learning effective club and body **alignments**, not club and body positions. It is very important to be aware of efficient impact **alignments** for the shot at hand. Where is the shaft, clubhead, and clubface?

Note: Eyes, shoulders, right arm, club, right foot, all on plane.

1980's | 1999 | 1920's | 1910

1990's #4 | 1999 #2 | 1980's | 1990's #4

EYES, SHOULDERS, RIGHT ARM, CLUB, RIGHT FOOT—ALL ON PLANE

1990's #7

1990's #7

1990's #7

1999 #4

1999 #7

1900's

1900's #4

1950's

1999 #7

Eyes, Shoulders, Right Arm, Club, Right Foot *All* On-Plane

2000 #2

2000 #2

1990's #7

1999 #2

1990's #2

1990's #5

1930's

1990's #4

1940's

Physical Basic #2

Standing Inside the Ball and Target Line

(I.e. Ball location, grip, alignment, posture)

1960's — Ben Hogan

1890's — Harry Vardon

2000 — Tiger Woods #7

1880's — Tom Morris

"Standing to the ball, takes little talent,
but does take a good deal of knowledge."
– Ben Hogan

"Hitting a baseball is hand/eye coordination,
but good golf is founded on efficient posture."
– Dr. Harold L Kalawan

"To control the ball—
a golfer must first learn to control himself."
- John Stuart Martin

1999

1900

1915

1905

Golf's Physical Basics #2 – Golfers have always stood inside the golf ball and target line.

Secret: **For five hundred years the roof like inclined angle of the shaft has required players to stand as they do – inside and to the side of the ball and target line at address.**

The physical basic of standing to the side of the ball and inside the target line has always **required** the players swing to move their club in an arc (not a straight line) as the hands, arms, and club stay in front of the player's body. An efficient golf swing arc for most shots goes back, up and in from the ball, then back down and out to the ball, approaching the ball from inside the target line. This arc also stays parallel to the inclined angle the shaft occupied at address through impact, (and for the entire swing of many world-class golfers).

Note: Baseball, tennis, and hockey players are also required to move their bat, racket, and sticks in an arc, because they too are standing to the side or inside the object they are hitting.

One of the main requirements of body alignments while standing to the ball at address is in the area of **The Balance State**. If a player is not balancing correctly at address, it is not likely they will be balancing correctly during swing motion. Human motion happens around the body's joints, and the brain will always introduce extra or compensating motion when the body goes out of balance. Keep in mind what you are doing in one segment of the body always effects every other segment.

The human body has 13 major joints. Two ankle, two knee, two hips, two shoulder, two elbows, two wrists and the neck. The efficient swings we like to watch are balancing these thirteen joints in three-dimensional space. **That is, side to side, up to down, and front to back.** One of the reasons efficient swings have this three-dimensional balancing capability is because of how players with efficient swings **stand to the ball at address**.

The following are suggestions you may want to consider as you develop your ideas about standing to the ball.

Powers of Observation

Two of the world's finest golf instructors are on either side of your nose. Many skills learned as children, (riding bikes, swinging bats, throwing and catching balls, etc.) we started to learn by watching others perform them, and not because someone told us what to do. Observation is also a very effective way of learning how to stand to the ball at address. My suggestion to readers who want to improve their game: **USE YOUR POWERS OF OBSERVATION**.

Watching LPGA and PGA Tour professionals, local club professionals, and outstanding amateurs play can help your own game. While there are studies that suggest using expert models to learn a **"swing motion"** is not the most workable approach, observing expert players standing to the ball at address does provide some general guidelines.

But please be forewarned! Everyone is going to look different. Body styles, swing shapes, tempo and rhythm, will all change from one player to the next. So what can we possibly learn? **When we know what to look for much can be learned.** As we begin to gather information about some of the basics that all good golfers share, these players gradually look more and more alike.

Ⓐ 1940's

Here are some suggestions on where to use the POWERS OF OBSERVATION: **It is my feeling, that unless suggestions for standing to the ball and holding the club are gave in person, they should be general in nature.**

Posture

Notice the posture of a world-class player does not change very much from club to club under normal conditions. The arms hang down from the shoulders and lay on the chest from the elbows up with every club. The shoulders do not change either, the right is lower than the left. With all clubs there is a small bend from the mid-section. There is also a slight flex in both knees. Most of all there is no discernible tension. As a club gets longer, the player will stand farther away from the ball with his feet wider apart to accommodate the length of the shaft.

1920's

Head

Notice where good players place their head in their stance. Draw an imaginary vertical line up from the ball, and notice the player's head is in back of the ball for most shots and especially with tee shots.

In efficient swings, the head is normally back behind the ball and only flows forward after impact. Also notice how a good player has the face looking down. The old saying of "keep your head up" does not really hold true for many world-class players, most have their face looking down at the ball, knee joints over ankle joints.

1930's

Spine

The spine is angled over (above) the ball and angled back from the target, with the lower, middle, and upper spine, at three different angles. Note: Ⓐ on pages 121-183, and Ⓐ above on this page.

1920's

1950's

2000 #2

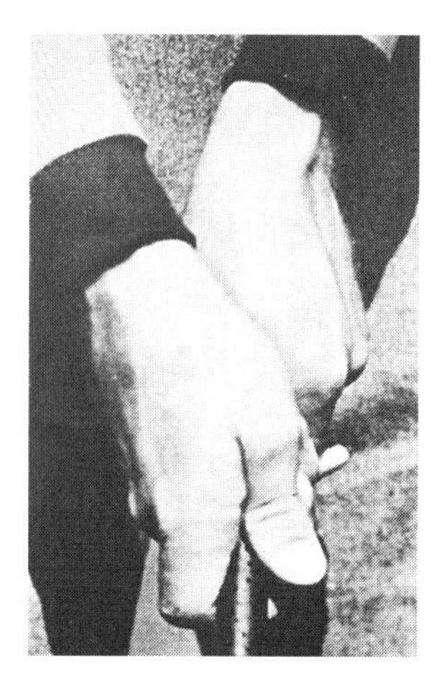

Holding the Club

It is useful to have your concept of holding the club go beyond the hands. When we look at professionals, we can see they don't give the appearance of hanging on for dear life. To achieve this same look, **expand your concept of grip to include wrist, shoulder, and elbow joints, all free of tension.**

Notice how the left thumb is right of center and right thumb left of center. One element of some effective grips that cannot be noticed by looking would be the last three fingers of the upper hand and the middle two of the lower hand are much firmer than the thumb and forefingers. This approach will give you the needed grip pressure to compress the ball, but it also keeps your **wrist joints free** during the swing (when the thumb and forefinger are firm the wrist joints are not as free as they could be).

Exception – with shots that you would like your wrists to be firm (e.g. Putting and chipping), be firm with your thumb and forefinger when holding the club.

"Leave the forefingers and thumbs loose so the club can work." - Alex Herd 1903. One general suggestion, hold the club more in the fingers than the palms, with the lower fore-finger spread somewhat down the grip.

"When players stand and aim wrong—they then try to pull or push the ball to correct for faulty stance and aim. In golf, faults covered by faults do not cancel each other."

- Sir W.G. Simpson 1887

Palm of lower hand feels firm against the thumb of the upper hand.

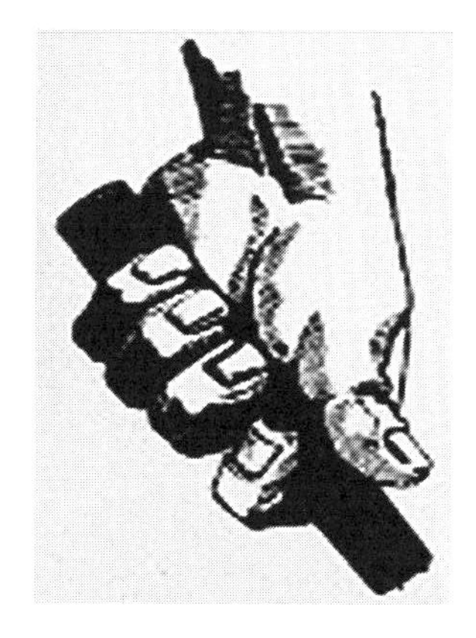

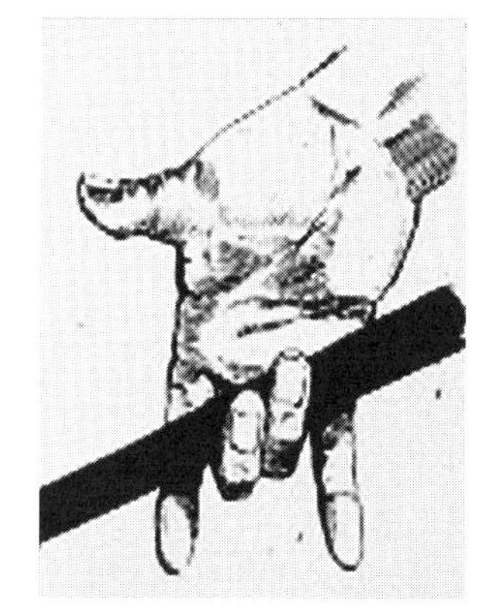

"The fore-finger and thumb play a secondary role. The middle fingers of the lower hand and the last three fingers of the upper hand apply pressure."

- Arnold Palmer

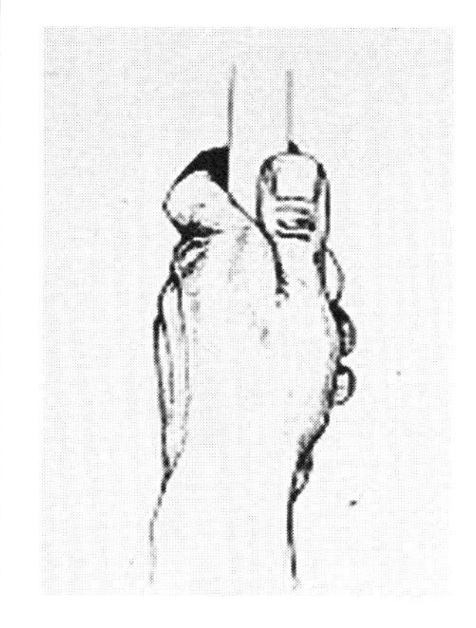

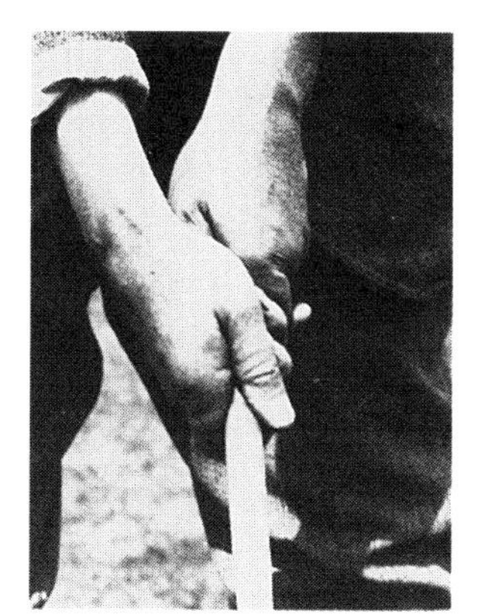

Harry Vardon

"The shaft is placed under the heel pad of the upper hand as the last three fingers pull the club up into the heel firmly."

- Ben Hogan

Note: The previous suggestion, while somewhat specific, are general in nature. There are always some suggesions, or exceptions to the rule that could be made in person.

PRE-SHOT ROUTINE

When watching a professional, you will notice that he or she will use the same (pre-shot routine) movements before each and every swing. These are learned motions and the first steps to consistent golf. Good golfers know by starting with a consistent pre-shot routine their chances of repeating their swing and ball flight increases. Every player's routine is somewhat different, but what ever the pattern is, it is the same time after time.

If you do not have what you would call a pre-shot routine, here some general suggestions

- Stand behind the ball; look at the target; gather information (distance, wind, lie, desired ball flight).
- Pick your club, stand with shoulders somewhat open (while facing the target); now place the clubface behind the ball with your feet together. Some good golfers place the clubface behind the ball holding the club only with the right hand, others only with the left, then they place the other hand on the club after aligning the clubface. Pick what works for you. I would **not suggest** having both hands on the club as you place the clubface behind the ball.
- Next, separate feet on a line parallel to the target line – all the while you are looking at the target (not at the ball), **with your eyes on-plane.**
- Now look back at the ball, picture the ball flight; one more look at the target (**with eyes on plane**), now back to the ball, then swing. You may find it useful to have your shoulders and hips somewhat open to the target line with your heels square to the target line at address.

Ben Hogan

Sergio Garcia #7

AT ADDRESS, SEE LINES BEFORE YOU SWING

What we see before we swing is as important as what we feel when we swing.

The saying "Well begun is well done," certainly holds true for both playing and learning golf. **Golfers who make progress normally have different background information than golfers who are not improving.** The following is some background information that players should be aware of before they try to improve their golf swing.

The cause of poor golf can change from one golfer to the next, but one very common cause is a player aiming both his clubface and body to the right of the target. This alignment normally causes the player to use a swing motion that comes down, into the body, and across the target line. When a player stands on one line and uses a swing motion that takes place on a different line (not parallel to the stance line) it can create both workable and unworkable pulls and pushes, slices, and hooks.

Tiger Woods #7

Golf is often described as a game of parallel lines, and it would be my suggestion that any efforts to improve one's current game should start by first seeing lines. Then, move on to learning how parallel lines can be used to change ball flights without changing swing shapes.

Note: These players all have their eyes on-plane when looking at the target.

Sam Snead — 1950's #6

Some lines golfers may want to be aware of before they swing include:

A. **The Target Line**: This line goes through the ball straight to the target.

B. **The Player's Stance Line**: This is the line the player stands on at address, which is normally parallel to the target line.

C. **The Clubface Line**: This is the line formed by the bottom edge of the clubface.

D. **The Plane Line**: This is the line or angle formed by the club shaft as it comes up from the ground at address. **The plane line (or angle) is the heart and soul of the golf swing.** At impact, the clubhead, club shaft, right forearm, hands, and right shoulder should all be traveling down and out, parallel to the plane line established by the shaft at address.

E. **The Base of The Plane Line**: This line is about one inch inside and parallel to the target line. This is the line the shaft of the club points to at address.

F. **The Shaft Line At Address**: As the player looks down, this is the angle players see the shaft on as the club is placed on the ground at address, (clubhead mass behind the grip).

G. **The Shaft Line At Impact**: This shaft line normally leans more forward to the target than at address, but is still parallel to the shaft angle present at address (or on plane) through impact.

H. **The Line of Separation**: This is the line or arc the clubhead travels away from the ball on after impact.

I. **The Line of Approach**: This is the line or arc the clubhead travels back to impact on.

J. **The Line of follow-through**: This is the line or arc the clubhead travels on after impact (when on-plane).

K. **Ball Flight Line**: This is the line the ball will travel on after impact. When the player can visualize the ball flight line they want before they swing (especially for the short game) it normally improves the results players receive for their efforts.

Arnold Palmer #4

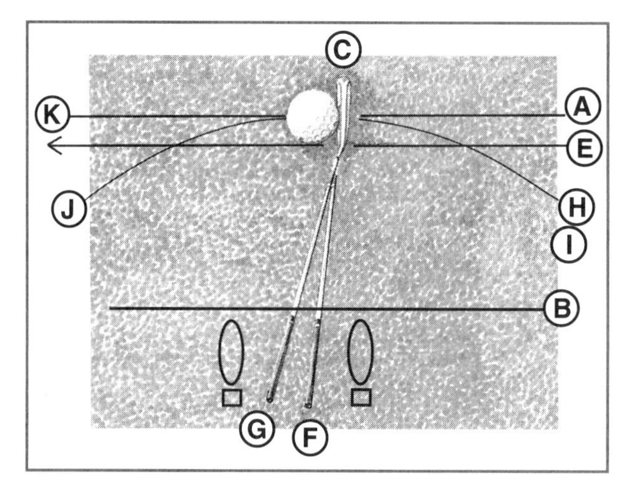

Jack Nicklaus #2

Some readers may feel this is a long list, but it becomes second nature soon after a player starts to be aware of these check points.

For the shot at hand: Players have choices. Should my stance line be one that is open, closed or a square line to the target line? Should my shoulders be an open line, hips an open line, and the feet a closed or square line to the target line? (This is how Ben Hogan and many other successful Tour players aligned their bodies.) Normally it depends on the shot at hand.

For the shot at hand: What line should ball location be on? At address, should the ball be located on a line that is forward, back, or in the middle of my stance? Another way of asking this question would be, where should the ball location be in relation to my spine line? Normally it depends on the shot at hand.

Before players start their swing, they should be aware of what line they want the **clubhead** to swing away from the ball on, and what line they want the clubhead to return to impact on. Also, what line does the player want the **shaft** to be on at impact? At impact, what line does the player want his **clubface** looking at: open, closed, or square to the target line? Normally this all depends on the shot at hand.

Impact — 1915

It is also useful for the player to be aware that during efficient swings, because his eyes are behind the ball at impact (looking both down and forward), **their hands and club shaft will give the impression or illusion they are leaning more forward of the ball than they actually are.**

Players should see lines before they swing: Lines that for the most part are parallel lines that can be used or adjusted for the shot at hand. Does the player want left to right, right to left, high, or low ball flight? By adjusting the parallel lines that exist in golf, players can change their ball flight without trying to change their golf swing.

- Normally aligning the shoulders, hips, and stance line left of the target, with the clubface aligned to the target at address, can produce a left to right ball flight.
- Normally aligning the shoulders, hips, and stance line right of the target, with the clubface aligned to the target at address, can produce a right to left ball flight.
- Normally ball location at address behind the spine can produce a lower than normal ball flight. Ball location at address several inches forward of the spine can produce a higher than normal ball flight (especially in the short game).

Lee Trevino — 2000 #4

Secret: **To make progress players must become aware of lines before they swing – period end of sentence! In the past no one may have asked you to see or be aware of lines, but once you start to be aware, it quickly becomes second nature. I know young golfers some as young as 6 years old who are aware of lines before they swing.**

Note: PGA Professional Ben Doyle has designed a training mat to help golfers learn to see lines before they swing. To order call Ben (831) 624-2526.

Address and Impact Are Not the Same

Perhaps the first step to create effective impact alignments is to know what effective impact alignments looks like before the swing starts. It seems effective impact alignments would be difficult to produce if the player did not know what they are. This would be like trying to get to Main street without knowing where it is or not having any directions.

Tom Watson — 2000 #2

Lie: Impact and address have the same alignments. This concept is the foundation for many causes of inefficient swings, including golf's most common and damaging habit, the clubhead passing the hands through impact.

Address - 1930's

Impact alignments are different from address alignments. At **impact** there is a forward leaning shaft, flat left wrist but a bent right wrist, with the right leg having more flex at the knee than at address. The hips are more open at impact, with the right elbow lower and down and in front of the right hip. At **address** the shaft has less forward lean, the right wrist is straight, the left wrist is bent, and the left shoulder is lower than it will be at impact.

Secret: When players have poor concepts of impact alignments and conditions, and try to return to impact with the same alignments they had at address, it's difficult to reach their potential. The angles an effective swing delivers to impact are created for the most part during the back swing. They were not present at address.

Impact

In 1922 Seymour Dunn made a useful observation when he talked about a effective swing having not one, but two pivot points, our two hip joints. He believed backswing turn is on the right hip joint, and the downswing turn is on the left hip joint. He felt his experience had taught him, *"It is no use to turn only upon an imaginary center line between the two hip joints."* He also noted during the downswing, when the swing turned from the right hip joint back over to the left hip joint, the players center of gravity or balance had also moved a little to the left. **Mac O'Grady calls this shift a second axis tilt.** Many instructors point out there is, or should be a slight bump by the hips forward before the left hip turns left in the downswing. (Today it is still possible to find copies of Dunn's "Golf Fundamentals" and you should try to find one. It is a wonderful and enlightening work that contains information that could help anyone's game.) I would like to suggest this slight bump of the right hip, be more out to the ball (across the line), than to the target (or down the line).

Address

Note: This very slight out and down bump of the right hip, or second axis tilt is simply **the bodies normal and natural shift of its center of gravity** (or balance) more forward and down. This allows the body to turn more effectively on the left hip joint in the downswing turn. Several very important elements of a effective swing are a result of this shift of the player's center of gravity. First, the center of balance is moved closer to the back of the ball, creating a more efficient application of body rotation through impact – the right shoulder also moves down plane, **not into the body**. The closer the center of balance is to the back of the ball, the smaller the turning radius of the hip girdle can be. The shift \(or bump) of the center of gravity causing the upper spine to stay back (second axis tilt), away from the target, is influenced by a down plane right shoulder.

Impact

Secret: Without this change (second axis tilt) in the spine angle, the right shoulder will come back down to impact off plane (too high), with the right forearm also going through impact off plane (too high).

The change in the position of the player's center of gravity (slight bump) at the start of the downswing turn, also contributes in a positive way to the players head staying back before impact. Imagine if you can, a hip bump and the head going past the ball at the same time (it is probably not possible).

Note: When the right hip is lower than the left hip at impact, the force coming from the hips is more parallel to other on-plane forces in effective swings, then when hips are turning level.

2000 #5

2000

1930's

1930's

A-B-C Spine Angle #7

What happens in any one segment of the bodies skeletal system, has an immediate effect on every other segment in the system. It should be the goal of every player to discover and employ effective body motions that can set off a chain reaction of other effective body motions automatically (without conscious effort).

Secret: **A slight change of the bodies center of gravity at the start of the downswing, is an example of one very small motion that sets in motion several other body motions. Ie. Right shoulder going down plane first.**

Baseball #7
A-B-C Spine Angles

A – B – C = Spine Angles

Above, **B**ack, and **C**entered **Spine Angles** are common elements found in efficient swings. The spine is bent over at two angles – with the upper spine angled **above** or over the ball, and angled **back** from the target. The lower spine is normally **centered** between the ankle joints at address.

When the lower spine moves more forward at the start of the down swing, the two spine angles **above** and **back** are held constant through impact. **All efficient swings transport the club under a spine that is angled over to the ball, and away from the target.** Good golfers swing down-plane under a spine that is angled away from the target.

Ben Hogan once said, *"the most difficult thing about the golf swing is staying bent over for two seconds."* If there was only one element I could make gofers aware of, it would be a spine angled **away from the target during down swing.** (This permits the club, hands, right forearm, and shoulder to travel down plane to impact.)

A-B-C Spine Angle #7

1930's — Jimmy Thompson — The Longest Driver of that Era

A — B — C SPINE ANGLES
GOAL: ABOVE—BACK—CENTERED

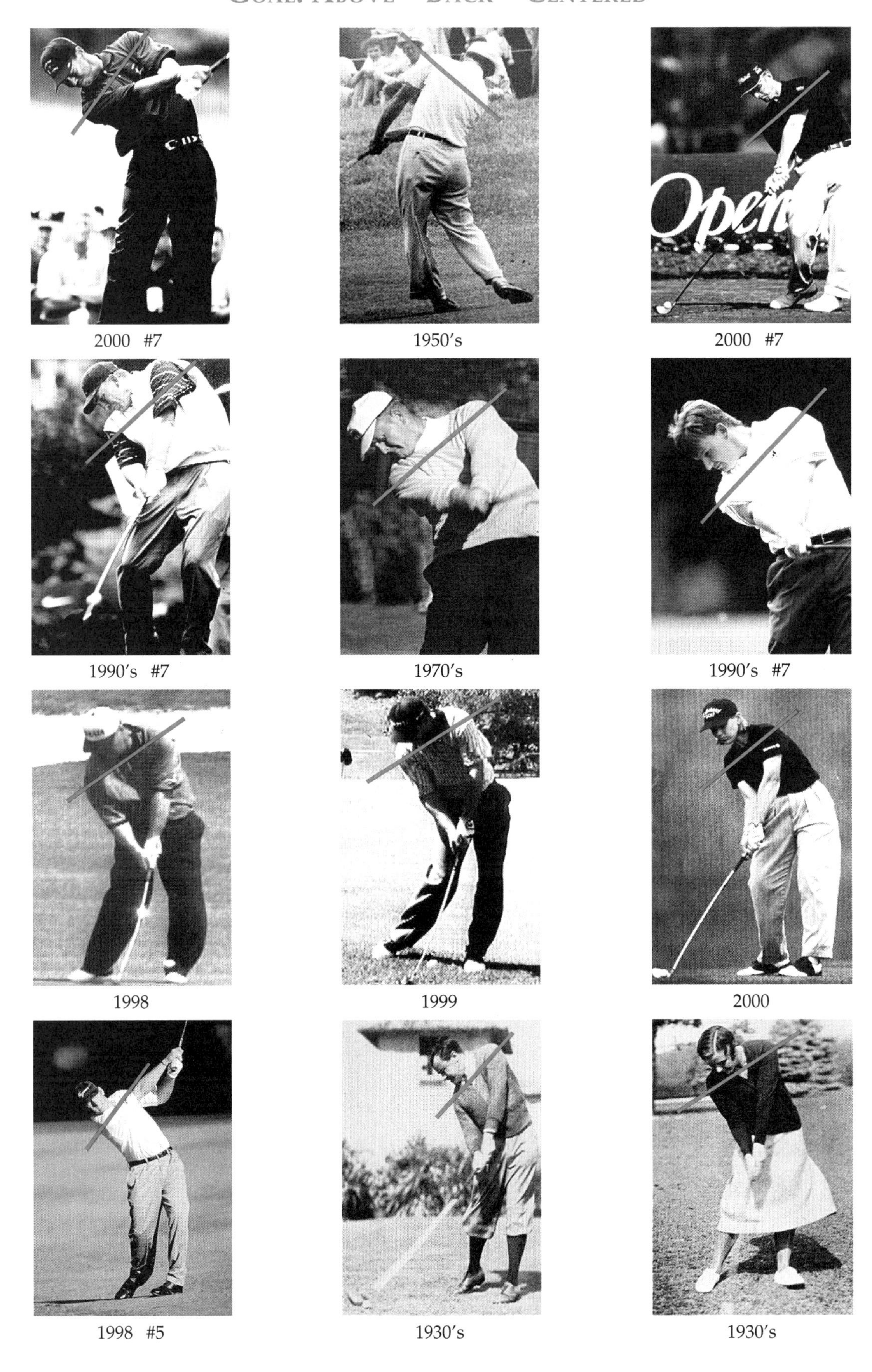

2000 #7

1950's

2000 #7

1990's #7

1970's

1990's #7

1998

1999

2000

1998 #5

1930's

1930's

PHYSICAL BASIC #3

Balls are Compressible

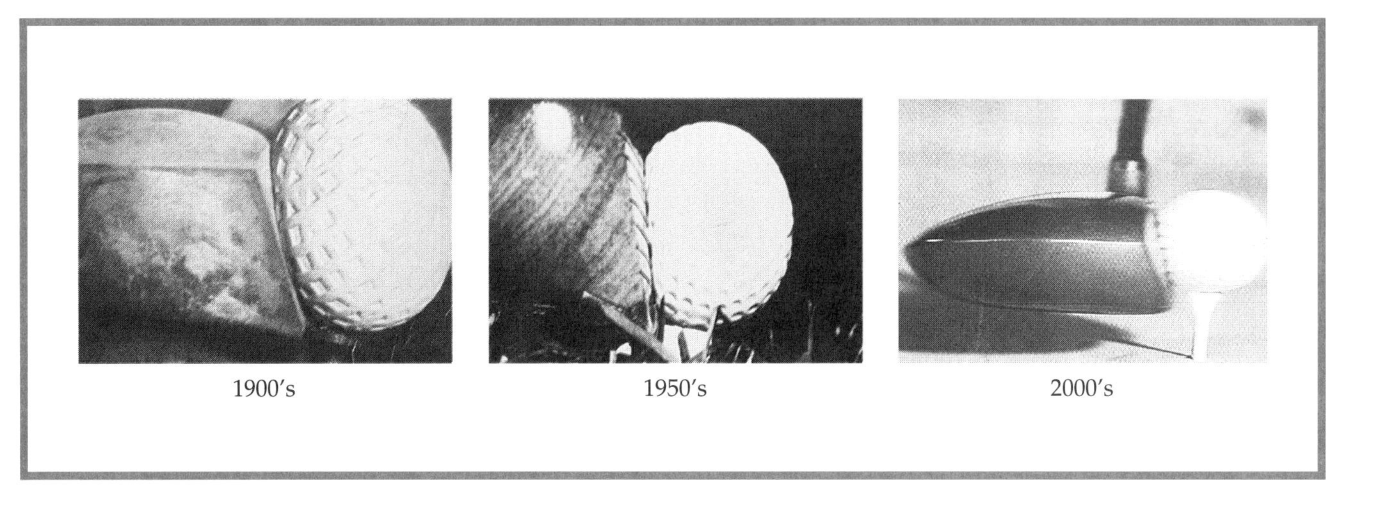

1900's 1950's 2000's

For over five hundred years,
after impact a golf ball has rebounded off the clubface into flight.

Velocity or miles per hour are normally associated
with impact and the effect of on-plane force gets overlooked.

PHYSICAL BASIC #3 – GOLF BALLS ARE COMPRESSIBLE.

Secret: **Efficient swings do not try to lift the ball. They compress the ball onto the clubface, (from driver to putter) causing the ball to rebound off the club at the loft angle of the clubface (i.e. wedges going higher than 5-irons).**

I will often ask golfers what they think moves a golf ball? In my mind what moves the ball is one of the most important insights for any player to have about playing the game. The soul object of a golf swing is to put the ball into flight under control, therefore the player's view of what causes ball flight should be a workable one. In fact, I have often found that when a player changes a poor concept of what causes ball flight for a more useful one, the results he or she receives from their swing immediately improve.

Golf balls are compressible

To gain effective insight into the cause of ball flight in golf, notice how a basketball rebounds up off the floor after it is compressed at impact. The conditions under which a floor applies force to the ball, are similar to the conditions an effective golf swing creates, when it impacts a golf ball.

Note: **Homer Kelly,** *"The basic principal of a boat; it can float. The basic principal of an airplane; it can fly. The basic principal of a golf swing;* ***it can create, apply, and sustain force or on-plane pressure."*** When a golf ball is compressed onto the clubface it then rebounds off the face into flight. In 1922 Seymour Dunn said *"flattened like a pancake, and goes off like a bullet"*. Unlike a basketball, where the golf ball is impacted and where it leaves the clubface are two different places. After a golf ball is **impacted** it then stays on the clubface for both some time and distance until it rebounds into flight, **separating itself** from the face.

Secret: **The only time the clubface has to be facing in the direction of where the player wants the ball to start into flight is when it leaves the clubface at separation.**

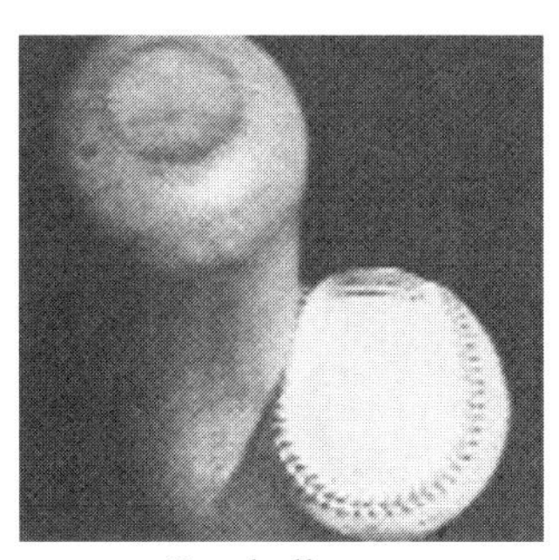

Baseballs are compressible

Note: During the very brief time and distance a ball is on the clubface (1/4" and five-one-hindrethsn of a second), it receives impulses from the clubface and swing path telling the ball in which direction and distance to fly. (It is very interesting to me that a ball is in contact with the clubface for less than a half a second in the entire round of golf.)

Tennis balls are compressible

Important: The golf swing should **never feel** like, **seem** like, or **look** like the club or swing is moving the ball. (There are a few short game exceptions.) **Golfers should use a swing that gives them the feeling they are compressing the ball (not moving it), with the ball then rebounding into flight.**

APPLYING FORCE

"How does one get the ball to rebound off the clubface into flight?" Answer, **by applying force**. Next question "How does a golf swing apply **force**." Answer; the same way a few everyday tools do. For many golfers clubhead velocity or miles per hour are normally associated with distance, and not more force at impact. Lets take a look at a **mop**, a **paintbrush**, and a **hammer** for some insight into how effective golf swings through impact create, apply, and sustain on-plane force.

- When using a mop, its handle is **on an angle** leaning forward of its strings. (**angled** in the direction it is being pulled)
- When applying paint to a wall with a brush, its handle is **on an angle** leaning forward of its bristles. (**angled** in the direction it is being pulled)
- When using a hammer, its handle is **on an angle** leaning forward of its head. (**angled** in the direction it is being pulled)

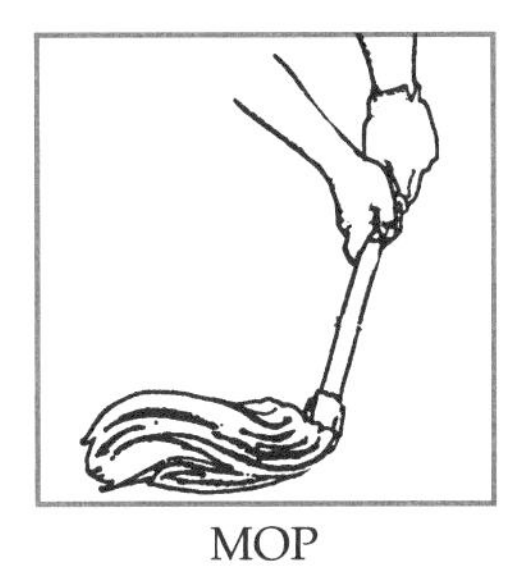
MOP

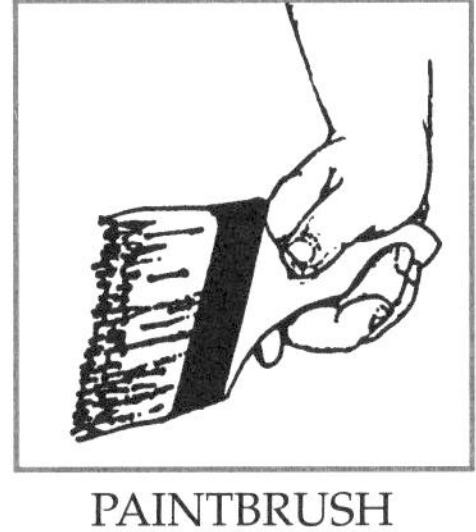
PAINTBRUSH

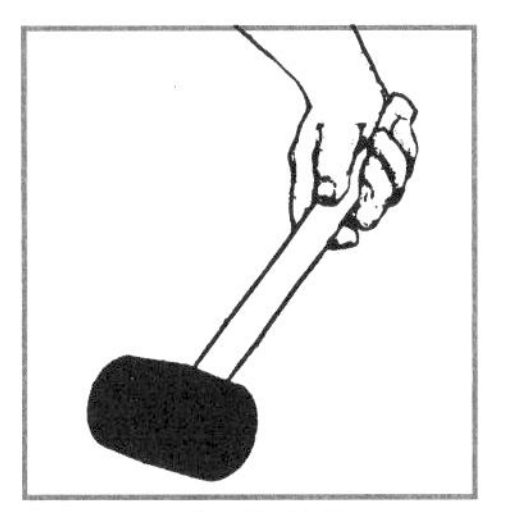
HAMMER

These familiar tools are everyday examples (if used properly) of how force is applied to a floor, a wall, or a nail.

Note: When in use, the handles of all these tools are **angled** in the direction they are being pulled. When the strings of a **mop**, bristles of a **paintbrush**, and a head of a **hammer** are pulled and allowed to lag behind the handles of these common tools, they can apply force. The hand that is holding the tool is also normally bent back behind its wrist, with the weight of the tool lagging behind that wrist.

Now note the similarities between these common tools and a golf club. A golf club is designed with its handle **angled forward** of its clubface and head (**Physical Basic #1**). When the swing's pulling forces keep the club and the clubface behind the handle through impact, the ball can be compressed onto the clubface and then rebound into flight. **(Physical Basic #3** - The original design angle, (face behind the handle), is being retained.

Note: A source of force can be a lagging component. Example: when a car is pulling a house trailer, the weight of the lagging trailer puts force on the hitch between them. When the weight of a baseball bat is lagging behind a players bent right wrist, the bent wrist angle is retained, keeping force (or an angle) in the system. A baseball is not impacted with a straight bat or one that has passed the players hands. The bat is behind the player's hands and leaning towards or angled into the ball at impact **(Physical Basic #1)**. When a bat or golf club passes the players hands before or during impact, the right wrist is no longer bent back, causing a loss of force at impact. (The player now needs to use the effort of pushing forces because the club is no longer being pulled.)

If the concept of what happens to a the ball at impact is seen through the eyes of **form follows function, and nature knows no other possibilities**, the

Initial ball speed after force is applied has a direct influence on ball flight distance.

1960's

1930's

1940's

1940's

1910

2000 #5

sticks in golf, baseball, hockey and tennis are all pulled through impact. Their tip end is behind the players hands, and the sticks are leaning toward the objects being impacted **(Physical Basic #1)**. The feeling of the ball being compressed on to the clubface then rebounding into flight, is an effective concept that every golfer should strive for. **(Physical Basic #3)**.

Secret: **During a effective downswing, the shaft of the club should feel like it is leaning in the direction it is being pulled, especially through impact.**

Imagine for a moment that a golf ball is a computer, the golf swing its program and the flight of the ball its printout. A computer can only printout what it is being told to print, just as a golf ball can only do what it is told to do during impact. **A computer follows directions blindly, so does every golf ball.** At impact the ball is programmed to go high or low, left or right. Whether the player likes or dislikes ball flight after impact, that flight was the only possible outcome from the alignment and conditions the players swing, clubhead, shaft, and face produced at impact.

Secret: **Where the clubhead, clubface, and shaft are at impact, and what they do through impact, programs distance and direction of ball flight, period – end of sentence! Nature knows no other possibilities.**

What moves the ball? Efficient swings compress a ball at **impact,** the ball then rebounds off the clubface into flight at **separation** in the direction and for the distance programmed at impact. When a golfer's concepts include; the swing and club are moving the ball, more often than not the clubhead and shaft are going to pass the player's left arm and wrist before impact. This causes a loss of force (or angle) that cannot be regained during impact.

The term's particular point and particular line are used when describing where force from a effective swing must go. *"Pressure must be applied to a particular point along a particular line."* **Greg McHatton**, (Southern California PGA Teacher of the Year). This particular line is known as the swing's plane, and the particular point is the **inside** back corner of the ball (not the back of the ball).

Impact Matrix

	WORST	BEST	O.K.
Path	Into the Body	Squaring	Inside-Out
Face Angle	Very Open	Squaring	Closed
Angle of Attack	Up	Down	Level
Horizontal Face Impact	Toe	Center	Heel
Vertical Face impact	High	Center	Low
Ball Flight	High	Boring	Low
Spin Ball Characteristics	Axis Tilted Right	No Axis Tilt	Axis Tilted Left
Distance Characteristics	Short	Pre-Determined	Long

1990's #5

No One Flips Their Hands

Many poor shots are caused by the clubhead flipping past a golfer's hands before impact (there are a few, short game exceptions to this rule). I believe, and have found that **no one really flips the club with their hands before impact**. It only looks like a flip of the hands.

The club is flipped past the hands, when the right elbow joint that folded up during the backswing, expands its angle before impact. Early straightening of the elbow joint **sets off a chain reaction** that can cause the club to flip past the hands, giving the impression hands were the cause.

Cause: When a swing's turning/pulling forces stop before or during impact, the right arm can straighten too soon, pushing and flipping the club past the hands. I.e. exactly like a car making a sudden stop, causing what's on the seat to fly forward.

In an efficient swing, pulling forces will keep the club behind a bent right wrist through impact. The weight of the club bends the right wrist back (not cocked) during backswing. Ideally a bent right wrist is maintained through impact by pulling forces (preventing any flip).

Secret: **In efficient downswings the left wrist uncocks without the bent right wrist losing its bend (angle), keeping the club behind the hands.**

Pull for Stability

Stable motions with the club mass staying behind the hands through impact are the two primary elements of efficient swings. Both actions can be more easily accomplished, when forces applied to the club are more pulling, than pushing forces.

Law: Any mass automatically aligns itself and **follows** the direction of a pulling force. A pulling force stabilizes a mass and keep the mass on a constant path (behind the hands). A pushing force on the other hand must be applied exactly through the center of any mass to keep it stable. Bobby Jones said, *"I feel a pull against something when I'm playing well"*. Bryon Nelson said, *"I am conscious of pulling the club down."*

Secret: **When the forces in a downswing are pulling forces, players improve their ability to have a stable motion and clubface stability through impact. Nature knows no other possibilities.**

It may help to feel no one really flips the club past the hands, when pulling forces stop the right arm expands, pushing the weight of the club past the player's left wrist. Again, much like a car making a sudden stop, causing what is on the seat to fly forward.

Rotational Pulling Forces

Principle of Pressure: Application of Force Over Distance

A golfer's left arm for example, could be anywhere from 30″ to 35″ long, and the club's shaft could be 35″ to 45″ long. You now have a 70″ to 80″ stick (from the left shoulder joint to the clubhead). When the shaft is in-line with the left arm through

A

1999 #5

impact, that's a 70" to 80" stick leaning into the ball (A). However when the shaft is passing the players left wrist (B) the player is now using a stick that is bent at the left wrist joint, and the shaft no longer has the ability to lean into the ball with the mass of the clubhead behind the handle. In fact, the shaft is leaning away from the ball when it passes the left wrist joint (B).

Visualize the #1 on your left arm, the #2 on the club shaft and the #3 on your mid section. In efficient swings #2 never passes #1 befor e or during impact, as #3 helps transport #1 and #2 thr ough impact (C).

When the weight (or mass)of the clubhead is pulled and stays behind the hands through impact. The clubhead is also behind the right elbow for most of the downswing. The way in which a player achieves these alignments are of course, personal in nature. Some visualization players I know use to pull the hands, arms, and club down plane to impact include:

B

- Moving the right shoulder down plane (to pull the club).
- Moving the left shoulder up plane (to pull the club).
- Moving the right elbow down plane in front of the right hip (to pull the club).
- Moving the right forearm down plane (to pull the club).
- Letting gravity move the hands down plane (to pull the club).
- Turning the mid-section of the body to pull the right forearm, hands, and right shoulder down plane.
- Letting the downswing be a reaction to the backswing (to pull the club).
- Unwinding back muscles away from the target (to pull the club).
- Ben Hogan, *"The left side pulls"*.

Very Important: Down-plane is not down to the ground. Down-plane is down and out to the inside – back corner of the ball. At the top of the back swing the shaft, clubhead, clubface, and the players hands and arms have moved back, up and in. The club is now more or less 6 feet up and 30 inches in from the ball. The downswing now has to return the club and players hands both down 6 feet and out 30 inches (not just down).

C

1999 #5

Up and In, 6' and 30"

Down and Out, 6' and 30"

Separate the Down From the Unwinding

It is useful to separate the **down** from the **unwinding** in your concept of the downswing. See the hands, right shoulder, and club moving on a line **down** and **out** on plane and then the lower body **unwinding**. In physics terms, this longitudinal acceleration (a line down plane) is being redirected by radical acceleration (a circle by body rotation) for maximum on-plane velocity and the application of force through impact.

Note: Angles create both the size and speed of motion. With the introduction of angles the size of a motion is increased (elbow joint folds to complete the backswing). Then the explanation of angles to re-seek an in-line condition increases velocity without effort.

1950's Down Plane #6

Most if not all motion in sport is transporting angles that seek an in-line condition, i.e. running, throwing, striking, and swimming.

Phil Mickelson - Down Plane - 1992

Note: Many swings are returning the hands and club into the body, instead of down and out. **If I may, I would like to suggest that golfers exchange the term "over the top" for "into the body." Inefficient swings move the hands and arms into the body.** These kind of swings are moving the clubhead outside the target line into the body. More often than not this happens because their upper spine was not angled away from the ball at the start of the downswing, thereby preventing the right shoulder from traveling down-plane.

1950's Down Plane #6

1st Down, Then Out and Around

1st Down, Then Out and Around
Alan Trammell

Application of Force: Seeking an In-line Condition

The term **seeking an in-line condition** refers to actions in a golf swing that creates angles during the backswing i.e. **bent** right elbow angle, **cocked** left wrist angle, **bent** right wrist angle, and a left arm **into** the chest that were not present at address. Then the golf swing expand these angles to seek, (or re seek) an in-line condition through impact. (The backswing aligns angles, the downswing keeps angles aligned and applies force when angles expand.)

1920's - Down Plane

1910's

Examples: When a ball or hammer are first picked up, the user's arm is straight. The ball and hammer then go up and back when the elbow joint folds. The wrist joint may also bend or cock. The arm is no longer straight. Now when the user wants to throw the ball or use the hammer, the angles now present at the elbow joint and wrist joint expand or release to seek or re-seek their in-line condition. This expansion of angles helps produces the necessary velocity and force for throwing a ball or for moving a hammer. Both apply the actions of seeking an in-line condition.

These same actions are elements of efficient golf swings. The golf swing creates angles during the backswing (left wrist, right elbow, bent right hand, left arm comes into the chest) that were not present at address. The downswing then expands these angles downplane to seek an in-line condition to apply force and velocity down into the ball at impact. Homer Kelly said, "*Expanding angles during the downswing creates four sources for applying force:*"

1930's

1. Muscle power (right arm expands)
2. Velocity power (left wrist un-cocks)
3. Transfer power (shaft going in line with the left arm)
4. Radius power (left arm swinging out from the body through impact)

Force or pressure in a golf swing must have a source, but force also must be exerted against something that can directly or indirectly drive the club through impact. (Force is defined as; energy that causes or changes motion, an effect against resistance of inertia)

1950's #6

A. The Right Hip – Exerts force against bent right arm.
B. Bent Right Arm – Exerts force against bent right wrist.
C. Bent Right Wrist – Exerts force against heel of right wrist.
D. Heel of Right Hand – Exerts force against the left thumb and shaft.
E. Upper Left Arm – Has upper left chest exerting force against it.
F. Cocked Left Wrist – Exerts force against last three fingers of left hand.
G. Angle of Shaft to Left Arm – Exerts force on the index finger of the right hand.

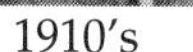
1940's 1910's 1940's

1940's

All of the above **points of force** are being pulled down-plane through impact by rotational forces that cause the club shaft and the left arm to seek an in-line condition through impact. The bent right arm is also seeking its in-line condition through impact. **The exact same results and conditions are present (expanding angles seeking an in-line condition) when we throw a ball or use a hammer.**

Secret: When the golf swing is moving the right shoulder at the same rate of rotation as the hands, all angles are normally retained. They do not expand until the right elbow expands them.

STRAIGHT BACK OR IN AN ARC?

There is some instruction advice states that the clubhead must **move straight** back from the ball, while other instruction says that the clubhead must move in an **arc**. If we take into account the design of the club: a shaft that comes up from the ground on an inclined roof-like angle (like a hockey stick), both points of view have some truth to them.

"The left hand should not roll at any point during the swing."

- Bryon Nelson

A motion that moves back horizontal to the ground moves in two directions, back and in (baseball and tennis). Motion that moves back vertical to the ground, moves in two directions, back and up. (Croquet). **Motion that moves back on an inclined plane (golf and hockey) has three-dimensions: back, up, and in.**

When a golf swing stays on plane, the **clubhead** is moving on an **arc** (back-up-in), as the **shaft** stays **straight,** or flat on its plane. **Efficient swings also have the hands going slightly down at the start of the backswing, (not up), as they react to the left shoulder moving down plane at the start of the backswing.**

On Plane Off Plane

MORE DISTANCE

Gaining insights into longer ball flight starts with knowing what elements of the golf swing that give ball flight "better direction". These elements will also give **more distance**. **Improving distance and direction requires improving the alignment then application of force through impact. Nature's truths simply know no other possibilities**.

Secret: While golf is always played in non-static, ever changing conditions, the game has several constants that do not change during a swing: the design and weight of the club; the design and weight of the ball; ball location at address; the form of a golfer's body parts; and of course all principles of motion and force are the "constants".

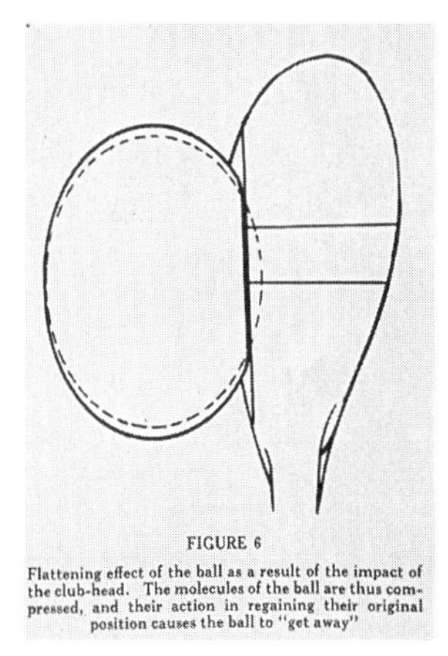

FIGURE 6
Flattening effect of the ball as a result of the impact of the club-head. The molecules of the ball are thus compressed, and their action in regaining their original position causes the ball to "get away"

Impact—1900's

Golfers at every level, who want longer ball flight and some overall progress, may want to pay **less** attention to "how to lists" and become more aware of the design characteristics of the club, the ball, and the principals of **motion** and **force**. **Motion is mentioned first because without effective motion there would be little chance of effective force for longer ball flight.**

Every golfer must develop a swing and game that works best for them. This individuality, however, cannot overlook **Golf's Physical Basics** (club, ball, field of play, time and balance) and the principles of motion and force. **Efficient golf swings always reveal what is true about them, "how to lists" do not**. Of course, improving one's physical strength and flexibility while using equipment that fits an individual's swing can also help distance and direction.

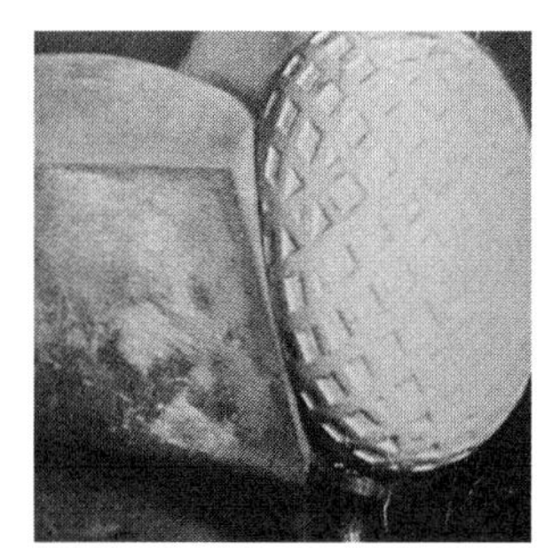

Impact—1910

To improve our insights into achieving greater distance and improved direction, let us discuss the four elements of **generating, accumulating, aligning**, and **applying force** through impact. Golf is a game of **force**. When golfers overlook this fact and also the fact that good golf comes from influencing the direction and application of force (nothing more, nothing less), any progress they may wish to make will be more difficult.

The human machine that swings the club which impacts the ball and creates ball flight has elements that can **generate** force and elements that can **accumulate** additional force when needed. This machine also has elements that can **align** and **apply** force. When playing good golf (golf with predictable outcomes), all these elements of force are in harmony **Golfers who are not happy with their distance and direction have elements of force moving through non-efficient patterns of motion.** (i.e. force lines that are not parallel, or moving at different rates of motion, etc).

Secret: All swings generate some level of force. At the same time a swing may not be efficiently aligning or applying force, or effectively accumulate additional forces when needed. It helps to realize that up to 70% of a swing's force comes from the right shoulder.

Impact—1950's

We are going to say that a golfer's hips and shoulders can **generate** force, even different amounts of force, by changing the size or velocity of their motion patterns. Smaller, slower patterns produce less force than larger, faster patterns. To add more force than is available from hips and shoulders, the swing must find a source capable of **accumulating** additional force as needed. Efficient swings have four sources from which to accumulate additional force.

1. **The right elbow joint**, if or when it folds, is capable of accumulating force that can be spent through impact.
2. **The left wrist joint**, if or when it cocks, is capable of accumulating force that can be spent through impact.
3. **The angle formed** between the shaft and the left arm is capable of accumulating force that can be spent through impact.
4. When the upper left arm **swings into** the upper left chest in the backswing, it is capable of accumulating force that can be spent through impact.

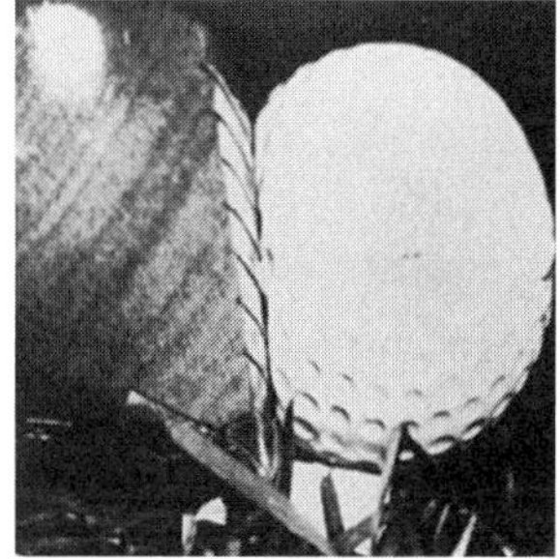

Impact—1970's

After one or more angles are created #1 right elbow, #2 left wrist and #4 left shoulder joints, these three (angles) sources of additional force can be expanded by rotational force to re-seek their in-line alignment. When these three angles are going back in-line, they provide additional force and velocity through impact. Additional force is also available, when the angle formed at address between the shaft and left arm #3, is held through impact. All four **accumulators** (A Homer Kelly term) are capable of adding **more force** through impact and, therefore, **more distance**.

It is useful to note that efficient swings use both **generated** and **accumulated** forces through impact. Less efficient swings use effort when trying to create more force. Efficient swings use **rotational forces** to generate force with the hips and shoulders. **Rotational forces** are also used to create the angles that accumulate potential for additional force. The application and alignment of force through impact is also done with **rotational forces**.

Through impact, the clubface rotates around its own sweetspot.

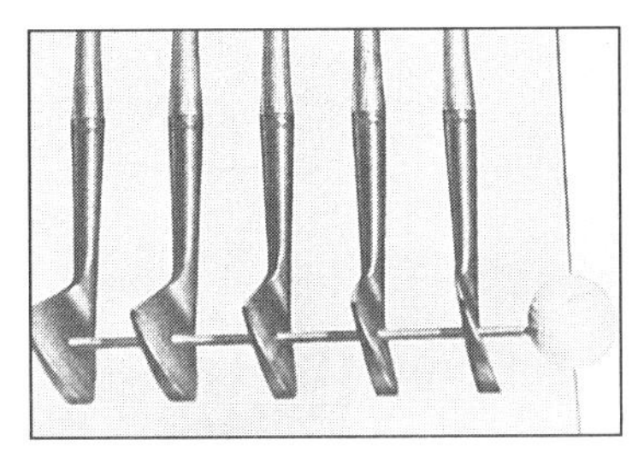

Sweetspot

Aligning and Applying Forces

After force is generated and accumulated it must be **aligned** and **applied** on lines that stay parallel to the lie angle, which the club's shaft occupied at address, before direction and distance can be improved.

Note: In efficient swings much of the swing force comes from the **right shoulder** as it moves down-plane creating a **force line** that is parallel to the lie angle the shaft occupied at address. In efficient swings the **right forearm** also travels through impact on-plane creating a **force line** that is parallel to the lie angle the shaft occupied at address. The **club's shaft** also travels down-plane creating a **force line** that stays parallel to the lie angle it occupied at address. The **player's hands** also travel down-plane creating a **force line** that is parallel to the lie angle the shaft occupied at address. All these **lines of force** give ball flight **more distance** when they travel through impact parallel to the swings plane. I could change my mind in the future, but if I could make only one suggestion about developing on-plane force lines it would be: use **pulling forces to transport the club down-plane under a spine that is angled both over to the ball and away from the target.**

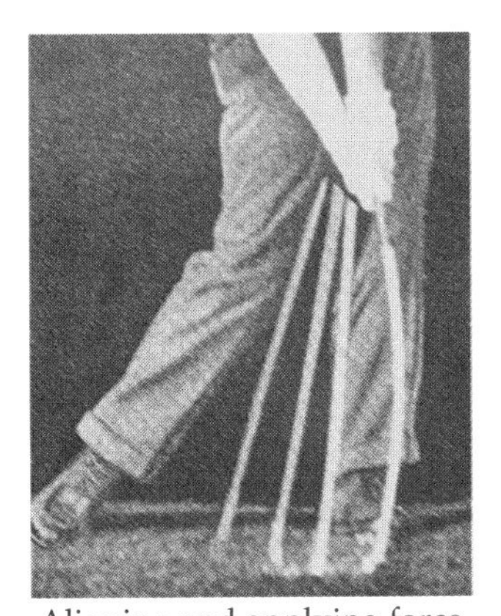

Aligning and applying force

Secret: What do golfers who want a controlled, powerful ball flight, have to learn? In a few words it is: produce effective forces, than use all those forces on lines that stay parallel to the plane of the swing through impact for the shot at hand.

Long-term progress, and the ability to know the causes of a particular ball flight (wanted or unwanted) is founded on **knowing what is producing and influencing the alignment and application of force lines.** Where do I want forces applied, and what do I do to produce those forces? These are questions golfers, who want a controlled, powerful ball flight, must answer and learn. **The concepts many golfers currently use overlook the fact that the alignment and application of force is at the very foundation of good golf.**

1950's Sam Snead #1

Left Arm or Right Arm?

Which arm is more important to the golf swing, the left or the right arm? Where does power come from? Is golf more of a left or right hand game? These are just a few of the many questions golfers have been asking

1960's #1

2000

1960's

1992

for years. I am sure, one hundred years ago in Scotland, golfers were looking for the answers to these same kinds of questions.

For any golfer to reach their potential, they should have some understanding of how both the left and right arms operate during the swing. It would be my suggestion to start by having a general concept that during the swing the left arm is always swinging and the right arm is always driving. Next, move along to a more specific concept that a bent right arm (as in baseball) is helping to support and drive the left arm and club down to impact.

It helps to understand that the swing's power and force are a result of rotational forces that transfer energy from one segment of the total swing system to the next. On their own, the left or right arm, or hand alone could not produce the kind of power for which most golfers are looking for.

The right and left arms work as a team to produce force. First, notice how, during a sound swing, the turn of the body can hold an inert upper left arm against the golfer's upper chest through impact. Then, the left arm is moved out into a swinging motion. This "swinging-out" motion of the left arm and club can be a reaction to body rotation.

When the left arm and the club are put into orbit by body rotation (and in an expanding right arm), it is much like the handle of a whip causing the end of the whip to expand and deliver its power. Keep in mind, the energy of an inner mass (the handle of a whip or the body of a golfer) can be transferred out to the end of the whip or to the arms and club of a golfer. By themselves, the left arm or end of the whip have little power. Their power comes from a transfer of energy outwards.

The other option available to golfers is right arm thrust. During the downswing, the bent right arm can be intentionally straightened to drive the left arm and club down to impact. For example, a golfer could use the triceps muscle of the right arm to straighten the right forearm and thrust the left arm and club down to impact. This procedure can be a very effective application of force for all short game shots, including putting. In my view, it is more useful to have on-plane right forearm acceleration, when putting, than right hand acceleration. Right hand acceleration will often cause the left wrist to bend, whereas on-plane right forearm acceleration normally will not break down a flat left wrist, neither will it break down a bent right wrist.

Arnold Palmer's, right arm goes straight through impact and is one example of rotation and the right arm thrust approach to moving the club. When a bent right arm is moved into impact by the triceps muscle, it is much like throwing a dart. (The forearm in a dart throw is being moved by the triceps muscle).

In the other hand, **Ian Woosnam's** swing is an example of a golfer whose right arm is straightened by body rotation, moving the club down and out to the ball at impact. This style of moving the club is much like throwing a discus into orbit at a track meet by rotating the body, causing the right arm to expand. This approach could be called swinging or body power. On the other hand, when we use the triceps muscle to move the right forearm, it could be called hitting or muscle power. It helps to recognize the difference.

If a golf shaft was made from a rope or a fly rod shaft, the only procedure that could possibly be used is swinging or pulling with body rotation. Hitting is similar to using a hammer, where body rotation is not as important as straightening the forearm.

Secret: As you can see, both arms are equally important. Golfers have a choice, and can develop force from body rotation, or right arm thrust. Keep in mind, the left arm is always swinging, and the right arm is always expanding or driving in both swinging and hitting approaches. The ultimate application of force uses both body rotation and on-plane right arm thrust through impact.

1990's #4

Some reasons swings do not create or sustain force through impact include:

- Believing address and impact have the same alignments.
- Trying to hit the back of the ball
- Trying to have a square clubface at impact
- Overactive knees and feet
- Not separating the "down" from the "unwinding" during downswing
- Over accelerating any of the swing's angle

1990's

Some elements of efficient force at impact include:

- Correct ball location
- Left shoulder joint behind the ball (tee shot)
- Clubhead behind hands
- Flat left wrist
- Bent right wrist and elbow
- Upper left arm on upper left chest
- Bent right arm expanding
- Player's head behind the ball
- Pulling and rotational forces
- Efficient clubface impact location

Note: In my view, some players have over done the concept of keeping the backswing wide. They have overlooked that a **golf swing can only be as wide as a players left or forward arm.**

1950's

More Clubhead Speed Equals More Distance – Maybe Not!

All golfers would like to hit the ball longer. Most believe they would have lower scores if they did.

"If I could only hit irons into par 4's, instead of woods, my scores would come down. If I used my short irons into green's more often, my handicap would be lower." These are familiar statements from players looking for more distance. While more distance may be an obvious step to lower scores, what really can give a player more distance may not be as obvious.

Some examples of how people have tried to increase their length include: an off-season physical training program, new clubs, different balls and of course putting more effort into their swing. While any one of these methods might seem as if they would guarantee extra yards, more often than not they do not.

2000 #2

Secret: So if stronger muscles, new equipment, and more effort do not guarantee more distance, what can? The answer is: proper application of the law of mass times velocity.

NO

NO

While new equipment and more strength cannot be overlooked, they can only help a player who is applying the **necessary elements of distance**, and more effort will not help under any conditions.

A popular belief, **is more clubhead speed will create more distance**. This is not always so! There are many club golfers who create more clubhead speed than some touring professionals, but have a considerably shorter ball flight. More clubhead speed achieved, but less distance, how is this possible, you may ask. It is, and for several reasons.

Often, when a player believes extra yards come from only making the clubhead go faster, it can cause the clubhead to pass the player's hands before impact. This causes a great loss of force. Efficient clubhead velocity is measured by how fast the clubhead goes through impact, not how fast it swings past the player's hands. Keep in mind, **speed by definition, has no direction and golf will always be a game of direction.** When **speed** is the player's main focus, the swing will often lack the precision needed for more distance.

Power and effort are not the same. Efficient power comes from the proper alignment and application of Mass times Velocity. Every swing has some Mass (club) and some Velocity, but to increase distance, Mass or Velocity, or both, must be increased.

YES

Most of us equate Mass with the size and weight of the clubhead, something that is not going to change during the swing. When golfers are looking for more distance, they are left with the assumption they must change the **speed** of the clubhead.

Studies and tests with high speed equipment and computers have come up with surprising results. They have found that clubhead velocity is harder to change than changing the effective mass of the clubhead. Please note: I said effective mass, not just mass.

Perhaps, it will help your understanding of how the proper application of Mass times Velocity leads to more distance to recognize a golf club has no moving parts, nor does a golf ball. The club is just weight and size. During the swing this mass is in motion. For it to be effective mass, it has to be applied efficiently and not just deliver a glancing blow at impact.

NO

The first element of more distance is impacting the ball with a clubface that is behind the player's hands. This allows for a maximum transfer of energy from the clubhead into the ball. (Ideally above the mid-point on the clubface).

Another element that promotes an effective transfer of energy and more distance is ball location. Where the ball is placed at address is very important. If the ball is behind or forward of the ideal location, maximum transfer of energy is not possible. **For tee shots, the left shoulder joint should be behind the ball at impact.**

NO

Next, golfers looking to increase the length of their ball flight, must use a swing that can fully compress the ball on the clubface. To increase the amount the ball is compressed on the clubface, we must increase the amount of force transfers down into the ball at impact. More on-plane force is a result of the proper alignment of angles and application of body turn.

The most common error in golf is a loss of force through impact. This happens when the clubhead is permitted or made to pass the hands before, during or after impact.

Again, a well-struck golf shot reacts much like a spaceship firing on all rockets, with the ball exploding off the clubface out into space. If your goal is more distance, find ways to keep the mass of the clubhead behind your hands and you will have more force on the ball at impact and a longer ball flight.

Thomas Kincaid, 1687, *"Play first with little strength, observing all the rules of poustaur (posture). When ye have acquired one habit of hitting exactly, then increase force by degrees. The knowledge of these degrees will serve for half chops, quarter chops, and for holling the ball".*

YES	**NO**

- Flat left wrist
- Head Back
- Bent right wrist

- Bent left wrist
- Head forward
- Straight right wrist

Secret: **It is useful to see a golfers hips performing like the clutch and transmission of a car. See the hips synchronizing power flow and transferring force. Don't see hips as a big source of force. They only produce 10-15% of an efficient swings force.**

Cary Middlecoff wrote in his book, The Golf Swing, *"If Ben Hogan was wrong about anything, it was his belief that muscles around the hips would automatically recoil or unwind to start the downswing. (page 70-71 of Five Lessons). Anatomists have told me that muscles do not have the elastic quality that Hogan believed they did. Muscles can be stretched, but they stay stretched, unless there is a positive action taken to make them contract."*

PHYSICAL BASIC #3—SUMMARY

- Golf balls are compressible
- A constant rate of rotation keeps the mass of the club behind your hands
- No one really flips their hands, angles normally expand early and cause the hands to flip when rotation stops
- Use pulling forces for stability and the alignment and application of on-plane force
- Separate the down from the unwinding during the downswing
- Efficient swings move the club away and back to the ball on an arc that is on-plane
- Goal: Learn to keep the club head mass behind the hands through impact

Physical Basic #4

Timing and Balancing
(Tempo – Rhythm)

For over five hundred years,
the core elements of effective swing mechanics
have been timing and balancing
(Not some swing secret).

"In every sport, success seems to be in proportion to the players sense of balance and force – whether it is innate or acquired. Off balance force is erratic.

We must master balance."

- Homer Kelly

PHYSICAL BASICS #4 TIME AND BALANCING

(Also discussed in lesson five)

Golfers must recognize, experience, and learn balance and rhythm when they make any attempts to improve swing mechanics.

The core elements of effective mechanics are timing and balancing (i.e. tempo and rhythm).

Efficient golf swings have a beat of time to them. They also accommodate balancing in a three dimensional space (up to down, side to side, front to back). **Efficient swings take more or less the same amount of time from startup to back down to impact for every club in the bag**. World-class players have blended their swing mechanics into a flowing motion with a time frame that non-expert players rarely produce.

Secret: Music notes have to have correct sound, but they also have to be played in the correct time frame without losing the correct beat. Golf swings can also be in, or out of time. When golfers lose their beat, they hit poor shots.

Studies about the nature of learning have always shown that the key challenge for long-term learning is to develop ways of creating the most relevant types of experience from which to learn. Recent research has shown that **the element of time seems to be very relevant to learning**.

In 1991 Peterlin did studies in Michigan indicating that when a person's **Beat** or **Time** competence is enhanced, inner control improves. **People with poor perception of time are more clumsy then people with a good perception of time.**

Secret: Basic timing, one's ability to feel and express a steady beat of time, involves both rhythmic **perception** and rhythmic **performance**. In 1987 Welkart concurred that rhythmic skill involves one's perception of time, and then synchronizing one's body motion with that perception. As one's ability to match movement to a steady beat improved, motor performance also improved.

"Timing is the secret! But timing is inside the player, timing is instinct. What we see outside is the result of how the players time instinct is functioning. You must develop timing."

- Steward Maiden 1922

Most unnecessary and unorthodox movements that can be observed in golf swings are often nothing more than compensations for a swing that has moved off its beat, are out of center and balance. **Many swing movements that golfers would like to improve or eliminate, can only be helped by improved balance.** These unwanted actions are being introduced by the central nervous system as an automatic reaction to the body and swing being out of balance. Most times, I have observed that the only way to stop unwanted actions is to improve balancing the bodies thirteen major joints throughout the swing.

STEADY YES! SLOW NO!

Efficient golf swings produce, use, and sustain on-plane force (i.e. pressure). Pressure is a constant force and any segment of a swing that is out of time with other segments can cause a loss of pressure. Swing steady, not slow. Efficient swings have the proper blend of body turn and arm swing, but they also have an element that is not referred to very often: an **effective rate of rotation (RPM's).**

Some understanding of rate of rotation is necessary for golfers to reach their potential.

- One reason efficient swings look so **rhythmical** and **smooth** is the: rate of rotation.
- One reason efficient swings are so **powerful** is: rate of rotation.
- One reason efficient swings are so **consistent** is: rate of rotation.
- One reason efficient swings stay in **balance** is: rate of rotation.

Secret: Efficient golf instruction often looks for one piece of information that could help golfers accomplish several elements of a effective swing. "Rate of rotation" is an example of one element that helps several others.

Often players try to improve their swing by swinging slower than they normally do. This approach, more often than not, does more harm than good. In fact, players are now left with a slow unworkable swing, instead of a fast unworkable swing. On the other hand, when a player has a swing that has a steady rate of rotation, many other elements of his swing improve. During a swing, the hands and right shoulder are both moving. During **ineffective swings**, these two elements are often moving at different rates of rotation. **In efficient swings the hands and right shoulder move at the same rate of rotation.**

To help understand rate of rotation, picture a disk (Figure 1) with dots painted in a line that runs out from the center of the disk to its outer edge.

When the disk turns, the outer dot moves faster than the inner dots. The dot closest to the center moves at the slowest speed. The inside dot has a smallest circumference to travel and therefore moves at slower speed than does the outside dot which is traveling on the largest circumference and at the faster speed.

What should be noticed is that while all of the dots move at different speeds, they are all moving at the same rate of rotation (different speeds, but same steady rate of rotation), as they stay in line.

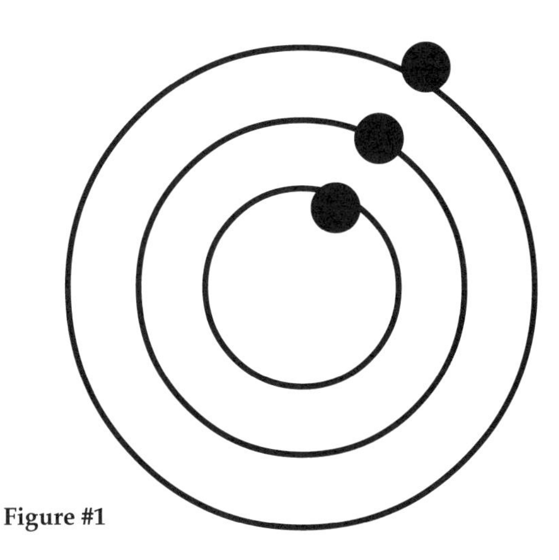

Figure #1

Figure 1: To help understand rate of rotation, picture a disk or record with dots painted in a line that runs out from the center of the disk to its outer edge.

The same results can be seen at the ice show. The inside girl on a skate line is moving at a slower rate of rotation than the outside girl on the line. A law of motion states: "*when the inside segment of a system moves slow and in a small circle, the outside segment is moved at a greater distance at a greater speed*". Just watch any door close and notice the door handle moves fast and far, while the hinge moves slow and a short distance.

The same principle applies to a effective golf swing. The hands move in a bigger circle than elbows, and the elbows move in a bigger circle than the hips, these movements give the system the natural result of the hands moving faster than the elbows, and the elbows moving faster than the hips. But along with the **hands and right shoulder all move at a steady rate of rotation.**

1990's

Studies show that during efficient golf swings, when the clubhead is moving 80 to 90 mph, the hands go 15 mph and the hips 3-5 mph. (Tiger Woods shoulders are moving four times faster than his hips.) At the same time, there is a steady rate of rotation with no over acceleration or jumping motions.

The **ineffective** swing can have the arms racing past the body (causing pulls or hooks) or the body moving faster than the arms (causing a push or slice), or the hands passing the arms (causing topped and skied shots.) **Efficient swings do not have any sudden stops or starts. They move at a steady rate of rotation.** At times, a player will try to speed up their hands through impact, feeling this would create more power or clubhead speed, only receiving poor results from a misapplication of force.

Secret: Once you have the feeling your hands and right shoulder are moving at the same rate of rotation, you can increase or decrease the turning rate of the whole system to hit the ball different distances.

1990's #1

When any swing segment (arms, hips, or legs) has any sudden changes in its rate of motion, the swing will not produce the kind of effective force a constant rate of rotation does.

Efficient swings produce, use and sustain on-plane pressure (force). Pressure is a constant force and any segment of a swing that is out of rate with other segments can cause a loss of force. Swing steadily, not slowly for efficient application of force.

When looking at professional tournament players, you will see different turning rates, some are slower than others, but they all have a rate of rotation with no sudden stops or starts. Craig Stadler, Lanny Wadkins, Tom Watson and Arnold Palmer swings all look faster than do the swings of Steve Elkington, Tom Purtzer, Steve Pate or Sam Snead swings. While their swings may not have the same turning speed in common, there is no one segment outracing any other segments in these swings that have an efficient application of force.

Note: Music education uses the terms "tempo" and "rhythm" as does golf instruction. In music the term "tempo" is used in reference to slow, fast, or medium time. Golfers should also refer to the pace of their swing speed as its "tempo". The term "rhythm" in music refers to the synchronization of all the time elements in a piece of music (these elements are either in or out of rhythm). Golfers should also have all the elements of their swing – shoulders, arms, hips, clubs etc. in "rhythm" or in sync.

1980's

Balancing

When deciding how to stand to the ball (with few exceptions) consider starting with the following general suggestions: (also refer to Lesson Five).

Ankle Joints: Ankle joints are placed outside the hip joints. This alignment will help keep the player's body inside the width of the feet from start up to the finish of the swing. When the ankle joints are placed outside the hip joints, rotation of body weight during swing motion is more stable and centered, then when body weight moves out and beyond the ankle joints in either the back or downswing.

Knee Joints: Bend the knee joints slightly at address, so they are aligned over the balls of the feet. This alignment not only meets the needs of a balanced state, it also prevents the hip joints or pelvic girdle area from moving to far back past the players ankle joints at address. The more the knees bend out at address the more the hip joints will have to move back trying to accommodate **a balanced state**.

1900

WARNING: When the knee joints are flexed inward or towards each other at address, this alignment can cause the left knee joint to move back past the left hip joint in the backswing. This posture causes the players upper spine to lean left into a reverse pivot to balance the body.

When the knee joints are correctly aligned over the balls of the feet, the player may feel somewhat bowlegged, with the upper legs (thigh) angled away from each other to accommodate **a balanced state**. (Some swing styles may require the right knee to be bent slightly to the target at address).

1950's

Hip Joints and Pelvic Girdle: To accommodate a balanced state the pelvic girdle can be placed more **under** the trunk of the upper body than out past the heels of the feet. The hip joints, themselves, should be aligned over the ankle joints, with the top of the pelvic girdle as **level** as possible.

Spine: The human spine is organized into four segments. At the bottom of the spine is the **Sacral** segment. Its nerves control the toes, groin, and some parts of the legs. The **Lumbar** segment is next, and it controls the hips and the legs. The **Thoracic** segment is next, and it controls the torso and some parts of the arms. The **Cervical** segment is the top of the spine and it controls the neck, arms, and hands.

To accommodate **a balanced state** the spine is angled over to the ball with all four segments at different angles. The bottom segment (**sacral**) is somewhat vertical to the ground. The next segment (**lumbar**), is over 5-10 degrees from the top of the sacral. The next segment (**thoracic**), is over 15-20 degrees from the top of the lumbar. The top of the spine, (**cervical)** or neck, is over 15-20 degrees form the top of the lumbar.

1940's

Note: The three different angles of spine.

Note: Picture the face of a clock, when the hand points to #1, or 5 minutes past the hour, it's angled over 30 degrees from vertical or 12 o'clock.

Important: The golfer's spine is also angled back from the target with the upper spine more away from the target than the lower spine. **Effective swings return to impact with the spine angled both over to the ground and away from the target**. (The spine is often thought of as only over to the ball at one angle, causing balancing problems and off-plane swing motion.)

Note: The neck of a player, who is accommodating a balanced state will be more over and out, **than up**. The neck (cervical segment) is angled out, more or less parallel to the ground with the player's face and eyes over to the ground. The chin is away and off the chest, but head is not up. I've rarely seen a world-class golfer with their head up at address. Their face is also down at impact.

When the eyes and ears are as level as possible to the ground at address (and hopefully, throughout the swing), both eyeballs can stay centered in their sockets with both eyes fully focused on the ball. When players stand to the

1950's

1890's

1990's #5

1930's

ball with their head up, their eyes must now rotate down to the bottom of their sockets, looking at the ball from a place which that no longer provides full focus. The brain will now have to make unnecessary compensations as it looks for **a balanced state.**

Shoulder Joints: To accommodate **a balanced state**, shoulder joints should be over the toes of the feet.

Wrist Joints: The needs of **a balanced state** will be met when the wrist joints, fall under the player's chin with short to mid-irons, and move out under the nose for long irons and under the eyes for woods.

Elbow Joints: When the arms hang down form the shoulder joints they move slightly away from the body as a response to the spine bending over to the ground and ball. But elbow joints and upper arms are still close to the body to accommodate **a balanced state.**

When it comes to where the elbow joints point at address, there seems to be several alignments that work. Some players have their elbows pointing down to the ground. Some have them pointing away form each other. During the swing motion, the elbows of world-class players are pointing down to the ground throughout most of the swing. (Some effective swing styles have the upper arms and elbows placed more to the sides of the chest than on top at address.)

Suggestion: If you tend to over use your arms, and under use your body when you swing, consider having your elbows pointing down at address, arms to the side of the chest. If you tend to over use your body and under use your arms, consider having your elbows somewhat together at address, arms on top of the chest.

Weight Distribution: Where body weight is placed (more to the left side or right side), is determined by what ball flight the player wants to create. Weight back at address can help the ball go higher. Weight forward at address can help the ball go lower. For wood shots weight can be more back, for iron shots weight can start more forward.

Secret: **At address do not feel flat-footed. When the foot is flat on the ground studies show the brain does not receive enough information about the balance state. Feel a high arch, toes slightly up, and some weight to the heels.**

Players should balance their body weight between the ball and heel of the foot, with the feeling of a high arch. I've been told professional hockey players use skates that are a size to small, so their feet are given a high arch, with the heel and ball of the foot providing balance information to the brain. Watch small children and ballet dancers. Most of their walking is done with a high arch, on their balls and heels, for maximum balance information going to the brain.

Feet: Golfers, who feel they don't turn their bodies freely when they swing, may want to consider having their feet turned out, or toe line away from each other, with the heels placed parallel or square to the line of flight on which you want the ball to start on.

Head and Ears: The length of the club, and the lie of the ball (uphill, side hill, etc.) dictate how far **behind** the ball a golfer's head is aligned at address, with the ears as level as possible to accommodate a balanced state. (Exception: Some short shots around the green, have the head placed forward of the ball.) One of the balance centers of the human body is located within the inner ear. During swing motion, when the ears stay as level as possible, the brain makes fewer adjustments for balance then when they are not level.

1915 — Eyes on-plane

1950's — Three Angles of Spine

1990's #5

Time - Balance - Motion

1940's

Everyone comes into the world followed, not led by their accomplishments. There are times, when these accomplishments are founded on the timing and balance of body motion. i.e. as in the game of golf. What is often overlooked by golfers who want to improve is, before **good golfers** made any key accomplishments in the game they first were people with efficient timing and balancing of body motion for the shot at hand.

People, who can influence the timing and balancing of body motion have a better opportunity to see improvement with their golf skills, then people who cannot. Good golfers, some by intuition, can tune their body and minds into effective motion, while some others have had to learn to develop timing and balancing skills.

Secret: **Efficient body motion is fundamental to good golf, and one way or another this must be addressed by golfers who want to see progress.**

Every golfer's **present** swing and game are based on the sum total of feeling experiences which they have taken away from their **past** golf experiences. All feeling experiences, old and new, positive and negative, mental and physical, are stored away in our subconscious memory, some say forever. As a good golfer approaches the shot at hand, they draw on and use these past experiences.

For a moment, let's look at our bodies as being dumb. i.e. world-class dancer Mikhail Barisnikov's feet are dumb. It's what he developed in his mind for the feel of timing and balance that allowed his feet and body to move with grace and ease. He's drawing on past feeling experiences. People can naturally, and we could say automatically, recall phone numbers. Golfers should develop the ability to recall and return to the feel of efficient body motion for the shot at hand.

1990's #5

T. Woods Early 1990's

B. Hogan 1950's

S. Snead 1940's #6

G. Middlecoff 1950's #6

Golfers who are not happy with their progress may want to consider staying aware of what the body is saying when it moves. **Do not analyze the golf swing – just stay aware of balance and timing is the message.** No motion is a wasted motion, every small or big movement is an opportunity to gather information about timing and balancing.

Secret: When we become partners with our feeling experiences, progress that is not available from "how to lists" is possible.

Free and balanced traits of body motion feel very different from body motion that is ill-timed and out of balance. Motion that has efficient timing and balancing has a loosening effect on both our body and mind. For example; the weight of a body segment (shoulder, etc.) has the ability to transfer its motion on to other segments in the system, or move the segment itself. Motion that takes place under this transfer approach unites the entire system in quiet, yet dynamic movements. Movements that are flowing and confident, not cautious and rigid, are the goal.

World-class golfers or performers from the arts, have a flow and rhythm of motion that is more than free. It is peaceful in its approach. World-class golfers have found their own ways of letting motion happen without effort. Effort of course creates tension which often comes from trying to follow someone else's "how to list".

Road blocks to free, well-timed motion are normally more mental that physical. Body motion is directed from one's mind or from what is in our subconscious from past motions we have performed. The integration of the body and mind is generally founded on feeling experiences. Every golf movement is an opportunity to ask, "Was that light?" "Was I balancing?" etc. Once the habit of staying aware is placed in a golfers mind, their own feeling experiences can now replace **less valuable tools**_for progress.

Secret: Changing ones body motion, especially when past unworkable feelings still exist in our subconscious, requires self-discovery and awareness skills, not someone else's "how to list". **Realizing what to do,** is always more useful than following "how to advice".

Muscle Guarding

Humans are born (hard wired) with reflexes and what is referred to as **"righting reactions".**

"Righting Reactions" are how babies have the ability to seek their balanced state after becoming unstable. As we grow in size and age, proprioception becomes a learned corrective response to where we are in space. All three **reflexes, righting reactions, and proprioception,** are members of a natural system that protects the body from injury.

Muscle guarding is also part of this natural system of protection that humans are born with (hard wired) to guard against stress, strain, or injury of muscle tissue. Muscles will **tighten** to guard against injury when the skeletons system of bones moves out of workable and safe alignments.

Secret: When a golfers body experiences a swing flaw that causes the body to lose its natural alignments, muscle guarding causes muscles to **tighten automatically** (for protection), causing poor results.

Golfers should become aware of how their body looks and feels when its thirteen major joints (ankles, knees, hips, shoulders, elbows, wrists, and neck) are aligned correctly during the swing, and when they are not. Again, when a golfers body moves away from workable alignments, the bodies natural protection system (muscle guarding) causes muscles to automatically tighten.

Balanced Finish

Tiger Woods #7

David Duval #5

Tom Watson #5

John Daly #2

PHYSICAL BASIC #4—SUMMARY

- Steady YES, Slow NO! A steady rate of rotation with no jumping or effort through impact

- Level eyes and ears at address and impact, helps golfers gain acceptable balancing of their bodies joints in a three-dimensional space during their swing motion.

- Golfers miss more shots because of unworkable timing, than non-workable swing patterns.

- Goal: A swing that balancing in a three-dimensional space, that has acceptable tempo and rhythm.

Physical Basic #5

The Field of Play and Ever-Changing Playing Conditions

When ball is above feet
Ball goes left, aim right

When ball is below feet
Ball goes right, aim left

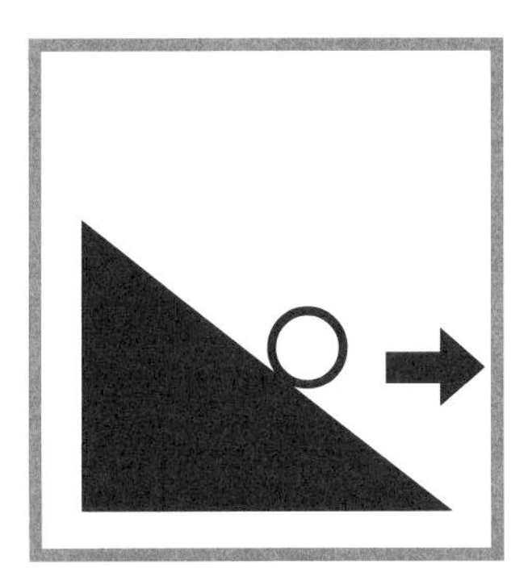

Playing downhill
Ball goes lower and further

Playing Uphill
Ball goes higher and shorter

For over five hundred years,
everything a player should do has been founded on
the playing conditions the player is presented with
(I.e. Golf's Environments)

1857 H.B. Farnie,
"By all means, let golfers play a system
that is adapting their swing to the lay of the land."

PHYSICAL BASICS #5 -
THE FIELD OF PLAY, AND EVER CHANGING PLAYING CONDITIONS.

Everything works back from the playing conditions the player is presented with.

The design angles of the golf club can be a blueprint for the swing's shape and as well as its source of power. The field of play and the ever changing playing conditions (i.e. golf's environments) also provide additional information. This is valuable information which can be used as a guide for a player's posture, alignment, weight distribution, and the swing for the shot at hand.

Secret: **Without taking into consideration the field of play and the current playing conditions, the results of the swing shape and its source of power, will be less than optimal.**

Most of the swings that people make either on the course; practice range, or putting green, are from ground that is more or less level. A high percentage of swings golfers make are under level ground conditions. They stand to the ball without making any adjustments to their posture (for balance), to their swing plane (for impact alignments) or to their alignment (for ball flight direction). But as we know, many swings are not made from level ground. When they are not, players are required **by the lay of the land** to make some adjustments to their posture, swing plane, and alignments (using reverse engineering principles).

The field of play has been one of **Golf's Physical Basics** from day one. The lay of the land has always had a direct influence on the player's posture, swing plane and alignment. Keep in mind, specific playing conditions require specific adjustments that are more or less non-negotiable **Physical Basics**. Former PGA Teacher of the Year, Chuck Cook, points out that someone learning to play golf in West Texas (where it is flat and windy), will develop a style of playing and swinging quite different than someone learning to play in conditions that are hilly and less windy. Hogan, Trevino, Nelson all grew up in Texas. Nicklaus and Watson in the mid-west and Snead in the South. All of their swing styles reflect where they learned to play golf.

Here are some general guidelines for playing shots from ground that is not level.

1) Players should make adjustments to their stance that neutralizes the slope of the hill. Creating as close as possible the feeling of a level lie.
2) Off slopes and hills (ball above or below feet), the flight of the ball will spin or fly away from the high side, in the direction of the low side of the slope. i.e. balls **above** the feet go left, to the low side of slope. Balls **below** the feet fly right, away from the high side of the slope.
3) From uphill and downhill lies, balls tend to follow the slope in the direction they are being played. Ball flight is higher and shorter from uphill lies. Ball flight is lower and longer from down hill lies.

BALL ABOVE FEET

The ball is now closer to the players chest, than from level ground. The swing now goes more around the body, and on a flatter swing plane. The ball is played more in the center of the stance. Use a wider stance with the body, weight equal heel to toes. Ball flight may be lower (hooking or pulled). The more loft the club has, the more the ball goes left. The steeper the slope, the more the ball goes left. Swing low to low with the slope of the hill. You may want to consider having a slightly open stance and open clubface at address, and holding the club a little shorter.

BALL BELOW FEET

The ball is now further away from the players chest, then from level ground. Accordingly, the player now stands closer to the ball. The ball in the center of your stance, use a wider stance, and body weight equal heel to toes. Ball flight may be higher (slicing or pushed). The steeper the slope, the more the ball goes right, the less loft on the club used, the more the ball goes right. Swing with the slope of the hill. More up than around. You may want to consider having a slightly closed stance and closed clubface at address, with more knee flex and spine tilt.

UP HILL

Adjust shoulders, hips, and knees (without changing balancing), parallel to the slope of the hill. Keep body weight with slope. Use a wider stance with the ball a little forward. Considering using a less lofted club. Aim a little left and swing flat footed with the slope of the hill.

Note: Balancing is always the first consideration for any shot in golf. When the swing is being made from slopes and hills, balancing becomes ever more important, (if that is possible). When playing down hill, the bottom of the swing will be more back by the right foot. Therefore the ball location at address should be more to the right foot. From an uphill lie it is more to the left foot.

DOWN HILL

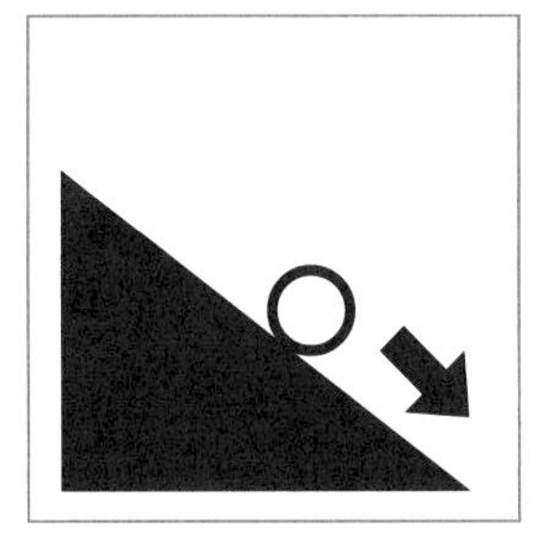

Adjust shoulders, hips and, knees (without affecting balancing), parallel to the slope of the hill. Keep body weight with the slope, use a wide stance, place the ball back in stance. Consider using a more lofted club. Swing flat-footed, aim a little right, and finish low with the slope of the hill.

Secret: **Hills and Slopes: The ever-changing playing conditions of the field of play, (from both grass and sand) are what dictate the players stance, swing plane, and alignment, not some tip form a well meaning friend.**

SAND SHOTS

A sand shot is just that, the sand, not the ball is impacted. The sand moves the ball. For sand shots, the club must go through impact lower than the ball, displacing the sand. The ball rides the sand out of the bunker. (Long fairway sand shots are the exception, the ball is hit before sand).

The bottom of a good sand iron is more V-shaped than flat or U-shaped like the bottom of other clubs. In an effective sand shot swing, the V or bounce on the bottom of the clubhead enters the sand. It acts somewhat like a plow and prevents the club from going down into the sand more than it should for workable results.

Improving sand shots is really learning to influence the size and shape of divots in the sand.

Note: Placing your hands behind the ball at address activates the back V or bounce of the club (plow) to hit the sand first. Use this alignment, when you have a good lie in the sand. The sand that is impacted is driven down by the V. Impact causes the sand which is forward of the spot the clubhead hits and under the ball, to go up and out of the bunker.

Sand Shots

General Information

- Learn to control the size of divots, and where the club enters the sand.
- For high shots, weight on back leg. Flex knees, and you may want to let club pass left wrist joint.
- Hit sand shots three times harder than putts.
- Swing size, club's weights, and its momentum influence downswing, not effort.
- Hold club in fingers, use little to no palm
- Feel like you hit sand down, then to the target

When your hands are over the ball at address, the front or leading edge (not the back V or bounce) of the club is activated to hit the sand first. Use this alignment when you have a bad lie, (buried in the sand, or wet compact sand). When the hands are over or forward of the ball at address, the club will go deeper into the sand with little or no plow effect. From bad, buried, wet, or compact lie in sand, at address, have hands and weight forward and have a short follow through. Take into consideration that the ball will now roll more than normal.

In general, for most sand shots the ball is played somewhat forward, off the left foot, with body weight forward. The shoulders and arms can swing the club up. Body turn and arms swing the club down. Also, feel as if the clubface is open always looking up to the sky through and after impact. Bad lies are played more in the middle of stance. **Keeping knees flexed after impact for all green-side sand shots seems to help.**

Players have two approaches, or a combination of both, they can use to control how far the ball will go from the sand:

1) The amount of sand the swing will take, or
2) How much the clubface is open at address and through impact.

For **short** shots either

1. open the clubface a lot, and have the ball placed inside left heel or
2. play the ball forward of the left foot and plow **lots** of sand down with a square clubface.

For both, use an open stance and swing on body line.

For **medium** shots either

1) open the clubface a little less and have the ball placed more in the middle of your stance, or
2) play ball off the left heel taking **less** sand, with a square clubface.

For both use an open stance and swing on body line.

For **long** shots either

1) use a square clubface and have the ball inside left heel, using a longer swing or
2) play ball back in middle of stance, taking little sand, with a square clubface,

For both, use a square stance and swing on body line.

Uphill sand shots normally go shorter. **Downhill** sand shots normally go longer. Adjust your shoulders and hips parallel to the slope of the sand, and swing along the up or down hill slope. **Downhill** shots from sand require player's to open the clubface more. **Uphill** shots require a more closed clubface.

From **compact**, **hard**, or **wet** sand the ball will fly longer, so the clubface should be opened more than from normal sand. Hands and weight are placed forward. From **soft sand**, the ball goes shorter, so use closed clubface, with the ball placed forward. For **long** sand shots from normal sand conditions close to the green, use a pitching wedge and open clubface.

For most sand shots around the green that are going to be hit with an open clubface, turn your right hand more to the left or on top of the shaft. This grip alignment will help keep the clubface open. Firmer, crisper, faster impact tends to stop the ball quickly. Freer, smother, slower impact tends to let the ball roll more.

From fairway bunkers, try to top the ball. Play the ball a little forward in your stance, dig your feet into sand and, grip down on the club shaft, feel a flat swing plane, taking little or no sand while trying to top the ball.

PUTTING

On most greens players are often putting over and through undulations. Putts can be up or down hill. Others can be of the side hill variety, where one side of the green is higher than the other. Ball flight, even when putting, has two elements, its **direction** and **distance**. When putting, keep in mind that **distance** control is more important because it influences **direction** control.

The speed of the green influences how fast the ball will roll. How fast the ball rolls influences the line (or direction) the player must roll the ball on. After players develop a feel for the speed of the green, they can make decisions about what line to the hole on which they want to roll their putt. Faster rolling balls break less than slower rolling balls. One must keep this in mind.

1960 PGA Champion Lionel Herbert told me he believed that because Jack Nicklaus played on faster greens growing up than most professionals, this gave him an advantage in majors.

My suggestions for putting always include some ideas I once heard Phil Rogers talk about during a golf school I had the pleasure of doing with him. Phil said he believes, *"great putters never try to make putts per se or try to hit putts straight. Great putters are tuned into the speed of the green and try to roll (not hit) the ball at the proper speed for the line they want to roll the ball on"*. Rogers said he believes that, *"great putters are letting the shape of the green and gravity roll the ball into the hole"*.

Secret: **Great putters pick the speed before the line. Only after you know the speed of a putt can you pick the line. When you have the ball rolling at the correct speed you will make a lot of putts.**

"You work all your life to perfect a repeating swing, then on the green you have to try to do something totally different. There should be no cups, just flagsticks, and the man who hit the most fairways and greens, and got closest to the flag would be the winner."

- Ben Hogan

The leading putter on the men's PGA Tour averaged 27.1 putts per round in 1998, with the highest putts per round averaging 30.5. The leading putter on the LPGA averaged 28.7 putts per round in 1998. A good goal for non-professional players would be to average 32 putts per round.

I know some very good putters, who play different kinds of shots on the green. For putts that roll left to right they play the ball more forward in their stance. For putts that roll right to left, they play the balls back in their stance. When a putt is going to roll very fast, players sometimes address the ball more on the toe of the putter and stroke it with the toe. When a putt is going to roll slowly, they firm up their grip. Most good putters I have seen, never let the clubhead pass their hands before impact. At address and throughout their putting stroke, good putters also have their, neck, upper back and face over and parallel to the ground.

"To be a champion, you have to find a way to get the ball in the cup on the last day."

- Tom Watson

I've heard several great putters say, *"they were not disappointed when they missed a putt, they were only disappointed when they miss-hit a putt"*. Greens are not perfect. After the ball is rolling, it could pass over a surface that has some irregularities which are hidden to the eye of the player. Players can only do their best to roll the ball at the correct speed and let gravity take over.

Putting
1890's to 2000

1950's 1890's 1900 1960's

1900 2000 1910 1960's

2000 2000 1960's 2000

Note: Face down, long neck, flat upper back, eyes and ears level.

Note: There are some good putters, who like to feel that they are trying not roll the ball past the hole, some do not. Noted short game instructor and friend, Dave Pelz, often asks golfers to roll the ball at a speed that would cause it to pass the hole if it does not go in, this is good advice. While it is true, and *"never up, never in"*, is good advice, our goal is to always have the ball rolling at a speed that would let it fall in from any angle (front, back, or either side). Learning to roll the ball at different speeds is very important to making progress and more putts. For what it is worth, **roll the ball into the hole (don't hit) would be my suggestion.**

"In putting let the balls momentum give way to gravity on breaking putts. If the ball speed overcomes gravity, all is lost. Putt to where the ball stops traveling under its own power, and then let gravity finish the task.

- 1933 Jerry Travis

At address, knowing where the clubface is pointing may be putting's number one fundamental. It seems to me that good putters hold the club more firmly than do bad putters. Good putters have less moving parts than bad putters. Most good putters have their right forearm and right shoulder on-plane through impact. Most good putters move the club at a steady pace throughout the swing. Good putting is very individual, and requires a personal feel for the speed of the green.

Pitching (High)

Ben Hogan 1950's

Chipping (Low)

Seve Ballesteros 1980's

"Around the green, play the club that keeps the ball nearest to the ground. Putt rather than chip, and chip rather than pitch. It is easier to roll the ball up to the hole, then flight the ball up and stop it by the hole.

– Billy Casper 1971

My preference would be to say *"I have a low shot (not chip shot) or I have a high shot (not pitch shot) into the green"*. When shots around the green are referred to as low and high shots, it is my belief they are easier to learn and repeat.

Around the green see golf as a ground game. The only reason you go in the air is because the ball will not roll far enough on the ground with control or the ball must go over some obstacle it will not roll through. (You always have more influence over the ball when it is on the ground, then when it is airborne.)

"The American Haskel ball has replaced the Gutta Percha, and I now suggest using the run-up shot over the lofted club stroke around the green for more control."

– 1903 H. Hilton

For low and high shots around the green, feel that all backswings are the same speed. When the downswing is a total reaction to the back swing, this keeps the tempo as constant as possible. As you train your tempo and make different size swings (not different speeds) and become aware of how the ball reacts. One suggestion I have is to try and let your downswing be a little longer than your back swing. This approach should avoid the tendency some golfers have to deceleration at impact.

Some players use one club and different swings. Other players use one swing with different clubs. Normally the club with which you decide to hit the shot with is influenced by both how far away, and how far up the green the hole is. More lofted clubs normally don't roll the ball as far as less lofted clubs after the ball hits the green.

*Lower and shorter air time (rolling shots) around the green are more controllable.

Secret: **It may help to see these swings as a steady putting swing with a lofted club. When training your chip (low) and pitch (high) shots, do your best to feel like you have a swing speed that is steady, like a putting swing.**

If you always use **one club** (i.e. pitching wedge) around the green, learn to change ball locations (forward, middle, back) and experiment with different weight distribution (50/50, 60/40,40/60). If you decide to use **different clubs**, before you swing, see the ball flying low more than high, and find the club with which you can best create the height you want and control the distance with. Also experiment with placing the shaft at different angles to the ground. I think you will find the more vertical the shaft is, the straighter the ball rolls. But always have the clubhead behind your hands at address (physical basic #1). Learn to influence the ball with the shaft, clubhead, and clubface. **Try to visualize or see the result you want before you pick the club.**

When using **different clubs** around the green (different lofts for different shots), consider always playing the ball in the middle of your stance, body weight 50/50 front to back feet. Experiment with different size back swings for different length shots, but always with a bigger downswing than the back swing. To add some softness to your shots into the green , let your hips turn with your shoulders in both your back and downswing.

Summary of Golf's Physical Basics

A short summary of Golf's Physical Basics shows efficient swings are based on these five basics.

Physical Basics 1 and 2 (the design of the club, and address alignment)

The location the player stands at address, and the path and shape of their on plane swing are both done to accommodate the shaft angles of a golf club. i.e. the player stands inside the ball and target line and swings their club, hands, arms, and shoulders through impact parallel to the inclined angle the shaft occupied at address (on plane).

Physical Basics 1 and 3 (the design of the club, and compressing the ball)

Efficient swings have the clubhead and clubface behind the player's hands through impact. The shaft is leaning in the direction of the target, leaning in the direction it is being pulled. This alignment, clubface behind the handle through impact, is the angle on which the shaft of all clubs are designed on. When the handle is forward of the clubhead through impact, the ball is compressed onto the clubface and then rebounds into flight.

Physical Basics 4 and 5 (Tempo – Rhythm, and the Field of Play)

Efficient swings meet the requirements of balancing and swing timing. The player must also take into consideration the field of play and the ever changing playing conditions before swinging the club.

Common Alignments
1920's to 2000

COMMON PUTTING ALIGNMENTS—2000

Face Down, Long Neck, Flat Upper Back, Right Forearm On-Plane

Classic and Timeless Hints

1857 to 2000

Classic and Timeless Hints

Like a classic blue blazer, some golf hints are timeless in their value. While the game has been played in some form for several hundred years, golf's first instruction book, The Golfer's Manual was not available to golfers until 1857. We could say formal golf instruction started when this manual was published, and I quote, *"Under the special patronage of the Royal and Ancient Golf Club of St. Andrews Scotland."*

As the game now moves forward into the new century I looked back over the thousands of golf hints published since 1857 and listed some useful ones from the past.

Every golfer will have their favorite, however the timeless value of these classic hints is easily recognized, especially when we consider the game has always had **a golfer** swinging **a stick**, to flight **a ball**, on **a field of play**; hopefully using effective **balance** and **swing timing**. As I have said, these physical basics have been the foundation of golf since day one, making hints from the past as useful today as they were when golfers first read them years ago.

1857-1900

1857 H.B. Farnie
The Golfers Manual

At first – practice the swing without the ball – swing at a particular spot on the turf. The sharp chirrupe of the grass will at once tell the accuracy of the stroke.

By all means let golfers play a system that is adapting their swing to the lay of the ground. **(Physical Basic #5).**

Nothing is more fatal to steady play than forcing additional strength. Pressing throws the golfer off his equilibrium, with little of any increase in distance. **(Physical Basic #4)**

There must be a difference in the driving club of golfers – agile and non-agile - the shaft must be made to ensure elevation in consequence of an imperfect swing.

1863 W.R. Chambers
A Few Rambling Remarks of Golf

The sand iron comes into play when the ball lies in a bunker – but it's also used to loft balls over hazards, for balls in loose whins, in roads, in deer grass, and a serviceable tool within fifty yards of the hole.

After shots that have more harm than good to them, play your next as if nothing in particular happened – and your next may be good – but press for good, and chances are you will bundle it.

So much depends upon golf clubs, gain some idea of their form. It is easy to start with a wrong idea, and difficult to acquire the right style, and all because of erroneous deductions. **(Physical Basic #1)**

1881 Robert Forgan
The Golfers Handbook

In every stroke there are three essentials:

1. Position of the player to the ball.
2. Players grasp of the club.
3. A players swing that is based on the first two essentials. **(Physical Basic #2)**

The forward swing should allow the club to follow. To manage this type of stroke is not easy, but it is deadly in the whole game. **(Physical Basic #3)**

1885 James P. Lee
Golf in America

Golfers should never just wave his club to and fro without purpose, when warming up swing back and forth with an intended flight in mind.

Always keep your eye upon the part of the ball which the clubface is to come into contact, but in a bunker aim and hit the sand back of the ball. **(Physical Basic #3)**

1886 Horace Hutchinson
Hints to Golfers

Let the gentle force of a swing expend naturally, without effort of your muscles. **(Physical Basic #3)**

In the sand – the looser the sand, the further back of the ball one must hit. The closer the ball is to the wall of the bunker, the further back of the ball you also must hit.

1897 Willy Park Jr.
The Game of Golf

As a general rule, at address feet are placed on a parallel line, ball tee'd opposite left heel. Arms hang easily and more into the body, rather than out. **(Physical Basic #2)**

1887 Sir W.G. Simpson
The Art of Golf

Don't treat the ball like a heavy object, it has no weight, and it ought to be swept away, not jerked. **(Physical Basic #4)**

When players stand and aim wrong, they then try to pull or push the ball to correct for stance and aim. In golf faults covered by faults do not cancel each other. **(Physical Basic #2)**

The body remains a fulcrum for the lever that is composed of the golfers arm and club. It is that lever that hits the ball. (Physical Basic #3)

1897 Willy Park
The Game of Golf

It is a mistake to try and do something that will aid in lofting the ball. Such effort is entirely unnecessary, and is the very thing that ruins 9 out of 10 strokes. Loft on the clubface is sufficient loft. **(Physical Basic #1)**

There is a difference in a player in practice, and a player out of practice. Through practice one will be able almost intuitively know what to do – especially in the short game.

1897 Encyclopedia of Sports

When the club is truly swung, it contacts the ball before it has commenced upwards. **(Physical Basic #3)**

There are different styles among good players – beginners would be well advised to pay no attention to details when they differ – and look only where the styles agree (at impact).

Half-shots should be part segment of the full swing – quarter shots are part segment of the half-shot. As far as possible different shots should be played the same way.

1897 John L. Low

Golf is a game of beginnings. Each step becomes the first beginning of a new series (alignment, grip, posture, start the swing). But it comes about; it's the conclusions of a man golf that are marked, rather than the beginnings.

1897 Spalding Athletic Library

The ideal "waggle" consists in a gentle to and fro, once or twice in the same plane as the arc which the clubhead ought to describe in the actual stroke. **(Physical Basic #1)**

1900-1925

1901 Harry Vardon

There are few methods of practice as valuable as making a round of the links with a single club.

1902 C.S. Hanks
Niblick

No stroke stands by itself – each must be considered in reference to the next.

If one swings within himself, and does not attempt to over accelerate any movements, there will be rhythmical harmony which all good golfers use in getting distance. **(Physical Basic #4)**

1903 Harry Vardon
1896,98, 99,03 Open Champion
1900 US Open Champion

Allow the body to turn until the left shoulder is opposite the ball.

1903 James Braid
1901 Open Champion

At the moment of striking the ball, be somewhat firm on both feet, then immediately after the right foot and knee turn through.

1903 Alex Herd
1902 Open Champion

Grip firm with the left hand, and last three of the right hand. Leave the forefingers and thumbs loose, so the club can work.

1903 Harold Hilton
1892-97 Open Champion
1900-01 US AM

Swing the same for all clubs, I always believed I played each club differently, and tried to. But now I see from pictures there is only infinite variations. **(Physical Basic #1)**

Now that the American Haskel rubber core ball has replaced the Gutta Percha, I suggest using the run-up shot over the lofted club stroke around the green for more control.

1903 H. Hutchinson
A Book of Golf

As in billiards, make each shot with a definite view as to the next one.

1903 J. Braid
Advanced Golf

For practice to have full value, make each swing with the care of a stroke from a tee on medal day. Short iron strokes and putting need the greatest amounts of practice.

1907 Harry Vardon

My counsel to all who love the game and want to excel – think out the connection between cause and effect. **(Physical Basic #1,2,3,4,5)**

1913 G.S. Brown
First Steps in Golf

During the downswing, **allow** the hands to go freely out to the ball, not into the body, letting the club pass **through** the ball as **freely** as possible. **(Physical Basic #4)**

1916 John Dunn
A B C's of Golf

Balance is essential. With balance the ball gets all the power, and none of the energy is put to work maintaining equilibrium. Body balance is common to good golf. **(Physical Basic #4)**

1920 Douglas Edgar
The Gate to Golf

The line taken by the clubhead is a curved arc through impact, not a straight line. **(Physical Basic #2)**

1920 Jack Hutchinson
"American Golfer"

There are only two ways of looking at the ball. One is mental, the other is physical. Look but don't think about the ball.

1922 Jim Barnes
"American Golfer"

Slicers – be careful that you are not standing up. When the body comes up, there is a pull across the body.

1922 Stewart Maiden
"American Golfer"

Timing is the secret! But timing is inside the player, timing is instinct. What we see is outside and the result of how the player's time is or is not functioning, you have to develop timing. **(Physical Basic #4)**

1922 Seymour Dunn
Golf Fundamentals

Begin right, learn and study principal first. Do not do what some golfers do – and pursue the details of some famous golfers style, (and not principals) and never play better. **(Physical Basic #1,2,3,4,5)**

A common mistake is buying clubs off the wall. There are no two players alike. The best ways is to have your measurements properly taken, and then have clubs made for you.

The golf swing is the proper blend of round about and up and down its plane. Always keep a third of your strength in your pocket, never press. **(Physical Basic #4)**

1923 Ted Ray

Into the wind make contact with ball before the lowest point in the swing. In cross winds play for the wind to move the ball.

1924 George Bedlam
The Key Book

When the hub moves the rim, its power from within to without. When the clubhead is the last to move, maximum effect is achieved with minimum effort. A wrist is the minimum through which power is transmitted outwards. A wrist does not supply the motive power.**(Physical Basic #3)**

1925-1950

1927 Ernest Jones
"American Golfer"

You must get a mental picture, that is the start of any swing, it is the basics that few golfers ever consider at all.

1929 Walter Hagan
"American Golf"

Putting is more mental than physical. Good putting is mental balance where you make a decision that is not guessing. Feel at ease, lack worry, and no guessing as you hit the ball.

1929	H. Fry "American Golfer"	Never under club – always have some club in reserve. Under clubbing is the bane of every golfer with optimistic belief.
1929	Harry Vardon "American Golfer"	Don't think of the club, or a throw or flick. This will only retard, not accelerate the speed of the club. The wrist is a hinge – and works automatically in the act of sweeping the ball away. (Physical Basic #3)
1930	Harry Vardon	The best advice I can give – you must obey the club and what the club wants you to do, letting results be natural. **(Physical Basic #1)**
1931	Joyce Withered	The two qualities that help me the most – honestly about my weakness, and a sense of humor. Don't try shots beyond ones ability, and don't get upset on the course.
1931	Fed McLeod "Cut Sand Shot"	Have feet firm in sand, clubface open, aim left, eye on imaginary bottom of the ball, have thumb and forefinger of the right hand on the club very light. It is a left-hand shot that must hit the sand hard.
1931	John Dunn <u>Natural Golf</u>	When turning the size of the pivot must be in accordance with the length of the swing. Three-quarter turn for a three-quarter swing.
1932	Alex Morrison	The excellence of anyone's game depends of self-control. The self-control that inner peace arises from What is a swing? The swing is a full flowing motion without mental or physical interpretations. **(Physical Basic #4)**
1932	Francis Ouimiet <u>A Game of Golf</u>	To get the necessary accuracy and crispness, play iron shots with three-quarter swings.
1932	Bobby Jones	Refrain from extending the arms away from the body. The feeling of ease is worth all the mechanical precision that is found in a dozen strokes. Rhythm and smoothness are desired. **(Physical Basic #4)**
1932	MacDonald Smith	The idea of hitting leads to tightness and trouble. Swing means the opposite. When you swing you can't tighten up. Swing from a good body turn and from inside the line. **(Physical Basic #4)**
1933	Fred Tate	Good fortune favors the brave in golf. Timid putters don't get lucky. Never up – never in.
1933	Craig Wood	Golf is a game of targets. Every shot in golf should be played to a defined target.
1933	Jerry Travis	In putting let the balls momentum give way to gravity on breaking putts. If the ball speed overcomes gravity all is lost. Putt to where the ball stops traveling under its own power and let gravity finish the task.
1937	Harvey Penick	Keep elbows the same distance from each other during the swing.

1940 Alex Morrison
A New Way to Better Golf

When standing, keeping weight towards the heels is about half the job of making a smooth powerful swing. **(Physical Basic #2)**

1946 Sam Snead
How to Play Golf

The hands are the key to transferring power from the body to the club. Club shaft is held more in the fingers than palm of hands. In the palm it is impossible to get any zip into the shot.

1950-1975

1950 Patty Berg
Golf Illustrated (book)

Playing into wind, grip club shorter, firm left hand, ball back towards your right foot, clubface slightly closed, use a little longer club.

1953 Tommy Armour
A B C's of Golf

Hands stay forward of the club for as long as possible in the downswing. **(Physical Basic #4)**

The average golfer tees the ball too low for the driver.

1954 Percy Boomer
On Learning Golf

The beauty and meaning of all music are both hidden in its rhythm and timing. Rhythm is also the soul of golf, where power is applied indirectly (hidden) through its timing. **(Physical Basic #4)**

1957 Ben Hogan

A full swing is nothing more or less than an extension of the short swing. The right elbow is close to the right hip and leads the right arm to impact. The right elbow is the part of the arm that is closest to the target as you approach impact. The forearm and hand catch up with the elbow as the players arm is extended. **(Physical Basic #3)**

1957 Ben Hogan

The body and the legs move the feet. Never worry about the left heel. Whether it comes off the ground 1" or 2" is a result of the body's actions.

1962 Byron Nelson

Think of the downswing as a chain reaction. It starts with the left side pulling the arms down, the arms pull the hands, the hands pull the clubhead down, into and through the ball. Down, into, and through are the key words. **(Physical Basic #3)**

1962 Byron Nelson

Good long-iron players position the ball a bit more forward than the less skilled. In a properly struck long iron the clubhead meets the ball and then the turf almost instantaneously, slightly skimming the turf in front of the ball.

1966 Tony Lema
Golf Hints

For backspin – play the ball in the middle of your stance, use a firm grip, little wrist action, hitting down and through squeezing the ball.

1966 Gary Player

On Practice: Always practice to a target, keeping the ball some distance away so you take your time between swings. Play the course on the range. Putt at home on the rug.

1968	Doug Ford	For high pitch shots, position the ball an inch or two forward of center in your stance. For low shots position the ball an inch or two back of center in your stance.
1968	Search for the Perfect Swing	Keep fades low and hook shots high. Play the ball back in your stance for fades, and the ball forward in your stance for hooks.
1969	Cary Middlecoff	Unfortunately too many golfers think of the swing as straight back, and straight through the ball (like a pendulum). See the clubhead path following the rim of a tilted wheel and yourself as the hub of the wheel. **(Physical Basic #1)**
1969	Peter Thompson	Use your brain, not your endurance when hitting on the range.
1969	Homer Kelly The Golfing Machine	Learn alignments not positions. Any short cut can easily turn into the longest route. Start with address alignments and see impact alignments. If there is one imperative, it is correct impact alignments. **(Physical Basic #2)** Treat the feel of after impact as though it was impact, even though the ball is gone. **(Physical Basic #3)**
1970	Lee Trevino	Every good golfer keeps their left hand leading through impact. **(Physical Basic #3)**
1971	Billy Casper	Around the green – play the club that keeps the ball nearest to the ground. It is easier to roll the ball up to the hole, then flight the ball up and stop it by the hole. Putt rather than chip, and chip rather than pitch.
1971	Bob Toski	There are a "few" mechanics anyone who hopes to play well must first master (i.e. aim and hold club). But without freedom of movement and a feel for the clubhead, knowing about mechanics will not help. (Physical Basic #4)
1971	Paul Runyan	I suggest you swing around a point, the nap (back) of your neck in the middle of your shoulders. Keep this point the hub of the swing, and as level as possible.
1972	Sam Snead	1. Swing only at 80 to 85 % of your strength. (Physical Basic #4) 2. Picture the club at impact, hands are forward of the clubhead. **(Physical Basic #3)**
1972	John Jacobs	The upper body leans slightly to the right at address, this tilt to the right remains to the right until after impact. **(Physical Basic #2)**
1973	Minden Blake Golf Swing of The Future	The ball has to be met solidly with the full pressure of the body behind the shot at impact. Its pressure that counts. Everything is subordinate to achieving maximum pressure. **(Physical Basic #3)**
1973	Eddie Merrins	Proper wrist action is up and down, not side to side. Proper wrist action gives the swing height and leverage, and also levers the clubhead during the downswing. Improper wrist action (side to side) misalign the clubface and moves the clubhead off tract.

1974 Johnny Miller

To maintain good tempo you have to be relaxed and don't have a fast backswing. **(Physical Basic #4)**

1974 Gary Player

From fairway bunkers focus on the front edge of the ball and swing through.

1975-2000

1975 Michael Murphy
The Inner Game of Golf

The prime causes of error are within the mind – doubt, tension and a lack of concentration cause more errors than ignorance of mechanics.

1975 Phil Rogers

Great putters, and I've seen some, learn to roll the ball at the correct speed and let gravity help them make the putt.

1975 Nancy Lopez

Every time I swing I am aware of tempo. Even and controlled tempo is at the foundation of my game. Keep practicing without swing hints until you find your natural swing tempo. **(Physical Basic #4)**

1979 Jack Nicklaus
Playing Lessons

The busier you keep yourself with the particulars of the shot at hand – the less room there is for negative thoughts.

1981 Henry Cotton
Thanks for the Game

Always, when you can, leave yourself a level lie. I would much rather hit a 5 iron from a level lie, then an 8 iron from a side hill lie.

1983 Jack Nicklaus
The Full Swing

The less you turn your upper body, the less clubhead speed you generate. The more up, rather than upward and rearward the arms swing, the sooner the body will stop coiling. If this seems contrary to what I have said in the past – with apologies I say golf is always a learning process.

1984 David Graham
Winning Golf

For the basic chip shot, turn the left hand to the left (into a weak position). This firms up the wrists.

1985 Jack Grout
Golf Clinic

Playing from long grass demands a firm grip, and a more up and down angle of attack. Also play the ball back in your stance, open clubface, and aim a little left.

1985 Bob Charles
Left-Hander's Golf

Never practice when you are tired. Always hit to a target. Work on one problem, not several, and don't have high expectations.

1985 Sandy Lyle
Learning Golf

Balance starts at address, flex knees, bent slightly from waist, arms hang down and extend until shaft points at belt buckle and hands are centered under the chin. Feet placed under the hip joint. Hip line, shoulder line, feet line all parallel to the target line. **(Physical Basic #2)**

1985 George Low
The Master of Putting

Putting: Use a heavy putter with a thin grip. Put both thumbs on top of the shaft, weight on your left foot, head is down, and don't move it.

1986	Dr. Frank Jobe 30 Exercises	Your body is your most important piece of equipment. Improve your golf with flexibility and strength exercises. Do exercises at a steady pace, with no quick or bouncy motions.
1986	Davis Love Jr.	On the take away – have the feeling you are going to shake hands with a person directly to your right. There is a little forearm rotation.
1988	Davis Love Jr.	Taking loads of mechanical thoughts with you onto the course is like inviting a back-seat driver along, and undermines the fun of the game and your swing.
1988	Greg Norman Shark Attack	On the take away turn your right back pocket for a good hip turn.
1989	Ray Floyd From 60 Yards In	**Pitch and run from a divot** – put the ball back in your stance, weight left, hands ahead of the ball, grip down and set the club down in the divot on it's toe. Turn the toe in so it contacts the ground first. Use the pitching wedge.
1989	Alex Hay	Always start your address by first aiming the clubface, then take up your stance. Many golfers take up their stance first. **(Physical Basic #2)**
1989	Ian Woosnam Power Golf	The follow- through is only the natural result of what happens before hand. See the bottom of the swing as few inches beyond the ball (divot starting beyond the ball) and imagine the follow through is a result of the right arm fully extended until the top of follow through.
1989	Charles Earp Down Under Par	Many golfers try to lift the ball into the air. Feel you hit the ball first, then squeeze it through the ground with a clubhead staying low after impact. **(Physical Basic #3)**
1990	Nick Faldo	In the downswing, keep the upper left arm on the top half of your chest as much as possible. Feel the left side and shoulders are moving at the same speed as the hands, so the hands don't take over. **(Physical Basic #3)**
1990	Bob Ford Golf, The Body, The Mind, The Game	The clubhead remains inside the target line for the entire golf movement. Inside to inside like a baseball swing. **(Physical Basic #1)**
1992	John Goodwin First Shot	Notice how a good backswing keeps the right knee in place over the right foot, more or less where it was at address. It is from this stable, balanced position the downswing starts. **(Physical Basic #4)**
1992	Gardner Dickinson Let'er Rip	At address, incline your head so you are looking directly at the ball from the center of your eyes. Never hold the club so tight that you can't feel its weight. **(Physical Basic #2)**
1994	Gardner Dickinson	For soft wedge shots, stand much farther away from the ball, bend your knees more than you've ever done, and don't stand up until the ball is gone.

1994 Corey Pavin
Shot Making

For the shots with extra carry, tee the ball so that most of the ball is above the top of the clubhead and move the ball forward one inch, and keep your head back through impact.

1995 David Frost

When the ball is below your feet, widen your stance to lower your body at address and your swing plane through impact.

1996 Gary McCord
Golf For Dummies

Swing plane is the path the shaft follows when you swing. The angle the shaft occupies at address is the angle the shaft is parallel to through impact in most good swings. Also your hands should not be behind the ball at impact. **(Physical Basic #1)**

1996 Nick Price
The Swing

Legs play a supporting weight – bearing role. During the downswing the legs move intentionally only after the hands are down in front of the right hip.

1997 Judy Rankin

In a fairway bunker – set feet firm into sand, keep lower body quiet, hold club one inch shorter, swing more with shoulder and arms, not legs. Use a flat swing.

1998 Brad Faxton

When practicing putting, make putts from the same place, but at different speeds to improve your rhythm. **(Physical Basic #4)**

1999 Tiger Woods

At the top of the backswing, the right elbow should be pointing down at the ground, but not be to close to the body. **(Physical Basic #1)**

Practice putting with one hand. Putts under five feet – swing straight back and straight through. On long putts – swing slightly to the inside in the backswing, squaring at impact then back slightly to the inside. Use only your dominant hand to feel your rhythm.

1999 David Duval

Don't change the amount of flex in your elbow joints during your putting swing.

1999 Bob Duval

The key to great ball striking – the body leads and the club follows through impact. **(Physical Basic #3)**

2000 Tiger Woods

I learned the short game first, my Pop believed in the importance of putting, chipping, and pitching.

2000 Tiger Woods

When I want to hit a long drive, I keep my head back longer.

2000 Tiger Woods

I always practiced with my Pop, we played games that were both **creative** and **competitive**. Who could hit the highest or lowest shot, etc.

SUMMARY OF CHAPTERS ONE, TWO AND THREE

- The tips and advice many golfers exchange with each other have always had **little common ground** and **dissimilar suggestions. Avoid tips.**
- Golf is a game of force. Improving the alignment and application of force is **the only way to improve ball flight.**
- People who have made progress in golf, have **adapted** their game and swing to golf's environment.
- **Golf's Physical Basics** have never changed, and have been the foundation of the game from day one.
- Golfers who experience long-term learning use **self-discovery** and **awareness skills.** They avoid tips and "how to" advice from fiends,
- Chapters I, II, and III were written to expose readers to information that could create **new insights** and **improve learning potential,** hopefully it did.

Concepts within the physical laws never change. Only the development level of the golfer or athlete changes. Golfers who want to improve should follow the suggestions below for skill acquisition Dr. Ree Arnold offers:

1. Look for a realistic (game like) environment to learn from
2. Use an approach that progressively increases the complexity of the movement task. (start with small motions)
3. Use specific feedback regarding techniques (use a mirror or video replay yourself)
4. Use specific feedback regarding results (ball flight)
5. Allow for learning to occur (there are no quick fixes)

Feedback acquisition is essential for success. This feedback must be from the learners motion., not from some expert model. Self-modeling and or non-specific learning models have been shown to be more useful from long-term learning of motion patterns than expert models and drills.

Golfers who are not happy with their progress often look in the direction of "how to" advice and "drills". Whereas expert after expert, and study after study in the field of skill acquisition all point away from "drills" and "how to" advice in the direction of **self-discovery in changing environments.**

Training and practicing in a variety of different situations normally facilitates more learning that static non-changing environments. The more variety the better. **It also helps retention of skills (for later use) the more closely training resembles game-like conditions.**

When people are trying to improve their golf, many fail to **identify the sub-skills** that must be learned in order to perform a full swing. People are aware of the sub-skills (grip, posture, alignment, etc.) but rarely have learned them on a level that supports learning a full golf swing.

Prerequisite skills, or sub-skills are necessary for people to participate in sports (I.e. golf) successfully. With the help of a useful source of instruction information, golfers must gain some insights on where each of these sub-skills fits into a hierarchy, or sequence for learning to improve their golf.

"Steps too large equals failure and frustration, steps too small equals boredom and off task behavior." - Stevie Chepko. Chapter Five, **The Nature of Learning and the Nature of Instruction** will make suggestions about learning and using any new insights readers may have gained from the first four chapters. The Extra Credit section contains detail that may only interest some readers. But can help every reader.

Chapter Four

Golf Questions and Answers,

Secrets and Lies

Helping people learn is not about
giving them the right answer,
it is about helping them learn
to ask the right question.

QUESTIONS AND ANSWERS SECRETS AND LIES

The following contains information for the most curious golfer. Golf is a game of creating and using force, and this section may give readers new insights about force. (This may not be required reading, but will be interesting for some golfers.)

Mr. Bob Bush is a highly respected engineer, whose knowledge and insights have influenced golf for years. He was a member of the team of engineers who designed and built the golf industries first mechanical hitting machine (Iron Byron) for True Temper in the mid 1960's. After working for True Temper for 30 years, Mr. Bush is now one of the most sought after consultants in the golf industry.

Bob has more knowledge about the swing than anyone I know. I asked him to answer a number of questions about the golf swing as if the mechanical laws and physical principles were giving the answers. Hopefully, readers of Golf Swing Secrets and Lies will find the answers useful. (Mr. Bush, thanks for your help).

What would the Mechanical Laws say is the most important element of an efficient swing?

Answer: *"Velocity is slightly more important than mass. Velocity becomes a vector when it has direction. In efficient golf swings its vectors (Lines of force) stay parallel to the plane of the swing throughout impact."*

Where is the primary center of a golf swing?

Answer: *"Golf swings have several centers but, the primary center for the efficient swing is just under the players left breast, (right hand golfers) and in the middle of the chest cavity. The distance from this point to the right shoulder is the longest lever in a golfer's body. This is one reason why the right shoulder delivers up to 70% of the swings force, (its part of a long lever)."*

1950's #6

1990's #7

1990's

1950's

1950's #6

Are there any noted differences in the swings of stick games, i.e. baseball, hockey, tennis, and golf?

Answer: *"Not many- But golf is the only stick game that has its shaft rotating about its own longitudinal axis during swing motion."*

As the club is moving with the golfers body turn, the club shaft also rotates about it's own longitudinal axis. We could say there is rotation within rotation. Without this shaft rotation, the swing would have less force. This shaft rotation is caused by both hand rotation and the clubhead's center of mass rotating to line up with the center of mass of the golfers hands.

Note: If the clubhead was turned over, with its toe now pointing to the ground, there would be little or no rotation because the center of mass of clubhead is now in-line with the hands center of mass.

How would centrifugal force in an efficient golf swing be defined?
Is centrifugal force a fictitious force?

Answer: *"First, centrifugal force is a real force. Centrifugal force is a pulling force that causes the center of the clubhead's mass to droop to go in line (on plane) with the hands through impact."*

Is the outward pull of the clubhead as much as 80 lbs as the shaft goes in line with the left arm in the downswing?

Answer: *"It's a down force, not out."*

"The centrifugal force, about 100 lbs, causes the club shaft and clubhead to droop through impact to go in-line with hands, not go in-line with the left arm. (Player generated rotational forces that expand levers cause the shaft to line up with the left arm not centrifugal force)."

1950's

2000

1960's

2000 #5

Is downswing or forward swing a more accurate term?

Answer: *"Downswing – The ball goes forward, but force goes down and out."*

1999 #2

1998 #4

1990's #2

1910

Are the major torque's in a golf swing produced by the shoulders and back muscles, with only some torque coming from the hips.

Answer: *"yes."*

1990's #5

2000

1990's #7

1920's

Do the shoulders travel faster than the hips during the downswing?

Answer: *"yes—three or four times faster."*

What percentage of clubhead speed are the hips responsible for?

Answer: *"Only 10%- 15%."*

Does a player's body mass have less than a 1% effect on initial ball velocity?

Answer: *"yes."*

Is 85% of clubhead speed produced by the right arm?

Answer: *"No – The right arm is supporting the left arm and club throughout impact, as it reacts to rotational force."*

1960's #1

1950's #1

1960's #1

1950's #1

Where does most of the clubhead force come from?

Answer: *"Rotational Forces transmitted through the hands."*

- A golfers body has several segments that are capable of producing force.
- The right shoulder delivers up to 70% of the swings force. This is why it's so important for the right shoulder to travel down plane to impact. As the left shoulder moves up plane, see the left shoulder as a guide, for the right shoulder in the downswing.

1950's #6

1950's

1999

1990's #4

1940's

Note: The importance of shoulder rotation to club head velocity was discussed in a study by Dr. Richard Nelson and Tim Aro of Penn State Biomechanical Lab, Bruce Knoth of Advanced Mechanical Technology Inc., and Ralph L. Robinson. Their findings follow.

The most significant element in a swing for club head velocity is wrist cock. Without ample wrist cock, maximum club head velocity was not reached (I.e. Putting has no or little wrist cock). The size of wrist cock during the first half of the downswing is very important.

The second most important element is timing, or when the wrist angle was released. Also the larger the angle, the faster the club head can move through impact.

The third most important element was the rate of rotation of the shoulder through impact (not hips). The study said some professionals retain their wrist cock well into their downswing, with shoulder rotation, above all other elements, dominating club head velocity through impact.

The fourth most important element was the rate of rotation of the hips during the downswing (Not impact).

Secret: While a wrist cock, and when in the downswing full wrist angle release happens is critical, without efficient alignment and application of shoulder rotation, club head velocity will be less than it could be.

1930's

1920's

1930's

1940's

What would the mechanical laws say starts the downswing?

Answer: *"Tensile Forces - Pulling forces that go down-plane into the right leg and ground."*

- The right shoulder is the swings main source or force as it goes down plane.

1999 #2

1999 #2

1999

1999

Is the crack of a whip a good example of what happens in an efficient golf swing?

Answer: *"No - Only if you put a weight on the end of the whip."*

Does each mile per hour of clubhead speed equal 2.5 yards of distance?

Answer: *"Yes."*

Are there any pushing forces of note in the downswing?

Answer: *"No."*

Is there more body weight on the right side then the left side just before impact in efficient swings?

Answer: *"Yes."*
(Studies, on page 225, by Dr. Greenwald also made this observation.)

1990's #5

1950's

1960's

1930's

Questions about sequencing:

- **Do shoulders start, and then stop, giving their energy to the arms?**
- **Do the arms start, then stop, giving their energy to the hands?**
- **Do the hands start, then stop, giving their energy to the club?**
- **Does the club's momentum go into the ball at impact?**
- **Does impact slow the clubhead down 20%?**

Answer: *"Yes that's the sequence - and the club slows down a little more than 20%."*

Does force on players hands and arms slow them down before impact?

Answer: *"It is a transfer of energy that slows them down, not a force."*

What is the velocity of a pro's hands?

Answer: *"Hand velocity reaches 15 MPH."*

Does the left arm stop for an instant during impact?

Answer: *"In an efficient application of force, the left arm stops just prior to impact."*

1960's #1

1950's #1

1930's

1999

Does the head of a golfer counter balance the pull of the club during impact by staying back and down?

Answer: *"No, hand strength does."*

1970's

2000

2000 #7

1999 #7

Is the firming up of a players left side a reaction or a caused action on the part of the player?

Answer: *"A caused action."*

1910's

1990's #2

1990's #2

1990's #5

Could it be said, the shoulders pull on the arms, the arms pull on the hands, the hands pull on the club in efficient downswings?

Answer: *"Yes"*

Does the left shoulder and hands go down at the start of the backswing?

Answer: *"Yes"*

When the clubhead starts its return from the top of the backswing, is it at 0 mph?

Answer: *"Yes."*

1900

2000

1999

1910

What should we know about the players' spine?

Answer: *"Shoulder turn is more or less at right angles to the spine. The upper spine, or neck is over and out more or less parallel to the ground at impact. Spine is also always angled away from the ball."*

1999 #7

1950's #1

1950's #6

1910

Where is the shaft loaded?

Answer: *"When the left arm is parallel to the ground and the shaft is vertical to the ground* Ⓐ *in the downswing is where the shaft is loaded. This is when the shaft goes from vertical to the ground to* Ⓑ *horizontal to the ground. At the start of the downswing there is a pull (from rotational forces) on the shaft and arms – a stretching, not a loading action."*

Ⓐ 1910

Ⓑ 1910

1940's

1950's #6

What would the Laws of Motion and Force say have more influence on the starting direction of the ball – Clubface or swing path?

Answer: *"Clubface."*

Does sidespin come more from swing path or clubface alignment through impact?

Answer: *"Swing Path."*

When the clubhead stops moving down, and starts up, does the club slow down?

Answer: *"Generally, yes."*

Are efficient swings impacting the ball on the up swing with a driver?

Answer: *"No, but because the Center of Gravity of a driver is located back behind the face, and also behind the axis of the shaft, the center of gravity of the driver is trying to go in line with the handle of the shaft. This action causes the drivers face to impact the ball 2 degrees up. The 2 degrees up is result of what the center of gravity of the driver is doing, not the swing."*

Where is the bottom of a driver swing?

Answer: *"It's certainly slightly ahead of a vertical line up from the ball."*

Is the bottom of an iron swing the bottom of the divot?

Answer: *"Yes – Ball location is ¾ behind the bottom of the divot at address."*

1950's

1950's

1990's

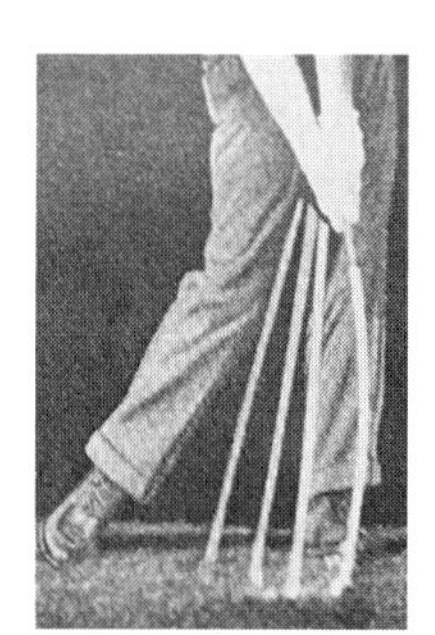
1970's

Where is the bottom of a fairway wood swing?

Answer: *"Fairway wood heads are more in line with the shaft at impact then drivers. The bottom of the swing is more forward then irons, but in back of drivers. Reason: the center of gravity of a fairway wood is closer to the face, then with drivers."*

Do the shoulders turn through impact parallel to the shaft plane?

Answer: *"Not quite – just a little lower."*

1990's #4

1999 #5

1999

1990's #7

1930's

1990's #2

1990's #2

1990's #7

1920's

1920's

Does the right forearm swing through impact parallel to the angle the shaft plane occupied at address?

Answer: *"Yes."*

1920's

1999 #4

1999

1930's

According to Mechanical Laws, is there a difference between iron swings and wood swings?

Answer: *"No – Learning one swing is hard enough. But irons are designed to impact the ball below the center of the clubface, and the drivers should impact balls above the center of the clubface for maximum distance."*

How does making the club longer influence distance?

Answer: *"Longer clubs are very difficult to control. They work only when the player can handle the increased inertia. – Few can. – Most hit wild shots."*

In Bob Bush's opinion – **the skills that create and direct force have been over looked.** Players with efficient swings know how to create, use, and sustain force through impact for the shot at hand. Most golfers focus on clubhead speed not force. **There is a huge difference in speed and effective application of force. Learning to align and apply effective force is the key, not clubhead speed at impact.**

1920's

1930's

1920's

1950's

1950's #6

Long Drives

The following is based on information I received from the Titleist Tour Van, and from other studies. Titleist invited me to spend some time with the men and women who travel the PGA Tour gathering information about clubs and balls.

The desired Launch Angle for the driver is 10 to 14 degrees. The desired spin rate (backspin) of the ball as it comes off the clubface is 2500-3500 Rpm's or lower. The longest drivers of the ball have a high launch angle but a low spin rate.

Tiger Woods has a launch angle of 11 degrees and spin rate of 2200 Rpm's, with clubhead speed of 130+ mph, and ball speed of 170 + mph.

The average launch angle on tour is 9.4 with a spin rate of 3000 Rpm's, with clubhead speed of 120 mph, and ball speed of 160.

When impact conditions can produce 15% less backspin, the ball goes 23 yards longer. Clubhead speed is normally 2/3 of initial ball speed. Initial ball speed is important for more distance.

The desired impact point on the face of a driver is above its center of gravity. This point of impact produces a high launch angle and a low spin rate (less backspin).

In wind, players should use balls, equipment, and swings that produce a low spin rate. (Less backspin)

Back strength influences clubhead speed. Flexibility influences accuracy. Studies have found, as the ability to increase clubhead speed goes up, handicaps go down.

Iron Byron

Since the late 1960's ball, shaft, and club manufactures have used a swing machine called "Iron Byron" to test and develop their products. The U.S.G.A has also used True Tempers Iron Byron for research purposes. Some manufactures have recently developed their own version of Iron Bryon. What follows is based on information gained from a precise sophisticated golf swing machine (Iron Bryon) developed by modern technology.

This swing machine is capable of using any length club, on any plane, with any clubface angle, from any ball location, at any swing velocity. It can be programmed to make good and bad shots. Iron Byron has a repeatable swing that can carry the ball at least 250 yards, and can control its swing within ½% of any measurement. For over 30 years the Iron Byron has been adjusted to test balls, clubs and shafts, as well as to demonstrate any claims a company may make about their product.

Tests Show The Following:

- A **minor** variation in the alignments of the clubface at impact will have a **significant** effect on direction and trajectory of ball flight.
- The alignment the clubface assumes at impact is **significantly** influenced by both the material properties and the geometry of the shaft.
- A golf clubs shaft has both torsional (rotational) and longitudinal (bending) – stiffness. Torsional stiffness dictates clubface alignment at impact. Note: the greater the torsional flexibility, the more the clubface will have to be open at address (up to 5 ° degrees), to give the ball the same directional flight a stiff low tension X shaft would.
- When the club head has less mass (lighter), there is greater twisting motion at impact. This causes shots to go more off-line than club heads with more mass.
- Regardless of the shaft's flexibility, in both tension and bending, ball and clubhead velocity were more or less the same.

- As swing weight of the club goes up (i.e. from D0, D1, D2, etc.) Clubhead velocity decreases ½° for each swing weight.
- There is a correlation between a golf ball's initial absolute velocity and how far a ball carries.
- The path of the club through impact (face, head, shaft) is a curved path, not a straight line. The ball goes straight; the swing is on a curved path.
- To hit the ball from 200 yards within 4 yards of a target, the ball must be placed within ¼" of the perfect location at address. As clubs become shorter, with more loft, the ball location becomes somewhat less critical.
- Ball location at address:

  Iron Byron hit high hooks with 2 irons when the ball was located 3" forward. By opening the clubface 4 degrees the ball flight became straighter, but still pulled off-line about 7 yards.

  With the 5 iron, ball located 3" forward, the clubface had to be open 4 degrees to stop hooking, but it still pulled 6 yards off-line. When the ball is placed back in the stance, the ball flies lower and to the right.
- The clubface closes at a rate of 6 degrees for every 3" of forward ball position. (2 degrees from the swing arc, and 4 degrees from club rotation.) Most top professionals are similar to the Iron Byron. For both, during the 140" movement from 9 to 3 o'clock (I.e. waist high to waist high), the clubface has rotated or closed about 180 degrees.
- The golf ball is in contact with the clubface for approximately .000500 seconds regardless of ball type or clubhead speed. Tests suggest there is no significant relationship between clubhead velocity and the amount of time the ball stays on the clubface. So whether the clubhead speed is 106 MPH, 96 MPH, or 83 MPH, the ball stays on the clubface for .000500 seconds.
- The clubface must be aligned within 1 degree of acceptable alignment, to hit the ball 200 yards with some accuracy.
- The shaft and its stiffness have no significance during impact relative to distance. The shaft should be seen as a timing element. The clubhead (not shaft) can influence ball flight.

The Shaft and Efficient Swings

The shaft of a club is very important to any golf shot for several reasons. But energy at impact is not really one of them. **The shaft transfers energy, it does not supply energy.** It is useful to first see the shaft as a timing mechanism, that helps the player deliver the club's head down to the ball at the most effective and efficient time.

When selecting a shaft, the main consideration is to match its dynamic in-swing characteristics (or personality) to the swing personality of the golfer. When and how fast or slow the players muscles fire and react during the swing, should match the shaft being used.

The tip, or the area of the shaft that is in the clubhead, is the most important segment of the shaft. In general, this end of the shaft can be made to have firm, flexible or medium bending characteristics. The softer the tip, the higher the ball will fly. The stiffer the shaft is, the more the clubface has the tendency to close. Flexible shafts keep the face more open. Low hooks come from stiff shafts and high fades soft ones.

The weight of the shaft is also very important. In fact, the lighter the better. When looking for a shaft that can match your swing timing, or muscle firing sequence, lighter is better than heavy. Light shafts have a low moment of inertia and are easier to move. This shaft should also be one with little or no torque (twisting properties).

One of the light shafts available to both the golfing public and tournament players is made from graphite. Most research has shown that manufacturers are still working to further develop the graphite shaft. Today, there is no strong evidence that can say graphite is a much better shaft than lightweight steel.

Research shows graphite does not hit the ball as straight as steel, and in truth, not much longer. Some graphite shafts are not lighter than some steel ones. The boron that has been added to some graphite shafts only makes them stronger, and does not remove the torque or twisting characteristics all graphite shafts have.

But perhaps the biggest or most important difference between steel and graphite is what science calls the "damping effect". When a ball is hit with a graphite-shafted club the player may receive less feedback than from steel. Graphite can or dampen the feel of the shot. The feel a shot provides is critical feedback for a player's next swing. With graphite shafts this kind of information is not available in the same quantities found in steel.

While we know the shaft is not where the swing's energy comes from at impact, shafts do influence several important properties of a sound swing.

- **Swing Radius** - The length of the shaft and the player's left arm establish a radius from clubhead to left shoulder joint.
- **Dynamic Lie** - As the club is moving or being transported down through impact, it is moving at an angle. This angle or dynamic lie is influenced by how the shaft reacts during the swing.
- **Launch Angle** - The angle from which the ball leaves the clubface is influenced by the tip end of the shaft. The softer the higher.
- **Spin Rate** - The rate at which a ball is spinning (when it moves off the clubface) is responsible for how high and far a ball travels. The shaft influences this rate.
- **Address Position** - The lie or angle of the shaft at address influences the plane or path of the swing. Any compensation a player may or may not be required to make when making a shot.
- **Swing Timing or Sequence** - The human body and brain have the ability to adapt very quickly. Even when using a shaft that is not matched to a player's natural swing timing - the golfer will subconsciously adjust after a few swings and hit some acceptable shots. However none of these swings could be called optimum.
- **Feel of the Shot** - A shaft will influence how the shot feels to a player. This information can influence his/her next swing. (Note: The ball is long gone before the player feels impact)

While all of the above are influenced by the shaft, the swing's energy at impact is influenced mostly by what is called a transfer of momentum through impact. Ideally, at impact there should be no energy being expanded or stored, it should have been spent -gone into the ball. At impact, the clubhead should be at maximum velocity. It should not be speeding up or slowing down. Ian Woosnam and Fred Couples are two examples of this swing principle. Bob Bush felt that these two swings were great examples of very efficient swings.

At impact, it may help to feel that the clubhead is like a free moving object which has been put into orbit by the swing. In truth, the clubhead could be attached to a garden hose or rope at impact. The energy the ball receives from the swing is transferred through, not by, the shaft.

During a typical 18 hole round of golf, the ball is on the clubface for a very short period of time, less than 1/5 of a second. That is not for each shot, but the total time the ball and the face of the club are in contact for the entire round. It is during this very brief time period that the ball is being told what to do. The clubface, swing path, velocity, and angle of approach determine ball flight.

Because of the forces provided by a sound swing, just before impact the clubhead's center of mass is trying to line up with the center of mass of the hands. This will cause the shaft to bow down, making the toe go down.

At address, to take advantage of the forces a sound swing can produce, the club face can be slightly open with the toe off the ground. Remember centrifugal force causes the toe down as the face is closing through impact. **A properly fitted club will sit with its toe off the ground.**

Research has found that when the shaft gives the club more loft, this added loft has more influence on impact conditions than the closing club face. Also woods and offset irons produce more loft and closing conditions than non-offset irons.

Research has found that the flight time of a properly impacted ball is always between 5 and 6 seconds. The drive is airborne for about 6 seconds, the wedge 5 seconds. The optimum height for all clubs is similar.

The height of wedge shots and drives should be similar. The driver should stay airborne slightly longer than other clubs.

Woods, even though they weigh less than irons, are longer. This gives woods a larger moment of inertia (harder to move). This is one of the reasons some golfers do not swing or hit their woods as well as irons.

The exchange of energy, when the clubhead and swing puts force into the ball, is the most important segment and principle of the swing. Everything you should do with your body, swing, and club is founded on maximizing force at impact, (transfer of momentum).

When the ball and clubface collide, friction between the two is created - this is called coefficient of restitution. Ideally, we want low friction and high compression at impact.

When the True Temper Shaft Company does research on the swing, they start by seeing the swing as having (5) five hinges or links: shoulders, elbows, legs, hips and hands-wrists. Their studies show these five segments all move together. However, they move in different, but parallel planes of motion (much like the parts of a watch). It is also useful to realize that when the bigger segments move or transfer energy to the smaller segments of the swing, it becomes more efficient.

Their studies also show the muscles of the back set the plane and help the hips to rotate. The pelvic girdles reacts to the bigger shoulders and lower back muscles when they start the arms and club back down plane.

True Temper research shows that the head of the club and its natural inertia loads the shaft of the club slightly as it changes direction at the top of the backswing. However the main loading or stretching of the shaft does not take place until the left arm is parallel to the ground and the shaft is vertical to it.

The Physics of Golf

When Theodore Jorgenson (University of Nebraska Physics Department) wanted to improve his own golf he started by reading what the experts had to say. His first observation after spending some time in the library was, *"It appears that a great deal of golf instruction is of the nature of teaching, rather than helping golfers develop a correct style of their own".*

"A careful reading of many books offered minimal help. These experts were not discussing fundamentals that had any meaning to my background in Physics." (I.e. a search for laws that govern behavior), *"I soon realized that my scientific curiosity (knowledge gained through experience) would only be satisfied if I did my own research".* He started in May 1968.

I never had the pleasure of spending time with Theodore Jorgenson. I know I would have enjoyed learning from him. What follows is from notes that I made while reading his book, The Physics of Golf.

It is important to keep in mind that when Jorgenson was trying to improve his golf he looked for information about the game and swing that was based on Force and Motion Principles. This is similar to Homer Kelly, who one day hit the ball better than he ever did before. Homer immediately wanted to understand what he did different that day to get improved results and using his engineering background, wrote The Golfing Machine.

Jorgenson felt that if a golfer was going to make progress that lasted, it was important that all of the events that make up efficient golf swings **should not** be initially taken into consideration.

Jorgenson, *"A general non-specific model that can stimulate confidence, is what golfers need at first. While this model and information should be manageable, it can't be so non-specific that the model overlooks the core element of the event"*. It's interesting to me that a physicist suggested that a non-specific model would help a golfers progress. Eleanor Langer a PhD from Harvard made the same observation in her book, The Power of Mindful Learning when she suggested using general non-specific learning models.

"There is more to playing golf than just swing a club. There is putting, bunker shots, deep-rough, wind, trees, choices of clubs, mental attitude, and the distance one can drive", Jorgenson.

A study at Nebraska's Physics Department shows that a tee shot's average distance has a direct influence on any golfer ability to shoot par. The shorter the tee shot, the more strokes would be lost to par on an average length course.

Average Distance	Strokes Lost to Par
160	15
170	12
180	9
190	7
200	5
210	3
220	1

Lesson One in this book states that golf is a "game of force". When we improve our alignment and application of force through impact, we can improve our game. Jorgenson, *"I soon learned that improving ones distance off the tee and lowering ones score, were often one in the same"*.

A Physical Event

Jorgenson pointed out that the golf swing is a physical event. A dynamic process governed by the principles of motion and force. There are three separate events in a golf swing:

1. The swing of the club
2. The impact of the clubhead with the ball
3. The flight of the ball

Jorgenson said that his book was not a "how to" book, but he hoped that the information in the book would bring some fundamental understanding of what golfers should do to improve their games.

Some highlights of Jorgenson's findings follow.

The swing of the club is what physicists call a double pendulum.

1. The arms
2. The club.

"Methods of obtaining the equation for the motion of a double pendulum had been worked out hundred of years before I began to study the golf swing. As I started to apply my understanding of physics and math to a golf swing, I noticed that most golfers used swings that lacked any scientific understanding", Jorgenson

The following concepts of work and energy, as used in mechanics, did not exist when golf was first played in the fifteenth century. Some of Jorgensons finding are listed below.

- A golfer's arms and therefore his hands slow up just before impact. Rotation of the club in the plane of the swing produces a force from the club on the golfers hands that slow the hands down.
- During the swing, the club turns about its shaft
- Golfers who swing the club efficiently use constant torque

- The club may have five different torques acting on it.
- The golfers arm may have five different torque actions on them.
- A standard swing has the energy of about two-horse power.
- A golfer needs at least thirty-two pounds of muscle to supply two-horse power.
- Efficient golf swings pull against the mass of the left arm and club.
- The large muscles of the back and shoulders act together to produce the largest torques in efficient golf swings
- Any motion that is not rotational is wasteful energy
- Any increase in the size of wrist cock angle at the start of the downswing can produce an increase in clubhead speed at impact.
- A golfer could reduce his backswing by 30 degrees, and only lose about 2.5% of possible clubhead speed.
- Anything a golfer does to **decrease** the wrist cock angle early during the downswing will result in less clubhead velocity.
- Bobby Jones, *"When playing well, I have the feeling of pulling against something".*

Secret: **Since any transfer of energy from the clubhead to the ball is determined by the physical properties of the club, the ball and by the Laws of Physics, golfers should learn how the club acquires its energy during the downswing.**

Golfers and the clubs they use have the potential for applying force. At the top of the backswing- there is a potential for energy, depending solely on how elements of potential energy are aligned.

Through impact, the total kinetic energy (its not longer potential energy) of the system consists of:

- 71% from the work of rotation.
- 13% from deceleration. i.e. (As arms slow the club gains).

Jorgensen said, *"A person can only learn by doing, but not haphazardly. Theoretical understanding of the swing puts limits on what should be attempted within general guidelines, as people develop their style of applying sound theory."*

In closing, Jorgenson pointed out that workable techniques are determined by the limitations of the human body and the Laws of Physics. We develop a skill by getting the "feel for it". It is a feel for things that should be learned.

RESEARCH CAN IMPROVE YOUR TEE SHOTS

At the risk of sounding obvious, one difference between high and low handicap golfers is the swing they use. This is especially evident when a few key areas of their swing are compared.

Biomechanical analysis and research of body and club alignments during a golf swing has gone on for several generations. However, most of the information gathered was often complex and difficult for players and instructors to apply.

For several years, Dr. James Greenwald, M.D., Anthony P. Feroan, M.A. and Greg McHatton, PGA, along with other staff members at the University Sports Biomechanical Research Center in Reno, Nevada, have been doing studies on the golf swing. The information gathered from these studies is very straightforward and "user friendly." The results have shown some significant and definable differences between a swing that is mechanically sound and one that is not. In my opinion, these studies have produced an objective checklist that could be used to improve anyone's swing.

Swings were analyzed from four different groups of players at the University Sports Biomechanical Research Center in Reno: Group 1 - PGA, LPGA Tour, PGA instructors, amateur with under 5 handicap; Group 2 - handicap 6 to 12; Group 3 - handicap 13 to 19; Group 4 - handicap 20 plus.

I am aware that many players and instructors have strong feelings about the information they use to improve golf swings. They all have their opinion.

Please Note: Information developed during responsible research is not someone's opinion. It is information founded on universally accepted procedures that were used and followed.

Driver Swings

Most golfers have heard the saying, "You drive for show, but you putt for dough." while that may be true, it is also true that you must be on the green to putt, and it's a lot easier to hit greens if your tee shots are in the fairway

My hope is the following will give readers some insights into their faulty tee shots and some suggestions for changing habits *not found* in mechanically sound swings.

Some key areas of the driver swing evaluated in Reno:

- Where is the left shoulder at address?
- Where is the left shoulder at impact?
- Where is the left wrist at impact?
- Is the club head path in-to-out, or out-to-in, when the club shaft is parallel to the ground in downswing.
- Is the angle between the shaft and the left arm 90 degrees or less when the right arm is parallel to the ground in the downswing?
- What is the relationship of the left arm to the club head at impact?
- Is most of the player's weight and swing force on the left or right foot at impact?

Where is the left shoulder joint placed at address?

In Group 1, professional and low handicap golfers have the left shoulder joint over or behind the ball at address. The players from Group 2 have it even or slightly ahead of the ball. In Groups 3 and 4, the leftshoulder joint is well forward of the ball at address.

Where is the left shoulder joint at impact?

In Group 1, professional and low handicap golfers have the left shoulder joint behind the ball at impact. In Groups 2, 3 and 4, the left shoulder joint is forward of the ball at impact. An **optimal two-lever function** of the left arm and club shaft is only available when the left shoulder joint is behind the ball at impact. Players in Group I have a significant mechanical advantage over players in the other three groups.

Where is the left wrist at impact?

In Groups 1 and 2, the left wrist is bowed out ahead of the ball at impact. In Groups 3 and 4, the exact opposite conditions (the most common error in golf) is displayed. The left wrist is bent back in a concave position behind the ball. Also, the club head is behind the hands through impact in Groups I and II, while it has passed the hands before impact in Groups 3 and 4 causing a loss of power and pressure on the ball.

Please Note: Research has shown that where the left shoulder is placed at address will influence both the left wrist and left shoulder at impact. Better players start, then get the left shoulder more behind the ball, developing a mechanical advantage that higher handicap players do not create in their swings.

When the shaft is parallel to the ground in the downswing, is the swing path in-to-out, or out-to-in?

Players in Groups 1 and 2 have in-to-out swing paths. However, players in Groups 3 and 4 have out-to-in swing paths. Studies show as handicaps go up, the swing path becomes dramatically more out-to-in, causing a loss of power and direction

When the right forearm is parallel to the ground in the downswing, is the angle between the shaft and the left arm 90 degrees or less?

Professional and low handicap golfers in Group I displayed the smaller loss of angle between the left arm and shaft before impact.

Players in Groups 3 and 4 **dissipate power** by opening the angle both early and more than Groups 1 and 2. Within Groups 3 and 4, Group 3 holds the angle longer than Group 4 because Group 3 has their left shoulder joint closer (but still ahead) of the ball than Group 4 both at address and impact; Players in Group 1 are behind the ball and create the greatest amount of power.

Where was the left arm at impact, in relation to the club head?

For the greatest mechanical advantage, the left arm should be ahead of the club head at impact or at least pointing at it, avoiding club head deceleration through ball contact.

In Groups 3 and 4, the left arm is behind the club head at impact (Group 4 more than Group 3).

Players in Group 2 have the left arm somewhat even with the club head at impact.

In Group I the left arm is forward of the club head. Studying the left arm relationship to the club head at impact is similar to evaluating the left wrist at impact, but research shows studying the left arm more accurately reflects a golfer's ability to deliver force to the ball through impact.

Is most of a player's swing force on the left or the right foot at impact?

Past research in this area did not report using large numbers of excellent golfers. The studies in Reno by Dr. Greenwald and his team used the swings of 50 excellent golfers. Also, the left and right foot were evaluated independently.

Swings were performed with each foot placed on an AMTI 0R6-6 Force Plate, bolted into a concrete floor. Three dimensional kinematic data was also gathered. Analysis of the vertical (down) forces during the downswing found 82 percent of the players had loaded their right foot prior to impact. "When I feel my weight has been transferred to my left side, actually it has not been, but it feels that way for every golfer." - Cary Middlecoff

Yes, weight is ultimately transferred, however, impact should ideally occur at a time of stability, preceded by an increasing load on the right foot at impact.

Fourteen of the golfers tested were successful Long-Drive competitors, who had reached national levels of competition, and 93 percent or 13 out of 14 increased the load on the right foot prior to impact.

Sound swings and excellent golfers comply with the universal laws of force and motion rather than fight them. To change is not easy, however, if you have been trying to drive your legs to get to your left side, in an attempt to deliver maximum force down into the ball at impact, you may be working against a natural law that can help your power.

Newton's Third Law is, "For every action there is an equal and opposite reaction." This would indicate to me that golfers should feel pressure and weight going down plane into the right leg and foot during downswing for maximum power at impact. They should not be driving their legs to get to the left side.

My General Suggestions:

- Address the ball with your left shoulder joint over or behind the ball. (driver swings)
- At the end of the backswing, the left shoulder joint should be more behind the ball than at address as a result of it moving down its plane.
- During downswing have the feeling the club head has been left behind, as rotation moves the shoulders down their plane, the arms and hands down their plane, and the club shaft down, its plane always with the feeling the club head is trailing the hands, and the hands trail the right elbow.

What Do Tour Players "Feel?"

At every level of the game, from tour players, to high and low handicap golfers, a "feel" for the shot at hand may be the most important element of playing good golf. Feel is a useful and important tool. With this in mind I sent eight questions to players on the PGA and LPGA tours, to learn what they feel. Some answers were predictable, others were not. Feel is personal in nature, and the foundation for learning to play good golf. Suggestions for developing your own feeling sensations are given at the end of this section.

Reading and learning about what the best players in the world feel when they are playing should help every golfer's game. As you look through the following, keep in mind that these players were describing what they feel, they were not describing a swing theory.

1. Do you have any thoughts about "feel"?

Most professionals said under the pressure of playing tournament golf, a "feel" was more important than a mechanical thought.

> *"By having a feel for the whole swing, (not its pieces) while under pressure, I know it was helpful in wining a US Open"*
>
> "I recall the feel of many great shots – then duplicate that feel."
>
> "Being a rookie on Tour, I've learned there are a lot of different looking swings on Tour, some are not pretty – but everybody has great short game feel."
>
> "Feeling a shot before I swing is just as important as pulling the right club, and having the right yardage."
>
> "Two weeks ago I was one shot out, going into the final round – The fog came up and I could not see the edges of the fairways or greens. I lost my feel, and finished 8th."
>
> "I think all great players rely on feel much more then theory or mechanics when the heat is on. Even though Crenshaw has different feel than Watson."
>
> "You have timing, pace, tempo, rhythm. With a good grip and feel you can be an excellent player."
>
> "It is a feel game, practice mechanics, play by feel."
>
> "When I play my best, All I am concerned about is my feel, not mechanics."
>
> *"We must know mechanics, but we need feel to play different shots on the course."*
>
> "Feel is how we reproduce trained skills."
>
> "Difficult to teach, but feel can be learned."
>
> "Feel is like your instinct. When you get into the hunt, I believe our feel is the most important thing."
>
> "Feel is possibly the most important word in my golf game."

2. What does address "feel like"?

The most common description Tour players used was "balanced," followed by "comfortable, stable, relaxed, ready to move".

We could say **motion** is the common denominator in all sport (i.e. we have baseball motion, tennis motion, etc.). The common denominator in efficient motion is **balance or balancing**. Balancing must be every golfers first consideration at address, during the swing and at the finish. By replacing the term balance with **balancing**, golfers may get a better feel for what is actually happening. Golfers with efficient swings are in motion and are balancing in three-dimensional space; side to side, front to back, up to down, from address to finish.

At Address:

"I feel balanced side to side and front to back."

"I try not to stop moving, keeping a good rhythm even before I take the club back."

It was interesting that many players mentioned they felt their hands hanging down (not arms hanging) at address.

"I feel hanging hands, that feel soft."

"I feel my hands hanging under my shoulder."

Many players said they feel the club is part of their body at address.

"I feel the club is like another arm, leg, or part of my body."

"I feel oneness with the club, a sense of control and awareness."

"I feel part of the club."

"I feel my club becomes one with my arms and hands."

Note: Just one player mentioned alignment and ball position. Only a few mentioned weight distribution. It is important that every golfer realize the importance of the elements of ball location and weight distribution. I can only assume that for Tour Players, ball location, alignment, and weight distribution are not evaluated through feel, but by the actual requirements for the shot at hand.

Tournament players say they feel relaxed and ready to move, balanced with nothing static. However, most club golfers look very tense and non-athletic.

3. What do you "feel" when you hold the club?

The most common answer Tour players gave is one I believe most club golfers would not. Tour players said they "feel" the weight of the club. Also, half the players said they feel a firm grip, and the other half feel a soft grip.

Holding the golf club:

"I want to feel my fingers melt onto the club and become one."

"A stuck feeling."

"The hands feel as a one piece unit."

"My hands feel like they are one."

"I feel like my hands are glued to the club."

"I feel equal pressure, and my hands keep equal pressure during my waggle, both hands working in unison."

"I want to feel a heavy club."

"I feel soft hands and arms."

"I feel the overall weight of the club."

"Lightness in my shoulders, firm in my hands."

"I feel the balance of the club and it's swing."

"I feel the weight of the club and flex of the shaft."

Efficient swings impact the ball with force. Players do need some pressure from their hands on the grip to accomplish force at impact. **It's my guess that golfer's with strong hands feel a light grip, golfers with less strength in their hands feel a firm grip.**

Tour players said they feel the weight of the club. Most club golfers fill their minds with distracting thoughts. Many club golfers never become aware of the weight of the club. But by not grounding the club at address, (Jack Nicklaus) you will start to be aware of the weight of the club. This is a very important feel.

4. What do you "feel" during the backswing?

Six players answered they "feel" everything – a one piece, all together backswing.

Five players answered they "feel" a hands and arms backswing.

85% of the players said they "feel" a shoulder turn, or a body coil; or hips and shoulder turning in the backswing.

Some players feel their hands and arm. Some have a one piece feeling. Others feel body, hip, or shoulder turn. Most everyone described a free flowing rotation and coil behind the ball.

In the Backswing:

"I feel a lot of turning and loading – I feel the shoulders turning into right hip."

"The main feel is a flow – power/energy throughout the body."

"I feel the body turn the club over the right shoulder."

"I feel the club flowing into a proper swing plane."

"I key on my hands for a feel of swing plane and clubface position."

"I feel controlled moves when I practice, but I don't play that way – I just feel the target."

"I feel a strong coil to my right heel."

"I feel coiled behind the ball."

"I feel coiled in my upper body."

"I feel shoulder coil."

"I feel a giant coil inside my body."

5. What do you "feel" during the downswing?

The most common answer had to do with a **lagging feeling** that players described in different ways. Only four players mentioned a feeling of using the hands or arms to start the downswing. More then half the players talked about some feel in their left side to start the downswing. No player mentions any pushing feelings in the downswing.

"A lag feeling in my upper body."

"The club lagging, following body motion."

"The club feels delayed, the shoulders pulling the club through."

" I feel my left side start, then my arms and hands follow with a lagging club."

"I feel my left knee drive to the target."

"I feel conscious movement to the left."

During **efficient transfer of energy during the downswing** the club is building up its velocity. If the downswing starts too fast, players miss the opportunity to experience this natural and powerful accumulation of force. Efficient swings on Tour have been described in these ways:

"I feel like I'm in slow motion."

"I feel I am holding the club at the top as long as possible."

"I feel the body uncoil, and a gun going off at the last second."

"I feel a smooth transition from the top, and increasing speed of the clubhead."

6. Do you have any special "feeling" at the end of your swing?

The most common answer, almost to a player, was "balance,". This was also the most common answer about address. If most club golfers would put aside all the tips well meaning friends offer and focus on a balanced finish, their game would improve. **A feel for balance** may be one key that would help every golfer.

"I feel like Fred Couples follow-through – when I'm swinging good."

"Awareness of Balance."

"Balance is usually the first feel that comes to mind."

"Balance and total release of energy."

"Nicely balanced on my left side, not forward."

"Balance with a tilted spine."

All efficient swings (no exception) have the players spine tilted both over to the ball and away from the target. Ben Hogan once said, *"The hardest part of the swing is staying bent over for two seconds."*

"I feel my right shoulder lower than my left."

"A feeling of holding my finish without trying."

"A feeling of completeness – as if all the air has gushed out of a balloon."

Again, Tour players are aware of balance before, during, and after their swing motion. A useful goal for any golfer.

7. During the swing – any "feels" for your head?

Most tour players said they were aware that the head may move a little in their backswing. However they still like the feeling of a steady head. Players say they feel the head staying back. Studies show the head moves back a little at the start of the downswing, but it is perfectly steady as the swing moves from waist high to waist high through impact.

"I feel my head resting on top of my body as the swing winds up and releases."

"I like to feel my head moves a little because of my body turn back."

"I feel the head behind ball contact, as weight is pulled through the hitting area."

"I feel I swing past my chin."

"I feel level eyes parallel to the target line."

"There should be no feeling of strain in the neck."

One key to proper or efficient head location is a spine that angled over to the ball and away from the target during address, backswing, downswing, and finish.

8. Do you "feel" any difference when playing short game shots?

Most says *"yes"*. The most common answers had to do with "lack of tension". Less body motion and pre-swing rehearsal of the shot was also mentioned. As they pay attention to **speed and feel**.

"I feel soft hands and light arms."

"A physical rehearse the shot to get the feel – and use imagery of results."

"I feel very light hands."

"I feel more linear and less circular."

Paul Runyan, the great short game player/instructor, suggests a feeling of the shaft being more vertical at address to produce a less circular swing for short game shots.

"I use more feel, less mechanical thoughts around the green."

"I try to feel the ball bounce off the club, instead of launching the ball."

"I feel softer hands, and I'm more aware of rhythm."

"I feel I use less angles and softer hands (no wrist cock, or elbow fold)."

"I feel no build up of energy and slow tempo."

Dave Pelz has a good suggestion – *"feel equal size hip turn and shoulder turn for less build up of energy in your backswing. When hips turn is less than the shoulder turn, it can buildup too much energy in the short game"*.

"Visualize a feel, then practice that feel."

"I feel more open posture."

"I feel light tempo and grip."

"I feel more vertical, and pay attention to speed."

SUGGESTIONS FOR BECOMING AWARE OF YOUR OWN FEELING SENSATIONS:

First, it is **not useful** for long-term learning to stand in one place making the same swing over and over.

**After every third putt, chip, or swing change your target, or size of your swing, or tempo. Golf is played in ever-changing conditions, therefore it helps our progress to train and practice in conditions that also change.

**Use one club (9 iron) and hit shots different distances, 70 yards, 90 yards, 110 yards.

**Putt one ball across the green, now putt the next ball half that distance, and the next ball half that distance, and so on.

When your are working on your **feel, keep your mind free of swing tips. Stay aware of the feel of your swing and the results that feel is producing.

**Hitting balls with your eyes closed, helps improve trust in your swing and awareness of what feel your swing produces.

**After a swing you like and you are pleased with the ball flight, call those results "vanilla", then just say, "vanilla" before your next swing, without any swing keys.

Poor Concepts, Misconceptions, and Lies

- Golfers must hold the club lightly.
- The legs are a swings major source of power.
- The clubface must stay on a straight line after impact for twenty inches.
- The clubface must be square at impact.
- The clubface must impact the back of the ball.
- The hips will spring back automatically during the downswing.
- The hips must be restricted in the backswing.
- The hips provide most of the golf swings power.
- The player's face/head must be up at address.
- The player's back or spine must be straight at address.
- The player's arms must be level at impact.
- The hips must turn out of the way to permit the passage of the arms and hands through impact.
- The hands must turnover through impact.
- Most of the player's weight must be over the left side before impact.
- The shoulders must turn level through impact.
- Player's must push off their right leg during the downswing.
- Centrifugal force causes the wrist to unhinge.
- The swing lifts the ball into the air.
- The club must swing back on a straight line.
- Swinging slow will improve ball flight.
- Shoulders must be square at address.
- The hands must speed up through impact.
- Clubhead velocity at impact is more important than at separation.
- Golfers must roll their hand at impact.
- Golfers must keep their left arm firm.
- Golfers should let their head move through impact (not after).

All of these concepts violate the natural principles of motion and force.

Chapter Five

The Nature of Learning
And
The Nature of Golf Instruction

Note: This chapter can be read as presented, or by opening to any heading and start reading there.

INTRODUCTION

This introduction is being written after the rest of the book has already gone to print and could be seen as a postscript. I am on a plane returning from the World Scientific Golf Conference for The Future of Golfers. It was held March 11th - 15th, 2001 at Arizona State University. The director of the conference was Debbie Crews, PhD., and Lori Lutiz coordinated it **with the hope it could influence and improve learning and playing golf in the future.** During the week scientists and educators from all over the world shared their ideas and research about learning motion patterns, some of which I had already included here in Golf Swing Secrets... and Lies. This was reassuring to me and I decided to write this introduction, we could say, postscript.

It was an honor for me to be asked to be a presenter at this prestigious conference, but it was also invaluable to be in the company of leading scientists and educators as they discussed current research and shared their experiences. This conference was one of the most, if not the most, useful conference I have ever attended. During the week some research pointed out the following:

Random Training supports long-term retention of skills more efficiently than drills. When training, it is always useful to change environments, or the size, speed and shape of motions.

Self-Learning – Education by "selection" or choice, is more effective for long-term retention of skills than "how to" directions. Being aware of "external" stimulus (i.e. the shot at hand, or where you want the club shaft at impacts) is more effective than focusing "internally" on moving body parts.

A Learning Model that is "general in nature" is more effective for retention of skills than a specific expert model. Highly skilled motions can be (and should be) acquired from models that are just "in the ball park".

Effective Learning Environments that support retention of skills, 1.) Focuses on the learner, not poor habits; 2.) Helps the "learner" discover the changes that are needed; 3.) Provides learners with the opportunity to "personalize information" and develop the tools of adapting to the shot at hand.

Neurologically learning golf's motion patterns is not different from learning other motion patterns. According to the National Learning Foundation, **agile learners** are not passive sponges of information or "how to" advice. **Agile learners** have mastered information and turned it into knowledge that is personal in nature with **reflections** and **choices** that were personal.

Secret: **It is education by "selection", not "how to" advice that leads to long-term progress. *"We have lost touch with own experiences as our main source of personal learning and development."* – David Kolb. Improving long-term learning skills often starts with reversing, recycling, restoring, any misconceptions and poor concepts about learning and the skill to be learned.**

There are a number of factors that can fragment learning including: stress, rigid systems, drills, rote learning, expert models, lack of core knowledge, little or no creative play, little sensory stimulation, little opportunity for developing imagination, few chances to solve problems, training in a "get it" or "did not get it" environment, and consistent low level skill testing.

Chapter Six is about the Nature of Learning, and I would like to end this introduction by pointing out that perhaps the greatest gift that anyone can receive, and really the only gift worth having (beyond health) is a **desire to keep learning.** But, keep in mind, some approaches to learning are more effective than others.

The Nature of Learning

Without some insights into the nature of learning, how can any approach to instruction or learning be effective?

"It's a miracle that the modern methods of instruction have not entirely strangled all curiosity of inquiry"

- Albert Einstein

Secret: **Experiencing movement is the only door to learning movement.**

"There are some things a man can be taught, but golf may not be one of them. The most a teacher can do is tell you his deductions, he can not give experience. Every golfer must have experiences of his own and use them to their best advantage. I do not believe any really good golfer has been taught their game."

- George Low 1899

"Learning is the ability to make sense out of something you observe, based on your experience"

- Art Winter

"All behaviors, good, bad, or indifferent, are learned."

- Author Unknown

OUR MOST VALUABLE LESSON—LEARNING WHAT CAN'T BE TAUGHT

What's written here in **Golf Swing Secrets...and Lies** mirrors portions of knowledge I've learned from others. It also shares insights I've gained over time about learning the game. Hopefully this book will also reflect the appreciation and feelings I have for the game. There is much to appreciate about golf: its courses and their architects; the game's great players and their memorable shots; the games ability to make a difference in someone's life; and of course its history and traditions. Golf is an activity where people can enjoy each other's company, what they are doing, and enjoy where they are doing it. As a golf instructor, I have the opportunity to possibly enhance these experiences, and it is in this spirit I've written what follows.

While helping people with their golf cannot be compared to helping someone with a serious medical problem, I have always tried to do my best to keep the information I use in my work about the swing, the human body, playing and learning the game as current and effective as possible. Golf equipment (clubs and balls) and the field of play (grass and playing conditions) have all improved over time. However, on the other hand, some people feel many golfers may not be moving in the same direction. If these golfers were improving the average USGA handicap would probably have gone down over time, but statistics show it has not.

Everyone who reads golf instruction, realizes that books by different world-class players will contain different suggestions. Putting these occasions and individual differences aside, I ask, *"Over time, how can so many well meaning suggestions from the golf instruction community be in such disagreement, sharing little common ground?"* For example, almost every book, video, and TV tip is in conflict with the next one. The title of a book I came across a few years ago was, 57 Ways to Get More Power (Can you imagine – 57 ways!)

For over 100 years, "how to" advice for improving ones golf has come from a variety of "recognized sources" and because of these sources, it has been accepted as quality information. However these sources are often in disagreement over, "how to". Are there any cracks in the quality? How useable can "How To" instruction be if recognized and accepted sources can't narrow their ideas. Some arrogance about ideas, like "some" of most things is not bad. But when arrogance to an idea reaches the point where it can possibly impede progress, that is another question. When it comes to the information available to golfers who would like to improve there has always been strong controversy, almost a rage of values within the golf industry. This should and can change.

It's not unreasonable to believe everything can be improved including how people have been trying to learn to play golf. Schools and informal education have been with us longer than we know, but learning has only been studied in detail over the last fifty years. Hopefully, as the world of education improves its understanding and approach to learning, golfers will be open to their discoveries and start to apply some different techniques and approaches for learning golf.

Secret: **The most valuable lesson golfers can receive from instruction maybe the awareness of what instruction can't teach.**

We have all heard the expression "street smarts". Good golf is founded on "golf smarts" and like "street smarts" gained mostly through self-discovery and not from someone's "how to" lists of do's and don'ts. Successful businessman and author Mark McCormick has defined street smarts (or golf smarts) as *"ability to make positive use of your instincts, insights, and perceptions to get where you want to go,"* In his book, What They Don't Teach You At Harvard Business School, McCormick said, *"In fairness to the Harvard Business School, what they don't teach you they can't teach you"*. Perhaps the sub title to Golf Swing Secrets... and Lies should be *"What golf instruction can't teach, and self-discovery can"*. In McCormick's opinion, an MBA or an LLB are both worthwhile endeavors and good introductions to business. However, as an education and an ongoing learning process they only provide a foundation.

Secret: Golfers should understand where a foundation for an efficient swing **stops**, and learning to play good golf in ever changing conditions **starts**.

When people read non-instructional books, they normally read to be swept away by the magic of a writer's imagination. The magic of words can cause readers to invent their own dreams, transporting people on flights only dreams are made of. A book can also be a reader's **private guide** to any noble plans they may have. Books can provide a pilgrimage of progress that can nurture old workable habits, or find ways to develop new ones. When people read golf instruction books, they are normally couriers for knowledge that can make a difference. Yes, some books can cause readers to dream. This book on the other hand was written to help people gain insights that start journeys into territories where new perceptions and progress have their start.

Studies referred to in this book show that the way people have been trying to learn golf, can be improved. Informed by some experience with subjects like **Anatomy**, (a players most important piece of equipment is their body); **Bio-Mechanics**; **Physiology**; **Geometry**; **Physics**; **Principles of Force and Motion**; the **Nature of Learning**; **the design of the club and ball**; (to name a few sources of information) I wrote this book.

There is a human tendency to have heroes in our lives, especially in sport. Many people make models out of sports figures that do well. At times they attempt to copy their styles, looking to them for guidance. But this very human tendency (copying heroes) can hurt and slow down progress when it comes to learning golf. **Golfers should always see themselves and be seen as individuals.** Each has their own personal style, and I have found progress is built on self-discovery and not by trying to copy someone else's approach. While there are a few (not many) important essentials that appear in all efficient swings, every champion applies them in his or her own best way. In this book I am suggesting that readers should develop an approach for learning to improve their golf based on self-discovery and awareness of Golf's Physical Basics, and not someone else's "how to do it" list. (The game has always had a golfer swing a stick, to flight a ball, on a field of play, hopefully using effective balance and swing-time.) These physical basics that have been at the foundation of the game from day one were discussed in Chapters Two and Three.

Ride Your Own Wave

Studies have shown that golfers don't need specific directions for their journey to a specific goal. By finding ways to let information about golf's environment in, progress follows. Long-term learning is never about giving people the answers, its about helping people learn to ask the right questions. *"Self-education is the only real education that there is. Schools and instruction advice can only make self-education easier. Beyond that, they do little"* - Isaac Asimou

What is learned "best" is learned almost unconsciously as we ponder questions and make mistakes. We learn "best" with rich experiences from self-discovery as we interact with the environment and the shot at hand. We learn "best" coming face to face with problems to be solved, not from drills and expert models.

Secret: **Every golfer has three systems. Their mind, their body and their emotions and we learn best when all three are in balance. I.e. our mind can see, our body can do, and our emotions allows it to happen.**

Any actual sensory experience is difficult to write down or talk about. For one person to express information about motion or abstract feels that would be useful to someone else, is a serious challenge if not impossible. Learning to make progress in golf normally requires an intellectual (learning) temperament that most forms of instruction advice do not mention.

This book is geared to life-long learners with little or lots of time for training. The content here hopes to help golfers develop pathways for progress. It is important that golfers train with "feels" and "insights" of their own choosing. **Ride your own wave.** By harvesting our own and probably unexpected insights, long term learning becomes possible.

While "how to" suggestions from experts may convey ideas about playing and swinging, they can never convey the "flavor" or "feel" need to make progress, that self-discovery provides. Any thrill of the unexpected insight will also be missing. Some golfers will always be convinced because "how to" advice is coming from experts, the advice is like Rumpelstiltskin, and will be able to turn straw into gold. I have found that there is little or no gold in "how to" directions.

"How to" advice may ease what ails people in the short term, but it also produces the harmful side effect of little long-term progress from our efforts. By improving ones learning potential, the "hope of progress" becomes a reality. Self-discovery and awareness skills are the only tools that I know of that are personal in nature. **What else could we ask for?**

It can help long term progress to say "there really are no experts". **We only have the gift of sharing personal experiences with each other.** The more opportunities and tools we use to share experiences the less limiting any learning experiences will be for both the given and receiving of advice.

Stopping the Struggle

Information only works when it is true and can be personalized. **Golfers who have experienced long-term progress had an experimental bend to them.** By starting with a workable approach for learning golf, progress becomes easier. I have said that golf can't be taught like subjects in school, but golf can be learned.

In a school class room, teachers use words and numbers to transfer information. Then students are expected to give back these exact words and numbers on tests. When trying to learn the motion of any physical skill **the most valuable information** does not come from the advice giver, it normally comes from the learner (player). When trying to improve, what golfers see, feel, and can remember is more valuable than someone else's "how to" directions.

Learning and skill acquisition studies indicate that telling someone "how to" feel this or that, or "how to" perform, is not as useful as asking the learner to describe what they see and feel when doing this or that. Having them explain their impressions of what this skill requires is a step in the direction of long-term progress. "How to" advice about moving body parts normally fragments personal insights.

People do not go to golf ranges and ski slopes and try to copy golfers and skiers who are failing to demonstrate balanced and coordinated motions. Everyone recognizes pleasant looking motion. While people can recognize orthodox motions, they often need to be guided past all the misconceptions and poor concepts they make when watching these workable patterns of motion.

People without core knowledge about any skill will often misinterpret and misapply information about that skill. It seems to me, that people who are not happy with the kind of progress they believe they are capable of, need to improve their approach to learning and avoid "how to" suggestions about performing motion. *"There is always one moment when a door opens and it lets the future in."* - Graham Green.

Goals and Dreams

We should not confuse a goal with day dreams and wishful thinking. Day dreams are merely fantasies that require no actions on the part of the dreamer. Dreamers say, *"Wouldn't it be nice if ________".* On the other hand, goals are dreams that are acted on. Goals involve defined plans that must be carried out.

It seems that the most successful goals and plans are organized into three stages: long-range, intermediate and short range. Keep in mind that long-range goals and plans tend to weaken without a short-range goal that is within our reach. Any short-range goal should be one that is reachable. Hopefully readers will find Golf Swing Secrets and Lies a useful tool for reaching your goals in golf and maybe beyond.

How any and all golf instruction (books, friends, videos, etc.) interacts with golfers, fully depends on the view held by both the giver and receiver about the nature of learning. If a golfer has always been told "**how to**" do it, and that is their perception of what golf advice is; when they are asked to consider a "**what to**" approach – the most frequent reaction is that it can't be done "that way", or this "won't work".

As I said earlier, I grew away from a "**how to**" approach to golf instruction years ago. Moreover I do not see myself going back to the approach to which I was first exposed when I started to play golf. Most of the information people are given over time about anything is gathered **unconditionally**. This information is accepted without questions or doubts – we could say **mindlessly** on blind faith (after all it's coming from some expert or a friend). Most of the information we are given is presented in a single perspective. People then process the information in that manner, as though it was workable in every situation.

The quality of any motion is founded on accuracy of the brains perception of that motion. Before effective motion can be repeated, effective motion patterns must exist in the brains motor memory.

Secret: **You may find that the most useful approach to any long-term learning (not only in golf) is open, not absolute. It seems that the more rigidly original information is presented and learned, the harder it can be for the learner to be open to new insights, and up to the task of creating options for different conditions and situations.**

Golf instruction traditionally has given students packaged "**how to**" information that is largely option free and not personally relevant. This information is then processed as absolute information to be memorized. "**How to**" information does not give any reasons to doubt. Unfortunately it also does not quite give people the tools to open or personalize packaged information. Packaged "**how to**" information may help a golfer for a few swings, but normally does not lead to any long-term learning.

In general, most education has focused on the outcome and not the process by which outcomes are achieved. Everyone is born with the **natural desire to explore**. Just watch small children. But, over time, "**how to**" education often kills off this natural desire to explore and to gain personal insights.

Note: Education for outcomes often creates mindless learners trapped by **"how to"** information with no personal insight into the process by which the outcome can be accomplished. Just watch most golfers and their friends at a driving range.

Of course by using our natural desire to explore, self-discovery and awareness skills, the information with which each person can best learn with is uncovered and forever known. When a "**what to**" approach is used, people see for themselves what information is the most useful for the outcome they want. By avoiding a "**how to**" do it approach that is not personal in nature, long-term learning becomes a real possibility.

A PHILOSOPHY

It would be difficult to fully describe someone's philosophy about golf instruction, but some of my feelings about learning golf can be found in the following quotes:

> *"A student must learn sooner or later to use their own judgment of play and not to depend on the assistance of others."* - John Duncan Dunn (1920's)

> *"There are at least six people who want to be taught golf for the one who wants to learn."*
> - Tommy Armour (1950's)

> *"Practice without a foundation is like the captain of a ship without a compass."*
> Leonardo Da Vinci 1500's (**Golf's Physical Basics** can be a foundation)

> *"Without recognizing the scientific basics of an effective swing, it is impossible to distinguish essentials from personal mannerisms in a swing."* - Alex Morrison (1920's)

Many of today's golfers know enough about the swing, but maybe not enough about learning one! You could say at times we are drowning in swing information. But at the same time we are starving for knowledge about how to learn the information.

Secret: **One challenge for golfers is to become personally aware of what is relevant information and what is not relevant information for them.**

It has been said that when children are learning, they have no pre-conceived ideas (or misconceptions) about how outcome happens. Children are open to self-discovery and have little blocking their learning/thinking minds. Children are in their own little discovery zones, **without others telling them what to do or how to see and feel motion.** Children are open to self-discovery. This leads to long-term learning that adults often do not achieve after being told what to do.

Today, in many cases, the natural process of learning directly from experience is often undermined by "how to" instruction (with expert after expert telling us what to do). The word **education** comes from a Latin word "educare" meaning **to lead out**. This indicates that the intelligence within us needs to be drawn out. **The primary function of effective instruction is to draw out what is already there and thereby help golfers to develop useful insights and perceptions for their game and swing.**

I am not so sure we can teach a golf swing. A golf swing is a little like someone's signature, it's very personal in nature. **Instruction that leads to long-term learning and not just a quick fix, is probably more an act of providing and supporting a learning environment.** An environment in which people are learning in their own best way is an environment in which they learn at their own pace. While penmanship and a golf swing are both personal in nature, they are both trainable. Looking back, we were taught how to recognize and be aware of correct letters and numbers, but no one taught us how to write. We were guided, (not taught) as we learned how to physically write in our own best way. **Hopefully "Golf Swing Secrets ..... and Lies" will help golfers discover and learn what really cannot be taught by someone else about the swing and playing the game.**

Secret: It is not what instruction information says that's important, it's what the learner **hears, understands** and **remembers that's important.**

Golfers normally do not reach their potential unless they understand what they are trying to do. Understanding from useful insights and accurate perception of information becomes the foundation for long-term learning.

Respected instructor and long-time friend Bill Strausbaugh once said, ***"It is not very hard to see the difference between good and bad golf, why then is good golf so hard to accomplish? Good golf of course is a combination of talent (God given) and technique that is learned and acquired."*** **Bill went on,** ***"Golf is a game where we are not looking at the target when we are in motion, applying principles that do not change in conditions that do change with every swing. It is a game where it is important to understand the whole before a person tries to develop its parts."***

Secret: **Many golfers want to simplify golf's curriculum as they look for ways to stop their struggle to make progress. Golf's curriculum is non-negotiable. It's based on the principles of motion and force. What can be made more effective is our approach for learning the curriculum. All golfers can improve, perhaps some more than others, but everyone playing golf today can improve by improving their learning potential.**

VALUE OF INFORMATION

It seems people tend to put more value in what could be called **conscious** information (books, magazines, the spoken word) than **experience** or **unconscious** information. This preference could be described as knowledge without experience. However, we all know that experiencing anything can be more valuable than reading or hearing about it. People often have impressions that are not accurate, and when allowed to physically experience the environment, they see that lack of accuracy.

Secret: **Being half-right accomplishes nothing! The real challenge is to acquire useable insights and allow them to happen.**

Studies show imagination and intuition are probably the **best tools** for learning a sports skill, with memorization the **lowest form.**

- We learn best when we are in the mood.
- We learn best when we are not in a hurry.
- We learn best when we accept we may have to go back to go forward.
- We learn best from people we like.
- We learn best when we realize we will never own the golf swing.
- We learn best with a desire to learn, not a desire to hit the ball better.
- We learn best, if we know more good rounds come from good thinking, putting and wedge shots then making perfect swings.

It may be useful to say people have two minds. One is their **thinking/knowing** mind, and the other is their **feeling/awareness** mind. To be aware of what you are currently feeling, is a good first step for golfers who want to make a change. Awareness skills improve, **when "how to" directions stop.**

Secret: The most useful approach to learning anything (not only golf) develops the tools to learn. Successful players have come to realize that **learning is something we allow to happen** and not something we do.

MORE LIGHT

Our ability to make progress is based on our ability to increase understanding and improve insights. Our ability to increase understanding and improve insights could be thought of as putting more light on the subject.

See yourself as a system of lights. Light represents consciousness and the brighter the light the more understanding of which you are capable. **To improve, you need to be conscious of information you may have overlooked in the past.** You could say, we need more light.

"Language is so removed from experience that words do not trigger the true sensations to which they refer". – Author Unknown

The light a book or instructor can provide is very important, but this is not light from your own understanding, and it can only travel at a certain frequency. The light from a book cannot be made to go brighter by the learner. However when a book or instructor causes the learner to turn up their own light, learners can now see things for themselves.

Secret: **When your personal perception or light improves, it will always be brighter than the light someone else can cast for you.** Your perception is now reinforced by the quality of your own understanding, and not just the light that a book or an instructor can provide.

TWO INSTRUCTORS

We could say there are two categories of instructors: PHYSICAL and NON-PHYSICAL. Both are important to our progress, **but in my view the non-physical is more important than the physical**.

PHYSICAL INSTRUCTORS stand with students. This type of instruction also includes "how to" articles, books, and tapes. The non-physical instructors cannot be seen, but they can provide as much, if not more useful information than can physical instructors for a student's progress.

NON-PHYSICAL INSTRUCTORS include memory, experience, fears, understanding, intuition, negative or positive thinking, self-image, creativity, knowledge, will, perception, commitment, insights and feels.

There is a line in the movie City of Angles, where Nicholas Cage asks Meg Ryan, *"What does a pear taste like?"* She replies, *"You don't know what a pear tastes like?"* To which he replies, *"I don't know what a pear tastes like to you."*

A physical instructor, book, tape, or article can help you to understand what your choices and experiences represent. They can provide you with the knowledge that will allow you to choose. But when non-physical instructors are involved, students can truly understand and personalize knowledge.

Secret: When we set out to learn, improve or change our golf game, in many cases we will not see improvement or progress initially. We may even regress, but this is only natural. **Learners must know and learn the differences between learning and performing, and train accordingly.** When learning we should be less concerned with the results, while focusing on **what** is changing habits.

AN ACTOR'S INSIGHT

Secret: **Golf Swings can be to complicated for words, but not too complicated for awareness and self-discovery.**

In a recent interview award-winning actor/director Ron Howard revealed some interesting insights about learning. He started in show business as a child actor and said, *"Most child actors are not taught how to act, they are taught somewhat like trained animals are taught how to perform. But I had a father who was an actor and he taught me to be aware and think about what I was doing. I always felt I was learning a craft."* (How many golfers can say that about their approach to golf?)

"I understood what I was doing, and I gained confidence." (How many golfers can say that?)

"I was not just performing like a trained animal...I was always working towards something." (How many golfers can say that?)

"I understood the process, and always enjoyed it, and was comfortable. (How many golfers can say that?) *"I felt other kid actors resented what they were made to do."*

"I saw passion and commitment in my dads approach to his own acting, he had a willingness to dig." (How many golfers can say that about their game?)

Golf is not only a worthwhile pastime played by both the young and not so young. The game has much to share if we are open to learning. **To play golf successfully requires prompt but careful judgment as golfers are faced with problems under circumstances that normally never occur twice.** Golf is an exercise of walking, thinking, and striking, all done when played successfully with cool judgment. It is a pastime of many advantages, and there are few things in all of sport that can compare to playing good golf.

I am aware that talking about awareness and self-discovery may be a thorny issue for golfers who have used and relied on "how to do it" approaches for learning. **The corner stone of golf's ultimate classroom is a golfers response**. Responses are more positive and long-lasting, when people are guided and given the freedom to adapt and modify their insights and body motion to golf's environment (i.e. **Golf's Physical Basics). The ultimate golf classroom is also prepared to guide people through unfamiliar terrain filled with secrets and lies that have little common ground.** Effective learning is a traffic cop, sending some ideas away, suggesting others stay.

Lessons in School

When we were first exposed to formal lessons in pre-school and then up through grade school and college, these lessons were all designed and determined by our teachers and schools. However, what was actually learned by students was less definable. In school, students are more often than not shown and told what they must learn. Teachers tell students what they themselves know and in some cases what the student must do. There is very little **self-discovery** in a setting in which teachers solely define and design lessons. This approach, is often carried over to golf advice. This may be one of the main reasons golfers don't make the kind of progress which they are capable of making. This approach lacks **self-discovery.**

- When subjects like math, English, history, foreign language, etc, are being **taught**, students give answers on tests using the exact words and numbers they received from their teachers. These exact words and numbers of course lead to good grades, but students may have no personal understanding or insights into the subject matter. Responses are often being parroted back to the teacher and required no self-discovery.
- It may be worth noting that most of what we were "taught" in school can no longer be recalled, but what **we learned** can be recalled. i.e. Many asked *"why do I have to take history? I will never use it"*. But if we look back we see that when taking history we learned to organize information, write papers, use a library, make an oral report, etc. Even though we can no longer recall most of what we were taught in History class, we did learn some skills we still use today. No one taught us the taste of vanilla ice cream or how to ride a bike. Even after time away from both, they are easily recalled. On the other hand, facts and figures that were taught, are often lost and can't be recalled. As was said earlier, golf advice can come in many forms. Advice has been around as long as the game has been played. Let's call this **conventional "how to do it" advice**. In contrasts the suggestions that are being shared with you here, let's call **alternative self-discovery advice.**

"Lets train the mind to desire what the situation demands" - Seneca

Alternative Advice

Self-discovery advice hopefully sounds like common sense to readers. It will help develop insights and self-discovery skills not used in the past. **This approach is not based on any guru-like secrets about the golf swing**. It's straightforward information about the swing, playing golf, and most importantly long-term progress. In the past conventional advice has focused on symptoms of poor golf rather than prevention and long-term fulfillment. Every golfer who has predictable troubles and untapped resources can benefit from moving away from conventional "how-to-do it" advice, and **into a system of awareness and self-discovery**.

Conventional advice is really secondhand information. It is not as valuable to learners as the first hand personal experience self-discovery offers. With self-discovery skills, players can discover and learn for themselves what must be done.

There are times during which conventional advice has its place. In a short-term emergency, where a golfer is mentally traumatized and is lacking in confidence, a conventional tip may put him or her more at ease mentally for a weekend tournament or important round. This in itself may lead to more enjoyment and a few good shots for a round or two. **But please understand that this kind of advice cannot provide the foundation for any long-term progress.**

- Only self-discovery and personalizing of information deliver the required insights to make changes from within that are personal in nature.
- Over time, most golfers have gathered information and taken advice from others. This is not all bad. Sharing information has improved the quality of life from one generation to the next, but this sharing has also caused people and golfers to overlook their most valuable source of advice – **themselves,** and their own feel and perception of information.

Secret: No one else in the world feels what you do. Two people seldom even describe events that they both see in the same manner. **When compared to self-discovery, any suggestion from the mind of one person to the body of another is not very useful.** Information about moving one's own body must be internal and personal in nature, if it's going to lead to long-term learning.

While it's only human nature to seek advice from others, there is probably more advice available about golf than anyone could or should use. Most of it is telling us what we are doing wrong and how to fix our broken golf game. But **only** when information comes from **within** the player, does he or she have advice that can lead to a change in perception. As you have read, studies show it normally takes a change in perception, leading to new insights, which can accelerate learning.

FIXING SWINGS

Add wisdom to information for **knowledge**, and **reasoning** to knowledge for **insights**.

When golfers are trying to fix what they believe are broken swings and games, they are very receptive to ideas about what to do. Just go to any driving range and watch. **Golf Swing Secrets.....and Lies** has asked readers to become more aware and is not telling people how to do anything, **per se**. You have been asked to become more aware of the clubface, clubhead, and shaft and to rely on your own capacity to develop new insights based on self-discovery and **Golf's Physical Basics**.

Secret: **If people are going to make progress in golf it is important that they believe in themselves and their own capacity to learn and improve. They should avoid some system or the latest "How To" ideas!**

Golf Swing Secrets...and Lies was written to help readers change poor concepts into useful insights and new perceptions. **You may want to look at this somewhat like Christmas at 5 years old and Christmas at 20 years old**, it is the same day, but seen from a new or different perspective. I am not familiar with each reader's information base, so I'm not sure what each of you will take away from reading this book. My goal with this book, as in every lesson, is to help golfers use an approach to learning that has no bottom, and is always interesting. **By combining the nature of learning with the nature of golf,** I'm trying to help golfers learn for themselves what is personally relevant and that which is not, for their swing and game.

Note: Every experienced or new golfer that I have ever worked with, has had the ability to recognize the differences between a relatively good swing and one that was clearly ineffective. Just go to any practice range with a new golfer and ask them which swing they believe would be a good model and which would not. Golfers (even new ones) can see a difference and do not need to be taught (in general) what a good swing looks like.

What they do not know is how to perform an effective swing. Often they cannot, because they have misinterpreted what they are seeing, and have been giving themselves poor concepts of what to do. Progress under such conditions will be slow or even doomed. If people can already recognize (in general) a swing that would be an acceptable model, without much help from me, I feel my time as a golf instructor is then best used **to help golfers learn what is relevant in those efficient swings and what is not**.

As Bobby Jones said, *"intelligent progress is difficult without accurate information."* I have found many golfers base their approaches to improving on their own **secrets**. When looked at from a more objective point of view, these secrets turn out to be **lies**. At times golfers use information they have received from of a variety of sources and have no personal insights or understandings of the information. This information is less useful than personal insights.

Secret: **Golfers often overlook important elements that are present in efficient swings, and misinterpret elements that are there, leaving themselves with poor concepts.**

As I said earlier, I see myself as a guide, someone who during a lesson helps guide golfers through a vast sea of prior information, or what could be called secrets and lies about the swing and game. At times this requires the player to gain an insight he or she didn't have in the past. This change in perception often makes information more useful.

DRILLS: MAYBE NO!

For years, many people have believed the fastest most productive way to learn any task was to rehearse and repeat them over and over using drills. Research found in two books by Dr. Eleanor Langer of Harvard, Mindfulness, and Mindful Learning, and other studies by leaders in the field of skill acquisition now show there are some **problems with this long-held approach.**

The approach of repeating and repeating does not leave much room for self-discovery and rethinking information. Studies now show there are more effective ways of mastering skills. Dr. Langer calls it "mindful learning" (as opposed to mindless), and points out long-term learning requires much more than drills founded on memorization, repetition, and rote. **Conventional learning (mindless drills) depends on behavior that stifles creativity and undermines self-esteem as people struggle and often fail to adequately learn techniques.**

Studies have also shown that using drills leads to boring, mindless, non-focused training sessions that leaves people with little or no insights into the skills they are trying to learn. Using a repeating, unthinking manner to learn can almost guarantee mediocrity.

All drills are based on a **"how to do"** the task approach, that is not giving individuals the opportunity to gain new insights and options. **Expert golfers become experts by developing various ways of using the very same basics some golfers are trying to improve with mindless repetitions**. Studies show learning happens best, when skills are performed in changing conditions (not static). Keep in mind that golfers are rarely if ever faced with the exact same shot or conditions. Experts adapt their skills to a variety of conditions.

Note: **Repetition can create mediocre performance and poor game condition skills.** Most people do not experience (self-discovery) thinking beyond the information they have been given when using drills. When we are learning like robots, rehearsing over and over, it deprives students of maximizing their full potential to learn the application of skills in **ever changing situations**. When using drills players never learn how to use their own unique physical skills, mental abilities, and personalities to their fullest.

Secret: **Simply memorizing the execution of information will not lead to the kind of long-term learning, that awareness and self-directed learning can produce.**

Moving away from the obsessions of trying to get it right in **drills** brings on the joys of learning. Fear of negative evaluation can take the fun out of anything. For example, Dr. Langer points out that *"if we were rated on how fast we completed crossword puzzles, how much enjoyment would we actually get from doing them"*. I suggest, that when lost for a word, having to search for ideas, often requires the mind to do work one feels good about when the answer is found. **Looking** and **finding** really can be more rewarding (Yes, I found it!) than immediately knowing what word the puzzle is looking for.

When learners stop judging themselves when doing drills, and become more involved in the whole experience of learning through awareness and self-help, pleasure and productivity become partners on the path to long-term progress. **I know asking golfers to move away from using drills is controversial, but a decision that studies (and my experiences) show will lead to long-term learning.**

Failing Can Improve Learning Skills

Columbia University Professor of Psychology, Carol S. Dweck, points to research in the field of learning that shows when students complete at task where success is almost assured (with little chance of failure), **learning skills are not enhanced.** When students are either given praise or assume they are making progress after experiencing success with little chance of failure, their **problem solving skills** are not being advanced. Their love of learning and confidence can also be damaged without a real challenge. Developing **learning skills** is often based on trying something we may fail to accomplish at first. **Golfers who continually put themselves in situations that require problem solving, accomplish long-term learning and retention of skills more easily than golfers, who remain content with doing drills.**

Noted psychologist, Dr. Leonard Berkowitz and others who have researched how individuals learn motor skills like golf, points out that human behavior can be classified as occurring in a persons **cognitive domain** (intellect), **motor domain** (physical motion), and **affective domain** (emotion). We learn through all these domains, many golfers overlook how their emotions (affective domain) influence learning and improving more than drills.

Note: Much if not most of our affective or emotional behavior is learned behavior, and is classified into five categories.

A. Awareness – is influenced by emotion.

B. Willing to receive – is influenced by emotion.

C. Responding – is influenced by emotion.

D. Organizing – is influenced by emotion.

E. Characterizing by value – is influenced by emotion.

Secret: For golfers who want to improve, behavior in the affective domain has a strong influence on ones ability to learn. Affective behavior has more influence than drills.

A. Golfers must be **aware** to learn

B. Golfers must be **willing to receive** information to learn.

C. Golfers must **respond** to playing conditions to learn.

D. Golfers must **organize** a plan to learn.

E. Golfers must find **value** in information to learn and reach logical conclusions.

Improving affective behavior, (not drills), influences learning skills that lead to the kind of progress which all golfers would like to accomplish.

RETHINKING THE VALUE OF EXPERT MODELS

When learning a motion (i.e. tennis or golf swing motions) the past common notion has been, it helps to watch an expert model. Expert models were thought to be good representations of what to do, and also a comparison for changing unworkable habits. In the past it has been said the more frequently learners see expert models the stronger the mental blueprint of the model would be, translating into increased abilities to perform and change unworkable motions. As we know coaches from many sports have supported the use of expert models for years.

After years of studies Professor Gibson F. Dardon of Radford University and many others in the field of motor learning now point to evidence that the use of expert models only encourages imitation (much of the following information is based on this work). **Expert models often do not guide learning into retention of the skills (or rules of motion) needed to perform in ever changing real life conditions and situations.** Schmidt, 1991 and Magill 1993 both point out; "*motor skill learning is largely rules learning*".

Typically expert models have provided demonstrations of motion we believed people were able to copy. In fact, there are any number of popular video instruction systems that compare expert models to a learners motion. **This form of training leads to a performance that is called a conditioned reflex**. (Lee, et 1994 p330). Since golf presents ever-changing playing conditions, golfers would be best served by developing **creative skills** that can make adjustments for the shot at hand. **It seems that developing a "conditioned reflex" using drills to copy expert models is not the most useful learning strategy for golf.**

Today, there is evidence that supports using "variable forms" of training (i.e. different speeds, swing sizes, paths, and clubface alignments, in a golf swing motion). Such a diversity of training techniques, does in fact promote more effective learning of the rules of a motion. This approach helps people learn the real nature of **cause and effect** motion patterns and ball flights. This increased variety during a training session often results in a stronger memory of the basic skills needed to influence the clubhead, clubface and shaft through impact.

Repeating an error-free performance (i.e. standing in some swing ring, swinging over and over) imitating an expert model appears to ignore what we now know about learning motions (Mangill 1993, Lee, Et al 1994) – Error free practice and repetition are poor learning strategies. **After a skill has been learned, repeating it over and over can have some value to highly skilled performers, but not for most learners**. Apparently there is real value in missing a foul shot, or missing a serve in tennis or missing a shot in golf. *"Players learn from their mistakes," "Players have to learn what it takes to win," "I must keep putting myself in position to win before I learn what it takes to win,"* are all familiar statements sports announcers and players make.

Secret: Information about workable and unworkable actions, (both mental and physical) must be available for long-term learning. A player's brain and feel system must become educated to a variety of motions. **Becoming aware of the differences in workable and unworkable motion is the first stage of the long-term retention of any skill.**

Golfers looking for long-term learning and skill retention must avoid learning a task under false pretenses (static conditions). Real life performance conditions require problem solving skills and adjustments strategies. If golfers must train and practice on a range I suggest making believe you are playing holes, or change clubs after two swings, as you change targets and size of swings. This kind of variation in training is more useful for long-term learning than imitating expert models using a "how to" list.

Golfers would be better off, when educating themselves about leaning a skill, not to look for immediate success. This approach often causes progress to leave as quickly as it arrived. Learning should be seen as problem solving. At times **problem solving** often does not lead to increased levels of performance during practice. However, since skill development is internal at first and therefore invisible, evidence of a learning transfer can show up at any time. **People should understand the difference in temporary effects of practice and the long-term retention of skills, or we could say, the difference in fixing a habit and changing a habit.**

Secret: **The use of self-discovery skills and problem solving approaches can open a path to long-term retention which "how to" lists and "expert models" can't provide.**

Learning Models

Studies show that people must believe they can achieve a models level of performance. **Often when expert models are used, self-confidence can be damaged**. Without some level of confidence, most individuals would not make progress. Studies now suggest using a **learning model** (not expert), a model that takes into consideration the strengths and limitations of the individual learner. **Any pressure to "do it like the expert" can prevent some people from discovering what can work best for them**. Trying to copy an expert model can stop people form exploring different personal "feels" for being on-plane, and overlooks the power of self-discovery and awareness. Golf is a game of personal adjustments, recovery, and finally numbers.

By their nature **"learning models"** are variable models. They have been found to be very beneficial for long-term learning (Schmidt 1991). **It is now believed when people become more aware in general, non-specific terms** (i.e. aware of on or off-plane swing motion, aware of a clubhead that is behind the players hands through impact, and a clubhead that is not) **its more useful than trying to imitate an expert model**. An expert model can get ones attention and may even increase motivation. But with respect to the process of learning or insights about the skill, **expert models fall short when compared to general descriptions and self-discovery**.

Studies show that it is more useful for people to receive **immediate accurate feedback** about **their** performance than to have information from an **expert model**. Accurate immediate feedback enhances motivation and guides learners away from just trying for results with their ball flight into observations about there current swing motion or about the process of learning. Accurate immediate feedback (using mirrors, and video replays of their own swing) can allow people to become aware of their own motions. **It seems expert models require an accuracy that most times is beyond the skill level of some learners**.

I feel it is very important to recognize while a particular golf swing may be effective, there are a variety of ways (not one way) world-class golfers could approach or may feel a workable swing motion. Yes, tour players all look more or less the same at impact, but they all can have dissimilar "feels" and approaches to similar impact alignments. These "feels" are of course personal in nature and most likely founded on self-discovery of what works best for them.

Using a non-specific generalization (learning model) can be a more effective method for allowing people to become skillful at their current level, especially when combined with accurate and immediate feedback. **It seems golfers would be better off if their model was more or less in the "Ball Park," and not necessarily a perfect picture.** Reference "In the Zone", in Chapter Two.

Secret: **A cutting edge hypothesis points out that the most effective demonstration (model) seems to be one that is only slightly above the learners current skill level. This promotes persistence and self esteem during learning** (McCullagh and Caird 1990).

Several studies question the need of giving people explicit information on how to execute motor skills (Rink 1994). People only need information about appropriate movement patterns to reach the goal of very accurate or explicit patterns of motion. Several recent studies suggest observing a learning model (a non-specific generalization) is more effective than using an expert model. **Allowing people to explore possible solutions is a critical aspect of the learning process**. From this view **expert models** may indeed, restrict learning.

Years ago I wrote about some research that showed when a **picture** (model) was combined with a **feel**, learning could improve up to 70%. It is now obvious to me, the picture used should be that of the learner or of a learning model. By using a mirror or video replay people can evaluate the relationships of their own motions to a general model.

It may be difficult for many of us who have used expert models (including myself) in the past to believe that replacing the expert model with a learning model, enhances learning. But I can say from experience that it does. Studies support these finding. I suggest working with general information rather than very specific details. You may want very specific results and alignments, and progress in that direction is possible for any golfer. **Based on what is now known about learning, golfers should consider moving away from expert models and drills into using a learning model, even when looking for specific alignments and results**. Hank Haney, *"Drills are not very effective, a waste of time"*.

Mindful Exercises

Instead of mindless drills, let's use what I would call **Mindful Exercises**. i.e. When you are trying to improve either your swing plane, balance, or alignment, etc.

- Use a few short swings, then long, and then medium.
- Hit shots left, then right, then some straight.
- Use different swing speeds and different clubs.
- Change something every two or three swings.

Golfers looking for long-term progress should avoid trying to learn a task under **false pretenses,** i.e. static conditions. Every shot at hand requires using problem solving skills to make adjustments for each swing. Golfers, who want long-term progress, must recognize that golf is not played under static conditions. **Consider whether your training is geared towards learning or practice**. Training for **learning** is geared towards problem solving and habit changing in game situations. Training for **practice** is geared towards physical exercise and motivation. **Note: in order to practice a skill, it must already be known. Training is acquiring, practice is applying.**

Don't just stand in one place repeating and repeating drill swing after drill swing. During lessons I often have golfers play their golf courses on the range. We start with a tee shot, then hit to the green, etc. playing all 18 holes.

With **Mindful Exercises** a thinking/learning mind will stay fully engaged and alive. We are not only training some basic element of our swing and game, but we are also making an investment in the direction of long-term learning in a non-static environment.

"Tis the mind that makes the body rich." - William Shakespeare

With **Mindful Exercises** we are adding some changes or distractions to our training sessions. By doing so we move away from mindless leaning habits in which we are not as mindful of the active as is possible. Distractions are just the mind paying attention to something else. We should ask, "can we learn something from this new stimulus?" (and not be distracted by them). When working on something (backswing, tempo, grip etc.) for any amount of time, the image or conditions must be varied to get the most from your time and effort.

Studies have shown that an image will actually fade from view when it is focused on for a long time. These studies also show varying the target of our attention, whether it's visual or mental, apparently improves our memory of it. To increase our ability to learn, look for novelty or create novelty within the stimulus. We should do this even if the instructor does not mention it. Varying the target of our attention seems to lead to and improve ones' ability to pay attention and recall what was being learned.

Note: We have all walked on to a putting green, dropped a few balls and made the first putt. This is an everyday example of a mindful approach. The first putt is the first time we are gathering information about the shot at hand. It is fresh interesting information. **We are mindfully engaged and fully aware – and bingo – the first putt goes in.** There is a good chance if we stayed in the same place, and hit putt after putt a mindless approach could take over then our practice/training time becomes less valuable.

It has been said, "*Variety is the spice of life.*" You may want to add some variety to your current approach to learning with mindful exercises that use different swing sizes, speeds, and targets, as you train and learn a particular element of your game. **By voiding repetition you will also avoid mindless learning.**

People are always learning different ways to accomplish the same goal. i.e. from day one members of any sales force are learning how to sell a variety of customers with different needs for their product. If salesmen only exposed themselves to one type of customer in their early years, they would not be as valuable to the company as the salesperson, who was exposed to a wide variety of business situations, customers, and context.

Parents may have a set of values they want to pass along to their children. While this set of values, could be seen as a constant (as are **Golf's Physical Basics**), they will have to be shared and presented in a variety of ways to accommodate each child. Without some flexibility in how these values are presented, some family members may miss the lesson they are meant to provide. There is no formal schooling on how to be a parent, there is no "how to" list. The skills of being a parent are learned in a non-static, ever changing environment where mindful thinking is a perquisite. **This state of awareness is also required when learning golf.**

The sales force that trained and learned to sell products in a variety of business conditions, and parents who learn to share their set of values with their children through the ever changing stages of their lives, are both examples of a mindful, **what to** approach. (Both avoided the limitation that a **How To** approach can create.) This is much like golfers, who learned to play and swing with an open, aware, mindful approach. They learned to handle course conditions that are always changing. Golfers with a mindful approach have developed insights for what they want to do, that **how to** instruction does not provide.

Secret: The human body runs on electricity. Every human body and emotional system is wired differently. Every person is a unique individual who feel, see, experience and create motion in his or her own best way. The message is **Learn to Control Your Swing -No one Else Can!**

When world-class players are interviewed before a tournament, most of their answers reveal how they will be **adjusting their games** to the course and conditions they are facing that week. *"Well you know, on this course you have to..."*, or *"This week all the players that do well will have to..."*, or *"They have made some changes to the course from the last time we played here and everyone will be making some adjustments."* **They adapt by using reverse engineering principles that are discussed later.**

Suggestions:

- Consciously try to vary your style and let your body and mind experience different feels. Doing so improves ones' ability to **recognize** workable and unworkable motions. Ones ability to recognize mistakes, learn from them, and move on is very important to long-term learning.
- Become more **aware** of where the clubface, clubhead, and shaft are at impact.
- Evaluate the feel of **the task** to gain insights for improving skills that repetitions don't provide.
- Distractions do not have to be enemies of effective learning. When the mind becomes distracted and loses its focus, it's actually telling us that the way in which a person is trying to learn isn't

providing enough novelty. This causes the mind to wander and boredom sets in followed by distractions. It helps to **acknowledge distraction**, then vary the ways you focus by using other points of view from which to learn.

Secret: The **non-expert** is always trying to fix his or her swing. But by swinging without trying to fix the swing, players can become more familiar with what the unworkable habit feels like. In the future they will be more aware of what they did to cause the ball flight they want to change. Expert players can identify workable and unworkable swings by knowing the feel of both. **It's very useful to know the feel of unworkable habits.**

I strongly suggest reading Dr. Langer's books, Mindfulness and The Power of Mindful Learning.

Secret: It appears that repeating and repeating a motion would only have value **after** the motion had been learned. One's ability to learn that motor skill is apparently impaired by repeating a drill. Don't memorize, understand!

Perceptions, Where It Starts

"Our beliefs at the beginning of a doubtful undertaking is the only thing that insures the outcome of our ventures – both successful and unsuccessful." - William Jones

Golf is a game that sometimes brings out the worst in people. Just look at golfers on the first tee. **It helps to recognize that the player's personal perception of what they believe the shot at hand requires is where good and poor golf both have their start**. Often poor golf is a result of poor concepts, and misinformation. Progress with golf is not a matter of mastering difficult techniques, it is more a matter of becoming aware of and learning a few essentials. These essentials in part are founded on **Golf's Physical Basics**, which existed long before any instruction books were written. Some say, one secret to good golf is: there is no secret, only a few essentials that must be applied and repeated.

Golf has always been a game of playable misses, with a few good shots in-between. This fact requires some patience. Patience, when trying to make progress is a learned skill. In many cases our patience is influenced by our emotions when our best shot is followed by our worst.

Please realize that it is better to miss a shot and know the cause, then to hit a good one and not know what you did. For me a learners awareness is always more important than instruction information. What players can understand, remember and do, is more valuable than what any book, video, friend, or instructor believes.

When golfers hit shots with control and power, (and they normally don't) many have the **perception** they were just lucky to get those results. Please understand, powerful controlled ball flights have **very different** impact alignments and conditions than swings which lack these qualities.

Secret: Things do not just happen, there are causes. Results, workable and unworkable are brought about. **There is a very logical order and reasons for things that happen in golf.** Every component of an efficient, dependable swing has a proper relationship to every other component in the system. A golfer cannot move or place one component without influencing every other component in the system.

I have said one reason for a lack of progress in golf can be poor perceptions. For example; the force a effective golf swing develops, uses, and sustains can't be seen, (it's invisible) leaving many golfers with misconceptions about force. There are also other elements of the game and swing that are not easily recognized or are invisible, leaving golfers with misinformation and inaccurate perceptions. Fortunately, **the effects** of force and other elements can be **seen and measured**, and when they are correctly applied, **the swing itself provides its own blueprint**. To be repeated.

"The ability to convert visions to things is the secret of success." – Harry Ward Beechem

Over time, the exchange of information probably happened first on the walls of caves, then on parchments, then on paper, then over telegraph, next through phones and now computer lines. **While passing information on has led to progress, it also may be slowing down the development of self-discovery skills**. Today our perceptions are often founded on second hand information. This can cause people to overlook the value of perceptions founded on their own self-discovery skills.

Note: Perceptions gained from second hand information will never be a valuable as perceptions gained from self-discovery.

LADDER OF INFERENCE

Perceptions

We see, select, interpret, believe, and act, - often on poor and inaccurate assumptions

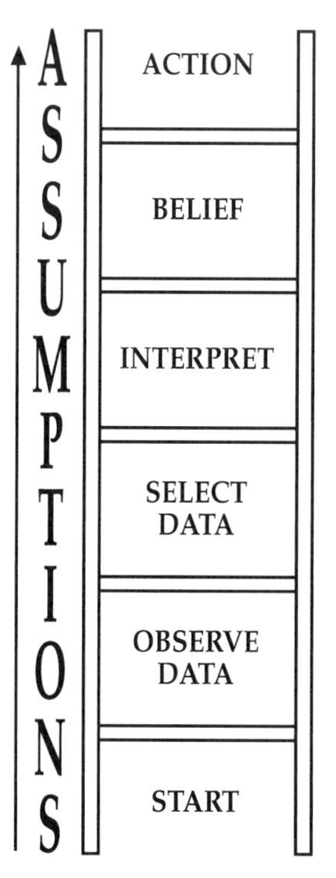

Assumptions

Unquestioned assumptions often cause poor results

Experts Have a Perpetual Advantage

The Biophysical Foundations of Human Movement, by Bruce Abernethy, Vaughan Kippers, Laurel Mackinnon, Robert J. Neal and Stephanie Hanrahan, contains information that when taken into consideration, will improve **any approach** to learning golf. The following is based on their research.

Their studies showed that there are a number of differences between the **expert** and **novice** golfer when it comes to processing information to acquire golf skills. These differences are apparent during every stage including; decision making, movement organization, execution of skills, as well as the observable movement patterns and outcomes produced by both expert and novice.

This team of experts found the information obtained from the three sensory systems key to movement, A) visual, B) kinesthetic, C) vestibule (inner ear for balancing), **does not differ** when it comes to improving skills of both the expert and novice. **The limiting factor to motor performance is not the sensory information needed but how basic information from these systems is interpreted and then used by the novice that limits performance of skills.**

Note: When performing golf swings, novices are often limited by how they **interpret** and **understand information** and then misinform the brain on how to guide movement execution. Experts have a **perceptual advantage** over the less skilled in this area. They rarely misinterpret and, therefore, rarely have poor concepts.

Thinking should be thought of as retrieving and recalling old information, whereas **new perceptions** and insights are gathering new information.

Secret: **Studies clearly show the role of perception is the most important element to learning golf skills effectively. Experts have better perceptions than the less skilled. Accurate perceptions not only enable a theory to be visualized; they can also simplify what may appear to be a complex system, advancing our understanding of how the system works is thereby improved.**

The findings of these motor skill experts also points out that perceptions are worthwhile only to the extent to which they **accurately capture the key characteristics** (what's relevant) of the skill we are trying to understand. Just as good perceptions can aid, poor ones can hamper understanding. There is a difference between observations and assessments. We could say, ***"it's assessments that revealed what is being learned".***

When golf skills are being acquired, accurate perceptions can provide relevant information for the brain to process. A computer uses information in a similar manner. Through its stored program a computer is able to convert the **input** of information from one form (a disk, the keyboard or other information system) into **out-put** information of a desired form. This **out-put** information can be numbers, letters, text, or graphics.

"Tell me what you pay attention to, and I will tell you who you are." - Jose Casset

"The voyage of discovery lies not in finding new landscapes – but in having new eyes." - Marcel Provst

The conversion of **input** information to **output** information is not a passive process. It is an active reorganization of information that is controlled by the commands within the computer programs. This active reorganization of information is limited only by two interacting factors; the computers **hardware** (memory) and its **software** (program). This is similar to how the nervous system uses input information from sensory systems (visual, kinesthetic, vestibular) for movement control. The **output** information is revealed in the patterns of motion we perform.

Secret: The success or failure of the golf swing depends on an accurate perception of sensory information which the central nervous system uses. Movement is the end product of a long series of information processing stages that take place **beyond observation,** within the confines of the central nervous system.

- The **first** and most important process the brain and central nervous system performs is **perception** of the shot at hand. Hopefully golfers are selecting **only the most relevant** information for further processing.
- The **second** important stage in information processing involves decision-making. The decision made is determined in part by the accuracy of the preceding perceptual judgments.
- The **third** stage is organizing the motion in the brain before it can be initiated.

Note: All three central processes – **Perception**, **Decision Making** and **Organizing** – are completed before any observable muscular contraction takes place or the golf swing motion occurs.

Again, perception is much more than the passive reception of sensory information by our receptor systems. It's a rather active process through which we **interpret** and **apply meaning** to that sensory information.

Warning: All of our prior golf experiences, including any accumulated knowledge, expectations, personal biases and beliefs contribute to our perceptions. Therefore it is not surprising that two people will often perceive and report different things after seeing the same pattern of stimulation (or golf swing).

Secret: **Studies show that humans are limited to storing seven items before they start to make errors of identification. To understand perception of movement, it is necessary to examine the potential input information which exists for that motion. However, after seven items the human brain gets lost.**

In his book, The Brain, Dr. Restak points out that the brain organizes body motion before the motion happens by telling the muscles what to do. **No one can perform and repeat effective motion until that motion pattern is established in out memory.**

When decisions about the swing must be made, the quality of those decision depends on the quality of the perceptual judgments as well as some **knowledge of the costs and benefits** associated with each particular option. Experts are more aware of the costs and benefits of decisions (expert golfers at times "play safe", and do not take the chance of "going for it"). Poor perception and/or poor decision making during a round of golf leads to errors and poor performance. **The perceptual and decision-making aspects of motion control can become the limiting factors to performance.**

"Experience is not what happens to you – it is what you make of what happens to you." - A Hurley

However, **both the novice and expert golfers more or less see and feel the same information,** but people who perform on a higher level than others have a more workable perception of golf swing information. Experts also make more workable decisions and understand the costs and benefits of their choice more clearly then the less skilled. **The lessons to be gained from this research: golfers should only use information that leads to accurate perceptions of relevant information, information that avoids poor concepts and misconceptions about the swing and playing the game.** Memories are enhanced by emotions. Getting emotional over unworkable swings makes changing the habit more difficult.

When learners are involved with golf instruction, it is not unfair to say (in general) that they want to learn how to hit the ball with control and understand what they did! Instruction for many golfers is filled with information they may not understand or consider very detailed. **The challenge for instruction has always been and will always be to provide information and knowledge that can be personalized by learners.**

Keep in mind that one of the reasons we play golf the way we do is our personal perception of information about the swing and the game. What we see and feel *before, during,* and *after* the shot is very important to our progress. To be informed (a "how to list") is not enough, when trying to learn or improve a physical activity. **Information must be experienced and personalized for anyone to learn from it.**

"Transformed perception could be called 'ordinary magic.' Ordinary because it is hidden from us by nothing other than our reluctance to see it and our habits. Magic because transformation of perception happens suddenly, even though it may have taken training, practice, and energy." - J. Hayward

"It is not that the instructor indicates and then you see, but in observing together you see for yourself." - from Flame of Attention by Kris Hnamurti.

Secret: When we just follow, we are not using our **intelligence**. It is only when we use our **intelligence** that there is an opportunity to learn. Motor skill instruction should be focused upon creating a big, clear window through which learners can gather information, information that can be personalized, remembered, and which can improve insights, perceptions, and feel.

A GOAL: MAKE GOOD GOLF OBTAINABLE

How is the **unique** power of playing good golf unleashed? Sounds like a very accurate description of how some players look at their golf. Many golfers are not happy with their level of play and want to improve, but **many do not know what will improve their games.** Handicaps kept by the U.S.G.A. indicate there are 90% more double digit handicap golfers than single digit players. These numbers indicate the ability to play good golf is indeed unique. This does not have to be the case.

The information that leads to any progress I have made as a golf professional, both in how I play the game and give instruction, did not come only from traditional golf knowledge. Information also came from other seemingly unrelated disciplines.

For example, the 1998 Spring-Summer issue of the American Educator, (a magazine published by the American Federation of Teachers) contained research about learning to read that I felt paralleled learning to play good golf. Every educator and parent knows that reading is the most important primary skill being taught in elementary school. As a golf instructor, I know that the primary information golfers learn, and what they should learn, is often very different.

"The Unique Power of Reading, and How To Unleash It" was the headline on the cover of the 1998 Spring-Summer issue of the American Educator. The entire issue was devoted to **why reading reform is essential today**. Some reasons include:

- 40% of all third graders are not reading adequately today
- In some major cities, one out of two children don't read on grade level.

Using the U.S.G.A. handicap records, the sport of golf could come up with parallel statistics about non-expert golfers, (even without including the 19 million who play without U.S.G.A. handicaps) that suggests that the way golfers have been trying to learn the game **needs to be reformed**.

Studies about poor reading suggest schools should use some of the new learning techniques available today. These studies show that if reading programs started using new approaches for learning today, we could ensure reading success for all healthy children born in the 21st century. All students would be reading at or about basic level by the age of 9.

By improving the techniques non-expert golfers use today for learning, **they too could unleash the unique powers of playing good golf**. Any golfer who would reform their current "how to" approach to learning, would see improvement. All golfers can lower their handicaps, just as all healthy children can learn to improve their reading skills.

The following are some parallels I found in learning to read and learning to play **good golf**. Earlier I defined **good golf** as predicting outcome of ball flight before you swing. Someone reading this can predict the ball will go 50, 100, 200 yards left, right, high or low, better than the rest of us can. That's what good golf is: **predicting the outcome of your swing**.

Parallels in Learning to Read and Learning to Play Good Golf

* A National Academy of Sciences study on reading found the most neglected components of effective learning are the very components research strongly supported for learning to read (perhaps golf should follow this approach).

A. Children need to have background knowledge about their own world – to make sense of what they read.

Golfers need to have background knowledge about impact alignments.

B. Children should be given the opportunity of putting pictures of a story into the correct order.

Golfers should be given the opportunity to explain what they see.

C. Children should be exposed to Science, History, and Geography to give context for understanding what they read

Golfers should learn there is no one way to swing, but there is one effective impact condition for the shot at hand.

D. Children should learn the letters of the alphabet.

Golfers should learn to see lines, (target line, plane line, impact line) and learn to hold the club and stand to the ball.

E. Children should learn the sounds of letters. Knowing basic speech sounds, lets children identify and manipulate the sounds with words.

Golfers should learn the feel and look of effective impact alignments, the feel and look of an on-plane swing, and learn how on and off plane swings hit different shots.

F. Letting children rhyme words in pre-school, builds effective awareness.

Letting golfers experiment with different swing speeds, shapes, and feels, builds awareness of swing shapes and feels

G. Hearing rhymes and producing rhymes for given words makes children focus on the sound inside words.

Golfers learning different speeds, and swing shapes improves awareness of balance and timing.

H. When children are comfortable and familiar with sounds that letters represent, advanced instruction is possible.

When golfers are comfortable and familiar with the design of the club, plane, and impact alignments, advanced instruction is possible.

I. Children should learn that text is written left to right.

Golfers should learn the cause of ball flight.

J. Children should learn that spaces between words matter.

Golfers should learn ball location at address matters.

K. Children should learn there is a one to one correspondence between words on a page and words they read and say.

Golfers should learn that weight distribution for different shots (up, down, and side hill shots) corresponds with ball flight with ball flight.

L. Children should be actively exploring new words – concepts.

Golfers should be actively exploring new ways to hit shots.

M. Children should be given the opportunity to make predictions about how the stories will end.

Golfers should be given the opportunity to make predictions about outcome of different swing shapes (good and bad).

N. Children should be given the opportunity to re-tell stories.

Golfers should be given the opportunity to use visualizations and recreate them.

O. Children should be given the chance to use new words.

Golfers should be given the opportunity to change clubs for the same shot

P. Research shows that the nine months of first grade can be the most important in a child's schooling. It is during this time most children define whether they will be a good or bad reader.

Studies show that the first few golf lessons can be the most important ones. They can either accelerate or slow down progress.

Q. Research shows that unfortunately the first grade is where common instruction practices are the most inconsistent.

Studies show that unfortunately in golf, the first lesson is often misunderstood, creating poor concepts.

R. Children should learn to blend isolated sounds into words.

Golfers should learn how to blend the isolated elements of a swing into the feel of a complete swing, when playing and training.

S. To write, children should learn to break works into their component parts.

Golfers should learn their own swing and to break down its elements into isolated feels.

T. The first grade should provide instruction and practice with **effective** structures that lead to a familiarity with spelling and effective conventions to use in identifying printed words.

Golfers should be provided with instructions about the swing plane and impact alignments that they can turn into personal feels

U. Creative writing instruction should begin in kindergarten. Research shows even **invented** spelling helps internalize effective awareness and alphabetic principles, (even though words are misspelled).

Golfers can invent their own way of playing shots, as long as they can produce effective impact conditions.

V. Failure to learn effective spelling of words is the most debilitating cause of reading difficulties.

Failure to know how the design of the club influences ball flight can be the most debilitating cause of golf difficulties.

W. Children should have solid comprehension skills, both for understanding material they read on their own and for material that is read to them.

Golfers should have a effective comprehension of swing plane, the angles of the club shaft, clubhead, and face angle, so they can understand their ball flight and any instruction they receive.

X. Children should spend more time reading than is available at school. Twenty to thirty minutes daily at home.

Golfers should spend more time on their short games than their full swings. Also spend time both before and after instruction working on habits. Time at home without a ball is time well spent. (i.e. grip alignment, posture, tempo, etc.)

Y. Everything a child does when learning to read is done to build the child's ability to understand the content of words and stories.

Everything a golfer is learning is done to understand effective application of Golf's Physical Basics for the shot at hand.

Z. The bottom line – all children who we expect to be reading and writing at grade level by age 9 – **have to learn to sound out words**.

Bottom line – no willy-nilly approach, or willy-nilly swing can produce good golf. The club is either on plane or it is not, and the swing can either be repeated or it can't.

NATURE OF LEARNING

What can or cannot accelerate learning will always be a topic worth investigating. It seems to me that any approach to instruction (not only in golf) would have to take **the nature of learning** into consideration. Without some insight into its nature, how else could learning be effective?

Golfers often say they understand the swing, but cannot perform one. Do they really understand if they cannot perform? University of California at Berkley Professor Hung His, points out, "*Education seems to be plagued by a false dogma that conceptual understanding leads to exertion of basic skills.*"

Secret: **Experiencing movement is the only door to learning movement.** Experience cannot be gained from a book, or from someone else's "how to do" it list. We must first experience effective movements to develop movement patterns that are considered workable. From tying ones shoes to writing, when we move (correctly or incorrectly), that motion was a trained pattern of motion. While learning is natural, this does not insure we will train a correct motion. Do not focus on "how to", focus on "what to", and realize desired ball flight tells us "what to do".

"No man's knowledge can go beyond their own experience." **– J. Locke**. Staying open and aware, experiencing the motion, is far more important than someone else's ideas about the motion.

Some of the following ideas are based on my thoughts and notes I've made while reading about learning over the last twelve years. Books by Ellen J. Langer, a PhD from Harvard University were especially useful. Mindfulness and The Power of Mindful Learning.

Dr. Langer and many others in the field of education have completed studies and research that revived some long-held beliefs about the **nature of learning**. The studies show how we have been trying to learn skills, actually may undermine true long-term learning. **Some myths (lies) include**:

- Drills, repetitions and memorization are necessary to learn.
- We must make basics second nature to learn a skill.
- There is a right and a wrong way of doing everything.
- We must focus on one element at a time to learn.
- Forgetting is a problem.
- It is important to have a goal, and delay gratification to learn.

All of the above myths can undermine the transfer of information that leads to true long-term learning (stifling creativity, silencing questions, and diminishing self-esteem, leading people away from being mindful, active, and aware, into a state of mindlessness). I will share some of my thoughts about learning and touch on some of these studies**, but I suggest reading Dr. Langer's books.**

Our learning/thinking mind could be described as either being active or inactive. People's minds can be **Mindful** and aware, or **Mindless** and inactive. When we are **Mindful** we are actively engaged in a learning/thinking process. On the other hand in the state called **Mindless**, there is very little going on, and a **Mindless** approach to learning, is really a **Mindless** attempt.

Secret: Another view of **mindful** and **mindless learning** would be to say a **mindless** approach takes in information without any input from the person receiving "how to" advice. On the other hand, a mindful approach has people actively involved and aware of the process. This of course makes the information more valuable to learners than **How to** information which does not empower people.

Note: Formal golf instruction got its start in 1857 when The Golfers Manual was published. From that time forward we could say there has been an acknowledged and accepted approach to golf instruction that could be accurately described as an approach that is telling people **How To Play and Swing**. "**How to**" approaches are built on accepted thinking found in many forms of instruction and education settings, they are not exclusive to golf.

I have had first hand personal experience with using a **"how to"** approach to instruction, and stopped using it in my work over ten years ago. My **"how to" approach** over time grew into a method that could be called a **"what to" approach**. There is a real difference between these two approaches to instruction. With a "**what to" approach** golfers are given choices to use in any and all context (ever changing course conditions and situations). In a "**what to" approach** people are learning what is personally relevant and what is not relevant for improving their swing and game (it is **Mindful** in nature). People are learning for themselves what is important when they are not being told how to do something (which is **Mindless** in nature).

Secret: It's not a matter of whether people want to improve – it's a matter of what is going to be the best way for that one golfer to make progress.

A "**what to"** approach is not asking golfers to follow someone's "**how to do it list"** without the opportunity to develop insights into information about their own swing and game for themselves. I fully realize the "**what to"** approach presented here in **Golf Swing Secrets...and Lies**, is a step and a shift away from methods that "**how to"** instruction employs. If you are currently satisfied with your progress and level of play, you may not want to consider a shift in how you now approach learning to improve. But, if this is not the case consider what is offered here.

A "**what to"** approach keeps the learning/thinking mind open, aware and awake. It has three elements that Dr. Langer calls: *"aware of more than one point of view; continuous creation of new categories; and being open to new information"*. On the other hand, the "**how to"** approach operates from only one perspective; it is entrapped in old categories and methods; and often relies on automatic behavior that can shut down any new signals. This shut down creates a mindless state that blocks true long-term learning and feel for the shot at hand.

Secret: Many golfers see the game and swing as a riddle – one that can't be "solved", they then look to someone else for answers that only self-discovery skills can provide.

"It's not what the eye sees, but that which makes the eyes see." - Frederick Franck

Many believe learning should take lots of hard work or even be a painful experience that must be survived before the rewards of learning happen. **This kind of mindset virtually guarantees a negative experience.** Discovering new information (i.e. the feel of on-plane) for ourselves and letting the mind exercise its powers, is interesting. When you stay interested, it is going to be easier to recall information you are trying to learn.

Note: Studies show emotions improves memory of events both workable and unworkable). **Being less emotional about unworkable swings will improve your ability to make changes in your game.**

No Pain/No Gain

Dr. Langer points out the "no pain—no gain" approach to learning is based on the long held belief of delayed gratification. With this approach people are practicing and training, looking ahead to the promise of a big payoff for their efforts in the future. At the same time they are over-looking the rewards that can be found in the present. **Accomplishments in the present are a fact and are certain. They are not just a promise in the future.**

"Don't look for results, just act and the results take care of themselves". - D. McCluggage

When golfers make a commitment to learning and progress, they should be open to the joys of learning all the small steps that lead to bigger ones. **True learning and progress is a journey, not a destination**. As golfers go from **not knowing to knowing more**, it is important that any future goals do not get in the way of feeling good about any progress, even the little steps.

Note: We do not have to create answers. Answers are always there, waiting to be uncovered. With new insights we solve problems. When we only focused on our goal (breaking 80), we may arrive once in a while, but we may not develop the insights needed to return on a regular basis with a swing and a game that is built on "how to" advice which overlooks self-education.

FORGETTING

While forgetting information at first glance may seem like harmful advice, it can help long-term learning. Studies show that certain kinds of previously learned and believed information can restrict creativity, and by forgetting it, the path to long-term learning reopens. When a **mindful approach** is used to learn, players remain open to noticing any little changes in future context (course conditions and situations) and make appropriate adjustments. *"When a **mindless approach** accepts information unconditionally, it blinds learners to options in changing contexts. We may be better off just forgetting information that was gathered without insights into options"*, Dr. Langer

There are always results – what we do with those results is where long-term learning and progress can have their start.

Again, I suggest reading Dr. Langer's books, Mindfulness and The Power of Mindful Learning.

LISTENING—A NEGLECTED SKILL

When people are listening to a speaker, they must adopt their listening to what is being said. **When it comes to improving our golf, "listening comprehension" is often an overlooked and neglected skill.** Studies have uncovered some startling information about listening that both golfers and the instruction industry may want to take into account. Studies have shown that when we are listening; often, the meaning of what is being said is not necessarily what the listener hears. Listeners draw support from any number of sources available within their own general intelligence while listening to new information. What is said may trigger past meanings of information in the minds of listeners. Focusing on these past meaning may well move their thoughts away from what is being said **now.**

Listening is hearing with a purpose. Listening requires attention and information processing. Hearing does not.

Often when people (instructors) are speaking, listeners (golfers) will start to subconsciously predict the next piece of information or reduce the number of possibilities they will consider from what is being offered by the speaker. I have observed that listeners will only take the time to use their **full processing capacity** in highly unusual situations (i.e. self-discovery golf instruction).

Note: When listeners cut down on their full processing time (researched by Piribram in 1971) this mechanism is called "Fast Forward." The central nervous system allows people to anticipate what is about to be said next. This causes listeners to not fully receive what is being said. **By anticipating what is next, the full message can be lost in assumptions that are based on past information.**

Our central nervous system has what could be called a **map of the external world** to which we subconsciously refer to continuously as we process new information. Much of what we hear is based on reconstructed scenarios that are consistent with past points of views of information about, the swing and playing the game. **What is particularly interesting is that information which does not fit the listeners past views often is simply not processed.** Listeners will just fit words into a scenario that they can easily construct from prior knowledge. This kind of inadequate listening, of course can cause troubles, if what is being said is to be used when or where precision is essential. (i.e. The game of golf)

Our present perception of past information about the swing and playing the game often influences what we are hearing today. i.e. Even as musicians are reading sheet music, they also hear the notes in their head. These musicians are being influenced by past perceptions of sound, just as golfers are influenced by their past perceptions of what has been said to them about their swing and game. People experience discomfort, when the **unexpected** shows up, in what to them is a familiar context. When golfers are hearing information that does not fit their prior preconceptions, it may not be fully processed.

Secret: Of all the elements in the learning experience that can assist the listener in gaining skills, the listener needs to deal with **authentic information.** Above all else golfers should not be listening to poor concepts and secrets that turn into lies.

Learning to Listen

"It's paradoxical that listening may be the easiest way to gather information, but at the same time the hardest skill to master. Schools have been able to help people learn to read and think, but the process of listening is almost entirely self-taught." – William H. Armstrong (1970 Newberry Award author of Study is Hard Work.) Some of the following is based on his work.

Listening is the process of decoding and interpreting verbal messages. If we can't say "I don't know," it is hard to learn. If you think you know, it's hard to listen. You may agree or you may disagree, but if you are using good listening skills, progress is possible. **Listening skills create curiosity.**

Before books and printing, the primary techniques used for acquiring knowledge were experience and listening. The practice of seeing (or reading), writing, and thinking are exercised from **within** the person. But an outside force often interferes with our mental powers to listen to the things that are being said.

Listening has the problem of a lack of "associated control." When we learn to read, our eyes control the speed at which we read. When we write, our hand controls the speed. In thinking, our thoughts travel at the speed capacity of our mind. **But when listening, our mind thinks four times faster than the average person can speak. That's four times faster!**

At times golfers may not understand what's being said and are to embarrassed to say so. This can cause poor listening. I suggest that golfers ask for the information to be repeated in a different context.

Secret: When learning to be a good listener, the hardest thing to learn is to adjust the rate of our thinking to the talking rate of the speaker. The easiest thing to do is misunderstand what is being said. **We tend to hear what we think we are going to hear. Too often, we make what we think we hear true; and long-term learning suffers!**

"Studies show in a lifetime, one is lucky to meet six or seven people who know how to listen and attend, the rest have short attention spans with fidgety ears. ***People seem to be afraid to lend their mind to someone else's thoughts, as if their minds would come back bent and bruised. This fear is fatal to learning."***
– W. H. Armstrong

When we learn to **adjust our speed of thinking** we have added two valuable elements to our ability to learn. **First,** we have disciplined our mind to the present; and **second**, we have become a follower. The mind performs in time. It wants to steer our thoughts either into the space of past time or into the future avoiding the present.

Listening transforms communication into the art of understanding. *"It takes a golden ear to be empty enough of itself – to hear clearly." – M.C. Richards.* Listening is more than hearing. Hearing is merely the physical component of listening.

Learning to listen is learning to follow. We must follow what the speaker is sharing. How many people do you know who want to be followers? Probably not many. People with good listening skills don't try to listen to two things at once. They are not thinking of what they are going to say while someone else is speaking. They do not miss opening remarks. They listen from the start. **Good listeners are not judging what the speaker is saying against their own beliefs, but are open to what is being said.** Golfers often wonder why they work so hard and make such little progress. For the answer, they may only have to look at their listening skills.

Secret: **There are only two kinds of listening, good or not listening at all.** Half listening maybe more damaging than not listening. Poor listeners can distort information, mixing truth with error, and can make the mistake of then learning mistakes.

Listening is more than hearing. Hearing is merely the physical component of listening. Listening takes will power. It requires actions that will train the mind to behave itself. Listening is not a passive act. Good listening requires keeping our eyes on the speaker and checking our every tendency towards permitting our minds to wonder. **Our eyes, ears, and mind must be working together if we are to hear what is being said and not what we think or believe is being said.** Good listening saves time. Good listening is time well spent. Good listening leads to new perceptions that can be the foundations of long-term learning. How would you rate your listening skills during golf instruction?

Feel

Words and descriptions can only act as a reference, **they are not the action itself**. When we are aware and pay attention to **the feel of an action or reaction, we can create a feeling image**. When the feel of our action is combined with a picture of our actions, studies show learning improves 70%. When you can, train and practice in front of a mirror or use video replay of your swing, this combines your actual physical body actions with mental pictures. A picture of ourselves is more useful than using expert models.

"The painter who has the feel of it is saved" - A. Renoir

A "Feel" can bring a personal point of reference to every element of motion or activity, and we must personalize information when learning golf. Feel can provide an immediate and direct connection to and from a physical action and its outcome. This "feel", of course, is very important for any skill that is performed by body motion that we want to learn to repeat.

Ben Hogan's Thoughts On Feel

In a 1943 interview, Ben Hogan talked about **feel**. The following is based on that interview:

Mr. Hogan said, *"I can harness your golf swing so you'll be converted from a high handicap hacker into a sensationally good swinger. The transformation will be made easily within a few weeks.* ***Sensationally*** *good is the right term to apply to the new and correct swing you'll have. Your swing will be founded on sensations".*

"Sensation, according to the dictionary is an impression made upon the mind through the medium of one of the organs of sense; feeling produced by external objects, or by some change in the internal state of the body. In the case of golf instruction, the "organs of sense" involved are those of feel. You can learn good golf if you use the sense of feel. If you're not happy with your progress, the chances are that you cannot recognize the sensation of a good golf swing."

Secret: *"Not knowing the difference between the feeling you should experience when your muscles, bones and nerves have collaborated in producing a good shot and the feeling you have when you make shots with any one of your numerous incorrect swings, leaves you without a foundation for your game."* –Ben Hogan

"Start with the feel of short shots. If you can learn a little swing you are on your way." – Harvey Penick

Ben Hogan said, *"If you don't know golf as a game of feeling, you are like a deaf man trying to play the piano by ear. Then you, and the professional working with you, are up against the extremely difficult challenge of trying to get words to describe sensations that are felt when a correct swing is made."*

Mr. Hogan was known for his right-to-the-point approach, when he gave his opinion. I thought readers would find his thoughts on feel and perception useful.

Perhaps, in the past you have tried to improve your swing by **only paying conscious attention to the description of different elements in the swing.** You may have overlooked feel. In the future, you should stay aware of what swing elements **feel like** when trying to improve. What is the feel of an on-plane shaft with the clubhead behind the hands through impact? What is the feel of a clubhead passing the hands before, during, or after impact? What does the shaft in line with the left arm through impact feel like? Does the shaft in-line with the right arm through impact feel different than when it is in-line with the left arm?

It's Personal

When we gather information that will be used for learning a golf swing, there are many different places one could start. **The best place for one player may not be the best for the next.** How and when learning takes place is very personal. Everyone has his or her own preference for how to receive (or best receive) learn information. Some of us learn best from pictures, some from feel, some by trial and error, and others from hearing.

How someone interprets information (i.e. pictures, words, feels, or motions) becomes the starting point for learning. The answer to the question: where is the best place to start? **The golfer's personal preference for information is the best place.** The body moves for one of three reasons, and it helps your insights about a golf swing to keep in mind that one of the following reasons is why a person's body goes into motion.

1. The body responds to motion (reflexes).
2. The body anticipates motion and then moves.
3. The body recreates a picture, feel or concept of motion stored in the mind's eye (perception).
    a. A baseball fielder's reflexes permit him to catch the ball.
    b. A batter anticipates a pitch.
    c. The baseball pitcher is recreating his perception of a throwing motion.

Players in a game of golf (unlike tennis, football, or basketball) have no opponents in motion to anticipate. **A golfer's body, club and ball motions are all based on the player's perception of what to do.** When your body, club, and ball motions are not what you believe they could or should be. Perhaps the answers to making more progress lies in discovering your **preference for information.**

PREFERENCE FOR INFORMATION

Dr. Cary Mumford, author of Golf's Best Kept Secret, suggests that golfers fall into four learning styles. At times we move from one style to the next. While there is no study that gives strong support for the use of learning styles, I have found people do have a preference for information when learning.

1. Driver – Doer
2. Feeler – Craftsman
3. Observer – Persuader
4. Analyzer – Thinker

Secret: **The more you can learn about your preference for learning information, the more useful your approach to learning will be. Therefore, more effective.**

Dr. Mumford believes that identifying your learning style is not as difficult as you may think. Students who are ***drivers – doers*** like to learn by trial and error. They like to do things rather than hear about things. They do not read directions when assembling things. During golf instruction, the *driver – doer* will not be very patient.

People who are ***feelers – craftsman*** are somewhat like the *driver – doer* but will have more patience. *Feelers – craftsmen* do not read direction but take more time to practice what the instructor has told them (the *driver – doer* does not have the patience for practice). *Feelers – craftsmen* listen very carefully, *drivers – doers* do not. The *feeler – craftsman* will have a sounder understanding of what the instructor has said then will the *driver – doer*.

People who are ***persuaders – observers*** will attempt to copy. They read directions but also rely on mental images. They like to have the instructor demonstrate so that they can observe. If they feel they are not getting enough information from observing, they will read about what they are trying to learn. Often this type of golfer has built a very good swing but has overlooked some details will be overlooked.

The ***analyzer – thinker*** wants to read directions. They like to analyze things. They like to have answers for everything they do. *Doers – drivers* could care less why things happen. They just want them to happen. The *analyzer – thinker* likes "how to" books, whereas the *observer – persuader* likes visual instruction. The *thinker – analyzer* is looking for perfection, while the *driver – doer* and *craftsman – feeler* just want to get the job done any way they can.

My suggestion is to keep in mind the descriptions of the different learning styles as you are developing your approach to, or style of learning and playing golf. You could also take into consideration whether you tend to be either a left brain or right brain learner. Studies have shown that one side of the brain, left or right, is our dominant side. **Left brain learners**, in general, tend to have logical and sequential skills, whereas **right brain learners** have artistic and visual skills.

Bio-feedback results at the Institute of Denver, after administering E.E.G. tests to more than 400 people, found accountants, chemists, lawyers, and mathematicians were clearly left brain dominant Artists, musicians, and athletes were right brain dominant. It also found that classical musicians were more left brain as expected, but that rock musicians were more right brain. Lawyers, who were involved with contract law, were more left brain, whereas criminal law attorneys were more right brain.

The left side of the brain tends to work with words, and the right side of the brain tends to work with pictures. To have this kind of insight would help any approach to learning.

Your right brain *doer – feeler* does not want a long detailed explanation of what to do. They learn better when they can see and feel it. They want to try the shot as soon as they can. They are in a rush to learn.

On the other hand, the left brain *observer – analyzer* wants the instructor to explain everything. The observer may also want to see a picture along with an explanation, and **thinkers** may read about what instructors are explaining and showing. *Observer – analyzer* type of students are willing to take their time as they learn.

Some General Playing Comparisons:

- Right brain golfers tend to have more natural talent than left brain golfers.
- Left brain golfers tend to have better techniques than right brain golfers.
- Right brain golfers tend to spend more time playing than practicing.
- Left brain golfers tend to practice more than they play.
- Right brain golfers must play well to swing well.
- Left brain golfers must swing well to play well.
- Right brain golfers should work more on their long game than their short game.
- Left brain golfers should work more on their short game than their long game.
- Right brain golfers are good at trouble shots and short game.
- Left brain golfers have good full swing abilities.

Research & Development Division

Setting up your own research and development division will help your progress using mindful exercises. Set aside some time in your day, week or month that will be devoted to creative thoughts and deliberate trial and error. Perhaps 5% of your practice and training time could be devoted to your personal research and development division. **It's in your own R&D department where you can run the risk of learning.** This is a place where you can acquire the new knowledge, and the understanding needed to refine what you do now with random training, avoiding drills.

After you discover what it is you have to learn, and the best way for you to go about learning, progress is not far behind. **Often tips and suggestions from our friends and other sources of golf instruction have little reference to the individual golfer who is receiving the advice.** Discovering what we have to learn or unlearn is always the first stage of progress.

"Self-education is, I firmly believe, the only kind of education there is. Instructors and schools can only make self-education easier, failing that, they do nothing." - Isaac Asimou

"The Knack of", Can't be Taught

Some readers may feel what follows is not relevant for making progress in golf, but I can assure you what follows is on the mark. The following is based on how humans have always experienced long-term learning (whether we realize it or not). **I have found that golf skills come and go because the approach used for learning them was not conducive to retaining skills.**

The "knack of" doing almost anything really cannot be taught by someone else. For example, the knack of regaining ones balance when falling; the knack of when to speak up, or speak softly; the knack of mixing up a special sauce, etc., all really cannot be taught. Fortunately, there have always been environments where the knack of good golf or any skill can be learned. These environments do not include "how to" lists.

How does the human nervous system go about learning the "knack of" any skill or playing good golf? First, it helps to understand that learning to strike a ball is no different neurologically (for the brain) then learning to speak, play the violin, or a game of Nintendo©. Dr. Harold L. Kalawan (author of Why Michael Can't Hit), a neurologist and leader in the field of skill acquisition, points out, *"Any neurological analysis of sports skills follows naturally, from the fact – all behavior has a neurological basis".*

Secret: *"Any athletic skill is merely one example of how the brains genes (not the athlete) have the ability to learn a skill* ***by adapting and modifying themselves to the environment they are exposed to****."* Dr. Kalawan, This is a very important insight for both golfers and any source of instruction advice (human genes have the ability to teach themselves the "knack of". **Our genes have the genius of being both learners and teachers.**

"What does neurology have to do with learning and performing sport skills? Everything!" – Dr. Kalawan.

We can plainly see the human form swinging and playing golf, but learning to swing and play occurs internally in the genes of our brain. The very same skills that brought mankind through evaluation, as our genes changed, adapted and modified themselves into this century's current model of human species, are the same skills upon which learning golf is founded.

The human species has gone through many changes throughout history, but when we are born, our brain is not yet fully developed. Many of our genes are still available to **adapt** and **modify** themselves to all of the different environments people may be exposed to. **This is why the first stages of learning any skill are so important.**

Any golfer who is starting to question the value of talking about our environment, evaluation of mankind, and the brains genes – stay on board – don't jump ship. While you may feel this is unusual information for improving one's golf, it is a starting point that has never failed the human species.

What is the best way for our nervous system to learn any skill or the "knack of" good golf?

Simply put – by adapting and modifying our insights, body motion and core golf knowledge, to the ever-changing environments presented by the game of golf and the shot at hand. Humans have done just fine for millions of years using their genius of adapting and modifying, and golfers who want to learn the knack of good golf may want to do the same.

Secret: **Our human genes were not designed to strike a ball. No physical skill was selected, and then passed down over time by our evaluating system to strike a ball. Humans have learned many skills without "how to" lists. Golfers who want to experience long-term learning, should consider using the skills of adapting and modifying themselves to golf's environments., not "how to" advice from well meaning friends.**

"Touch can't be taught, it can only be acquired." – Paul Runyan

"The best thing Mr. Grout did for me was, I learned to teach myself." – Jack Nicklaus

Golfers can learn something about improving a habit from the game of basketball. After a player misses a foul shot to the left, this player simply adapts and modifies the next shot to go more to the right. This ability to make a quick adjustment is possible because **information about the environment was both available and recognized by the player.** i.e. the height and distance of the basket and previous shot. All this information influences the next shot, not someone else's ideas, or "how to" list. When golfers become aware of and adapt to golf's environments (**Golf's Physical Basics**), they can learn the knack of good golf.

Note: A golf swing either has efficient alignments and application of force or it does not. When learning good golf our genes must be given the freedom to adapt and modify themselves to the environment to which they are exposed. Some world-class players are more comfortable in some golf environments than others. Since people learn golf in different or unique environments (i.e. wind , type of grass, lay of the land, etc.), we can see why even a world class player may be more comfortable on one course and less on another.

Every good golfer has learned to adapt and modify. Such as, long irons require different modifications of golf skills then shorter more upright clubs; up hill shots require different skill modifications than down hill shots. I could go on. Alignment and application of force (modifications) are determined by the shot at hand and by principles of motion and force, not "how to" lists.

Golfers wanting long-term progress should recognize **human genes have always learned best through adapting and modifying themselves to ever changing environments.** Learning golf in its ever changing environments should be no different. Golfers must stay open to and aware of golf's environment, then adapt and modify their approach for the shot at hand. This process is refereed to as reverse engineering and has been used by human's genes for long-term learning from day one. **At least 75% of a humans brain fully develops after birth, as the environment helps write the software.** It's during this period that most environmentally dependent skills (i.e. knack of good golf) are acquired by the brain.

Secret: *"Our ability to make progress is hard wired or genetically encoded in our brain, but the level of acquisition and development depends on the environment people are exposed to. Nature determines the limits of what nurturing can accomplish. This is an absolute. But where, when, and how the brain and environment interactions take place is the key to learning skills that are not hard wired at birth."* – Dr. Harold L. Kalawan

Self-Learning

Golf is a motor skill. Golf advice probably should not try to teach the swing, but should try to help the golfer redefine his or her personal perception of the swing. It's always the golfers perception of the skill that is going to create the most useful information for his or her brain. Often golfers have inaccurate concepts.

The most useful role for motor skill instruction is to help students focus and interpret the most relevant parts of the physical experience. I would say, most of the time avoid "how-to" advice. It's an order from the mind of one person to the body of another.

Secret: It's useful to see advice as catalysts to self-learning and improvement. The whole process of long-term learning is essentially based on three things: self-awareness, self-analysis, and self-teaching.

Golf instruction for the most part should be imparting ways to learn. Someone can either be "on purpose" or "off purpose" in his or her action. **Effective instruction can help learners stay on purpose.** Many golfers do not make progress because their thoughts and actions are off purpose. We can only change or improve upon what we already have or are currently doing.

Secret: The first step to long-term progress is for golfers to become aware of what their current swing pattern is before any useful change can be introduced.

More About Self-discovery

Secret: Most would agree that when it comes to golf instruction saying less and giving golfers less to think about are both steps in the right direction. Unfortunately, this is only true, when golfers already know what they have to learn, and what they are trying to do is not based on misconceptions.

"New consciousness is not a new thing – it's a long, painful return to what has always been." - Helen Luke

More than a few studies point out that up to 85% of what people know was learned through their eyes. The eyes can be windows to the world, but when watching good golfers, many people misinterpret what they are looking at. These misconceptions often fragment future progress. Another way of saying this: when what we believe is based on misconceptions, **it's not true!**

Russell Smith, a leading expert on learning said, *"Our concepts are first derived from our perceptions, or someone else's language."*

There are several reasons golfers can misinterpret what they see. First, there are both visible and invisible elements upon which efficient swings are founded. Alignment, swing shape, grip, etc, of course, are all **visible**. Force, pressure, energy, thinking, etc. are all **invisible elements** upon which most misconceptions are based. Visible elements can also be misunderstood, but to a lesser extent. Where does effective force come from? How do I develop and transfer energy? I could go on, but it seems it's in the area of **invisible elements** that many golfers have the most misconceptions with.

As golfers go about comparing what they believe they know with what they are still learning, it is useful to have an open mind. Many times what we know may not be as valuable as what we are still learning.

Respected PGA Professional Deck Cheatham from The Farm CC in Rocky Face Georgia, uses the term "Book of Right" for all the tips golfers receive from their golfing friends and other sources. Deck points out this "Book of Right" can cause golfers to use terms like: "good, bad, right, wrong, could have, should have, etc." Cheatham suggests throwing away every "Book of Right," all its rights and wrongs, and simply use the flight of the ball and self-discovery to learn what should be done to improve and make progress.

"In a world that is doing its best to make you everybody else – be yourself." – E. E. Cummings

I have heard Dave Pelz say, *"immediate accurate feedback is essential to progress and long-term learning."* I ask, what could possible be more accurate and immediate than the flight of the ball? Ball flight provides non-negotiable information.

Secret: **When golfers become aware of how the alignment of force from the clubs shaft, head and face at impact can influence ball flight, long-term learning becomes possible.**

While golf instruction can help make golfers aware of what impact alignments correspond with specific ball flights, instruction cannot teach anyone the feel of these alignments. **Feel is based on self-discovery and its personal in nature**.

Learning to recognize the feel for impact alignments for the shot at hand can start by realizing that after we put on a watch, the conscious feel of that watch against our wrist will last for a few seconds. Golfers can also use the feelings that last for a few seconds after every swing for learning workable alignments for the shot at hand.

When golfers are filling their minds with swing tips and "how to" advice, their feel system (brain) becomes less aware of what motion has just taken place. The ability to recognize the feel of effective motion is an important insight for learning and recalling any motion not only a golf swing. Recognizing "the feels" of unsound motions is as valuable to long-term learning as knowing "the feels" of effective motions.

Secret: There is often a gap between what we experience and what we want. Scott Grafton who is from the University of Southern California found that when people are first learning a new task, at first several areas of the brain are active at the same time. **People can be literally scatterbrained** during early stage of learning a new motion, but as proficiency improves the brain becomes more focused, or less scattered.

These observation by Grafton and others points to the importance of training longer in areas that players have some level of competence and a shorter time span in areas of lesser competence.

For example, to stand and miss-hit drivers for a half-hour would not lead to the same kind of progress using the driver for 5 minutes and then a club you can control for 25 minutes. By using clubs in which you have some control over ball flight, golfers have the opportunity to feel workable motions that can be transferred to other swings. When miss-hitting the driver time after time, people are only reinforcing the motion that miss-hits. They are not learning to be aware of "the feels" that control ball flight.

Secret: **Brad Hayfield of the University of Maryland found that during peak performances the mind has relaxed its analytical side and is in a flow state with the body. Golfers should train more with clubs and swings they can use to control the ball, and less with swings they are trying to improve. Then, as the feel of effective motion becomes more repeatable they should move on to the other clubs and swing sizes. As the feel of effective motion becomes easier to recognize, swings also become more effective.**

Simple Information

Over time, most of us learned that the kind of information which has **proved to be the most valuable to us** appealed to our logic, and was presented in a logical manner. This information was not necessarily simple, but it always led to some insight that we did not have in the past. When golfers look for ideas and suggestions to improve their game, many golfers want them to be simple. But when asked if they would rather receive suggestions they understand or simple ones, everyone I have ever asked, votes for ideas they understand. In truth, at times some simple ideas are incomplete, and learners are left confused and misled, with results that are unsatisfying.

"Train the mind to use its own powers, rather than fill it with the ideas of others." - T. Edwards

For information to be useful it must be understood. Many times what is simple and what is understood are worlds apart. For example there are no simple directions from my golf course on Long Island to the Long Island Expressway. Any attempt to make them simple would only add time or get people lost on their way to the expressway. Another example: When learning to write, we first learn our "A, B, C's", then words, then sentences, then paragraphs. That's a simple description of learning how to write. It's also painfully incomplete. There is no mention of rules of grammar, punctuation, or capitalization, to name a few elements of writing left out of our simple but incomplete description of learning "how to" write.

Many, if not most golfers, are frustrated with their level of play, this frustration causes them to look for simple answers, which can lead to the "any port in a storm" approach to learning. As I said, at times it seems golfers are saying, "I know this may not be the best idea, but at least its something upon which to work on."

Secret: **Insights that leads to an understanding you did not have in the past are not necessarily simple, but they are understood.**

Awareness Instruction

Fred Schumacher, *"Great coaching is really a conversation - but it is important to note, it's not what we say, it's what we listen FOR that's important. Listening TO, normally takes place through our current beliefs. But listening FOR, is normally without expectations and preconceptions"*. Both parties, (learner and instructor) have to be **Aware**, **Observant**, and without **Exceptions**, before any long-term learning occurs. **When players listen FOR what balance, rhythm, and their feel have to say** (and are not thinking about some golf tip a friend gave them), **it can lead to long-term learning.**

Secret: **Practice halls in the far east are called "The place of enlightenment" (Dojo in Japan, DoJang in Korea, and Kwoon in China). They are places to make contact with ourselves, and a source of self-enlightenment where true learning starts.**

When you are training your swing, I suggest at times staying away from swing thoughts, and become more aware of other things. Ask questions like: "Was the clubface open or closed at impact?" "Was the shaft *above*, *below* or *on* the same lie angle through impact it was on at address?" "Was the clubface behind the hands at impact?" "Where was the shaft pointing at the top of the backswing?"

- Answers to these kinds of awareness questions can give the kind of insights upon which long-term learning is founded. When the mind is filled with swing tips, a player's ability to be aware is less than optimistic. World-class golfers and masters of other skills are more aware and, therefore, better prepared not necessarily more talented and gifted. They also tend to be better learners and have insights others do not. **World-class players realize the difference between knowledge of information and insights into its application**. There is a huge difference between them.

Secret: **Your approach to learning golf should first help you become more focused and aware. Focus gives feedback and distracts negative thoughts. Being aware personalizes information.**

Note: Over time, language has, of course, greatly improved the quality of life for the human race. The history of sharing ideas and information shows that human language probably first took place in early speech and pictures on the walls of caves, then on paper, then by a printing press, then the telegraph, then phones, then computers. Now we have the Internet. All this has improved the quality of life we all enjoy, but there has also been a cost. Namely, these inventions may have slowed down personal awareness, self-discovery and learning skills, as people have come to rely upon on second hand information.

The world can now use secondhand information. I am not so sure how useful this is if people start to overlook their most valuable source of information, themselves. Awareness and self discovery lead to the kind of insights that secondhand information cannot possibly provide.

Advice!

Many people who take up the game of golf, will not reach their potential! **Many** golfers do not break one-hundred, even with "gimmee" putts! **Many** who play use a motion that bears little or no resemblance to effective swings. They lose their balance more than once during their swing (every time they swing). **Many** use a swing that is either too fast or too slow - a swing that is "out of time", "beat" or "rhythm". They are using clubs that do not match their physical strength or posture, and have preconceptions of what to do that does not lead to progress and long-term learning.

The above **statements are all true. The following may give insights into some of the reasons why:** First, golf is a very hard game and it is difficult to play good golf for several reasons.

- The game is never played under the same conditions. Everyday, every course, every hole, every green are all different. The back nine often present different conditions then the front nine.
- From day one millions of golfers have made trillions of swings - and no two swings have ever been exactly alike.
- More often than not, it takes a fair amount of time for golfers to learn how to "play the game" and to perform up to their potential.
- There is little common ground and much disagreement within most golf instruction. This can make things very difficult for many golfers looking for help.

It also seems that there is very little about golf that is natural or **comes naturally** to people. Just watch new golfers make their first swings. But some who give advice to golfers ask them to look beyond all the conflicting advice that is available. They encourage learners to put aside the many difficulties the game and the course present, and suggest that the game and swing are as natural as walking and throwing a ball.

Secret: Keep in mind when a golf ball is hit correctly, an area about the size of a pinhead on the ball is impacted by another area about the size of a pinhead on the clubface. The clubhead moves somewhere between 70 and 100 MPH. The player also coordinates over 700 muscles and 200 bones, to make the ball go where the player predicted it would. **Precision in, precision out.** That is what efficient swings do, and what inefficient swings can't do!

Advice about how natural or simple golf can be may encourage and support a player's mental and emotional state. But, I do not know how **inefficient swings** are going to hit more fairways and greens, or how **inefficient swings** are going to have any measurable improvement from this kind of advice. Given a choice between information that gives the impression the swing and game are as natural as walking or information that can lead to insight and understanding about the game and swing a player did not have in the past, **there really is no choice.** Without some understanding of **Golf's Physical Basics** and the requirements of the task at hand, I do not see how players are going to hit more fairways and greens.

On the other hand very good advice points out that a golfers' self-image and self-worth should not be based on how good one plays the game. Advice that points out that golf can be an outdoor activity where we enjoy the companionship of others, while testing our ability to trust and let go is also **good advice**. Advice that points out that trying to look good and not hit bad shots in front of others will get in the way of your progress and enjoyment of the game, is **good advice**. To accept what the game and your swing are giving you on a given day is also **good advice** (much better then not accepting and complaining).

Secret: It's been said that any information that humans have been exposed to may still be recorded in our brain. My question is, if a golfer has **never** made a effective swing or when watching one it has been **misinterpreted**, or if the advice the player has received is **misleading**, how can any amount of trust, letting go, and being natural, lead to progress and efficient swings *without a useful learning model?*

Golf is a game that rewards precision, especially if part of your enjoyment is lower scores and solid shots. Efficient swings not only hit the ball solidly; more often than not they also control the height, distance and direction of the flight of the ball. **Any old swing cannot give those kinds of results. Any old advice will not help build a swing that can.** When golfers are inconsistent, I understand how this opens the door for seeking advice from almost any source. When that advice does not seem to work, people look for more and different advice. This, faulty cycle is often repeated again and again.

TODAY'S PROBLEMS ARE OFTEN BASED ON YESTERDAYS ADVICE

Golfers cannot see themselves swing. This fact opens the door for advice. But most of the advice comes from a friend or playing companion who is also inconsistent. When golfers are trying to improve, they often become prisoners of their own thinking which may well be founded on misconceptions. This weak foundation causes today's swing problems. Unless you ask for advice by asking someone to watch something specific, **STOP LISTENING!, AND STOP GIVING ADVICE NOW!** People in your golfing life may be very qualified in their chosen line of work, but most advice they are going to give will only slow down or prevent any long-term progress of which you are capable of. In saying this I feel I am making an understatement.

There is a good chance most of you who are reading this do not know me personally. We have never met or talked about your game. You have no reason on earth to take my suggestions to heart. It's going to be very hard to stop taking advice when it's human nature to be open to advice when things are not going well. It's also human nature to give advice. But these two acts of human nature may be one of the main reasons many golfers do not make the kind of progress which they are capable.

Note: Poor advice leads to poor perceptions, providing results below one's potential.

Some people reading this may feel I have crossed the line by suggesting that all of you stop giving each other golf lessons, especially without me hearing or seeing the advice. If we are going to be honest, more friends with few exceptions have been hurt rather than helped by advice given by golfing companions.

Secret: Because the golfer, ball, club and playing field are located here on earth, the physical laws that govern all things on earth also influence the golfer, his ball, club, swing, and the field of play. Most of what takes place in a effective swing is really not negotiable. It is governed by natural physical laws and the **physical basics** of the game that have not changed since day one.

While golf has some science and natural laws at its foundation, it's also an art. Golf (like art) is felt, experienced, and created differently by everyone who has ever played the game and this is one of the reasons there has been very little common ground in golf instruction information.

In some cases you can believe what you read. This is one of them – **many golfers have not improved or experienced any long-term learning because of the approaches to learning golf they are now using**. It may be time to change your approach from a mindless **How To** system, into a mindful **What To** approach based on self-discovery and new insights. If you can recognize any logic in this, maybe **Golf Just Got Easier to Learn**.

NEW INSIGHTS

Information does not have to change to handle the problems of learning golf. You just have to change the way information is viewed and used. New discoveries can be built on old discoveries; and surprise upon surprise.

When the once unobservable (but present) is seen through a new light, the unknown becomes self-evident, and that is my suggestion to golfers who are not happy with their games or rate of progress. Change your point of view not your information. **It is my guess as you change your view of golf instruction information, most of it will no longer seem as valuable as it once did, and small amounts will become very valuable!**

Stephen Toulmin, a professor at the University of Chicago said, *"If there is a point, where we do not know for certain what we do know, or what we understand, don't let this frighten you, and do not ignore it either - because we do know it - its just unobserved as yet."* Things can really become self-evident when seen from a new perspective making what we see, feel, and interpret more recognizable to the individual learner. One of the goals of **Golf Swing** Secrets...and Lies, is to have readers develop new insights which can lead them in the direction of "mastery".

Secret: **Golfers need advice for awareness and comprehension, not short-term memory. Golfers need advice for above the eyes (the brain), to improve our body motion below the eyes.**

The How of Mastering

The following thoughts on mastery were based on notes I made while listening to a lecture by George Leonard. I highly recommend his book Mastery.

"The skills of mastery have always been very hard to define, even though everyone can easily recognize them. Mastery is based on a few unchanging laws (as are golf swings). Mastery is not just for the gifted and those who start early in life, it has always been available to anyone. It's available to anyone who will get on the long road to mastery, and is willing to stay on course. Regardless of age, sex, or previous personal growth individual mastery can be achieved." – George Leonard

- Mastery shouldn't be seen as a goal, it's more of a journey on a path of learning.
- Mastery starts with a commitment to the journey.
- It helps mastery to honor your dark side.
- The path to mastery must start with small steps.
- Masters of skills are also prepared to spend most of their time on plateaus
- Masters practice and train for the joy of it.
- People who have gained mastery have stayed away from getting ahead of themselves. They are always cultivating the mind and heart of a beginner.
- People who gain mastery always stay students.

There are no maps to guide us or even point out a path to mastery. People may ask "how long will it take?" but if the mind is on results, one's ability to be aware of what causes results gets lost. Mastery is made up of small short spurts of progress and learning. They are always followed by longer lasting plateaus. Learning happens in stages. At times there may seem to be no progress. In fact when golfers are scoring in the mid 90's stuck on that plateau for some time, they can really be learning how to break 90 and score in the 80's. Working on your game without expectations leads to mastery. People who are willing to stay on a plateau and learn, are on a path to mastery. **Plateaus are where learning happens.**

Masters of any skill are always cultivating the mind and heart of a beginner. They love to train and practice. **They see a path to learning as a verb, and training and practice as nouns.** They are involved in the joy of the journey. They are not in it for what they think they are going to get. They are committed to the process of learning and not only to achieving the end product. They realize it is "a" path, not "the" path to mastery they are on. Masters have discovered they gain energy by working and thinking, as they try and try, again and again, staying open and aware in the present. **Unfortunately today's modern world is filled with messages of quick fixes, instant success, and fast temporary relief.** All of their solutions lead people away from mastering anything with results that lead to long-term learning. How many people would start to learn something new, if they knew how long it was going to take?

Secret: The body and brain naturally resist change, both good and bad changes. This is called homeostasis.

This natural resistance to change is not all bad. For example, if the body's normal temperature of 98.6 were to change only 10% (higher or lower), we would probably be dead. When practicing and training, if golfers are aware of **the natural resistance to change,** it gives insights into how long it takes to make changes. What takes most people out of their "golf comfort zone" when making a change is the **anticipation** of poor results that are both predictable and natural. (I recommend reading Mastery, by G. Leonard.)

SEQUENCE OF INFORMATION

While we recognize that poor concepts and perceptions can slow down the progress of which golfers are capable, we should not overlook another very important area that must be taken into consideration, **the sequence of information**. The sequence in which information is presented or gathered is as important to progress as the information, itself. When the sequence of information improves, a road to learning opens. This is a road on which players may not have been on before. The six lessons in Chapter Two are given in the sequence of information I use more often than not.

Information in most cases does not have to change to make it more valuable, just change the way it is presented, or interpreted to add to its value.

Valuable information, when presented or gathered out of sequence (before or after what would be the most useful time), is of less than optimal value. For example; gathering information about the backswing **before** a golfers posture and alignment are taken into consideration **could slow progress**. Another example: the elements of balancing and swing timing are discussed in this book before moving on to golf swing elements. **If balancing and swing timing are not what they should be, any efforts put into improving swing mechanics would go un-rewarded.**

"Golf is an exercise in perceptions: every shot requires that you estimate where you are in relation to your target." - Shivas Irons

The most valuable sequence for instruction information first presents information that is clearly a foundation for the next piece of your golfing puzzle. Information when gathered or presented randomly sits by itself without a foundation. It does not lead to the next element of the swing or game to be learned. In many cases golfers with swings below their potential, built that swing without a effective sequence of information, developing motion that is also out of sequence.

Secret: **We learned letters before words, words before sentences, sentences before paragraphs and so on. This kind of sequence provides both a foundation for the next piece of information, and leads logically down a path of learning that provides long-term fulfillment. (Out of sequence golf information cannot offer this.)**

Former PGA Teacher of the Year and highly respected instructor, Hank Haney (Mark O'Meara's coach) has always pointed out the importance of sequence of information.

SIMILAR STRATEGIES

Strategies for people who are learning golf and sculptors who are creating art have several similarities. The artist starts with their perception of what they want, a hammer, and a block of stone. The golfer starts with a club, ball, and their perceptions of what they want to do. The sculptor now chips away pieces of stone to reveal their finished work. The golfer also removes bad habits on his or her way to making progress. **Both the sculptor and golfer use a process of subtraction to reach their goal.** It is useful to recognize the chips of stone that fall to the floor are as important as is the finished work to any artists progress. The bad habits golfers remove are also very important. Our ability to return to a desired end result is founded more on knowing what was subtracted, than what we may believe we should add. Often after we subtract, no additions are necessary. **Many golfers unfortunately may go about trying to improve by looking for additions, rather than learning what must be taken away, never reaching their potential.** "More" is normally "less" when it comes to making progress in golf.

The strategy that leads to progress in one area of our life often leads to progress in other areas, this is also true for what slows progress. Golfers can gain some insights into learning golf by looking into the field of art education.

Peter Plagens, a noted art critic said, *"Art schools today are trying to teach art, but at one time art students were learning art skills in school."* Art historian, Barbara Rose, said, *"Unfortunately, today most art looks like homework. It is art that follows some teacher's rules."* **Unfortunately golfers, who are not making progress often look like they are following someone else's "how to" list.**

Debra Soloman, New York Times art critic, said, *"Art is very popular today, and within this market-driven business climate, there is no shortage of new artist and new art.* Debra also points out this is not the same as important art, art that promises to last. **Golf is also very popular today, and within this business climate there has been no shortage of new golf swing ideas**. As with art, an abundance of new ideas is not the same as providing important instruction information that leads to long term learning.

While golfers and artists may need some help to become aware of workable approaches for any problems they face, **golfers and artists must also be given the freedom to use their own awareness and self-discovery skills in solving problems.** *"Students do not understand you have to make your self into an artist. A masters degree in art means little."* said Nancy Rubin, a noted sculptor. Many golfers make a parallel mistake by putting more faith in someone else's "how to list" then in their own awareness and self-discovery skills, and don't see the kind of progress of which they are capable.

Some golfers are like sports expansion teams which spend money to buy players in pursuit of a dream, and go quickly from the excitement of expansion to the realities of being a new team. Expansion teams do not cultivated talent within a farm system. This is much like golfers who embrace someone else's "how to" advice and overlook cultivating skills through their own insights. There is a long list of things money can't buy. Learning motion pattern skills is one of them . **When learning golf, don't go out for dinner, stay at home and enjoy the pleasures only a home cooked meal can offer.**

Today while buying things is in vogue, you can't purchase knowledge that is personal in nature. For both the golfer and the artist, the "knack of" a skill is cultivated by staying open and aware of what our bodies are saying.

Fred Shoemaker, *"People are born able, but self-interference gets in the way on the course. The shot you don't like is not what makes golfers mad, it's people believe they will do it again. What we believe the future will be, effects how we act today. Golfers see threats to their ego. They see hard shots with bad results, all with people watching. You will see little or no progress until negative self-doubt and lack of trust are both removed."* I would also add, subtract any "how to" list you may now be using with which to learn the game. **For years, golfers have been asking for answers they can and should learn to answer for themselves.**

By finding ways to enhance our learning potential, we can enhance our performance potential. When someone's golf game needs strong medicine, they should find an approach to learning that easy to swallow. It's time golfers learned to take advantage of their past experiences and self-discovery skills to improve future experiences. A bright future for anyone's golf game requires a plan, **and the heart and soul of that plan is the golfers awareness and self-discovery skills.** For many golfers the door to progress stays closed for several reasons including: misinformation and poor concepts, and using someone else's "how to" list.

Secret: Self-discovery is the only approach to learning that can accommodate everyone's potential.

U.S. Secretary of Education, Richard Riley made some observation about schools and long-term learning in November of 1999 on the Learning Channel. All of us can gain some useful insights from those observations. I have used several of his statements throughout this work.

"Schools give information, give tests, then grade tests. There is little self-discovery or real world experiences in traditional schools." – Richard Riley, U.S. Secretary of Education

Secret: Golfers may feel they have no influence over the instruction information they now can receive from a variety of sources, but every golfer can choose the type of instruction information they use. Words and images form a sound track in our mind. **Learn to distinguish the sounds of enlightenment, from the sounds of distractions; the sounds of connections, from the sounds that fragment; the sounds of what is personal, from the sounds of impersonal; the sounds of causes from the sounds of results.**

"Schools should be more than getting grades. Schools should be about falling in love with learning and keeping a students natural curiosity active." – Richard Riley

"Our life is what our thoughts make it" - Marcus Aurelius.

"Why don't I teach? You can't find anyone who wants to learn." - Ben Hogan

Virtual Science

Golfers who are not happy with their progress need more "learning power". On April 4, 2000 Section Four of the Sunday New York Times was titled "Education Life". In this section Nancy Beth Jackson wrote Virtually Science, an article that discussed the value of science experiments done on computer screens. Since the early 90's, what education refers to as virtual experiments using computers are being performed at most leading Universities by students studying Physics, Chemistry, Biology, Science, Human Anatomy. **Consequently learning power is not what it once was.**

Virtual Science occurs when a traditional classroom science experiment, using Bunsen burners and frogs, etc. (wet labs) is replaced by doing experiments on computer screens (dry labs). **Leaders in education believe that something is getting lost in dry labs.**

I bring this up here because there were many parallels in Nancy Jackson's article about dry labs and their negative impact on learning science with the lack of progress golf drills, how to lists, and expert models gives golfers

Dr. Lawrence J Kaplan of Williams College said, *"In dry labs, tactical experience gets lost, the learning that comes from mistakes that can refine technique is not available. Some experiences can't be duplicated in dry labs using computers. Computers can lull students into believing they have learned something, and never understand the concepts to master them."*

This of course is similar to how drills, "how to" lists and expert models can lull golfers into believing they are on the road to long-term learning.

- Nora Sabeilli – National Science Foundation. *"60-70% of the student studying science never do a real experiments."* Most golfers who are trying to improve do so under false pretenses in environment that do not support long-term learning.
- Arthur Levine – President of Teachers College at Columbia University. *"I'm worried students will miss the froginess of a real frog, or the opportunity to learn through Murphy's law. The advantages of the real experience can't be duplicated on computers."* Golf "drills" and "how to" lists cannot duplicate what self-discovery can when learning to make progress in golf.
- Dan Jang – University of California, Berkely – *"You really need to experience an actual cadaver to thoroughly learn anatomy. Arteries and veins can look alike, but you can feel the difference by touching them."*
- Linda Grace Kobas – Cornell Spokeswoman. *"Most of our faculty does not think the quality of the learning experience is the same in a dry lab."*
- Luis Auila – Columbia University Physical Chemistry Professor. *"Without the experimental exercise in wet labs, the students will never learn how, even with the best virtual reality software."*

- Dr. Edward F. Redish – University of Maryland Physics Professor. *"Dry labs is what I call the computer gets an A, the students get an F in experience. If they did not understand it before they saw it, they will not learn much from an experiment on a computer.*
- Golfers who have already learned a skill do gain some value from drills, but golfers who are trying to acquire don't improve their learning power from drills, "how to" lists, and expert models. Dr. Redish goes on to say, *"Students can be turned off by dry labs. Computer experiments don't provide insights into how science makes sense of the world. Computer experiments are often treated like a collection of meaningless revealed knowledge"*. Sounds like what can happen when golfers use someone else's "how to" list and drills; it's information without personal insights.

LONG-TERM LEARNING AND HUMAN EVALUATION

The following is based on notes I made when driving down Interstate 95 from New York to Florida. Maybe its not the safest way to drive, but I felt it would be good use of my time. There were several books I had wanted to read, but had little time in my schedule, so I listened to them on tapes as I drove. The books; How the Mind Works, by Steven Pinker; The Secret of the Soul, by Stuart Wilde; and How to Think Like De Vinci – Seven Steps to Genius, by Michael J. Geib.

The brain is an information processing system, designed with the ability to solve problems by reasoning. Our **mind** should be seen as what the brain does. Our mind thinks to retrieve information and **intelligence** turns that information into knowledge. Intelligence is the ability to pursue a goal in the face of obstacles (sounds like golf). Humans can combine abstract thinking (a skill unique to our species) with awareness and self-discovery to accomplish long-term learning.

Note: Causes always give **results** that can provide information for future use that no one's "**how to list**" could possibly provide. To retrieve and use the most useful information for future use, any past assumptions about how we have been trying to learn should probably be removed. It is always the eye of the beholder that is in control of how information is interpreted and then used.

Secret: **Long-term learning is not accomplished by following the old masters, but by seeking what old masters seek in your own best way.**

The ideal mind for learning is probably much like a clear mirror. It can see things as they are, and gives them back as they are. **We all improvise learning with assumptions and associations**. People can spend so much time on what they think something is, that they miss what it is. Unquestioned assumptions often cause poor results.

Long-term learning is really no more or no less than developing skills that solve problems. Learning does not come from using "**how to lists**." Today, the human species no longer relies on insights, intuition and innovation to grow, as often as we once did. What did hunting do for mankind's mind 1000's of years ago? It did everything. Hunting not only provided food, it developed every mental and physical skill mankind now has. **Because humans can now rely on others and upon their information, we often overlook our own capacities to learn.** You may ask why is a golf instruction book talking about the history of man? Simply because everything in life has a similar foundation and is connected in some way. Someone's lack of progress with golf often parallels much of mans lack of progress in history. Accomplishments also have parallels.

In some areas of education, what has been learned by others in the past does in fact help future knowledge. But when it comes to learning motion patterns, what has been experienced in the past by others has no real value to anyone else but the person who experienced that motion pattern. That person knows what it feels like to them; they know what it looks like to them; and they know how they would explain what they did. **Does anyone reading this book believe that any "how to list" developed by one person would have any real long-term learning value to anyone else?**

Secret: **Because Nature knows no other possibilities, anyone's efficient actions are influenced and controlled by external natural laws, not by someone else's ideas about motion patterns.**

Our beliefs and desires cause actions. We should do our best to narrow options to suitable perceptions. There are ways to explain, but some are more workable for an individual than others. Studies show people underestimate their potential. **Keep in mind your brain is better than you are now thinking.** Training and new insights can help the mind remember and develop information that lets people apply knowledge that is personal in nature. **There is a difference between information and knowledge. This fact cannot be overlooked.**

When learning, look for thoughts inside thoughts. Stay curious to learn. Commit to experimenting and learning from bad habits. Never overlook mistakes, if they happen, be open to gaining information from them. Long-term learning often happens when we are on a plateau, giving the impression of little progress. When golfers are shooting scores in the 90's, some are really learning to shoot scores in the 80's. Other golfers are learning very little.

Secret: It helps to realize that everything is connected; both the workable and the unworkable; the high and the low; the slow and the fast, are all connected Evolution operated with no goal in sight. **Use what you see and feel, not someone else's words.** Combine science and art. Efficient motion patterns are personal and artful, but their precision will need the guidelines only science can provide. When learning, **keep knowledge modifiable.** Use whole brain thinking combining logic and imagination. Use system thinking to see the connection in everything, then use those connections.

Reverse Engineering

For millions of years both mankind's body and mind have gone through an evolution process. Changing to adapt to the ever changing environment in which mankind was living. To be accurate, this re-engineering of mankind's body and mind should be seen as **reverse engineering**. Engineering designs and builds to create, **reverse engineering** designs to adapt. People who make progress in golf have adapted to **Golf's Physical Basics;** the club, ball, and field of play. Good golf and good golfers are a product of **reverse engineering**. Their swing and game were not built. Rather they are a product of adjusting and adapting to a changing golf environment. **Golfers slow down progress when they use an approach that tries to build a swing and style of play (using drills and expert models) and overlook the value of adapting and adjusting or reverse engineering.**

Man on all fours needed different physical and mental tools than man walking upright on two feet. The genius of natural selection would step in every so often and perform reverse engineering allowing mankind to adapt to the environment as it went through changes. **Designing a workable golf swing and style of play is also a reverse engineering process in which golfers adapt to the field of play, playing conditions, design angles of the club, and ballistic properties of the ball.**

At times people will pick up an object in an antique shop and don't understand what it is, or how it should be used. But after they find what the mysterious item was designed to do, a light of understanding goes on. Often, when a golfer, who is not making progress discovers the club was designed to return impact parallel to the lie angle upon which it was designed – it is my experience a light of understanding goes on. People now adapt their motion patterns to that angle, or plane of motion.

The human body and brain were both designed with principles of reverse engineering discarding some things along the way, while keeping useful regulators through natural selection. Mankind survived and rose to the top of the food chain through a process of mistakes and uncertainty as he learned to adapt. **Golfers who make progress have also learned to adapt to the uncertainties of the game, and used the mistakes their swings made when they were making progress.**

Note: There is a way of learning something that does not come from facts. Everyone has the ability to gain information from a sixth sense, an inner knowing called intuition that often works outside reasoning and intellect. Our ancestors (cave men) used intuitive skills or inner skill of knowing, to survive. **Good golfers use intuitive skill every time they are faced with conditions of play with which they are unfamiliar in tournament play.**

Today there exists a heightened state of gathering information upon which people often rely on that is **dulling the self-discovery, awareness and intuitive skills every man was born with.** Today, the golf instruction industry provides so much information that many people no longer use their intuitive skills to learn. Bombarded with information that can over-stimulate the mind, it becomes difficult to pick up any hidden information that is personal in nature.

Today's world is often just developing information. **It is not developing the intuitive skills which expand our sense of knowing, or our sixth sense.** Often, our eyes see what they have been told to see. Nothing of personal value registers. **Our intellect receives information but our intuitive skills do not**. By training the eye to observe first, without judgments, much can be learned. What we first see is often a misconception. It helps to recognize everything is some form of energy. The less energy you use to judge, the more energy you will have for insights. Our fears and intellect block insights that are personal in nature. When a golfer believes the shot is difficult, their fear of failure blocks their ability to play the shot.

Secret: There are really no experts. We only have the gift of sharing experiences with each other. The more tools and opportunities we use to share experiences, the less limiting the learning experience will be for both the giver and receiver.

Hopefully we are in a time of deep change regarding learning golf. In school we often learned information and alignment of thoughts, with our five senses. But what about the sixth sense? **The skill of intuitive knowledge**. We know people can touch and not feel, listen and not hear, look and not see, bite and not taste, smell and not recognize. Our 5 senses are not completely reliable. Our sixth sense, or intuitive knowledge, is more reliable. Smell, touch , see, hear, and taste can all be going on without learning or developing insights that are personal in nature.

Our intentions start every action. Therefore every result is caused by our intentions. But many people believe they are responsible for only some of their actions. However this cannot be so, if intention starts every action. Golfers, who intend to improve, must be aware of core golf information. Then they must use self-discovery skills, not "**how to**" lists.

Before the explosion of information, and **"how to lists,"** the world learned through adjusting to its changing environment. In the past, long-term learning happened, when the intentions of our inner powers (insights, intuition) outworked the elements of external power (i.e. fear, effort, control, money and position).

To learn what has to be learned for our own progress, we do not have to disagree with others. **We must only move away from someone else's interpretation of nature through their five senses and external powers**. When position, money, control, effort, and fear influence interpretation of information, the knowledge which has to be learned for our own progress, gets lost. When we read or hear about someone else's touch, taste, sight, smell, or hearing, **what has to be learned by us gets lost**.

The truth—**Golf's Physical Basics** contaminates no one! They are physical in nature and non-negotiable and effective for every golfer.

Emotions are currents of energy that pass through everyone, that could otherwise be used by our intuitive skills. Emotions are based on judgment, and judgments block insights into what has to be learned that is personal in nature. All emotions effect perceptions. Keep in mind, truth is what does not contaminate you or what you are trying to do. Truth empowers everyone (I.e. **Golf's Physical Basics**). Truth that does not contaminate, is the only real truth. **There is a difference between personal truth and impersonal truth. They are both true, but one is not true for you**. Truth can be contaminated by emotions and outside influences like our physical powers. Look for the non-physical realities that our insights and intuition offer. Learn from our non-physical teachers, not "how to" lists.

Sometimes, our answer (not someone else's answer) comes in the form of a feeling, memory, or a realization that comes later. **But we first have to learn what to ask.**

Secret: **Learn to ask for guidance not answers from golf instruction.** "Thought" is energy, or a light that has been formed by consciousness and awareness. You can change your thoughts by changing your awareness.

Quality of actions are based on intentions. You can't chose intentions until you are aware of what your real intentions are (often people will fool themselves) (i.e. are you trying to move the ball or compress the ball?) There are both external and internal forces that compete for out intentions. A wise choice of intentions takes into consideration results. (Form follows function).

In closing when we are learning through our personality and our five senses, we lose power at times as fear and doubt join the process. We gain power when we make choices through the clarity of insights that intuitive skills provide. What do you harvest when you are learning to play or improve your golf now? Once humans recognize problems, we either resist changing or try to change. Short cuts are warning signs, and are an opportunity to show off your physical power and avoid the empowerment of internal knowledge and our sixth sense. **Commitment to long-term learning is commitment to our internal powers of awareness, self-discovery, intuition, and creativity**.

Volume of Golf Information and The Renaissance

Michael J Gelb, a renowned innovator in the field of **creative thinking** and **accelerated learning, in his book, Seven Steps to Genius,** points out, even though mankind made many advances over time, he made no discoveries of note about the world and objects in it from the time of the fall of the Roman Empire up to the 14th century. During this time period the church was seen as the all knowing supreme authority on everything. All knowledge was believed to already be known. **People believed there was nothing new to learn.**

But soon, because of the birth of the Renaissance (1450-1550) people would no longer see the church as the only source of knowledge. The Renaissance was a time in history in which Leonardo Da Vinci and other great minds gave the world ideas and discoveries (from beyond the church) that would change the world for ever. i.e. Gutenberg's printing press, John Widman's math symbols, and Peter Heinleins hand-held time piece; to mention only a few.

The Renaissance would cause the world to change, but what caused the Renaissance? Many historians point to the Bubonic plague that swept across the land several times from 1350-1400, (killing the rich, the poor, and church authorities), as one reason for the Renaissance and for the great discoveries of that time.

This plague caused several important events. First there was a huge decline in population leading to a shortage in labor and significant redistribution of wealth. In the minds of many, there was now a sense of equality that did not exist before the Renaissance. After all, the Black plaque killed both nobles and peasants. No one was spared, even those who were looked upon as noble and special.

In what could be categorized as strictly business decisions, some of that redistributed money would now be invested to support efforts to find knowledge beyond church authorities. **With the hope of making a profit**. We could say the Renaissance gave the world its first IPO's and a flood of ideas about everything. **This flood was driven in part by a capitalization of business opportunities.**

Let's now look a the money that was redistributed after the black plague as similar to the non-golf money which started to come into the golf industry about 1985. That money also expected a return on investment. History informed the world about the great discoveries and ideas of the Renaissance. But history often overlooks the money invested for profit that did not improve our way of life or make a profit. **The golf industry has some similar examples.**

The golf boom that started in the mid 80's was also founded on a capitalization of business opportunities. There was less of everything in the game before what I call the "non-golf money" that expected a profit came into the game. While I will leave it to others to debate the real value of having more of everything in golf – **more instruction information (driven by business opportunities) has slowed progress and long-term learning.** Especially, when there is little common ground in the volume of golf instruction information available from a variety of sources. Today's golf advice has more forgettable mediocrity than quality information. Because there are more golfers it does not mean the world needs more "how to lists."

The freedom of thought given to the world by the Renaissance, cannot be measured in its importance. But today individual thinking is rare, and, therefore, more important than ever when it comes to learning to improve ones golf. **The flood of second-hand golf instruction and advice (driven mostly by business opportunities), in many cases is just too difficult for the unsophisticated golfer to avoid or evaluate.** The value of personal insights is being overlooked for the convenience of "how to lists." Humans are born with intuitive curiosity. In my view intuitive curiosity has been hampered by the volume of "how to instruction."

On the other hand long-term learning can be helped by both a high tolerance for the "uncertain" and being a disciple of "gaining by experience". Good learners are seekers of connections and learn to understand systems. A human is made of three systems: the mind, body, and soul (emotions). When you are trying to learn, are all your systems in balance and agreement? When they all agree, the mind sees it, the body does it, and our emotions allow it to happen.

"We need smart goals when learning," M.J. Gleb

S Specific goals
M Measurable goals
A Accountability goals
R Realistic goals
T Time line goals

When learning, do I ask myself the most useful question?

- Am I learning from both my workable and unworkable experience?
- Can I improve how I learn from them?
- What can I do to develop an independence of thought, with so much information available?
- Do I balance my body and mind?
- Do I hold creative tension and consideration?
- What are my plans for improving?

Secret: **Good learning skills joins: Experience with new perception. Logic with imagination, Reason with romance, and Science with art.**

When people are performing or creating a motion pattern for the first time, one's ability to move is based first on our perception or upon someone else's description of the act. **Doing something a second time is consciously or unconsciously based on what was done the first time, even if we are being told how to do it.** Progress in how we move our body through space is clearly based on becoming aware of the feel of both workable and unworkable motion patterns.

When we are not happy with our actions, in many cases, there was not enough internal information available to make the needed adjustments. Many golfers miss the internal information available after a motion pattern, because they are following someone "how to do it" list. When it comes to performing and creating golf swings, I question how many golfers use the internal information that makes long-term learning possible.

GOLF SWING INCORPORATED – A FABLE TO PONDER

*While Golf Swing Inc. is a fictitious company, we can gain real insights into the value of self-discovery and awareness skills from its approach to business.

Let's imagine there is a small company Golf Swing Inc. (GSI) located in the city of Linksland in the country of Everywhere. The company has one product. They produce golf swings. They have made them for millions of golfers for over 500 years with less than 30 employees. These original employees are the only workers GSI has ever had. This staff when left to do what the conditions of play require, have always done their job without help from others.

The only staff GSI has ever had, includes 12 sets of twins; two shoulder joints, two hip joints, two elbow joints, two wrist joints, two knee joints, two ankle joints, two arms, two legs, two eyes, two ears, two hands, two feet, a spine, mouth, and brain. You may now realize why it has never been necessary to hire new employees to produce swings. For over 500 years GSI has had the only staff it needed to make swings for a worldwide customer base that varied in age, size, and gender.

Like all successful companies, GSI has a broad-based goal. In their case it is to produce an effective golf swing for the shot at hand. Meeting this goal has required all employees to understand the company's goal, and for each employee to use their individual skills to the best of their abilities, adapting to golf's environment.

To accomplish their goal, GSI was careful to take into consideration each employee's individual skill, they did not expect any staff member to work outside their area of expertise. For example, GSI would not expect the knee joints to work before the hip joints have gone into motion in backswing, nor would they want the wrist joints to uncock before the shoulder joints or elbow joints move down-plane.

The management team at GSI has always received help from outside consultants; including balance, timing, transfer of momentum, gravity, rotation, mechanical laws, bio-mechanical principles, and some psychology to support the efforts of their staff.

From day one, GSI ran training programs for its staff. It should be noted that these programs have gone through several changes over time. **The changes in training came about to improve the way in which information during the training/learning programs were being shared, not to make any changes in their product, a golf swing.** GSI realized from day one an effective golf swing was a constant founded on **Golf's Physical Basics**. The company also realized that the training programs needed to undergo some changes, if golf swings were going to become less difficult for the staff to learn and repeat.

GSI is very proud of many swings it has produced over time. For example, there was the Harry Vardon model, the Bobby Jones model, the Sam Snead model, the Ben Hogan model, the Jack Nicklaus model, the Mickey Wright model, etc. GSI was also aware many swings were not as effective as they could be, and management wanted that statistic to change, so golfers everywhere could lower their handicaps. *"Students should be in a setting where they are not only responsible for today's results, but see how what they are trying to learn is used in the future."* – Richard Riley, U.S. Secretary of Education

In the past, the training programs at GSI were telling employees what to do for the shot at hand i.e. *"Shoulder you must..., Hips have to..., Arms you must feel...etc."*. From day one the discoveries of Sir Isaac Newton guided GSI's thoughts about the properties of efficient swings but the company had no guidelines when it came to helping their employee's learn the elements of efficient swings and their application. Recently GSI started to take into account their insights. If their training did less dictating and more empowering of staff through self discovery and awareness of golf's environment, (i.e. **Golf's Physical Basics**), the staffs ability to repeat effective golf swings would improve.

GSI's management recognized that because both staff and management were used to an approach that had always told employees what to do, introducing self-discovery and awareness would at first meet with some resistance. For hundreds of years GSI's staff (arms, legs, shoulders, etc.) were making golf swings based on directions they were given by the company. Under these conditions the staff was trying to make the "company's swing". The staff was not producing a swing that was based on their own discoveries and their own feel for the shot at hand. GSI hoped that after their staff learned and was empowered through self-discovery, the quality of golf swings they were producing would improve.

When empowerment works, it comes from the top down (i.e. management, parents, instructors, and coaches). Empowerment is a journey where some unexpected things are going to occur, especially if people are used to having decisions made for them or having been told what they should feel. In the past, traditional "how to" approaches to sharing information often got in the way of any journey to self-discovery, empowerment, and self-reliance at GSI

At first, some in management felt that if empowerment, self-discovery, and awareness skills were to take hold, management would soon be out of a job. This of course was not the case. When management became less controlling and directing their time was now used to guide employees into new insights that set the boundaries for the task at hand. One key to self-discovery is how management perceives information.

Secret: GSI discovered information was more valuable when used as a guide, then a how to list.

If there was going to be any long-term progress, learning had to become a team effort, in which there was no perceptual division between the thirty GSI employees and management. Both groups must be on the same page, when it came to determining what core knowledge they were to take away from the company outside consultants (balance, timing, transfer of momentum, gravity, rotation, mechanical laws, bio-mechanical principals, and psychology).

If the staff at GSI was going to make workable decisions which would result in making repeating golf swings easier, **management discovered that staff members did not need directions, they needed information that is personal in nature**. When information is enhanced by self-discovery, the end product is also enhanced. When the end product is based mostly on someone else's directions, (management, parents, instructors, and coaches) long-term learning is not optimized. People who are following "how to" lists, do not have the same commitment as those who feel they are involved and feel equally responsible for the end product.

Balls and Clubs Speak

GSI has recently developed technology that made it possible for golf balls and clubs to reveal how they believe the employees at GSI used clubs and balls, when the Bobby Jones model, the Ben Hogan model, the Mickey Wright model, were used.

The golf ball pointed out that many unworkable swings did not realize golf balls were born with out wings, but that balls did understand the dynamics of propulsion by on-plane force through impact. The golf ball also believed as more swings realized their cover was soft, and balls would fly after being compressed, swings would learn more about impact alignments. The golf ball wished the swing understood it should always swing down and out, and not up after impact, with the clubhead trailing the grip end.

Golf clubs said they were always willing to work for any swing, but felt at times they intimidated most golf swings. Clubs revealed most swings were clumsy in the way they treated them and that people did not realize clubs respond best to gentle and careful stroking. Many swings also don't realize clubs work best when they swing on an inclined plane that the shaft established at address. Clubs believed that most swings don't realize that the shaft, clubhead, and clubface should hinge and unhinge in the same groove through impact. Clubs said most swings try to have the hands unhinge, when they should let clubs, by means of their own built up force and momentum do the unhinging through impact.

Clubs also pointed out that many swings do not understand the need for constant acceleration in the downswing often complaining about being over accelerated with some golf swings always jumping at the ball at impact.

GSI was excited to have the ability to learn from balls and clubs what they expected from golf swings. Because GSI training programs were now including self-discovery, the company felt its staff would become aware of what golf swings and balls expected of them in the future, without using "how to" information.

LEARNING QUOTES

"Loyalty to an opinion never broke a chain or freed a human soul." – Mark Twain

"It takes a golden ear to be empty enough of itself – to hear clearly." – M.C. Richard's

"It is not enough to study action under a microscope, you need to know what it feels like." – Roger Fisher

"Each time we see motion, it is our own ideas of the action which we recognize." – M. Proust

"Education consists mainly in what we have unlearned." – Mark Twain

"When I was a kid I drew like Michelangelo, it took me years to learn to draw like a kid." – Pablo Picasso

"One can change things by the manner in which one looks at them. We can change perception." – Tom Robbins

"Finally you understand that the real motorcycle (or swing) you are working on is yourself." – Robert M. Pirsio

"A mind that is stretched to a new idea never returns to its original dimension." – O.W. Holmes

"Whatever authority I may have rests safely on knowing how little I know." – Socrates

"Artistic growth is a refining of the sense of truthfulness." – "the stupid believe the truth is easy." – only great artists know how difficult it really is." – Willa Cather

"80% of life is just showing up prepared." – Woody Allen

"All golfers are ready to play, but most are not prepared, and there is a difference." – Michael Hebron

"Words are like angels, they have invisible power over us." – James Hellmann

"We have to stop overvaluing words – we should realize they are only one of the many bridges that connect our thoughts to common life." – Rainer Maria Rilke

"He who knows that enough is enough, will always have enough." – Lao-Tzu

"Healing has nothing to do with books – and can't be learned from another person." – It is a matter of feeling, having a fresh mind, knowing how to listen to what no one else listens to." – Dominganga Nancufil

"I learn through my hands, my eyes, and my skin what I can never learn through my brain." – M.C. Richards

"To know truth one must get rid of labels – nothing is more powerful and creative than emptiness." – Lao-Tau

"I don't paint things. I only paint the difference between things." – Henri Matisse

"The voyage of discovery lies not in finding new landscapes – but in having new eyes." – Marcel Proust

"Tell me – I forget"
"Show me – I remember"
"Involve me – I will understand" – Confucius

"Like fingerprints and voices, each person's learning style is a little different. It determines how students approach a task and remember information." – Lynn O' Brien

"Our minds want clothes and food, as much as out bodies." – Samuel Butler

"Tell me what you pay attention to, and I will tell you who you are." – Jose Casset

"Don't stop exploration, at the end of exploring we will arrive where we started, and know it for the first time." – T.S. Eliot

"Ah – if I could dance all that you've just said – then I would understand." – Zorba the Greek

"Minds that do not change are like clams that don't open." – Ursla LeGuin

"The soul should always stay ajar – ready to welcome the next experience." – Emily Dickinson

"It is in fact, it's nothing short of a miracle that the modern methods of instruction have not entirely strangled all curiosity of inquiry." – Albert Einstein

"Telling ain't teaching – and listening ain't learning." – Bob Barkley

"All real truth touches not only the mind but also the imagination and an unconscious depth in a person. After years it may come to the surface of consciousness to yield new insights." – Helen Luke

"New consciousness is not a new thing – it is a long painful return to what has always been." – Helen Luke

"Learning is the ability to make sense out of something you observe, based on your experience." – Art Winter

"Learning is being able to take an observation and associate it with meaning." – Ruth Winter

"The maintenance of present knowledge requires review and the constant addition of new information." – Art Winter

"If a little knowledge is dangerous – where is the man who has so much he is out of dangers." – A. Huxley

"Iron rusts from disuse. – Stagnant water loses its purity. – Cold freezes still water. – and inaction saps the vigor's of the mind!" – Leonardo Da Vinci

"We can begin to experience fulfillment as soon as we choose to create environment permitting us to do so." – Bob Samples

"Learning can be defined as the process of remembering what you are interested in." – R.S. Wurman

"Does it then follow, the responsibility of instruction is to create interest?" – Michael Hebron

"Anyone who stops learning is old – the greatest thing in life is to keep your mind young – so keep learning." – Henry Ford

"Cultivate faith in yourself as a learner. Research now shows that adults are better learners than children when they act like beginners." – M. Ferguson

"If the brain is a computer, it is often run by unskilled labor." – David Lewis

"The experimental man improves after experiments – he learns how to learn. He not only solves problems set for him by the experimenter – he becomes more skilled in solving them." – G. Bateson

"When the brain is an open system, it can become intimate with what lives outside of it." – Bob Samples

"We are not troubled by things, but by the opinions which we have of things." –Epictetus

"Self-education is, I firmly believe, the only kind of education there is. Instructors and schools can only make self-education easier, failing that, they do nothing." – Issac Asimor

"Learning is not a task or problem – it is a way to be in the world. Man will learn as he pursues goals that have meaning for him." – Sidney Jourard

"There are no limits to the process of leaning how to learn – find new ways to structure knowledge and you will never again be bored." – R. Theobald

"A teacher is like a fire – get too close and you get burned. Stay away – no heat. Sensible moderation is recommended." – Tibetan Proverb

"Ancient Greeks knew learning came from playing – their concepts for education (Paideia) is almost identical to their concept for play (Paidia)." –Rroger Von Oech

"Transformed perception could be called 'ordinary magic.' Ordinary because it is hidden from us by nothing other than our reluctance to see it and habits. Magic because transformation of perception happens suddenly, even though it may have taken training, practice and energy." – J. Hayward

"Learning is a matter of attitude, not aptitude." – G. Lozanov

"Experience is not what happens to you – its what you make out of what happens to you." – A. Huxley

SOME CLOSING THOUGHTS

Secret: Perception of information is where learning and decisions have their start. **How we see, hear or feel information can prevent, slow down or lead to progress.** By stepping away from conventional tips into self-discovery alternatives, we gain more useful information than "how to" lists provided.

- Self-discovery requires being aware.
- Being aware leads to new perception.
- New perceptions lead to new concepts.
- New concepts can lead to long-term progress.

Suggestion: Re-conceptualize information (if it is valid) and use new perceptions, and don't look for new information every time you are not happy with your golf.

Adults often try to learn and fail because of their need to succeed fragments any gestures of freedom and enthusiasm. Children often break the rules of **what** to, **when** to, and **where** to, on their way to progress. Adults at times use such a careful application of motion little learning occurs.

Picasso said he painted and trained all his life, so one day he could paint like children do. When trying to improve our golf, information may not be as important a imagination. After all, imagination is a preview of coming events. When learning I can't think of anything more important or more fun than imagination.

Secret: **Look for progress from innovation, the unknown, the untried, and not by trying for optimization.**

When learning to play golf, try the untried and expect the unexpected as you look from different angles. Be playful as you get in touch with your feel for timing and balance. The possibilities are endless. There really are no rules when it comes to imagination. There is no chance for self-discovery or individual greatness when we try to learn from "how to" lists. When learning, consider playing "what if." After all, things are often not what they seem to be. **It is more important what someone can take away from a book, then how it was written.** Every golfer in the world has the capacity to create and improve!

Chapter Six

Extra Credit

Reading this section is similar to
extra credit work in a classroom setting.

The following contains details that may only interest
some readers, but it's information that could
be used by every reader.

General Thoughts

"People who want to learn how to play better golf must understand information can only inform and explain. Golfers must absorb and apply information to improve their game. The principles that govern the operation of a golf stroke (it is motion, force, structure) have been known since the days of Isaac Newton. Any short cuts around them can easily turn out to be the longest route. People can't play the game with more precision than their game possesses. The process of adapting and adjusting ones game has a degree of latitude. The precision that a prospective champion would need, is not the same as that of the occasional player. A step by step approach is needed, much like building a house. The only useful shortcuts come from more know how. A careless beginning can be disastrous." – Homer Kelly

Secret: **Learn to distinguish basic information from individual techniques, and observe how the basics are applied by skilled players.**

For some, golf has become, "the in game to play" requiring: Interest, Information, Inspiration, Intelligence, Interpretation, Intention, Intuition, Interaction, Industry, Inquiries, and Insights!

People who are familiar with my work as a golf instructor – know I'm not trying to teach physical actions. Rather I use an approach that tries to provide and support an environment for learning physical actions. Subjects like math, history, and English are taught. Physical actions are learned. Today, unlike 20 years ago, there are many studies and research that supports this approach.

In 1940's a well known golf instructor Ernest Jones, said "Swing the clubhead," Ernest also said he could teach his method to anyone in a few minutes, and believed he did. But this was far from teaching someone to play golf. "After we learn to swing like Hogan, we still have to learn how to play like him."- Author unknown

To physically swing a golf club is not too difficult, but we have to do more than just swing. An efficient swing impacts the ball on an area the size of a pin head with an area the size of a pin head on the clubface, without the clubhead passing the left wrist joint. The shaft, hands, arms, and shoulders also travel through impact on their individual but parallel planes of motion at a speed appropriate for the shot at hand.

No golfer, tour professional or high handicapper, brings these two small areas of the clubface and the ball together every time. PGA and LPGA tour professional have the highest percentage of effective impact conditions, but no one has a 100% success rate. As we move up the latter of handicap golfers from scratch to 36 and beyond – many golfers never have had a effective impact condition – NEVER.

Secret: **The goal is to know what was just done – and what should be done. These awareness points are where learning starts.**

Impressions

The following is based on my notes and impressions of what I believe to be one of the most important golf books ever written, The Golfing Machine by Homer Kelly. To some degree, the ideas and information that are in Mr. Kelly's book have been the foundation for information used by many successful players and instructors. In fact too many to mention all of them. (The following was written with Mrs. Kelly's permission, and edited by Greg McHatton).

Homer Kelly presents information that represents ideal conditions. Whether or not anyone on earth has ever achieved them is not important. They are a goal and not necessarily common practice. While the laws of motion and force dictate ideal conditions for any desired result, The Golfing Machine does not present one way or one swing. This book presents a series of principles that show the many ways golf can be, and is, played.

Secret: Golf will always be a game for thinkers. At the very least, we must be able to concentrate as long as our pre-shot routine and swing takes.

It is important to understand **learning** and **playing** golf are both a creative process. Your ability to make progress is influenced by the information your brain receives from your eyes and other senses (studies show that up to 80% of what is in our brain came from our eyes). How you use and react to that information is also important. Mr. Kelly points out that there are no real short cuts to learning golf. Progress and increased skills can only come to learners as clubface control **increases** and inferior and disturbing motions are **subtracted.**

Learners and instructors really should not move along to new information until what is being discussed and practiced is fully understood by the "learner." Learning golf or any motor skill is a step by step process that only grows when all parts are understood so they can be used as one swing.

Secret: Efficient swings have precise components. Golfers must find their way of translating these concepts into individual sensations, personal feels and pictures.

Learning research shows that when pictures are combined with "feels", learning increases at a greater rate than when pictures or "feels" are used separately. Muscles do not understand words, but they can and do respond to pictures and feels, especially when they are combined. **It is only by correct translation that a golfer can be led to correct application.** Any change introduced *must* make sense geometrically and technically or the translation will be faulty. **Never move the club without being aware of what you are feeling, or with proper rhythm.** If properly translated and the change fails, then there is faulty execution. Never move anything unnecessarily or more than necessary.

The goal of Mr. Kelly's work is an "Uncompensated Stroke." Any compensation for physical limitations is a personal preference or for special purposes, they are actually special techniques. The swing has two basic elements: its shape and its source of power. The more precision a golfer can build into these two elements, the greater his/her success will be. The swing has one responsibility, to control the club, (shaft, head, and face) as the body that performs the swing stays on balance. *"In every athletic activity success seems to be proportional to the player's sense of balance and force. Off balance force is very erratic. Most mechanical devices have little balance but the human body does."* H. Kelly

We must first learn to translate sound techniques and sound alignments into personal feels. Learning and building a sound swing is a step by step process. Golfers who are only concerned with returning the clubhead to the ball will make very slow if any progress at all.

When golfers are learning new information and sound alignments, where the ball goes is immaterial. **If you are concerned about ball flight when introducing a change, you are concentrating on the wrong things.**

The first wobbly point in your total motion is where you should be working. The inability to execute a full pivot swing at one half and one quarter speed as smoothly as you do at full speed indicates a flaw in your procedure. Homer Kelly suggests that learners should never trust feel alone. He said to watch closely - to *"look, look, look,"* and notice every detectable and distinguishable "feel". I suggest using mirrors. The single most important step you can make to improve your game, in my opinion, is to watch yourself in a mirror and look and learn sound alignments. *"Thousands of man hours are lost when effort is substituted for sound technique - trying to eliminate the effect instead of the cause, will not lead to progress."* – Homer Kelly

Work on one segment of your total motion at a time -with no regard for what is happening to the rest of the pattern. Translating each component from mechanics to feel letting everything melt into your "total motion." **Make balanced motion and efficient alignments your primary concern.** The shot is merely the inevitable results of impact alignments.

Working in front of a mirror in or outdoors is unquestionably the most effective place to perfect, assemble, and adjust your golf stroke.

Mr. Kelly divided the strokes into 12 sections.

1. *Pre-Address* - Assessment of the situation.
2. *Impact Fix (Forward Press)* - Final Club selection, a preview of impact, ball behavior, target line.
3. *Return to Address* - Practice swing, waggle, and return to address.
4. *Start Up* - The initial take away.
5. *Backstroke* - Stoke safely on its way.
6. *The Top* - A static period of alignment of hands, shaft, right shoulder.
7. *Start Down* - Where the stroke changes direction. The period of *shoulder acceleration as* right shoulder and elbow move down plane.
8. Down *Stroke* - The stroke has settled into its delivery line. This is the period of *arm acceleration,* bringing shaft parallel to ground.
9. *Release* - This section is the period of *clubhead acceleration.* Right elbow is in front of right hip as all angles seek their in-line condition.
10. I*mpact* - This section is the period of *all acceleration.* The interval between impact and separation. All angles are reaching an in-line condition.
11. *Follow-Through* - Both arms are straight for the first and only time at this section. Club shaft and left arm are in-line at 45 degrees.
12. *Finish* - The left arm has folded and the right arm has become the radius of the swing as the stroke traveled from follow-through to finish.

ZONES

Mr. Kelly referred to the golf stroke as a three-lane highway. Three separate but simultaneous and synchronous zones and lanes where the action of his 12 sections occurred.

Stroke actions are neither cause or effect. Law is cause. Ball behavior, intended or unintended, is effect. Strokes are means only.

Zone #1 Body Control

Zone #2 Club Control

Zone #3 Ball Control

These three zones are a natural division of action. Their identities must be maintained in practice and in playing. Unless zones are developed in sequence, a very weak, compensated game is inevitable.

Zone #1 includes: body turn, shoulder turn, hip turn, hip action, knee action and foot action. Body turn is completely uncompromised by either arm or by the club's motion.

Zone #2 - *Arm Lane* - Club Control. This zone adds the arms and club to the circular motion of the body for the generation of power rather than ball manipulation.

This zone defines the geometrical alignments and relationships that will produce precision impact at all speeds without throwing away clubhead power.

Zone #2 components are power components. Good golf is power golf. As you master clubhead control (power) you will gain basic clubface control (accuracy).

Zone #2 includes: grip, strokes, fix, address, points of pressure, left wrist action, lag loading, trigger power package triangle, assembly point and loading action.

If the flat left wrist, lag pressure, or delivery line become lost or vague, stop and find them before they become a habit.

Zone #3 - *Hand Lane - Ball Control.* This zone includes all elements of ball control. The path of the hand, the plane of the shaft and the alignment of club face through impact.

This zone defines the geometrical alignments that apply force to the ball for the situation at hand.

Zone #3 includes: plane line, plane angle, hinge action, power package, triangle delivery path, plane basic, plane angle variation and release.

Components from this zone should be practiced without a ball until reasonable skill and understanding are evident in one total motion.

Grip Variations

Overlapping—most common - unite both hands

Baseball—low clubhead acceleration

Reverse Overlap—reduces left-hand control

Interlock—used by small hand-short fingered players

Crosshand—strong right hand cannot overpower flat left wrist

Mr. Kelly felt it was very important for golfers to always know where their right elbow was and what it was doing during the swing. **Understanding the role of the right forearm and elbow can improve anyone's golf.**

DOWN STROKE - Elbow Position Variations

1. When the right elbow is at the **side of body** (back of right hip), normally a straight-line right hand *Punch* is delivered through impact.
2. When the right elbow is **down in front** of the right hip, normally a right forearm under hand *pitch* is delivered at the aiming point. The right elbow can lead the hands into release much farther and create a greater delay, (with the same amount of hip travel).
3. When the right elbow is **up and out** from the body, keeping the hands between the elbow and the ball, normally right arm must *push* into impact from this position, opening and putting loft on clubface.

Preparation

Impact and address are not the same alignment, except for club shaft plane angle. The left wrist can be bent at address; it is not at impact. Therefore, precision grip alignment can only be taken at impact. The left shoulder is higher at impact so the player must be positioned for proper shoulder to ball distance.

During pre-shot routine, players should forward press (to impact fix) and visually check impact alignments, They also should picture where they want to go during down stroke. The hands should appear forward covering the left toe and not to the back of the ball, (because the eyes are behind the ball looking forward).

Secret: Hand location at impact, without exception, determines the in-put and out-put power ratio. **Most golfers receive a low return for their effort.** See and know the difference between impact and address alignments.

Classically, at address hands are more or less mid-body, left wrist bent, right wrist flexed, shoulders somewhat level, but the right is lower. The more forward the ball, the lower the right shoulder.

At impact hands are forward of the ball, left wrist is flat, right bent, with left shoulder higher than right, right elbow bent. The more forward the ball, the lower the right shoulder will be.

Body Turn, The Pivot

The body turn uses multiple centers (hip, shoulders, etc.) to produce a circular motion for generating force on an adjustable plane while maintaining balance.

The pivot is the massive rotor supplying angular momentum and throw-out rotational force.

The term pivot is relative in that it can be classified as anything between full and zero motion.

Plane

A flat plane has a straight base line. A circle can lie flat on a flat plane, but if the plane line loses its straightness, precision is also lost. The path or plane of a sound swing is *inclined* like the roof of a house, (not horizontal like a floor, or vertical like a wall). During a efficient swing, the shaft stays in line with an inclined plane throughout its entire journey from address to finish.

The design of the club and the posture of the golfer establish the inclined plane (angle) of the shaft at address. The 14 different clubs establish 14 different shaft planes the swing follows.

The shaft and head of the club travel *back, up,* and *in* from the ball, target line, and bottom of the inclined plane simultaneously (at the same time), when the swing is staying on plane, during the backswing.

The corresponding on plane responsibility of the down swing is to return the club *down, out* and *around,* on plane.

The club is on plane when it either points to or is parallel to the bottom of the inclined plane established at address. At the end of the backstroke, when the shaft has finished its travel, it should be parallel to the bottom of its inclined plane in line, or the top of the roof.

Downstroke

The clubhead is more or less 6′ up and 25″ in from the ball, requiring it to go *down* and *out to impact.*

The *down* is straight line or longitudinal acceleration, (downplane).

The *out* is radial or rotational acceleration (downplane).

Secret: **Maximum force and pressure are available when downplane (straight line, or longitudinal acceleration) is redirected by radial, or circular acceleration, (body turn).**

When using a hammer it is a combination of a straight-line motion and a circular motion that produce a maximum force. First, the head and handle of the hammer move down. Then as the object is about to be hit, the butt end of the handle moves in a very small circle permitting the head to develop maximum velocity and force.

If the handle and the head of the hammer were moved only in a straight line, or the hammer was moved by only letting the butt end of the handle move in a small circle, velocity and force would be much less than when the down line is intercepted by, or combined with, rotation.

Straight Back or In An Arc?

Because we play golf on an inclined plane, (a) the club shaft stays flat or parallel to its plane and, (b) the clubhead moves in an arc.

Faults occur when the clubhead moves straight (not in an arc), or the shaft does not stay flat on the plane (and moves under or over plane). Some instructors will suggest moving the club straight back from the ball, and others tell us to move the club in an arc. When the club stays on plane, both have a valid point. The on plane swing will move the shaft flat or straight on plane, as the clubhead moves on an arc (back-up-in). Faults can occur when the clubhead moves straight and the shaft does not stay flat on its plane. Therefore, the on-plane swing moves the shaft straight back on plane, and the clubhead in an arc, on plane.

Approach

The path on which the clubhead moves, and the line of flight for the ball are not the same line. They only touch for a moment during impact.

The angle of the arc of approach and the plane established at address are the same. This angle can be seen both on the ground and on the inclined plane.

The arc of approach for the hands can be defined by laying the shaft of the club on the ground with the leading edge square to the target. The flatter the shaft angle, the more inside the target line the arc of approach of the hands will be, the more upright the closer to the target line.

It can help any golfer to see and understand that all reference points, planes, and lines of swing motion can be inscribed on both the inclined plane and the ground. When a player can only visualize the swing in one dimension, progress will not be what it could or should be.

Example:

A. The *Target Line* can appear to the player as only being on the ground. It is also parallel to the bottom of the plane.

B. The swing's *low* point is the bottom of the divot, but it also is the low point on the inclined plane.

C. The swing's *shaft plane* line can appear to the player as only being on the inclined plane, but it is also on the ground at the same angle and define angle of approach.

D. The *arc* of *approach of the* hands can appear to the player that it is on the inclined plane, but it is also on the ground at the same angle as the shaft.

E. The arc or delivery of the *clubhead* can appear to the player as an arc on the ground, it also moves down the plane.

Ball position and angle of the shaft at address define the angle of approach for the hands. Plane angle determines the angle of attack. This geometry requires the physics of the right forearm motion to be three-dimensional - down, out, and around. Because the design of the shaft is inclined, the ball must be impacted on its inside corner (not its back).

The arc of delivery is the curved line the clubhead travels down to the low point of the true plane, then back up plane, but the swing's force and momentum travel down and out to right field.

The true plane (shaft plane) is the basic delivery line for the right forearm, right elbow, hand, clubhead, and shaft. I.e. right forearm stays parallel to the shaft plane through impact.

At the start of the swing - unless the motion is three-dimensional (back, up, in) instantly and simultaneously - true plane and its precision are lost.

Basic Plane Angles

Mr. Kelly said: *"The shaft must start its journey on the plane of its address angle of inclination."*

No plane is technically too flat or too steep, unless it allows only the heel or toe of the club to touch ground before separation.

You never try to take or not take a divot. Divots should be an automatic result of ball placement and plane angles (**forward** for shallow, **back** for deeper divots).

*You must always adjust the plane angle and ball position to bring the **right forearm location** into agreement with the intended purpose of the shot.

Planes and Shaft Control

Basic planes are classified and verified on the basis of pre-selected reference points on which an inclined plane can be set.

Mr. Kelly considers five such settings. Three are fixed, one moving, one moveable. Each is named for its particular reference point.

* Remember that the only way the right forearm can be on plane is when the right elbow is on-plane.

ELBOW PLANE - At address, the right elbow can become the reference point. Draw a line up from the ball through the elbow to define this plane. When the hand, right elbow and shaft start and travel on this plane, reduced backspin is produced (putting).

TURNED SHOULDER PLANE - The reference point is the point the right shoulder reaches at the end of the backstroke. Draw a line up from the ball through this point to determine this plane. When the hands, right elbow and shaft start and travel on this plane, no plane shift is required.

SQUARED SHOULDER PLANE - This reference point is the point where the right shoulder is at address. Draw a line up from the ball through this point to define this plane.

TURNING SHOULDER PLANE - The pivot gives on-plane motion to the hands and arms in both directions. It brings the hands directly to a square shoulder plane **location without any turn or roll, left wrist vertical to the ground.** The player who takes the clubhead straight back from the ball and straight down to impact, is using this plane. When the hands, elbow, and shaft start and travel on this plane, it produces a vertical steep angle.

HANDS ONLY PLANE - The position of the hands at address is this plane's reference point. With the hands and shaft on this plane at address and throughout the stroke, some short game shots may improve.

Most successful golfers have some plane shifts in their stroke. This shift may happen during backstroke, down stroke, or at the top. My instruction and playing preference is for the shaft to start on the shaft plane, go to a turned shoulder plane at the top, and then return to its shaft plane. While doing these motions the elbow never leaves its original elbow plane.

Lag - Drag - Thrust

Secret: **Clubhead lag should be the first factor learned in club control, allowing nothing to alter the habit of proper lag of the clubhead mass. Nothing else matters when proper acceleration (lag) is lost.**

In efficient swings every lagging component places *drag* on its proceeding component. *Lag* defines the condition of following or trailing. Sound swings establish lag, then *drag*, and have *efficient force at impact*.

It's useful to have the feeling the weight of a lagging clubhead is first dragged slowly down plane then thrust by effective pivot into impact.

To some degree at every point in the sound swing, big, long, heavy bones have smaller, lighter, shorter bones lagging behind with a drag on them. Clubhead drag promotes even steady acceleration and control of distance.

The power package triangle (shoulders, arms, hands and club) can use four types of thrust control of a lagging clubhead:

1. Rotating forces pulling the clubhead towards an in-line condition.
2. Right triceps applying pressure and structure for the power package triangle.
3. The four points of pressure always sense a lagging -clubhead:
   1. Heel of right hand on top of left thumb
   2. Last three fingers of the left hand on the grip
   3. Index finger of right hand (1st joint) on shaft
   4. Upper left arm on side of (trunk) body.
4. The four power accumulators are left wrist, right elbow, angle of club shaft to left arm, left arm angle to left shoulder. All of them can drive levers and angles into impact.

Homer Kelly felt the secret of golf was the ability to **feel clubhead mass lagging** on any one or any combination of the four points of pressure.

Clubhead lag and the four points of pressure influence: *rhythm, force, pressure, velocity,* as well as how the shaft reacts through impact and separation.

Suggestion - train with small swings to learn clubhead lag and points of pressure. Some examples to help learn the four points of pressure are:

1. Put several blades of grass on top of your left thumb and under the heel of the right hand - now be aware of the pressure the heel of the right hand must apply to keep the grass in place and make some small slow swings as the clubhead mass ***lags*** behind this point of pressure.
2. Hold the club, feeling pressure only from the last three fingers of your left hand on the club (the other seven fingers very light), make some small slow swings, being aware of the pressure in these three fingers as the clubhead mass ***lags*** behind this point of pressure.
3. Hold the club with your right index finger lightly or slightly off the club. Now as the rotation of the swing starts, the weight of the club moves onto the right forefinger. Again, make some small, short, slow swings. Be aware of the weight of the club on your right index finger as the clubhead mass ***lags*** behind this point of pressure all the way down through impact to follow through.
4. Put a head cover under your left arm and hold it in place as you hit some short pitch shots. At all times be aware of the pressure between your arm and body as the clubhead weight ***lags*** behind this point of pressure.

These small training swings can help golfers learn sound impact alignments: I.e. a bent right wrist, flat left, club shaft leaning, hands forward of ball and bent right elbow.

To learn how important these four points of pressure are, make some short, slow swings and at impact let the club come off your right index finger; or let the grass fall off your left thumb; or be loose with the last three fingers of your left hand; or let your left arm move away from your body.

Secret: **When the pivot moves the right shoulder at the same rate of rotation as the hands, the levers and angles of the swing normally will not be released until the right elbow straightens (the right shoulder should travel at the same rate as the hands).**

When all of the **points of pressure are maintained**, a steady smooth thrust of the power package and a constant rate of acceleration of angles and levers down to impact is possible.

Secret: **The orbiting clubhead should never seek out the ball, it seeks out the plane. But never directly, only through right forearm location and by right forefinger pressure point being transported to the inside corner of the ball.**

Ball location, right wrist bend, and plane angle determine the precise angle of approach for the right forearm.

Any early extension of the swing's radius (loss of angles) decelerates the hands. Unless angles are supported and retained by rotation and thrust, or moved by throw-out from rotation forces, the result is a great loss of clubhead velocity

When club mass releases and the swing radius gets longer for any reason other than thrust or pulling rotation, it has been caused by an early loss of lag pressure. Lag creates and sustains points of pressure, thus maintaining the lag and drag of clubhead mass

Over accelerating any body segment at any stage of the swing **kills** lag and drag. When the hands reach maximum speed before release, they are out of rate with the other body segments and lag is lost. Mr. Kelly's suggestion would be to strive for *"low speed, high thrust"* with impact feeling *"heavy"* not *"quick"*.

Clubhead Lag

Efficient lag is exactly like dragging a heavy wet mop through impact -with a constant load in a constant direction.

Efficient lag pressure is totally inert. The slightest push away with the hands will produce clubhead throwaway and a loss of angles.

When you find yourself swinging too fast, whether you want to or not, you may have introduced clubhead throw away. Instead of pulling or driving the club, you will find yourself chasing it and never catching up.

When the angles and levers of the power package triangle are released efficiently, they apply force to the ball as the third side of the triangle (right arm) releases its angle and expands the swing's levers down and through impact.

Secret: The motion of the right arm is monitored only through the activity of the right elbow. **We could say the right elbow controls the right arm, by both its location to the plane, and when it expands.**

An angle (wrist cock) between the left arm and club shaft must be created some place during the stroke. This loading could take place as soon as possible, as late as possible or somewhere in between.

The amount of loading can be controlled by the speed of the entire motion, or by the sharpness of the specific procedure or both.

Normal delivery of motion is on-plane, with thrust being delivered down, out, and across the bottom of the plane-line, to low point (not to the target).

Secret: **The change from linear speed (down) to angular speed (rotation's release) will increase clubhead speed *without* changing hand speed.**

Timing

Maximum force is delivered when maximum thrust occurs *prior* to full extension of angles. This condition requires the right arm to be bent as the left shoulder is traveling up through impact for maximum pressure and force. At full extension (and full velocity), acceleration ceases and the flex in the stressed shaft is lost.

Secret: **Learn that all motion should drive the hands not the club down to the aiming point. It is hand location not clubhead location that must be understood, learned and used.**

- Training must focus on the moment of truth -impact *alignments.* Learn a pulling motion from the top, through follow through, without the slightest disturbances to impact the inside ¼ of the ball (or aiming point!)
- Acceleration of a lagging component stops the instant it achieves an "in-line" condition with its preceding component.
- For maximum force, the lag and drag of club mass should not be completely lost until after impact, or past the line of sight of the ball (from a player's eyes). The sequence of release always is left wrist, right elbow, bent right wrist, and finally the angle between the left arm and club shaft.
- By increasing the time between each releasing component, we can increase velocity. The *earlier* the down stroke release happens, the *slower* the release arc for both clubhead and hands will be.

Impact

Homer Kelly said, *"Every alignment in golf must be built with the desired alignment requirements of impact in mind. Golfers can and should set up and review the required impact alignments during their pre-shot routine."*

- During impact **rotation**, player induced rotational forces pull the club shaft in line with the left arm to square the clubface to the target line.
- When the face is slightly open and the ball is placed slightly off center (out to toe) at address, you can take full advantage of rotational forces.
- Because forces present in sound swings are forcing the clubhead and right forearm down and out; the swing's radius expands and becomes longer during impact than it was at address. When the ball is played in the center of the clubface, golfers are required to find a way to shorten the expanding radius. They do so by making any one or more combinations of adjustments:
  1. Raise the head to pull the arms and hands in.
  2. Bend the left arm.
  3. Pull shoulders back.
  4. Raise the spine.
  5. Standing up.

To take full advantage of the down and out rotational forces a sound swing creates, the ball is placed ¾ of an inch before low point (low point is bottom of divot or below and forward of the tee). The ball is normally impacted *before* low point and full extension of right arm with hands forward of the leaning shaft.

Secret: **The ball is gone before the club hits the ground with irons, or the tee with a driver. When the shaft is leaning forward at impact it still has the capacity to do work. The clubhead continues to have positive acceleration until the shaft reaches an in-line condition with the left arm. Ideally the ball is hit before this in-line condition. When the ball is impacted beyond low point or on the up swing, the club is decelerating, and impact does not have maximum pressure and force going down into the ball**

Impact Fix

Most shots are lost before the swing starts (at address) or by not being prepared mentally or physically or both. **Poor address alignments and faulty pre-shot routine cause most missed shots.**

During pre-shot routine, golfers should take the opportunity to check impact alignment. A forward press that fixes impact so that it can be visually verified is very important. Then address is resumed.

Checking impact fix:

Club face to target line slightly open

Grip to clubface, flat left wrist

Hands to ball, slightly forward - shaft leaning

Plane angle, shaft angle

Pressure points firm

Right forearm alignment on shaft plane

Head back of ball, face down, both eyes on inside corner of ball

Right elbow in front of right hip

Right shoulder slightly lower than left

Left leg straightening

Hips open

Spine angle both over to ball, and away from the target

Hands and club are never flipped or swished around haphazardly at *address,* forward *press* or *during the swing.* Be very deliberate, positive and heavy - never dainty. **Make short, heavy, slow strokes to learn how the clubhead lags and drives pressure into the ball at all speeds**. When a golfer has a flimsy power package triangle (arms and shoulders) they are misunderstanding how the right arm gives structure to the triangle. Learn, one step at a time and how to maintain the essential geometry (shape) of the swing.

Flat Left Wrist

Mr. Kelly felt that the *most important* alignment in golf is a flat left wrist during impact. Without a flat left wrist other information is useless and confusing.

Secret: **When the responsibilities and location of the right arm and elbow are not understood, any real progress will be difficult.**

To reach their potential, golfers should develop a total motion that can *support* the shaft, flat left wrist, bent right wrist and elbow as they drive force down *into the ball at and through impact.*

The foundation and source of all force, support, lag, and drag is **rotation** when swinging.

- Support and force on the shaft, and flat left wrist can come from a bent *right wrist*.
- Support and force on the bent right wrist can come from the *right forearm*.
- Support and force on the right forearm can come from the hips when the right *elbow is* down in front of *the right hip*.
- Support and force on the arms can come from the *body*.

Any impression during impact will permit a "leak" or loss of force and compression of the ball. Once you leak you cannot recover. Remember, the club should not feel like it moves the ball. A compressed ball moves itself off the clubface.

Secret: **The action and location of the right elbow determine how the right forearm, clubface, shaft, and clubhead operate during the swing. The right forearm of every "hacker" comes into impact too high (or off plane).**

Normally "steering" the swing can cause the number one fault in golf - a bent left wrist at impact! Any one of the following steering faults can cause the left wrist to bend through impact by trying to have:

Club face square at impact.

Clubhead on the target line much before and long after impact.

Clubhead on a level or upward path at impact.

"Quitting" will also cause the left wrist to break down. Stopping the hands (quitting) can be a sub-conscious action to change the natural down-out clubhead path to an **incorrect** on-line through impact path. Quitting is actually impossible with proper and continuous rotation and rhythm.

Secret: **Efficient swings keep the clubhead behind the hands and force on the shaft as the swing sustains the lag of clubhead mass through impact.**

Any excessive bobbing of the head, (caused by faulty back and knee movement) disrupts the shoulder to ball radius.

In-Line Condition

Efficient swings produce a condition that is called "in-line" from the clubhead to the left shoulder socket, at and through impact. The clubhead, shaft, left hand, left wrist, left arm and left shoulder socket make up this line which sound swings produce, use and sustain.

Homer Kelly called this line "A Line of Compression" referring, of course, to the requirement that the swing should compress the ball. A line of compression (force) must be present before, during, and after impact.

The direction of a compressing force is important. When the force direction does not pass through the center of the ball, the ball has sidespins. Sound swings compress the ball through a particular point, along a particular line, at and through the arc of impact. The result of this desired procedure is maximum compression.

The triangle (shoulders-arms-hands) can change shapes and size by changing the length of the right arm.

The primary lever of the swing is the left arm, with the left shoulder socket being its fulcrum.

The secondary lever is from the wrists down to the clubhead, with the left wrist being the fulcrum.

When the secondary lever moves by itself, we create a bent left wrist and have clubhead throw away, not clubhead lag.

Secret: The left arm can bend too much in the back swing when the right forearm-elbow has more than a 90-degree angle. The extension from the right forearm during the backswing gives the primary lever (left arm) its support and structure. When it bends past 90 degrees, the left arm bends too much.

THROW-AWAY

BIG SECRET: Any breakdown of a flat left wrist before or during impact will cause a loss of force (clubhead throwaway). Until a player knows how to avoid this condition (consciously or subconsciously) power golf is impossible. Working on anything else is a waste of time. Some reasons for throwaway or a loss of force are:

- The urge to move the clubhead from the wrist often caused by poor rotation (ex: when the handle of the whip stops rotating, the whip passes the handle).
- Over Acceleration - when acceleration is not constant, excessive hand speed throws the clubhead into release orbit prematurely. Proper speed may feel incredibly slow especially from the top. **A surprising low rate of sustained acceleration of the lever system is what's needed.**
- Trying to line the clubs face up at impact from the wrists (false wrist action) forces the left wrist to bend (stop) and the right wrist to flatten.
- Straightening of the right (elbow) forearm before impact can cause the right wrist to flatten and left wrist to bend.
- Trying to have the clubface square to the target at impact can cause the left wrist to bend.
- Trying to impact the back of the ball at impact can cause the right wrist to flatten and the left to bend.
- Trying to move the clubhead in a straight line before or after impact causes clubhead throwaway.

HANDS AND WRISTS

Homer Kelly said, *"The key to ball control is educated hands. Players must know where hands are and what they are doing at all times. It's best to picture that rotation during the swing is transporting hands. Whenever hands move the hands it can cause a loss of balance".*

Hands or fingers (except thumbs and forefingers) should be firm, and the wrists flexible. *"Everything written about a light grip should have been written about the wrists."* Jim Petralia

We would not hold a hammer with light fingers and tight wrists. The same is true for a golf club - flexible wrists but firm fingers.

Three grip motions moving horizontal to the plane **control the shaft.**

- The left wrist is neither bent outward, or
- Arched inward, or
- *Flat*

Three wrist motions moving perpendicular to the plane **control the clubhead.**

- The wrist is either cocked up, or
- Uncocked down or
- Level to the plane.

Three hand motions (forearm rotation) on plane **control the clubface.**

- The hands turn to the right, or
- Roll to the left or
- Stay vertical to plane as they are transported.

When learning the different motions and alignments of the hands and wrist, Mr. Kelly suggests practicing without a club, using firmly clenched fist as well as open hand.

Wrist motions and hand motions are **independent**. However they must be **coordinated**. The left wrist uncocks the clubhead, but clubface alignment at impact is the function of hand rotation.

With any loss in the angle of a bent right wrist during release, left wrist will break down and bend back. These actions start the club swinging from the wrist on an "inside" and "upward" path. This action causes the face to close and shaft to line up with the right hand instead of staying in line with the left hand.

Secret: **Remember, both hands must be transported down-plane to impact and not just the clubhead.**

Learn how the right arm moves or straightens on-plane through impact without losing a bent right wrist.

Learn to float down-plane from the top through impact with an inert right wrist.

Secret: **The hands are much easier to monitor than the clubhead. Never monitor the clubhead directly. The hands are moved much more slowly and more evenly than the clubhead, therefore they are easier to monitor.**

Regardless of the amount of technical know how and practice, uneducated hands can nullify it all and never be suspected of doing so. Learn to monitor and transport the hands, not the clubhead.

Using Levers – Retaining Angles

An efficient swing develops angular velocity (motion) by using two divergent forces. The linear (down) force of the shoulders, arms, hands, and club is diverted by the rotating force of the turning body, creating a fly wheel (throw-out) or natural expanding condition of the swing's angles and levers.

This throw-out action pulls the center of gravity of all the moveable segments (shoulder sockets, upper and lower arms, wrists, hands, shaft and clubhead) into an *in-line* and on-plane condition.

This expanding or throw-out action is a reaction. It propels the clubhead into maximum velocity at impact. At maximum velocity the clubhead is no longer accelerating.

Longer, larger, heavier components **transfer** force to shorter, smaller, lighter components causing them to move around their axis of rotation.

A small radius permits faster velocity than larger ones. This is why *efficient* swings retain full wrist cock and a lagging clubhead until **player induced rotational forces** cause a throw out action. Unsound swings have a misapplication of muscle force creating clubhead throwaway, or early release and expansion of angles and levers (large radius or long right arm).

Secret: **Any attempt to bring the angles and levers of the swing forward will cause early expansion or release around a large radius. They must move down plane first.**

The angles formed by the left arm and club shaft, the right forearm and upper humorous bone, the left arm and shoulder socket MUST GO DOWN PLANE, (not forward), if angles are to be retained and move around a small radius delivering maximum force to the ball. Picturing the left arm as #1, and the club as #2, with the wrists a hinge between the two may be useful.

In poor shots and unsound swings #2 passes #1 befor e impact. In efficient swings #1 leads #2 into impact. #2 receives a transfer of energy *from* body rotation and moves around the wrist joint seeking a natural in-line condition with #1.

The center of gravity of #2 is trying to line up with the center of gravity of #1. It does when the wrist joint is free to respond to a rotational force.

After follow through (the only stage where both arms are expanded and straight) efficient swings seem to float to their finish because all the force has gone down into the ball. Where as the unsound swing moves very aggressively to finish by using force that could have been applied to the ball. **Force not spent during impact is often being misapplied after follow through.**

FORCE AND POWER

> *** No law of motion and force can be annulled, even for a moment. These laws can only be *avoided, overpowered,* or *harnessed.***

Clubhead power is directly proportional to its kinetic (potential) energy. How do we increase the kinetic energy of the golf club?

Clubhead velocity is developed by thrust, which is a constant accelerating force provided by rotation.

Clubhead velocity is proportional to the angular speed of the swing's rotational center (under the left breast in the center of the trunk cavity). The clubhead reaches maximum velocity almost instantly after release and should remain constant.

Power and force can be regulated by:

- Rate of rotation
- Size of the swing's radius
- Length of stroke
- Where release occurs

Secret: **Believing that "effort" is power is one of a golfer's greatest hazard. No amount of effort can produce more power than a player's turning speed.**

Muscle effort must be avoided. A mechanical advantage must be introduced to make clubhead acceleration an "overtaking process."

The power package (shoulder, arms, hands, wrists) develops power and force through sound alignments; and through effective pivot thrust. Releasing and expanding its levers and angles down-plane into an in-line condition through impact.

When conflicting alignments exist, tremendous energy will be consumed in trying to offset their damaging influences to a player's full velocity potential. (I.e. muscle guarding)

The hands hold on and attach the arms to the club for control and clubface alignment, as pivot thrust drives these components through impact. By themselves, the arms and hands can move the ball only a short distance.

The muscles of the arms, hands, and upper torso have these assignments:

- Biceps - Bend elbows
- Triceps - Straighten elbows
- Deltoids - Raise arms
- Pectorals - Pull shoulders and arms forward
- Latissimus Dorsi - Pull shoulders and arms backward

The less we use the biceps and the latissimus dorsi muscles the better off we will be. The biceps can bend (move) the right forearm beyond a 90 degree bend during the back stroke, this causes the left arm to bend, shortening the radius of the swing and its structure.

The latissimus dorsi can bring the arms away from the center of the body during backstroke, causing the right arm and elbow to slip out and behind the trunk. From this position, it is almost impossible for the right arm and elbow to return to impact on plane.

It may be useful to picture the power package triangle as essentially inert - only moving because body turn starts to accelerate it. Pivot thrust blasts the levers and angles into orbit toward impact with momentum sustaining its journey to finish.

Bio-mechanically the right triceps and pectoral muscles can handle most of the muscle requirement of down swing. The left arm has very little power on its own. As the upper left arm stays on the trunk, energy from the upper body is transferred into the left arm and the power is considerable.

The tricep muscles can help expand or release the right forearm through impact, and the pectoral can give support to the humorus (upper right arm) bone.

Generating and Accumulating Power

The shoulders and hips can "generate" power by applying rotation. Additional power can also be accumulated then spent when an out-of-line condition of the power packages triangle components seek their natural in-line condition. There are four power accumulators that can supply four types of power:

Muscle	#1	Right arm (straightening)
Velocity	#2	Left Wrist (cock)
Transfer	#3	Angle between left arm and shaft (left hand roll)
Radius	#4	Angle between left arm and shoulder socket (left arm motion)

MUSCLE POWER: The #1 accumulator is the **right arm**. As it bends, it gathers potential power to be spent this power is spent when it seeks its in-line condition through impact and when it is supported by rotation of the hips and trunk.

Maximum muscle power is gathered (accumulated) when a **bent right elbow** is down in front of the right hip, with the "feeling" it has passed the ball before it is released by generated rotational force.

The bent right arm, from the start of the swing into follow through, should be making a steady slow effort to straighten. This stretch does not move the left arm. It provides pressure and structural **support**. This support is a deterrent to its (left arm) collapse in both the back stroke and stresses of acceleration through Impact.

The force (from the right arm) is a natural stretch, which keeps the right triceps active. This may be felt as a constant stretch with the **right arm** stretching away from the chest it provides:

Full extension of the left arm

Full extension of the right arm at follow through

The correct rate of clubhead acceleration.

Proper non-accelerating (passive) support for clubhead lag pressure (wrist cock).

This extension action and muscle force of the right arm through Impact (without rotation) can be used for less than full power shots, especially around the green.

At the start of the swing this natural extensor action from the right arm can pull the club shaft and left arm into a straight line. The bent left wrist at address is moved to a flat left wrist during the backstroke by the steady stretch of the right arm. This action can also creates a bent right wrist which remains present for the rest of the swing.

VELOCITY POWER: The second power accumulator is formed when the angle between the left hand and club shaft is created, retained and applied (wrist cock).

The weight of the club and the folding of the right forearm (when the wrists are free) create wrist cock during backstroke.

The longer the wrist cock is retained, the greater the velocity and force can be at impact, because the in-line condition of the shaft, left arm, and flat left wrist is re-established over a short travel time.

Secret: **A sound swing retains wrist cock (lag) longer than an unsound one (clubhead throwaway).**

TRANSFER POWER: The third power accumulator is formed by the angle between the club shaft and the left forearm (as in baseball and tennis). When there is no angle between the arm and bat/racket, or club shaft, there is less power.

When this angle is formed, several important conditions are introduced:

- The radius of the swing (from the left wrist socket to the clubhead) is smaller. The clubhead's velocity increases for the same work.
- The travel distance of the clubhead is greatly increased without increasing the amount of rotation.
- Keeping the arms closer to the body, reducing the size and space the mass which the swing occupies, increasing rotation speed improving the balance of body.

For maximum *transfer of power* there should be an angle between the shaft and the arms through impact.

For maximum power, the left arm should be as vertical as possible as the shaft is returned to its original shaft angle established at address. The right forearm is on the shaft plane angle supporting the #1 lever (left arm, hands, and club shaft) through impact.

When the right forearm is on plane, it will always establish the correct club shaft - left arm angle through release and impact, providing *maximum transfer* of force, energy and power into the ball.

When the club is held down in the fingers of both hands, (away from the wrist) maximum velocity and transfer power is available. When the club is more in the fingers at address, the wrists are in position to be transported pre-cocked

Secret: **The more the club is held in the palm of the left or right hand the less wrist cock, clubhead velocity, and transfer power is available.**

RADIUS POWER: The fourth power accumulator is the angle formed by the left arm and left shoulder socket.

As the left arm hangs at address there is an angle formed between the humorous bone and the left shoulder joint. As this angle decreases it gathers power. When it returns to its in-line condition it spends it.

The upper portion of the left arm should stay on the upper portion of the chest until follow through is completed. When the upper left arm leaves the body, it no longer has the support from the body, and this creates a large power leak for the swing.

When the angle between the upper left arm and shoulder joint gets smaller and then is moved back out (but not off the left side of the body during impact), power and force are added to the swing. Ideally the left arm will not move into the body very much (45 degrees) during the back swing because of the support and pressure being supplied by the right arm. But as the swing changes directions, the right elbow, and right shoulder move down plane. These movements bring the left arm into the chest more, reducing the angle between the shoulder joint, and upper left arm. This reduction in space or angle between the left arm and shoulder socket becomes a source of power. When the left arm is moved back out by rotational forces, the radius and in-line condition of the *left* shoulder, arm, wrist, hand, and the club is now re-established and automatically creates more velocity and force at impact.

There is another advantage of the left arm moving closer to the chest during the start of down stroke; It can now receive greater support from the body during the swing.

The left arm is not only a power accumulator, it also reacts to the triggering function of the right elbow. When the right elbow releases, the left arm and chest angle begin to release, effectively beginning their journey to the in-line fully released conditions. We could say radius power is really another name for body power.

Application of Thrust

Secret: **Power must have a source and it must be exerted against something that will drive the club through impact (directly or indirectly).**

The swings four power accumulators and four points of pressure combine in the application of thrust.

1. The *bent right arm* exerts pressure against the heel of the right hand, the thumb of the left hand and bent right wrist.
2. The left *wrist cock* exerts pressure down against the last three fingers of the left hand.
3. The *angle* between the club shaft and the left arm exerts pressure against the index finger of the right hand.
4. The *angle* between the left arm and shoulder exerts power and pressure against the contact point between the left arm and left side of the body.

All four accumulators can be used, or a golfer can use just one or any combination of these. The on-plane use of pressure points by, or with the power accumulators should transfer their potential energy into the clubhead always at right angles to the club shaft. This transfer of potential energy would not be possible without lag and drag.

Direction of Thrust

Secret: **The aiming point for an intact Power Package Triangle and the lagging clubhead must be on a *pre-selected* delivery line and angle of approach.**

The aiming point can only be pinpointed by the player, **through experiment and experience.** Ball position changes the aiming point. **The aiming point is never the ball but always a path down-plane to the inside corner of the ball.** The faster the hand speed the more back ball location. The slower the hand speed the more forward the ball is played. Always transport the hands and Power Package Triangle, not the clubhead, on the shaft plane through impact with effective pivot thrust.

Due to the Laws of Conservation of Angular Momentum, shorter clubs take less time to reach the in-Line condition than longer clubs. The wide face of the shorter clubs move its center of gravity (sweet spot) back from the leading edge allowing rotational forces to square club face up earlier.

Secret: **Mentally, see a line from the right forefinger to the aiming point (inside corner of the ball). All thrust is delivered and directed down and out, trying to drive the ball into the ground, not into the air.**

Even though rotation is a circle path, its "thrust" is **a straight-line force down plane** to the aiming point. Force can be applied from the right elbow expanding and right shoulder going down plane.

Spine and Shoulders

The spine should be viewed as the center or axis of the shoulder turn. The left shoulder socket should be viewed as the radius or center of the swinging left arm and club.

The shoulders are not only a great source of generating power, but their plane of motion is very important - **especially the plane of the right shoulder.**

Ideally, the right shoulder should travel down plane at the start of the down stroke. This down plane path of the right shoulder helps create several important actions of a sound down swing. **Seventy percent of the swings force comes from the right shoulder.**

- It helps move the bottom of the spine to the back of the ball.
- It helps move the right elbow down plane in front of the right hip creating maximum trigger delay.
- It starts the journey of the left shoulder up and away from the ball and target, creating the swing's longest radius.
- It helps bring the hands down plane with the left arm as close to the body and vertical as possible.
- It helps the back muscles to rotate properly away from the target (back tilt).

An on plane down stroke shoulder motion is only possible when the spine **stays** bent over to the ball in the backstroke; and when the bottom of the spine moves forward (2" to 4") at the start of the down stroke without changing the degree of bend of the spine over to the ball.

When the lower spine moves forward and out to the back of the ball, the upper spine also moves back or away from the target. **These simultaneous actions, permits the right shoulder to move down plane, as the original (over to the ball) spine angle stays constant.**

When the lower spine does not move forward and out to re-establish itself at the back of the ball, the right shoulder cannot move down plane and under the spine. It can only move out and in to the body.

Secret: **The right shoulder has several responsibilities and does not move around haphazardly. Moe Norman of Canada considered one of the world's premiere ball strikers, pictures hitting the ball with his right shoulder. Some other greater golfers have said that they try to swing it under their spine.**

The right shoulder is part of the pivot and the Power Package Triangle. **Because the right shoulder is behind the left in the down stroke, it has more influence on the power, pressure, support and direction of impact.** See the left shoulder as a steering wheel for the right shoulder.

During the backstroke, the right shoulder has more influence on the location and action of the right arm and elbow than does the left shoulder. It could be said that the right shoulder has a very precise job to perform. The geometry of the stroke is strongly influenced by the movement of the right shoulder. As was said earlier, seventy percent of the power for efficient swings comes from the right shoulder.

Accelerating or Loading the Club - Mr. Kelly uses the terms drive, float, and drag to describe three methods of loading the club or putting lag pressure into the stroke and the right elbow influences all methods.

Drive Loading - is pure right arm thrust against the lagging clubhead pressure. Short shots can be executed by pulling the lagging clubhead mass through impact with right arm thrust. Clubhead throwaway, (with drive loading), is caused by over acceleration. Use shorter, slower strokes. Backstroke can stop when the right elbow stops bending. Drive loading is hitting with an expanding right arm.

Float or Downstroke Loading (Acceleration) - This procedure delays wrist cock until start down. The cocking motion should be gentle or even lazy, never sharp, and can be completed by either driving or dragging the club into impact with a bent right elbow being moved down plane by lower back muscles and right shoulder.

Drag Loading (Acceleration) - Feels as though the club shaft is on your back. Then drag the club back down with your back muscles. This is only possible if inertia can hold the clubhead back and inside the arc of the hands and on the delivery path until rotational force sets in.

Loading Action - there are 3 actions available:

- Sweep
- Random
- Snap

1. Full Sweep - This loading (wrist cock) starts at the beginning of the backstroke.
2. Random Sweep - This loading (wrist cock) action starts at any point during the backstroke.
3. Snap - This loading (wrist cock) action starts at the last instant of the backstroke.

Stroke Power Variations

In his book, The Golfing Machine, Mr. Kelly used the number of power accumulators to classify the stroke: single, double, triple, and four barrel strokes.

Single Barrel - is using only one accumulator, it produces a stroke with very little power or variations - ideal on and around green.

1. Only right elbow bend
2. Only left wrist cock
3. Only left hand to shaft angle
4. Only left arm angle to shoulder

Double Barrel - using any two accumulators can produce a wide variation of force, but less than is available. Mr. Kelly felt a very satisfactory game could be developed using only two accumulators: (1 + 2), or (1 + 3), or (1 + 4).

Triple Barrel - using three accumulators requires more skill, but power and versatility increase: (1+2 +3), or (l + Z +4), or (1 +3 +4), or (2+3+4).

Four Barrel - this high performance combination can produce problems as the player tries to master it. But it can make a difference in top competition.

Plane Guide Lines

Planes are classified and based on a combination of positions. The first term refers to the plane line, the second term to the stance line (feet only) with reference to the line of flight.

- Square – Square
- Square – Open
- Square – Closed
- Open – Open

Open - Square
Open - Closed
Closed - Square
Closed - Open

Shifting the stroke from any one plane to any other, however slight the shift, results in a bent plane line and bent left wrist syndrome.

The relations among plane line, angle of approach, and ball location are constant. Changing one changes all three and usually plane angle as well, but not necessarily club face alignment.

EXAMPLES:

Square - Square - sets up plane line and stance line parallel to each other and the target line.

Square - Open - sets up stance line open to plane and target line.

Square - Closed -sets up stance line closed to plane and target line.

Open - Open - any of the above combinations that are now open to the target line.

Closed - Closed -any of the above combinations that are now closed to the target line.

CLUBFACE

The alignment of the back of the left hand can control clubface alignment, and the face controls the ball's starting direction. **Golfers can train and educate a flat left wrist and hand to close, hood or lay back the face through impact, creating a variety of ball flights.** It is not suggested that a player use independent hand roll to close the clubface. The back of the left hand can close the clubface, when the left forearm rotates, and reacts to the left shoulder rotation introduced by effective pivot. **Any effort to roll the hands independently can cause loss of precision.**

Any independent hand roll can cause over acceleration and a loss of constant rate (rpm's) of motion available from a turning torso and orbiting arms. When the left wrist stays flat, the arms, shaft, and clubhead all feel like they rotate at the same rate of rotation.

To learn different ball flights and the importance of a flat left wrist, practice short slow swings. The end of a short slow swing can finish:

1. With the face of the club and flat left wrist to the sky (laid back - vertical)
2. The toe pointing along the plane line and a *flat* left wrist (horizontal target line)
3. The face across the plane line and flat left wrist angled (closed).

When practicing these three different face and flat left wrist angles (vertical, horizontal, angled), make sure there is an angle between your hanging arms and club shaft (max. 45 degrees) and notice how the travel time of the clubhead for each procedure is different.

1. Vertical (face to sky) is the shortest.
2. Horizontal is the longest. This points out how the angles between the arms and shaft influence clubhead velocity and rhythm of the swing. The larger the angle the greater the velocity. Practice these shots without an angle between the arms and club to discover the differences.

GRIP - RIGHT ELBOW

Perhaps it would help if the grip was thought of as free wrists, strong fingers (except thumbs and forefingers), flexible shoulders and oily neck.

The fingers and hands hold the club – (clamp like with free wrists). The grip should support the shaft and stroke from behind the shaft at impact.

Secret: **The right elbow must be some place. Its location and action (on or off plane) play a dominant roll in the motion of the right forearm in every golf stroke.**

The right forearm should be in line with and directly opposed to the motion of the club shaft during loading, release and impact.

The right forearm, not just right hand and club shaft, must be driven down into impact. Ball position and right elbow location influence the angle of approach and application of force.

The right elbow raises and lowers the left arm and cocks the left wrist without bending, flattening or cocking the right wrist.

The right elbow action either powers and/or controls the three elements of the down-out and around downstroke motion.

Shoulder Turn

Secret: **The shoulder is the fastest and longest moving component of the pivot and actually transmits the pivot motion to the arms. (Normally 4 to 5 times faster than the hips).**

An inadequate backstroke shoulder turn, or inadequate down stroke shoulder lag will *always* produce an "outside - in" impact path.

Keep the right shoulder going down (on plane) or you will lose right elbow bend before impact alignment, causing the hands to react (an automatic throwaway).

The rotated shoulder turn moves the shoulders in a normal path at right angle to the spine.

The angle of the waist bend and spine tilt influences the plane of shoulder turn.

Hip Turn

Secret: **Use the turning hip to carry the right elbow around into release position after it has been moved down in front of the right hip.**

Some golfers over exaggerate hip turn before the right shoulder and right elbow move down plane, causing off plane downstroke. When right shoulder moves down plane, moving the right elbow in front of the right hip, golfers may feel a 2" to 4" hip slide as the lower spine reacts to the upper spine going backwards as the right shoulder moves down plane. Feel the right hip staying under the shoulders as it goes out to ball, before left hip rotates.

Hip turn is a by-product of waist and knee bend. The motion of hips and shoulders are independent but must be coordinated to avoid right elbow, and right hip interference. These motions which should be avoided, causing a round house throw away action during start down.

Correct hip turn **permits** rather than causes other effects, actions, and motions of the pivot. **The more the knees are bent, the less the hips can turn.**

Knee Action

The primary function of knee action, as with waist bend, is to maintain a steady head during the pivot stroke.

Ideally, address knee flex is maintained through backstroke. The slant of the hips determines knee flex during pivot. The amount of flex will also determine the amount of back turn and down stroke slide-turn.

Legs—Feet

The heels should not be lifted off the ground - they are pulled off and then no more than necessary. Lifting the heel accomplishes nothing and may cause a loss of balance.

The legs support and react to rotation. They do not create movement.

Mr. Kelly suggested that the weight be evenly distributed between both feet with enough on the heels so that the toes can be lifted without a loss of balance at address.

Secret: **Swing with a feeling that rotation puts pressure into the ground during the backstroke and also at the start of the down stroke.**

Learn to halt the back swing with the feet. Let this same force begin the down stroke pull, and continue through impact. This is swinging from the feet, which gives the stroke its maximum radius.

Left Wrist Action

"Player induced" rotational forces during the down stroke help to uncock the left wrist through impact until both arms are straight at follow through and you have full extension.

Clubhead surface (MPH) velocity increases in reverse proportion to the size of the angle (wrist cock) between the shaft and left arm (the smaller the faster). Note: The earlier the release, the bigger the angle and slower the velocity.

Arm Motions

Either arm can pull the club. The club can be moved with a putt motion and a completely motionless body, especially by the right shoulder. When the wrist action only moves the club it is called *peck* stroke. When both elbows are bent and forearms are on plane, it is called *pick* stroke. When both arms are frozen and the body only rocks, it is called *paw* stroke. When the hands make a pecking motion towards the ball, causing the left hand to stop and the right arm to drive hard against the stationary left wrist with little or no follow through, it is called *pause* stroke. Its called swinging, when pivot thrust (rotational force) moves the center of the clubhead orbit from the left shoulder joint; (the right elbow and right forearm, the clubhead, a bent right wrist stay in place and on plane into impact).

Ball Separation

Point of impact and the place where the ball separates in front of the clubface are two different places in the swing. The ball is on the face for a measurable amount of time and distance (¾" and 50,000ths of a second). **During the average round of golf, the ball is on the face of the club for less than 1/20th of a second total.**

The ball will normally separate itself at practically right angles to the face of the club or square to the leading edge. It is gone before the clubhead hits the ground. Separation (not impact) is the only time the face is required to be in-line with the players desired starting direction of ball flight.

Efficient swings transport the clubhead on an arc. It is of little value to have the club face square to the target at impact for most shots.

Ideally, the face will be slightly open at impact and square to the target at separation.

When golfers try to have the face square to the target at impact, they can cause a breakdown of bent right wrist causing a collapse of the left wrist. This creates clubhead "throw-away" as the shaft lines up with the right arm.

Another important principle to understand about separation is that the IMPACT VELOCITY of the club is not as important as its SEPERATION VELOCITY. When the clubhead impacts the ball, the ball pushes back causing at least a 20% reduction in clubhead velocity. In an instant 100 MPH becomes 80 MPH.

A sound swing that *produced, used,* and *retained* its angles and line of compression can retain this reduced clubhead velocity of 80 MPH until the ball moves itself off the clubface. Unsound swings do not, retain this velocity after impact.

Secret: One reason some golfers are unable to achieve the same distance others can is because of a breakdown of angles (lag pressure) during the time the ball is on the clubface.

This breakdown is a misapplication of force, which cause loss of force. The unsound swing has less separation velocity and ball distance than do sound swings which retain their angles and line of compression (flat left wrist) through and beyond separation.

The clubhead moves from 0 MPH at the top of the back stroke to 90-100 MPH in .02 of a second, causing the ball to accelerate from 0 MPH to 80 MPH in ½ of an inch. This is faster acceleration than any jet plane, racecar, or rocket can produce.

Any breakdown of the in-line condition from the left shoulder socket to the clubhead reduces the separation velocity of the clubhead and ball. Accordingly, this can be the main reason for poor golf and lack of distance.

RPM'S - Revolutions Per Minute

When the left wrist is flat, the clubhead can "feel like" it travels at the same rate of rotation as the hands. Ideally, sound swings will "feel like" all body parts (legs, hips, trunk, shoulders, arms, and hands) and clubs are moving at the same rate of rotation, (**but just the hands and right shoulder are**).

Secret: Sound swings do not have any one-body segment out racing another.

Because all the separate body parts travel different distances and different size circumferences, they all naturally travel at different speeds - but they all should feel like they move at the same rate of rotation keeping the left wrist is flat.

Example: The inside portion of a door moves much slower than that of the outside portion, but both arrive at the door jam at the same time because both are moving at the same exact rate of rotation.

Secret: Rate of rotation may be the secret of all sports. In coordinated well timed athletic movements, body parts move at different speeds but *feel* like they move at a steady rate of rotation.

A sound rate of rotation must be recognized, created and applied before a player can reach his or her potential.

One key to achieving a good rate of rotation is the right forefinger. At address the right forefinger should not apply any pressure to the club. But as the swing starts, rotation causes the shaft to put pressure on the right forefinger and keeps it there until finish. When a traveling clubhead moves in front of its shaft, the club moves off the forefinger and the all-important pressure on the shaft is lost - the left wrist bends and the right goes straight. Unsound swings move the club off the forefinger *before, during,* or *after* impact.

SUMMARY OF THE BASIC FUNDAMENTALS OF THE GOLFING MACHINE

The mechanical definition of a golf stroke is: The HINGE ACTION of an ANGULAR MOTION on an INCLINED PLANE, i.e., a gyroscopic motion on a slanted plane with club face control.

A golf stroke has two basic elements: its GEOMETRY (shape) and its PHYSICS (power). Geometrically, the golf stroke consists of the CIRCLE (orbiting clubhead), the adjustable RADIUS (left arm and club), and a CHORD (ground).

The Star System Triad:

The player using the THREE IMPERATIVES (must have)

1. The flat left wrist
2. The lag pressure point and
3. The straight plane line

To Control THREE FUNCTIONS

1. The inclined plane controls the club shaft
2. The flat left wrist controls the club face
3. The pressure points control the clubhead

Through the THREE STATIONS

1. Address
2. Top
3. Finish

The TRIAD is accomplished while observing the THREE ESSENTIALS (nice to have)

1. Stationary head
1. Balance
2. Rhythm

See Lines	**Feel Circles**
Target line	Shoulders and Arms
Plane line	Hips, Back, and Butt
Stance line	Chest
Spine line	Hands

When rotation is applied, a law of physics is introduced. Energy increases as straight-line acceleration is interrupted by radial acceleration as large bending forces are introduced.

- Force is applied to the ball through levers.
- Power is applied to the levers through pressure points.
- Power is applied to the pressure points by power accumulators.
- Power is gathered (to be used) by out-of-line conditions of the power package components.

All golfers have hands and wrist joints, arms, elbows, and shoulder joints: add a club which now make up their power package. This power package travels away from the ball at the start of the swing and goes to the end of the backswing then back down to the ball and swings through impact. Every swing in golf has power package participation. However some shots requiring more power than some others.

An effective golf swing has the ability to both generate and accumulate (gather) power during its backswing. The swing generates power with shoulder and hip rotation. When needed, it can gather or accumulate more power by creating angles during the backswing at three body joints (left wrist, right elbow, and left shoulder).

The First Power Accumulator – bend the right arm at its elbow joint.

The Second Power Accumulator – cock the left wrist.

The Third Power Accumulator – the angle formed by the shaft and the left arm, when the left hand is in a normal impact position. The greater the angle the greater the accumulation of power.

The Forth Power Accumulator – the angle formed by the left arm and the left shoulder joint. This is the master accumulator.

After potential for more power is gathered, (by creating angles during the backswing), the stored potential for power can be released down into the ball. This release happens when the angles of the power accumulators expand to re-seek their in-line condition through impact.

Note: By varying the amount of out-of-line or the amount of muscular effort, the golfer can vary the power that can be released.

Secret: **One of the real secrets of golf (if not its main secret) is to have the clubhead lagging behind all the pressure points of the power package through impact. This alignment develops points of pressure. Also notice that golf clubs are all designed with angles for impact alignments – not for address alignments.**

Pressure Points:

1. Heel of the right hand
2. Last three fingers of the left hand.
3. Right forefinger where it touches the shaft.
4. The point where the left arm contacts the left chest.

When the clubhead mass is resisting the change of direction, the resistance starts a chain reaction that puts force on all the points of pressure. The clubhead lags behind the third pressure point (right forefinger). The right forefinger lags behind the first pressure point (heel of the right hand) and bent right wrist. The bent right wrist is lagging behind the second pressure point, (last three fingers of the left hand) and flat left wrist that is lagging behind the fourth pressure point, where the left arm touches the left side.

When the swing is maintaining **lag pressure** on all the pressure points, the stressed shaft is also maintained – to be transported down to impact. When the turning components of the swing move the right shoulder with the power package (hands, arms, and club), the accumulators (levers or angles) are retained until the bent right arm releases and expands them to seek (or re seek) their in-line condition to produce velocity and force through impact.

As the swings accumulators (levers and angles) are releasing to seek an in-line condition, the swing's radius expands, this increases the mass of the system and decelerates the hands. Unless they are supported by the power package thrust, a great loss of clubhead speed can result.

Note: As the right arm expands and drives the hands not the clubhead, this expansion of the arm or extensor action is supported by thrust and clubhead lag pressure. The expansion can significantly increase the effective mass of the power package against the deceleration of forces in release and impact.

Any **over acceleration** kills all lag and drag. It lets the hands reach maximum speed before impact and dissipates lag pressure.

A full body turn delivers the power package as near as possible to impact before the release of the master #4 accumulator (upper left arm on chest). This allows the right elbow to straighten to drive the levers into impact **late** rather than early.

Ball Location – shorter clubs take less time to reach impact after release than longer clubs. Ball back (at address) for faster head speed. Ball forward for slower head speed.

Body twist (turn) will only be as good as your base.

Backswing A swinging left wrist cock.
Downswing Right shoulder goes down plane to the ball and then pulled to finish by momentum.
Impact See the ball on the clubface.

While techniques can differ, physical basics do not. At impact the club is either on its **plane** or it is not. The clubface is either **behind** the players left wrist joint or it is not. The clubhead is either approaching the ball from **inside** the target line or it is not. The ball is either being compressed by **on-plane force** or it is not. The player and their swing are either **in balance and time** or they are not. The player has either **adjusted** to the hill and slopes of the course (stance, alignment, and swing-plane) or they have not.

Fencing, Zen, and Learning Golf

By taking a short look back into the history of Japan's original fencing halls, golfers may become aware of some things that will improve their golf. The first Schools of Kendo, (which means "the way of the sword"), appeared in Japan in the late 1300's. However as early as 792 AD the Japanese army was training its soldiers to use swords. **Golfers of today could apply many of the principles used to learn the efficient use of swords thousands of years ago, to improve their golf.** These old Kendo schools were also where people often looked for enlightenment through fencing. They are still popular in Japan today.

It seems very logical to me that any principles that lead to learning the efficient use of swords could be applied to a golf club. After all, they are both long sticks. While I was doing research for Golf Swing Secrets...and Lies I came across a translation of The Book of Five Rings by Miyamoto Musashi, who was born in 1587, died 1647 and wrote the book in the last years of his life. The following is based on the notes I made while reading Five Rings (written over 400 years ago).

The Way of the Sword is not just training for fencing, it also means living by a code of honor. Golf, as we know, also has its code of honor that goes beyond learning a golf swing. The rules of the game, care of the course, consideration of fellow competitors are all important elements of playing golf. Kendo Schools also embraced the philosophies of Zen that go hand and hand with the art and skills of war.

Note: I know that when some people hear the term Zen philosophy, a red light can go off. This may happen because Zen is something that cannot be seen or touched, attaching some mystery to it. This of course should not be the case, especially when everyone reading this book has experienced some Zen in their life. While Zen itself is not measurable, its results can be seen and measured.

A Zen approach simply means you are on your own! With a Zen approach people are not going to depend on someone else to tell them what to feel, see, hear, or what to take away from an experience. Zen is being open to self-discovery. Its not following someone else. Zen is personal, like the feel for a putt or a swing. Zen always aims directly at the true nature of things and not at someone's description of them. i.e. the club is either on plane or it is not, as the player learns to feel and know the difference between on and off-plane swings.

Secret: With a Zen approach there is no teaching or even any elaboration, only personal discovery of new insights. As with any long-term learning, with a Zen approach, people are guided (not taught) by instruction. With a Zen approach the beginner and master see and understand together with knowledge becoming a full circle. With a Zen approach (or self-discovery) every intention becomes no intention, where there is spontaneous knowledge for every situation. (I.e. the same way world-class golfers can develop a feel for the shot, even if it's the first time they are faced with it.)

When Learning To Use a Sword (or playing golf)

Keep in mind:

- Everything can collapse when rhythm becomes deranged – (as in golf).
- Danger can cause a loss of balance – (as in golf).
- If you rely on strength, you will inevitably hit too hard – (as in golf).
- Without the correct principles, the fight cannot be won – (as in golf).
- Never lose control of your feet, they move as you walk, in rhythm – (as in golf).
- If you interpret meaning loosely, you will mistake the way – (as in golf).
- Meet the situation without tension, yet not recklessly – (as in golf).
- An elevated spirit is weak, as is a low spirit weak – (as in golf).

Holding The Long Sword (or playing golf)

- Grip with a rather floating feeling in your thumbs and forefingers. The middle and last two fingers should be firm. It is bad to have play in your hands – (as in golf).
- As you cut the enemy your hand must not cower. You must not change your grip in the swing – (sounds like impact to me).
- Above all, you must be intent on cutting the enemy in the way you grip the sword – (in golf we hold the club for the intended ball flight).

Foot Work

The top of you toes somewhat floating, firmly with heels, the left side open, feet moving in rhythm of walking, and never on one foot – (as in golf).

Strategy

When the swordsmen (or golfer) has attained the "way of strategy," there will not be one thing that they cannot understand. They will see the way in everything not only fencing.

The "way of the sword" applies not only to military strategy, but to any situation in which plans and tactics are used. This includes playing and learning golf. Japanese businesses still use this approach as a guide to doing business.

Effective learning engages people into understanding why some actions are more workable than others – effective instruction can guide people in the direction of new insights. Effective learning does not control improvement as much as guides it. Guidance and direction may be better descriptions for what is going on in shared experiences that leads to long-term learning.

Learning grows from differences in expertise. Collective and comparative learning is the goal. Instructions authority to lead does not mean much if instruction does not join the learners current skills and make both the golfer and instruction more effective.

Hence, the role of effective learning environments is to represent situations that create and engage people in learning new forms of training, learning, and practice. We train to learn, and then practice what we learn. Golfers should approach changing habits with a training and acquiring mind set. We practice law, medicine, etc., only after we learn by training appropriate skills. Many golfers don't train enough and practice more than they should, there is a huge difference.

Improvement is more likely to come from what people learn on the job, than from what they knew when they began the job. Remember, what we know is not as useful as what we can learn about what we know. Problem solving skills for unforeseen difficulties on the golf course should be recognized as tools for improvement, rather than as ends in the themselves.

Art, Music, Physics, Acting, and Golf

The goal of useful golf instruction is to help people learn how to get more enjoyment from their golf. Over time, I came to realize that instruction information and suggestion can come in many forms, using many different methods. Humans have been around for a long time, and from the time of the caveman up to the present day computer sciences, the world has gone through many changes that have improved our quality of life. Every idea, invention, and breakthrough that has led to modern day thinking has used some of the same elements for their foundation. I am going to suggest that what has made other disciplines (i.e. Art, music, physics, acting) work, can also improve your golf. At first glance, information from different disciplines may appear to have little in common with each other.

Art, we all know has its origin in the artist's imagination. It is meant to create emotion and illusions. **Art is the skill of using space**. Music has the structure of sounds called notes, and a flow to time called rhythm. **Music is the skill of managing time and sound**. Physics is an exact science that uses relationships between quantifiable properties to explain illusions and what happens. **Physics is the art of finding the exact**. Acting is the physical and mental expression of someone else's thoughts and ideas to create and tell stories. **Acting is the skill of recreating**. It is going to help your golf to recognize the elements that are common in all these disciplines are found in golf (i.e. good golf is the skill of managing illusions, time, space, and sequencing).

What's Common?

In any efficient approach to playing the game, golfers use mental pictures, their imaginations, depth perception, and the illusions the course presents (sounds like **art** to me).

In efficient swings, the relationship of the parts to each other (body, arms, hands, club) are all quantifiable and organized so they can be exact and repeatable (sounds like **physics** to me).

Efficient swings have a rhythm and timing that unsound swings do not. It is also a fact that short and long putts, short and long iron swings, fairway woods and driver swings all take the same amount of time from take-away to impact (sounds like **music** to me).

Golfers who make progress have the ability to take in information and recreate images physically (sounds like **acting** to me).

Successful golfers with effective swings use their imagination, have repeatable swings, good timing and rhythm based on recreating mental images physically (sounds like art, music, physics, and acting to me).

ACTING

*The following has already been said, but is worth repeating.

Ron Howard said, *"most child actors are not taught how to act, they are sort of taught how to perform, somewhat like trained animals are taught."*

He went on to say he was fortunate to have a dad who was an actor and he taught him to think about what he was doing, so he was actually learning a craft. (**How many golfers can say that about their approach to golf?**)

"I understood what I was doing, and gained confidence," continued Howard. *"I was not just performing like a trained animal. I was always working toward something. I was excelling and comfortable."* (**How many golfers can say that about their approach to golf?**)

"Other kid actors may have resented what they were made to do, but I always enjoyed it. I understood, and I was growing". (**How many golfers can say this?**)

"I saw passion and commitment in my dad's approach to his acting, his willingness to dig," concluded Howard. (**How many golfers can say that abut their game?**)

Golfers looking for progress keep in mind, *"The glory of a mortal's life is that we never arrive, we are always on the way."* – D. Elton Trueblood

Short Thoughts

The "short thoughts" that follow have been gathered over time from here and there. Having the pleasure and privilege of taking part in numerous PGA Education Programs both as a speaker and student for over 30 years, I have had the opportunity to fill many notebooks with idea from others. Some of the following is original but much of it is not. I thank everyone for sharing their insights. Hopefully the "short thoughts" presented here will lead readers to their own insights. (In Chapter One of the book I mentioned several instructors from whom I have learned.)

Perhaps the most useful way of using the following "short thoughts" is to go to one of the headings and pick one "short thought" at a time, to use when training.

Secret: **Short thoughts should be seen as "What To" thoughts, not "How To" directions.**

Golf

- Before every swing, verify grip, stance, and balance.
- Actions can be:
  Non-productive
  Counter-productive
  Productive
- Golf has two aspects – facts and illusions – and both are **useful**.
- Reproduce a motion from a feel, not tips.
- We play range every 20 seconds and play golf every 4 minutes.
- Training is acquiring – practice is applying
- Golf is a game of controlled misses. The better you miss the shot, the better you play.
- Swing properly, not hard –swing so you feel like the ball is going farther than it feels like it should.
- The golf swing can react to the target, but at times the players set up gets in the way.
- The fairway is about 1050 golf balls wide.
- There are laws of motion, physics, geometry, cause and effect, but no laws for swinging golf clubs, so use the laws we have.
- Enthusiasm without truth equals frustration.
- Golf is not fair however it can be fun.
- Anyway can work, but there is a **most** efficient way.
- Develop swings that can resist clubhead deceleration through impact.

Natural Laws

- Our feel can change, but the laws of motion do not.
- Behind every successful technique is a fundamental scientific concept or natural law.
- The golf club will not and cannot break any physical laws – it is the player who violate laws.
- Movement from the center can create movement away from center.
- Laws of motion and force can be **avoided**, **over-powered**, or **used**!
- Alignments and relationships govern hands, clubface, clubhead and shaft, not positions.
- Energy and work govern mechanics.
- Law of lever – no part of the swing's primary lever should move forward independently.
- Law of triangle – never changes shape, only size, because of right arm.
- The right arm can support the left. The right arm, (not wrists) is always trying to go straight.
- Law of parallels = law of plane. At the start of impact interval club shaft is parallel to the shaft plane at address.
- Laws enforce themselves.

Address

- The planes of motion are determined by the fourteen different club shaft angles.
- The flatter the plane the more important ball location is. Poor ball placement causes short irons to have too much backspin and long irons to have side spin.
- Start with zipper or belt buckle behind the ball so this area can rotate through the ball during impact.
- Spine is angled both over to the ball, and away from the target.

Grip

- Never change grip pressure; never lead from wrists; never prepare to stop hands.
- Have strong fingers, flexible wrists, and free shoulders.
- The weight of the club can establish its own grip pressure.
- Hold the club firm, not lightly; with no pressure from thumbs and forefingers, as your wrists and shoulder joints are free and flexible.
- When the left thumb is placed behind the shaft (right of center) the arms can hang vertical.
- A constant grip pressure and good turning rate (RPM's) go together.

Wrists

- Wrists should be in a condition that permits them to respond to the weight of the club (free – flexible).
- Wrists do not apply force, they permit application of force.
- Everything written about a light grip should have been written about the wrists.

Balance

- Starting the swing with the hands or arms instead of body turn can raise the center of gravity causing the body to sway.
- Never move hands with hands; never move feet with feet: hands just hold on, feet stay on the ground until they both react.
- Loss of balance occurs when the body's joints move out of position.
- Keep eyes and ears as level as possible.

Swing

- Most shots are missed before the swing starts.
- Eyes on ball – mind on hands.
- Force goes down into the ball – the ball goes up and down fairway.
- When most of the body is behind the ball you, can have a flat left wrist.
- Clubhead, shaft, hands, arms, shoulders, chest, hips all move in arcs.
- Swing is circular, but checkpoints and references are straight lines (plane, target line).
- To hit high or low shots, move the body's center of gravity at address. Back for high, forward for low.
- When hands are being transported by rotation they can feel like they are not moving. When you can feel the hands moving they are being thrown.
- To learn the feel of a "free swing," train by swinging without trying to correct bad shots.
- The less the center moves the more constant the circle can be.
- How do you use your hands? By holding on and aiming them down-plane with your turn.
- Develop sources and applications of power, force, rhythm, balance, pressure, distance, direction and timing.
- Golf shots really have no bad luck!

  Path = 20% of error

  Face = 90% of error

  Impact = 95% of error
- Path, face angle, and impact point should be worked on separately, and must be good before correct feel and touch can be learned.

- Effort is not power.
- Hitting is pushing, swinging is pulling.
- Goal – One-piece total swing.
- Improve one step at a time, start with a rotation.
- To be consistent, the right forearm should extend in both back and downswings.
- Know what you want, set it up.
- The brain can translate information from pressure points.
- A bent right wrist, and bent right elbow are transported down-plane.
- Larger muscles can be programmed more easily than small ones.
- The ball is met (impact) between the left facial cheek and the left armpit.
- Improve your starting position and change of direction.
- Doing anything with hands will cause loss of lag pressure, power and force.
- You can turn as fast as you want, as long as it feels steady.
- See how steady you can swing and how far you can hit the ball.
- The right arm helps keep the left arm swinging (and straight) from the left shoulder socket.
- Power = mass x velocity (wrong!) – it is effective mass x velocity.
- Left shoulder joint can be the center of circumference of the swinging left arm and club.
- Rotate club weight onto right forefinger during backswing.
- Right forefinger should feel like it is transported to the inside back corner of the ball with the weight of the club on it.
- When wrists uncock too early they will then be moved too far from the body by rotational forces.
- The hands involvement gives a low return on its investment.
- Arms for structure, wrists for flexibility
- Know the difference between impact and address alignments.
- Swing in the "state of grace."
- Short club swings are more vertical than long club swings.
- Club velocity comes from body rotation and expansion of angles, not effort from the arms and hands.
- See how steady you can swing but how hard the club can go into the ground.
- Never swing faster than you can turn.
- Golfers react more to the clubface than to path of swing.
- The swing feels slow when left shoulder socket is the radius, fast when the club moves from hands, wrist, or arms.
- At address, be as prepared as possible.
- From the top, be smooth and as even as possible.
- If your head moves, let momentum do it.
- The backswing can put hands on-plane with the right shoulder; the downswing can put hands on-plane with shaft plane at impact.
- Right arm can keep left wrist and arm to full extension, or from collapsing through impact.
- Whether it is a good or bad swing, always go to follow through, before finish.
- Never make or let the club do something the laws of force and motion do not want it to do.
- Center both eyes on the ball for depth perception.
- Look up after the ball is at the apex of its flight. Because of clubhead lag pressure the head is back.
- The shoulder turn should feel bigger on the backswing and smaller on the downswing than hip rotation.
- You transfer power as the shaft gets in-line with the left arm.
- You have radius power when the left arm comes off the chest.

- You have velocity power when the left wrist uncocks
- You have muscle power when the right arm expands
- Right elbow can help control the club path in a swing.
- Butt end of the club should travel in the smallest possible circle through impact.
- Understand where the hands are at all times.
- It is a mistake to stand on one plane line and swing on another for straight shots.
- Circumference of the swing is only as good as its center.
- Brace the right leg on angle to target, as turn puts hands on-plane over right shoulder, then over left shoulder.
- The left shoulder during the swing -
  (1st) Moves back = hands high (backswing)
  (2nd) Moves up = hands low (downswing)
  (3rd) Moves back = hands through (follow through)
- During efficient swings, lag pressure leaves the club and force goes into the ball.
- Learn alignment golf, not position golf.
- Learn to feel where the right forearm is at all times.
- The swing can get fast when arms out race the body turn.
- Waggle on-plane, waggle on to right forefinger.
- It is nice to have a steady head, balance, and rhythm, but we **must** have a lagging clubhead, flat left wrist, straight plane.
- Everything tries to move in a straight line – it does not because of body turn and inclined plane.
- You can use the body to thrust arms and hands through impact.
- Turn can put right shoulder, hands, left arm on-plane at the top.
- Use shoulders for direction
- Use hips for centering
- Use knees for flexibility
- Use feet for support
- During efficient swings –
  1. Left chest moves back to ball in back swing
  2. Left chest moves up and away from ball; to get the right elbow downplane.
  3. Left chest moves behind left leg; gets arms to finish.
- Loss of balance is moving hands with hands or feet with feet.
- Feet are pulled or rolled – they don't move independently (important).
- Eyes always look down-plane at the inside corner of the ball.
- Waggle on-plane to inside corner of the ball.
- The golf swing has two clubfaces – one is the club's face, the other is the back of the left hand. Wherever the back of the left hand points, so does the clubface.
- Show yourself impact, then go back to address and start the swing. Bad golfers try to return to address, good ones return to impact alignments.
- Address – bent left, straight right wrist. Impact – flat left, bent right wrist. (Know the difference.)
- Power is turning and pulling, shape is plane.
- Loss of balance occurs when joints get out of position.
- Any over acceleration kills the golf swing.
- Never drive hands at the ball, let the hands that are not changing their rate of motion be moved by rotation down-plane.
- Maximum compression comes from concentric circles (one inside –one outside). In golf, the shoulders and hips make up the inside circle and the clubhead the outside circle.

Backswing

- Shoulders turn ninety degrees , then right elbow can influence a swing by folding and moving the club up-plane.
- Shoulders can swing the arms, arms can swing the hands.
- When the right elbow slips behind the body, it pulls the left arm into the chest and is no longer supporting the shaft and left arm.
- Feel the toe of weight of the club hinge the left wrist and bend the right elbow in front of body.
- Right elbow can cock left wrist when it folds up.
- Right elbow points down in backswing, not out or up.
- Right leg is braced for backswing and it's angled to the target.
- At the top of the backswing, right leg leaning to target – right forearm and humorous leaning away from target (important).
- Left shoulder turns more than left knee.
- If the right elbow slips behind the hip, it is in a hitting, not swinging, position.
- Feel the right forearm face the sky and right elbow point down and in.
- Reverse pivot can happen when right elbow folds too late, causing the shoulders to tilt or turn too vertically.
- Club moves up-plane because right elbow folds, and left shoulder goes down.
- When the left foot is turned out, it is hard to slide back or outside right foot.
- Shoulders turn 90 degrees with driver. The turn can be smaller with shorter clubs.

Downswing

- Good downswing rotation can correct a bad position on top
- When the club hits the ball, it creates more than 2000 pounds of pressure. This drives the club down and makes divots. Bigger iron heads go down more than small ones (more mass).
- Downswing has leverage – not leakage (which is compensation for sliding). The backswing has lag not sag.
- When feet and legs lead, a bad rate of motion occurs. Legs should **respond**, not lead.
- The downswing is three-dimensional (down, out, and around). Right shoulder and lower back muscles cause **down**, hips and thighs cause **out**, total body rotation causes **around**.
- The downswing has longitudinal acceleration (straight line down-plane) **before** radial downswing acceleration (rotation).
- There is a vertical on-plane tilt of the shoulders through impact.
- The bottom of the spine can move forward as a reflex reaction to downplane forces.
- Club goes down plane first, not forward or out.
- The left thigh muscles turn hips after right shoulder, right elbow and club go down-plane.
- Force is going down and out (not forward), as the club goes up the plane after separation. Motion is always on-plane.
- The back turns away from the target to get the club going down-plane into the middle of the back.
- The right shoulder centers the hips as it goes down-plane and puts pressure into the ground and into the right forefinger and wrist.
- Both eyes level and on the ball as hands hold on while shoulder turn moves arms.
- Through impact, the right arm straightens as left leg straightens through pivot thrust.
- In the downswing the right elbow and right shoulder should feel heavy.
- When the swing hits behind the ball, it is because the hip did not turn and the right arm expands early.

- Shoulders should feel like they do not turn until the shaft gets parallel to the ground – (feel down-plane **before** turn).
- Right shoulder travels down through the **same space** the left shoulder used during the backswing. Right shoulder must move down plane to do this.
- When the right elbow is behind the body, the right arm will start downswing.
- Have the left thigh and lower back muscles turn hips – when the hips turn by themselves, the body alignments get lost.
- Duffers often develops more clubhead speed than do the professionals, and much more deceleration; therefore, they has much less effective mass.
- Let rotation blast the left arm back out to impact after it moves in a little during backswing.
- Feel like you go to impact with flat feet.
- Bring the whole club shaft to ball; have the feeling the hands are being driven past the ball by rotation.
- We must stress the shaft.
- Mid-section can throw left arm out to impact alignment.
- The left thigh and butt firm up through impact.
- Ball is gone before the club hits the ground, or driver hits the tee.
- Spine tilt gets right shoulder on –plane, feel the club coming out of the center of your back
- Right shoulder has to be low enough to swing up, not around.
- Low point is the bottom of the divot.
- Just keep the body ahead of the hands, hands ahead of the club.
- On-plane shoulders – feels like you hit the ball with right shoulder or elbow.
- Stay back – the more you are back the more time you have – keep right foot down until pivot moves it.
- Never drive hands with the hands at the ball. Control hand speed with rotation.
- After impact the club goes left as a reaction to the rotation of the body – (not the hands).
- Fat and thin shots have hands in same position but fat shots have no rotation, and right arm throws the clubhead. Thin shots have no gravity and right arm flips the clubhead.
- Right arm will look straight at follow through because it is extending down, as body turns and expands the arm.
- Left arm and right elbow swing down-plane under spine angled away from the target.
- When your spine goes up during downswing, the arms and club come into body not down, out and around.
- The longer the left wrist stays cocked, the longer the hands stay in. Then the throwout action of rotational forces moves the club down and out.
- Long shots feel and seem like you sling the weight of the club.
- During downswing feel, the right forearm going down-plane and the left shoulder going up plane.
- Have the feeling you have gotten into an underhand position in the downswing.
- Legs come apart in downswing as a reaction to right hip moving down-plane.
- Thighs can pull the arms through impact.
- Head back until after follow through, then momentum will move it up and forward.
- When the shaft is parallel to the ground in the downswing, the hips take over as momentum from the upper body is transferred to the lower body.
- Width of stance influences how far the hips have to move. When the stance is too wide the hips must travel too far to move the center of gravity to the back of the ball in the downswing.
- In the downswing the right knee stays flexed as long as possible, and really should not move until the shaft is parallel to the ground and the hands are down and past the right knee.

Through Impact

- Picturing a square clubface at impact can cause a throw-out from the right hand and arm.
- Upper left side should be behind the left foot.
- Right leg and hip stay together.
- Right elbow is still bent and in front of right hip at impact, and straight by follow through.
- Muscle power is a bent right arm, straightening through impact into follow through.
- Too much right arm is a right arm that is too long at impact.
- Without a flat left wrist we are pushing the ball.
- When the right forearm is on-plane, the clubface sweet spot can be driven through the ball as you rotate.
- The circle of the left arm and the circle of the body should meet at the bottom of the swing.
- The right forearm should be on the shaft plane through impact.
- Proper knee flex and hip bend will let the body respond to hip rotation (thigh muscles), causing clubhead lag, drag and line of compression to be present at impact.
- Clubhead velocity can receive "thrust" from pivot, then an expanding right forearm going down-plane through impact.
- Lateral body motion through impact stops rotation and causes the left wrist to break down.
- Hand location (at impact) determines how much effort will be needed.
- Ball always leaves at practically right angles to the clubface.
- Impact is the same for all shots, but the more forward the ball is located, the lower the right shoulder will or must be.
- Develop an inside-out path to impact, not an inside-out swing path. (Important)
- The line of flight of the clubhead and the line of the ball are not the same. They only touch during impact.
- Just before impact the arms have stopped accelerating and their momentum (energy) has traveled out to the club.
- Hand acceleration has stopped through impact (i.e. Ian Woosnam).
- Through impact the left thigh and hip are going back, around and up, straightening the left leg, giving the swing its longest radius., and on-plane hips
- Impact is a down-plane alignment – not forward.
- Right side is moving faster than the left through impact and is traveling a greater distance and a larger circle.
- Feel the clubhead behind the shaft until the shaft is parallel to the target line at follow through (This is important).
- Arms are moving slower than clubhead through impact.
- Clubhead, shaft, hands, shoulders, arms, chest, hips and thighs are all moving in an arc through impact.
- The left hip opens, or goes around to the left through impact.
- Arms may feel like they are squeezing together at impact, because they are being stretched down by rotational forces from internal rotation.
- At impact arms are in front and on the body as the clubhead is being thrown down and out to the ball by a rotational force that expands the right arm.
- Hands close to body, left arm as vertical as possible (right arm on-plane) so rotational forces can help throw club down and out.
- Club should always appear that it is leaning forward. (exception—some short game shots)
- Body turn brings full club shaft on the ball, not just the clubhead.
- Front view – club in-line with left arm
- Back view – club on-plane with right arm.

After impact

- Left arm rolls because the body turns and right arm expands, and design of the club.
- The eyes, shoulders, right foot, right arm, hands, and club all feel on-plane.

Follow Through

- Even on short shots, follow through is more important than finish.
- Arms go down not forward to follow through.
- Club shaft in-line with the left arm at follow through.
- The only time both arms are expanded (straight) is at follow through.
- The hips are starting to brake (stop) after follow through and momentum takes over and moves them to finish.

Finish

- There is no vertical support from a bent left leg, a straight left leg gives support and balance to finish.
- Thighs and knees together, same distance from target

Rotation / Pivot

- When the body moves in a straight line, the club will not be thrown out by rotational forces.
- Rotation can load the shaft onto the right forefinger and keep it there through follow through.
- The lower back muscles can pull the club to impact.
- Lower back and hips for backswing and downswing. Hips and left leg for follow through.
- Rotate in the smallest possible space.
- Use all the back muscles for backswing. Use lower back muscles and left thigh for downswing.
- Learn to feel the forward lean of the shaft as the left thigh rotates through impact.
- Left leg going straight or turning, gives swing longest radius through impact.
- No quitting or leaking during impact = line of compression (a principle) – straight line from left shoulder to clubhead.
- Impact interval – looks and feels like everything (right elbow, forearm, hands) have been turned past the ball with mind and eyes on the inside ˇ of the ball.

Feel

- Learn feel from mechanics.
- Produce feel from mechanics.
- Look ...look ... look... until you can really feel it.

Physics

- Range of motion, force, pressure and velocity are more important than speed (speed has no direction).
- When the club is moved from the hands it will feel very fast and uneven because of the short swing radius.
- Effective force (steady pulling) eliminates over acceleration.

Velocity

- Clubhead velocity, when the ball separates itself from the clubface, is as **important** than clubhead velocity at impact.
- No amount of effort will produce more velocity than a player's maximum turning rate.

Plane

- After impact, clubhead goes down and out to low point of divot, then in and up.
- The right elbow and club shaft are on the same plane at impact.
- Hands, left arm and right shoulder should be on the same plane at the top of the backswing.
- Spine stays tilted (over and back) until follow through, so that the club can stay on-plane.

Right Arm

- Right arm should not provide movement in backswing. It provides extension of left arm, and it is a non-accelerating mass in the backswing.
- Back view – at the top, upper right arm (humorous bone) in front of chest then it disappears, moving down-plane in front of right hip because of the right hip and right shoulder going down plane.
- Expands to impart impact alignments.

Body

- Hands move down at the start of the backswing, as the left shoulder goes down-plane and the right shoulder goes up-plane.
- Arms – have the feeling you could never pull the arms apart.
- Hips – influence shoulders in the backswing and spine angle in the downswing.
- Hands that move out, not around at the start of the backswing causes off plane shoulder turns.

Support

- Downswing is down – out – around
  - Down is supported by the left leg going straight.
  - Out is supported by the heels staying down.
  - Around is supported by the head staying back
- Right arm is always supporting the swinging left arm.

Golf Mind

- Cause and effect are the two sides of one fact. Nothing exists without cause. The brain must know the cause, so we can repeat or avoid the effect.
- The brain does not swing the club, but it can stop the swing.
- The brain controls the body. The body controls the club, and the club controls the ball.
- Let's train the mind to decide what the situation demands. (Very important)
- A golfer's game will only be as good as his/her concepts.
- We must change on the inside first. Golfers must know and understand what they are trying to do first.
- Understanding leads to a sound swing.

- Learning requires interpretation. Golfers need help to interpret what is going on, they don't need how to lists.
- To educate means to draw out, not put in.
- The brain needs accurate feedback; progress is not possible without it.
- Principles of development, effective training and coaching allow the brain to package information. The brain must learn how to package information before the body can perform.
- Once you know how to draw al little circle, you can now draw a bigger one. Learn small swings first.
- Mental rehearsal = motion blueprint.
- When people often have thoughts based on the past, they don't develop new perceptions. Thinking is retrieving, not creating. Look for new insights.
- The mind, body or emotions are not completely reliable –commitment is reliable. So commit to your future golf game.
- Learning behavior has 3 categories:

  Movement – organization (motor)

  Intellect – Abilities (cognitive)

  Feelings – motivation – Interest (effective), and this emotional category often gets overlooked.
- The eyes do not see, the mouth does not taste, the ears do not hear. Everything happens in the brain first.
- Distraction is merely attention gone some place else.
- The brain receives feedback –verbal (conscious) and unconscious (body language, feels and mental pictures).
- Understanding for the brain must be as important as achieving for the body.
- Things do not just happen They are brought about and they have their origin in the brain.
- The body will normally do what the brain tells it to do.
- The brain learns by doing. Emphasize the process of learning, not results.
- Think like a man of action but act like a man of thought.
- When the brain is full of words "how to" advice, it no longer has original thoughts, and it can be creative or solve problems.
- Play golf with pictures, feel and concepts, not with words.
- When the brain hears, it can forget. When it sees and you do, it understands.
- The eyes are the window of the brain
- Muscles receive their directions from the brain, 85% of the information in the brain comes from your eyes, and misconceptions are our downfall.
- Memory, or the brain's capacity to remember, may have more influence on learning golf than any other skill. Forgetting is a close second. Forget poor concepts.
- The brain's short-term memory span has a limit of 6 or 7 words.
- The brain learns better if it is given a plan, instead of just trying to do its best.
- The brain and the central nervous system automatically make balance adjustments during the swing.
- One of the purposes of training and practice is to tell the brain what to feel.
- The first step for a player is learning to learn.
- The brain remembers better when things are repeated 4 times. Retention rate goes up 90%.
- The brain knows what is different, not what is good or bad.
- Letting the brain personalize instruction information is more useful than using someone else's thoughts or words.

- Effective instruction and learning improve by removing self-imposed interference.
- The body should use suggestions within 5 to 10 seconds.
- Do not focus on what may happen. Rather stay focused on what to do. (Important)
- Brain to muscle information travels at 350 feet per second.
- A good golfer plans for success.
- Go with what got you there.
- Players don't choke, they just over-try.
- There are two aspects: physical (ball striking) and mental (how in control you are).
- Manage your game better, concentrating on strategy not swing thoughts.
- Play the shot at hand.
- Give your best every time you tee it up, and then look forward to the next time.
- Playing golf at a competitive level is a year round project.
- A routine allows you to be on "automatic pilot" when on the course.
- *"Playing with Jack Nicklaus at Pebble Beach did more for my game than all the balls I had ever hit. He showed me course management and personal discipline. He turned my career around, showed me how to win."* –Cal Pete
- Winning is a result, not a cause of confidence.
- Being nervous (adrenaline) brings you to a higher level – you think better and are stronger.
- We have to be willing to fail – stop trying not to three putt!
- Do not "pre-determine" skill level.
- Long-term memory of success, short-term memory of failure (learn to forget).
- Let action just happen. In golf we have to get out of our own way – don't over think!
- Always picture success, talk about good things.
- Some things are learned better when we do not try to teach them.
- Some things are learnable, but not teachable.
- Everything we try works.
- We learn from calamities, not from virtues.
- What is true for children is probably also true for adults.
- Students often learn more from each other than from the teacher.
- We learn to play golf in winter and we learn to snow ski in the summer.
- We should change the mind (inside) first, and then the physical outside can improve.

Glossary

ISAAC NEWTON (1642-1727)

English physicist and mathematician who was born into a poor farming family. Luckily for humanity, Newton was not a good farmer, and was sent to Cambridge to study to become a preacher. At Cambridge, Newton studied mathematics, being especially strongly influenced by Euclid, although he was also influenced by Baconian and Cartesian philosophies. Newton was forced to leave Cambridge when it was closed because of the plague, and it was during this period that he made some of his most significant discoveries. With the reticence he was to show later in life, Newton did not, however, publish his results.

Newton suffered a mental breakdown in 1675 and was still recovering through 1679. In response to a letter from Hooke, he suggested that a particle, if released, would spiral in to the center of the Earth. Hooke wrote back, claiming that the path would not be a spiral, but an ellipse. Newton, who hated being bested, then proceeded to work out the mathematics of orbits. Again, he did not publish his calculations. Newton then began devoting his efforts to theological speculation and put the calculations on elliptical motion aside, telling Halley he had lost them (Westfall 1993, p. 403). Halley, who had become interested in orbits, finally convinced Newton to expand and publish his calculations. Newton devoted the period from August 1684 to spring 1686 to this task, and the result became one of the most important and influential works on physics of all times, *Philosophiae Naturalis Principia Mathematica (Mathematical Principles of Natural Philosophy)* (1687), often shortened to *Principia Mathematica* or simply "the *Principia.*"

In Book I of *Principia,* Newton opened with definitions and the three laws of motion now known as Newton's laws (laws of inertia, action and reaction, and acceleration proportional to force). Book II presented Newton's new scientific philosophy that came to replace Cartesianism. Finally, Book III consisted of applications of his dynamics, including an explanation for tides and a theory of lunar motion. To test his hypothesis of universal gravitation, Newton wrote Flamsteed to ask if Saturn had been observed to slow down upon passing Jupiter. The surprised Flamsteed replied that an effect had indeed been observed, and it was closely predicted by the calculations Newton had provided. Newton's equations were further confirmed by observing the shape of the Earth to be oblate spheroidal, as Newton claimed it should be, rather than prolate spheroidal, as claimed by the Cartesians. Newton's equations also described the motion of Moon by successive approximations, and correctly predicted the return of Halley's Comet. Newton also correctly formulated and solved the first ever problem in the calculus of variations which involved finding the surface of revolution which would give minimum resistance to flow (assuming a specific drag law).

Newton invented a scientific method, which was truly universal in its scope. Newton presented his methodology as a set of four rules for scientific reasoning. These rules were stated in the *Principia* and proposed that (1) we are to admit no more causes of natural things such as are both true and sufficient to explain their appearances, (2) the same natural effects must be assigned to the same causes, (3) qualities of bodies are to be esteemed as universal, and (4) propositions deduced from observation of phenomena should be viewed as accurate until other phenomena contradict them.

These four concise and universal rules for investigation were truly revolutionary. By their application, Newton formulated the universal laws of nature with which he was able to unravel virtually all the unsolved problems of his day. Newton went much further than outlining his rules for reasoning, however, actually describing how they might be applied to the solution of a given problem. The analytic method he invented far exceeded the more philosophical and less scientifically rigorous approaches of Aristotle and Aquinas. Newton refined Galileo's experimental method, creating the compositional method of experimentation still practiced today. In fact, the following description of the experimental method from Newton's *Optics* could easily be mistaken for a modern statement of current methods of investigation, if not for Newton's use of the words "natural philosophy" in place of the modern term "the physical sciences." Newton wrote, "As in mathematics, so in natural philosophy the investigation of difficult things by the method of analysis ought ever to precede the method of composition. This analysis consists of making experiments and observations, and in drawing general conclusions from them by induction...by this way of analysis we may proceed from compounds to ingredients, and from motions to the forces producing them; and in general from effects to their causes, and from particular causes to more general ones till the argument end in the most general. This is the method of analysis: and the synthesis consists in assuming the causes discovered and established as principles, and by them explaining the phenomena preceding from them, and proving the explanations."

Newton formulated the classical theories of mechanics and optics and invented calculus years before Leibniz. However, he did not *publish* his work on calculus until afterward Leibniz had published his. This led to a bitter priority dispute between English and continental mathematicians which persisted for decades, to the detriment of all concerned. Newton discovered that the binomial theorem was valid for fractional powers, but left it for Wallis to publish (which he did, with appropriate credit to Newton).

In *Optics* (1704), whose publication Newton delayed until Hooke's death, Newton observed that white light could be separated by a prism into a spectrum of different colors, each characterized by a unique refractivity, and proposed the corpuscular theory of light. Newton's views on optics were born out of the original prism experiments he performed at Cambridge. In his "experimentum crucis" (crucial experiment), he found that the image produced by a prism was oval-shaped and not circular, as current theories of light would require. He observed a half-red, half-blue string through a prism, and found the ends to be disjointed. He also observed Newton's rings, which are actually a manifestation of the wave nature of light that Newton did not believe in. Newton believed that light must move faster in a medium when it is refracted towards the normal, in opposition to the result predicted by Huygens's wave theory.

Newton also formulated a system of chemistry in Query 31 at the end of *Optics*. In this corpuscular theory, "elements" consisted of different arrangements of atoms, and atoms consisted of small, hard, billiard ball-like particles. He explained chemical reactions in terms of the chemical affinities of the participating substances. Newton devoted a majority of his free time later in life (after 1678) to fruitless alchemical experiments.

Newton single-handedly contributed more to the development of science than any other individual in history. He surpassed all the gains brought about by the great scientific minds of antiquity, producing a scheme of the universe which was more consistent, elegant, and intuitive than any proposed before. Newton stated explicit principles of scientific methods, which applied universally to all branches of science. This was in sharp contradistinction to the earlier methodologies of Aristotle and Aquinas, which had outlined separate methods for different disciplines.

Although earlier philosophers such as Galileo and John Philoponus had used experimental procedures, Newton was the first to explicitly define and systematize their use. His methodology produced a neat balance between theoretical and experimental inquiry and between the mathematical and mechanical approaches. Newton mathematized all of the physical sciences, reducing their study to a rigorous, universal, and rational procedure, which marked the ushering in of the Age of Reason. Thus, the basic principles of investigation set down by Newton have persisted virtually without alteration until modern times. In the years since Newton's death, they have borne fruit far exceeding anything even Newton could have imagined. They form the foundation on which the technological civilization of today rests. The principles expounded by Newton were even applied to the social sciences, influencing the economic theories of Adam Smith and the decision to make the United States legislature bicameral. These latter applications, however, pale in contrast to Newton's scientific contributions.

It is therefore no exaggeration to identify Newton as the single most important contributor to the development of modern science. The Latin inscription on Newton's tomb, despite its bombastic language, is thus fully justified in proclaiming, "Mortals! Rejoice at so great an ornament to the human race!" Alexander Pope's couplet is also apropos: "Nature and Nature's laws lay hid in night; God said, Let Newton be! and all was light."

In my view, golf instruction information must rise above all the "confusion" that can be associated with the swing, human motion, and how motor skills are learned. It would be useful therefore, to have a set of defined terms, principals and concepts.

The intent of this section is to provide an objective information base for discussing motion and the golf swing. This requires attention being paid to precise definitions and terms.

Perhaps one of the problems for golfers who are trying to improve their level of play is the terminology that must be used to describe movements and forces present in sound swings. This terminology is not used very often in every day conversation.

This section contains terms and definitions that are common to any understanding of mechanical application of laws of motion and their principles.

The first stage in making progress with golf is having a new understanding of information we did not have in the past. The following is my attempt to add some understanding to terms and definitions that are not commonly used in some approaches to golf instruction.

ACCELERATION – Rate of change in velocity with respect to time.

> **Golf Application**: Over-acceleration of any body part kills a sound swing. In sound swings, segments should "seem" like they rotate at the same rate. The hands are being moved faster than the elbows, the elbows faster than the shoulders, and the shoulders faster than the chest – but they all should "feel like" they move at the same rate of rotation.
>
> No segment for a sound swing is over-accelerating or decelerating. However, the outside segment (clubhead) of a rotating system with its bigger circumference always moves faster than the inside segments (body) with its smaller circumference. The outside portion of a door moves faster than the inside portion – but both parts arrive at the door jam at the same time. They are both moving at the same rate of rotation (RPM's) around different size circumferences.

AGONIST – Muscle(s) whose activity causes the movement under consideration.

ANTAGONIST – Muscle(s) whose action opposes that of a the agonist.

AXIS OF ROTATION – The imaginary line or point about which a body or segment rotates.

BALANCE – A state in which all opposing forces cancel each other out. It is the ability of the body to perform purposeful motion while resisting the force of gravity.

> **Golf Application:** Balance in three-dimensional space (up to down, front to back, side to side) must always be the first consideration for a golf swing. The central nervous system automatically returns the body to an on balance condition whenever it moves off balance. This is why the young baby waddles and does not fall over.
>
> The balance centers located in the eyes, ears, and neck tell the brain when to readjust the center of gravity whenever the conditions require a compensation to return to a balanced state.
>
> There are always some unwanted movements in a swing that cannot be corrected by golf instruction. This is because these movements are caused by automatic compensations the central nervous system is making as the swing is in motion and moves off balance.
>
> Most, if not all, movement in the human body is a reaction to and out of balance state. The body has no natural movement when it is on balance.

BALLISTIC – describes a movement or part of a movement in which the motion of the system is the result of its own momentum and is not due to external forces. Ballistic is often used as a synonym for rapid. However this is incorrect.

Golf application: The ball moves itself ballistically off the clubface (after it is compressed by the force a sound swing delivers). The club should not feel like it is moving the ball. Unless this principle of force is understood, practiced, and applied, a golf swing cannot reach its potential.

BASE OF SUPPORT – That region bounded by body parts in contact with some resistive surface that exerts a reaction force against the body.

Golf application: Ideally, the inside measurement of our hips should be placed under our shoulder joints – with the toes turned out wider than the heels (left 20 degrees, right 5 degrees) feet flat on the ground.

BIOMECHANICS – The area of study wherein knowledge and methods of mechanics are applied to the structure and function of the living system.

Golf application: An area of study that can give both player and instructor objective information and knowledge for developing a sound swing.

CENTER OF GRAVITY – The balance point of a body; the point around which the sum of all the torque's of the segmental weights is equal to zero; the point of application of gravity's force on a mass; the center of mass.

Golf application: We should develop a swing that does not disturb the body's center of balance or gravity. This center is located in the middle of the pelvic area in the mid-section of the body. Ideally, the center of gravity is the axis or one of the centers of rotation of a sound swing.

CENTER OF PRESSURE – The point of application of the ground reaction force.

Golf application: Sound swings put pressure into the ground during both the back and downswing. The pressure that's applied to the ball is a reaction force coming from the ground.

CENTER OF ROTATION – Points around which circular motion is described.

Golf application: The center of axis of the swinging left arm and club is the left shoulder socket. When the left shoulder socket is the center or axis of the swinging left arm and club, it gives the swing its longest possible radius. (Swings have several C of R's)

CENTRIFICAL FORCE – A force directed outward that is exerted by a rotating body on a structure or mass.

Golf application: This force moves out from the center of a rotating system and is available and present in golf swings that have rotational forces causing the clubhead to droop through impact.

CENTRIPETAL FORCE – An inward directed force (toward the axis of rotation) that is responsible for changing linear motion into angular motion. This force is directed radically toward the center of rotation by a mass on a rotating body and causes that body to travel in a circular path.

Golf application: This force helps keep the clubhead moving in a circular and predicable arc or path.

CLOSED-LOOP CONTROL – The use of sensory feedback signals to provide continuous guidance of a movement.

COEFICIENT OF FRICTION – The ratio of the magnitude of the maximum force of friction to the magnitude of the perpendicular force pressing the two surfaces together (normal force).

Golf application: This force is present at impact in sound swings. The ball attaches itself to the clubface for a time and distance. During this time and distance (¾" and 55,000th of a second) the ball is being programmed to go long or short, left or right, high or low.

The ball could be thought of as a computer; the swing a program; and the ball flight the print out. The ball reacts blindly to the information it receives at impact from the swing and club. The shot you have made was created, it did not happen by chance. The ball's flight is not awful – it is obeying the laws of motion and is lawful.

COLINEAR FORCES – Forces whose line's of action lie along the same line.

Golf application: In a sound swing the shaft, hands, right forearm, and right elbow, are all being transported on a line of action down to impact.

COMPRESSIVE FORCE – A pulling force.

Golf application: This force is available when the club is being influenced by rotation in the downswing. A pulling force has more value than a pushing force in a sound swing. This is why the right elbow should be in front of the right hip before full rotation of the hips.

CONSERVATION OF MOMENTUM – A concept stating that when a system is not subject to an impulse its momentum remains constant.

Golf application: A constant rate of momentum is present in all sound swings. This condition can be altered when golfers make any sudden impulsive movements anywhere during the swing; (ex.) trying to drive the hands or legs will cause the system to lose its constant rate of motion and therefore its momentum. Momentum is created by a constant rate of motion.

CONSTANT LOAD – A condition during which the load experienced by a system remains constant, both over time and over a range of motion.

Golf application: A constant load (force or stress) is present when the club's head trails its shaft. This load, force or stress against the right forefinger and bent right wrist, is created by the clubhead's inertia or resistance to change and the constant rate of rotation in a sound swing.

Sound swings put force or stress on the club shaft. When we allow the clubhead to pass the hands we create deceleration or clubhead throwaway and have no pressure or stress on the shaft.

Sound swings have a lagging clubhead, flat left and bent right wrist during impact. Sound swings have a constant lead, force or stress on the shaft from the right forefinger and bent right wrist much like using a broom or mop, a paintbrush, or cast a fly rod in fishing. None of which could be used without a constant load or bent right wrist.

CONTRACTION – The internal state in which muscle actively exerts a force and shortens its length.

CROSSBRIDGING – This is the activity that causes muscles to move bones. Muscle is similar to Velcro – a series of little hooks and loops. When all hooks attach to all loops the muscle has maximum power potential.

Golf application: Maximum muscle power is reached when it moves at 30% of its maximum velocity – when it moves faster some of the hooks an loops (cross-bridging) do not attach and the muscle produces less power.

CURVILINEAR – Refers to motion along a curved line or path.

Golf application: This is the condition of a clubhead during a sound swing. Inertia would like the club to move in a straight line. But the rotation of a sound swing produces centrifugal or outward forces that prevent the club from moving straight.

The equal and opposite inward force to CF is centripetal fore. This is the force that moves the clubhead in an arc (curvilinear) during a sound swing, not effort from the golfer.

An inward force (rotation) creates an equal and opposite outward force (centrifugal) causing objects to be moved in an arc when the equal and opposite force to centrifugal – centripetal, applies its influence. Without these forces, inertia would move the clubhead in a straight line.

DECELERATION – The decrease in velocity per unit time.

Golf application: Sound swings must comply with the laws of motion that require a constant rate of motion – not motion that suddenly decelerates or accelerates the club. An example of deceleration is a clubhead that is moving up at impact – normally, when the club starts up, it is decelerating.

The main cause of clubhead deceleration is a bent left wrist at impact.

DISPLACEMENT – A change in position.

Golf application: I ask learners to displace body mass. They are not told to transfer weight.

Students are asked to develop a swing that can move their trunk (chest and back) behind the ball. Develop swings that displace body mass or changes the position of body mass.

I have found that the thought of transferring weight causes golfers to lose their balance.

DYNAMIC – A mechanical state in which a system experiences acceleration.

Golf application: By definition, dynamic means acceleration. But, it has been my experience that when golfers want to develop a dynamic swing with acceleration, they overlook the law of motion that requires acceleration to be at a constant rate throughout the motion. Students often develop swings that have sudden bursts of speed that kill their swings.

DYNAMICS – The study of mechanical factors associated with systems in motion.

Golf application: Objective information and knowledge from this subject can be used by both student and instructor to improve or learn a golf swing.

ECCENTRIC – The mechanical condition in which the load torque is greater than the muscle torque: this is not a type of contraction.

ECONOMY – The minimum use of energy to perform a task.

Golf application: This is one of the conditions under which sound swings take place. Sound swings do not use or require extra effort. Sound swings use the work laws of motion provide.

EFFECIENCY – The relationship between work output and energy input; often confused with economy.

Golf application: This is one of the conditions under which sound swings take place. Minimum input for maximum output.

ELASTICITY – ELASTIC FORCE OF MUSCLES – The passive property of a stretched material which allows the material to return to its original shape and size after being deformed.

Golf application: Some golf instruction has incorrectly suggested that our muscles can react like springs and rubber bands when they are stretched, and add power to the swing as they spring back. (A stretch reflex only starts the motion.)

Muscles can and do produce more work or power when they are moved or stretched to 120% of their resting length. This is because they now have a longer distance to apply work or force (F X D = W) not because they spring back.

Keep in mind that when a muscle group is moving, its opposing muscle group resists this action with what is called eccentric muscle control. Without this opposing muscle force controlling the speed and velocity of the contracting muscle, actions would be uncontrollable. This includes motions like walking, swimming or playing golf.

ENERGY – The capacity to do work.

Golf application: A property of sound swings, energy for and from sound swings is produced by efficient, economic work – not by effort from golfers.

EXCITATION – CONTRACTION COUPLING – The electrochemical processes involved in converting a muscle action potential into cross bridge activity.

EXTENSION – The position of the joints of the extremities and back when one stands at rest, or the direction of motion which tends to restore this in-line position; the opposite of flexion.

FATIGUE - A progressive increase in the effort required to exert a desired force and the progressive inability to maintain this force during sustained or repeated contractions (i.e. increased effort force failure).

Golf application: A condition that prevents some golfers from reaching their true potential (over trying, too much effort).

FINAL COMMON PATHWAY – An expression characterizing the function of motor neurons as the route by which the nervous system controls muscle activity.

FLEXION – Movement involving the bending of a joint whereby the angle between the bones is diminished; the opposite of extension.

FORCE - An action which changes the shape, state of rest, or motion of a body to which it is applied. It is a push or a pull, a blow exerted by actual contact or the pull of gravity on a body within its field. The force a sound swing creates goes down and out (not forward) compressing the ball onto the clubface. Now because of the Law of Coefficient of Restitution, the ball moves itself off the clubface at a rate equal and opposite to the force the clubhead produced at impact. Many golfers only produce speed, not force, velocity, power, torque, pressure, and do not reach their potential.

GRAVITY AND GRAVITATIONAL FORCE – A force produced by gravitational attraction by the earth on a body.

Golf application: A force, when permitted to influence the swing, helps eliminate the physical effort many golfers use in their downswing.

GROUND REACTION FORCE – A gravitational force produced by the weight of an object against the surface on which it lies.

Golf application: The greater the force going into the ground, the greater the force the swing can produce. Feel pressure going into the ground during both the back and downswings for maximum force production.

A basketball player can only jump as high as the force he puts into the floor.

For golfers to take full advantage of this same ground reaction force. They should have the feeling of a slight sitting down motion from the legs as the swing changes directions.

The greater the force going down into the ground, the greater the force the swing can produce. Feel pressure going into the ground during both the back and downswings for maximum force production.

GYROSCOPIC ACTION AND STABILITY – The resistance of a rotating body to a change in its plane of rotation.

Golf application: A golf club swinging on-plane (or off-plane) will resist any attempt to change its plane of rotation.

INCLINED PLANE – A flat surface positioned somewhere between horizontal and vertical.

Golf application: Picture a house – the floor is horizontal (like a baseball swing) the wall is vertical (like a croquet or bowling swing) the roof is an inclined plane (like a hockey stick and swing or golf club and swing).

When correct at address, the club's shaft is placed at the angle it was designed (on an inclined plane). During the sound swing, the shaft will point to or be parallel to the base or bottom of the original inclined plane created by the club shaft at address. The shaft stays flat and in-line with the roof during a sound swing. (There are exceptions)

INERTIA – The resistance of a body to a change in its state of motion. Once matter is moving it will stay in the same path, unless it is affected by an outside force.

Golf application: Inertia is one of the reasons a sound swing stays on –plane when it starts on-plane.

Inertia is one of the reasons a sound swing can stress and put pressure into the shaft. When the head of the club is left behind, its resistance to movement (inertia) causes the shaft to flex.

KINESIOLOGY – The study of human movement from an anatomical or mechanical perspective or both.

Golf application: provides objective information for a swing and body movement study.

KINETIC ENERGY – The ability of a body to do work by virtue of its motion.

KINETICS – The branch of mechanics that deals with the motion of a body under the action of given forces.

LEVER SYSTEM, WHEEL AND ACEL MECHANISM – Mechanisms for doing work consisting of a body with an axis of rotation and eccentrically applied force.

Golf application: Our body has both a lever system and a wheel and axle mechanism. Both are rotational systems, but the wheel-axle mechanism has an adjustable radius of rotation for the point of contact.

If a baseball player was to hold the bat straight out level, or in a line with his arms, he would have a lever system. When he holds the bat in the traditional manner (arms out, bat up) he has a wheel-axle mechanism.

The longer lever system (with out an angle) has a greater radius of gyration causing a greater moment of inertia and rotational inertia.

A reduction in a system's radius will increase its angular velocity. This reduction will create a smaller moment of inertia, which also increases angular velocity. (I.e. Angle between the left arm and shaft)

The rotational inertia of the baseball player holding the bat with an angle between the bat and his arms is five times smaller than the player who holds the bat straight (same for a golfer).

Thus, with equal muscle torque's acting for the same amount of time on the two different systems, the smaller inertia of the wheel-axle system allows for five times greater acceleration and velocity than the longer lever system.

This greater acceleration in a wheel-axle system gives this system 2½ times the velocity of the longer lever system. This is why the wheel-axle system is used and recommended for high-end point velocity striking skills like baseball, tennis, and golf. (I.e. Angle between the left arm and shaft.)

Golfers who maintain an angle between their club shaft and arms at address and through impact, can create more velocity than those who do not, and with less effort.

MASS – The measure of a body's inertia; the measure of a body's resistance to changing its state of motion.

Golf application: Body mass is displaced in sound swings. Weight is a force, mass is not.

MOMENTUM – The quantity of motion possessed by an object. A system's resistance to change in its state of motion (inertia) multiplied by its velocity.

Golf application: Sound swings do not place the club – the sound swing gives the club momentum. Momentum transfer is the most important component of a sound swing's power and force. At impact in a sound swing, the motion of one segment is transferred to another segment. This transfer of energy is what gives the sound swing its effort-free look and feel. Lighter, smaller, shorter segments cannot give much energy to bigger, heavier, longer segments. The ball receives a transfer of momentum at impact.

MOTION – A change in position that occurs over an interval of time.

MOTIVE FORCE – A force that causes motion or change in shape. The most significant motive force causing motion is the pull of gravity.

MOTORNEURON – A neuron whose action connects directly to muscle fibers. Since it represents the final stage in the output from the nervous system, and is the only means by which muscle can be activated, the motor neuron is referred to as the final common pathway.

MOVEMENT PATTERN – A general series of anatomical movements that have common elements of spatial configuration, such as segmental movements occurring in the same plane of motion.

POWER – The product of an applied force times the velocity with which it is applied.

Golf application: Research has shown that maximum muscle power is produced when muscle moves at 30% of its maximum speed or velocity.

At maximum force there is no velocity. At maximum velocity there is no force. Power is created at one third of its velocity.

When golf instruction lets learners become aware of tempo, timing, constant rate of rotation, smooth rhythm, it is heading in the right direction. But, when golf instruction tells golfers to fire their muscles as fast as they can, it is not.

POSTURE – A neuromechanical state that concerns the maintenance of equilibrium.

Golf application: The golf swing's first consideration is always balance (at address, during the swing, and its finish).

POTENTIAL ENERGY AND KINETIC ENERGY – An object possesses potential energy when it has had work done on it to counteract the effect of another force. Potential energy is the energy of position – kinetic energy is the energy of motion.

> **Golf application:** When a body or object (clubhead) is in a position to be lowered, it possesses potential energy. As the object descends it loses its potential energy and develops kinetic energy, the energy of motion.

POWER ABSORPTION – A system absorbs power when it does negative work.

POWER PRODUCTION – The flow of mechanical energy from the system to the surroundings. A system produces power when it performs positive work.

PRESSURE – The amount of force acting over a give area.

> **Golf application:** Pressure is the force a sound swing puts into the ball; the force a sound swing keeps on the shaft; the force a sound swing puts in tot he ground; the force a sound swing keeps on the right forefingers; the force a sound swing keeps on the left hand; the force a sound swing keeps on between the left arm and chest.

QUANTITATIVE – Describes the quantity or how much.

RADIUS OF GYRATION – A measure of the distribution of a body's or segment's mass about an axis of rotation.

> **Golf application:** I.e. The smaller the radius of gyration of the swing, the greater its acceleration and velocity. The bigger the angle between arms and shaft at address and through the swing, the smaller radius of gyration.

RANGE OF MOTION – The maximum displacement of mass about a joint that does not cause tissue damage.

RECRUITMENT – The process of motor-unit application.

REFLEX – A phase and state dependent input-output relationship in which the input is a sensory stimulus and the output a motor response.

RESTRICTIVE FORCE – A force that resists motion or change of shape. (Very important force in a golf swing.)

ROTARY MOTION – Motion that describes a circular path about an axis.

SHEAR FORCE - A side-to-side force (swaying).

SIMPLE JOINT SYSTEM – A biological model comprising five basic elements (rigid link, snovial joint, muscle, neuron, and sensory receptor) which are necessary for the performance of movement.

SKELETOMOTOR – The skeletal muscle fibers that exert the force associated with muscle activity.

SPEED – The magnitude of a body's displacement per unit of time without regard to direction.

> **Golf application:** By definition, speed has no regard for direction. Constant acceleration and velocity are more important to the sound swing than speed. By definition velocity has both speed and direction.

STABILITY – The ability of an articulation to absorb shock and withstand motion without injury to the joint; also, the resistance to disturbance of a body's equilibrium.

STATIC – A mechanical state in which the system is in equilibrium, stationary or moving at a constant velocity, the system is not accelerating.

STEERING – This is any attempt to hold the clubhead path and the clubface square to the target during release and or impact. There is no steering in a sound swing – in sound swings the clubhead is reacting to the Laws of Motion, especially momentum, gravity, and rotation.

STRENGTH – The magnitude of the torque exerted by a muscle (or group of muscles) in a single, maximal, isometric contraction of unrestricted duration. The ability of a muscle or group of muscles to exert force against a resistance.

SYSTEM – A body or group of bodies whose state of motion is being examined.

TECHNIQUE – A particular type, or variation, of the performance of the same skill.

TENSILE FORCE – A pulling force. (I.e. At the start of the downswing)

TERMINAL VELOCITY- The speed of an object under free-fall conditions when the weight and air-resistance vectors have equal magnitudes.

THREE-BURST PATTERN – Sequence of agonist-antagonist muscle activity that is associated with an indirect movement to a target.

TORQUE – A turning or rotary force; the product of a force and the perpendicular distance from the line of action of the force to the axis of rotation.

> **Golf application:** Sound swings create torque, retain torque, and use torque.

TRANSDUCTION – A process by which energy is converted from one form to another.

TRIPARTITE MODEL – A three-compartment model of the neuromuscular process associated with movement. The compartments include the high-level controller, the low-level controller and muscle, and the peripheral receptors.

VECTOR – A quantity having both magnitude and direction.

> **Golf application:** The sound swing gives the club magnitude and direction, or a vector.

VELOCITY – The speed and direction of a body.

> **Golf application:** the sound swing give the clubhead direction – or velocity.

VOLUME – The three-dimensional space occupied by a body (length, width, and height).

> **Golf application:** The sound swing stays in three-dimensional balance. The space an object occupies (golf ball or balloon).

WEIGHT – An expression of the amount of gravitational attraction between an object and earth.

Some Afterthoughts

When it comes to improving ones golf, it's science and true play that can guide any golfer in the direction of progress. If that was the first sentence in a golf book it may cause some golfers to stop reading, believing what was going to follow will be complicated and hard to understand. This should not be the case, but these golfers may be unfamiliar with the definitions of "science" and "true play."

Learning from experience, is one definition of science. Science is also defined as experimental investigation, or self-discovery. By definition, young children are doing science every day, as they interact with their environment. Young children could be called young scientists when they are engaged in true play. True play by definition is filled with imagination, creativity and is free from judgmental observations.

Golfers who want to experience long-term learning should rely on "science" and "true play," and avoid all the "how to" directions and criticism that well meaning friends and perceived experts have to offer.

There is a "stereotype" that many golfers have been putting on themselves for hundreds of years. This very common "stereotype" has golfers believing that they need someone else to tell them "how to," swing and play. These "stereotypes" are supported by the large volume of "how to" directions that have always been available.

In some ways, "how to" advice parallels the illegal drugs that are always available. Some people believe the only way their lives will work is by using illegal drugs. Some golfers believe the only way they will improve and be happy with their game is by following "how to" directions. Both drugs and "how to" are market driven. Illegal drugs keep coming into the United States because there is a market for them.

A market for "how to" directions exists, not because "how to" directions work, but because golfers believe and hope the will work. Believing someone else has the answer for improving our own swing and game is golf's first and biggest lie. "How to" advice givers are overlooking the long term value of doing science and true play, (i.e., self discovery experiences,) in favor of quick fix "how to" directions.

"How to" advice fragments new insights and problem solving skills that first hand personal experience offer golfers and long term learning has always required. It's a dangerous error to believe that the passive thinking act of following someone else's "how to" directions will accelerate learning golf. By its definition, the very act of "playing" golf requires imagination and creative thinking skills. By definition, learning and playing are founded on doing "science" and experiencing "true play".

We clearly must play to learn. We do not learn to play.

Golfers who experience long term skill acquisition 1) have improved their understanding of core golf knowledge, 2) gained more insights about Golf's 5 Physical basics, 3) and developed and use an approach to improving golf that has increased their learning potential and therefore improved their performance potential. Golfers need environments that support true play and science.

While modern technology may be improving the world we live in, some advances may be fragmenting learning and self-discovery skills. For example, when young children are said to be "playing" on their computers, this may not be true. Play is based on imagination and creative thinking skills. When young children are using computers, they are really being programmed, managed and told what to do, by what is on the computer screen (more often than not). Now if these children were writing and developing new and original programs for these computers, this would not be the case.

Often there is more memorization of information, than opportunities to put to use and improve creative thinking skills when 1. children sit in front of computers, and 2. golfers using "how to" directions.

Geography, Geometry, and Swing Plane Location

In my approach to helping golfers learn to improve, I point out everything in life has some common ground or is connected in some way. It's from this point of view I suggest reading the following.

Geography is a subject that all golfers were probably exposed to during their school years. In the spring 2001 issue of *The American Educator*, Walter A. McDougall, a professor at University of Pennsylvania wrote, "Why Geography Matters." This article could easily have been entitled "Why Swing Plane Matters" because of all the parallels to how important the location of force is during golf swings, that were in the article.

Professor McDougall said he is disheartened that so many Americans emerge from their schooling illiterate in geography. "People overlook geography is fundamental to the process of a true education. Geography serves as a springboard to virtually every other subject in the humanities and sciences." Many golfers and their sources of advice also overlook a "subject" that is fundamental to long-term learning in golf, *i.e.* the shape (plane or geometry) of a golf swing through impact.

Swing shape matters. Understanding the shape of your swing is an insight that also serves as a springboard for learning to solve any problems that the shot at hand may present. The heart and soul of every golf swing is the location of its plane (swing shape) through impact.

In 1997 the National Research Council reported, "The central tenet of geography is that location matters, and this helps us understand a wide variety of phenomenon and process." This statement reveals the universal insight that we need some knowledge to gain more knowledge. Golfers know a fundamental truth that leads to progress when they learn the required location of a golf club's shaft, face, and head, that the lay of the land requires (geography),

"You can not argue with geography. Geography concerns itself with the way things are, not the way we imagine or wish them to be and it is fundamental to any child's maturation." Professor McDougall "Geography does not argue, it simply is." Robert Strauss – Hype. Likewise, the location of force through impact, is either efficient or it is not, and golfers who want to make progress should know the difference. This fundamental truth leads to long-term learning and progress in golf.

Leaders in the field of education have many good reasons to feel geography is at the heart of a true education. Golfers likewise have many reasons to learn that the location of force through impact is at the heart of their golf education.

For example: as professor McDougall points out, the Mississippi River exists and while its name is a social convention, the river is real, and no student could claim to know American history without understanding the importance of the rivers location. It would also be difficult for a golfer to expect to make long-term progress without some insights into the shape (plane or geometry) of their own swing and the required location of force for the shot at hand.

The shape of the golf swing is not just a "point of view," it is grounded in reality. The plane or geometry of any efficient golf swing is a conventional and fundamental truth. We really cannot understand history without knowing how geography influenced history. Any hope of making long-term progress when learning golf must include the opportunity to learn about the application and location of force through impact.

Studying geography is learning about the lay of the land, doing maps and learning to get to specific locations. Learning and experiencing long-term progress in golf is also learning about location. i.e., The location of force through impact for the shot at hand. The shape (plane or geometry) of a golf swing matters.

Note: Geography is the study of locations and their relationships to each other. Geometry is the study of relationships and alignments. Swing Plane defines the location, alignment, and relationship of the clubs, shaft, head, and face through impact. As we said before, everything has some common ground and is connected in some way.

We Play to Learn

The following is worth reporting ,

If you have been trying to improve, and have not, the answer is, we must play to learn! This answer holds the reason for long-term progress.

Studies have found when we are engaged in "true play," the genes in the nervous systems are totally involved with gathering the kind of information that long-term learning is founded on. *Webster's Dictionary* defines *play* as "movement giving full play to one's imagination." During "true play," we are playing full out with our imagination, interacting with the environment. The greater the variations, the more opportunities there are to learn.

Studies also show we do not really learn motor skills, like typing, swinging, throwing, etc. However, the body can be conditioned to perform these and other motion patterns. Almost magically, motion patterns can go from being uncoordinated one day, to being acceptable motions the next day. "We get it!" But what is often overlooked is how "we got it," and why some people take so long to make progress.

During "true play," the genes in the nervous system are encoded with learning information about dynamic balance, timing, sequencing, touch, sight, the environment, eye-hand coordination, etc. Because our genes have the genius of being both learners and teachers, they can take all the information they have learned during "true play" that is personal in nature and condition the body to perform motion patterns.

During "true play," all actions, workable and unworkable, and the reactions to these actions are being encoded into our genes. (Unworkable motions are very valuable for learning.) During "true play," our genes have the opportunity to adapt to a variety of problem solving opportunities, which in turn improves one's ability to condition the body to perform different motion patterns. The skills and tools of adapting, not "how-to" directions, promote long-term learning.

When golfers use self-discovery (true play), with total freedom to investigate and interact with: 1. golf's environment, 2. golf's physical basics, and 3. the shot at hand, our genes are encoded with information that is personal in nature about timing, sequencing, dynamic balance, etc. for future use and long-term learning.

Secret: In the end, we must play (true play) to learn.

Studies indicate that "true play" can help one's progress. It also helps to recognize learning and conditioning are not the same. We can be conditioned to perform efficient motion patterns when we use the information that is gathered during "true play."

The culture that many golfers learn and play golf in is divided by high and low handicap golfers. This culture has golfers who have "gotten it," and golfers who "don't have it." In this culture of "got it" and "don't have it," golfers often attribute their unsuccessful learning experiences to their own perceived disabilities. Poor shots are tied to their belief that they are not "getting it." Within this culture, golfers define themselves in terms of their perceived limitations and this is unfortunate.

Rarely do golfers relate their lack of progress to "how" they have been trying to learn and assume that they are just not "getting it." I have found approaches to learning the game that use "true play" and self-discovery skills, while avoiding "how to" directions, always promote long-term progress. Keep in mind that we play golf not "golf swing," and when we are learning by experiencing "true play," we can gain long-term progress.

Golf Swing Secrets... and Lies,

To Be Continued...

"We never know what the future holds,
especially when it comes to what may be possible.

I know I will keep looking –
Best of luck pursuing your goals."

– Michael

COLOPHON

The preliminary design direction for GOLF SWING SECRETS...AND LIES SIX TIMELESS LESSONS began as a golf lesson. Upon learning of the project, I asked Michael if I could produce the book. The art of communication during this electronic age has made it possible to produce a book which reflects both the traditions of golf, as well as, a tool to better understand the learning process. The entire book was produced using a digital workflow. Prepress consisted of PostScript computer-to-plate technology.

CYBERCOLOR INC.
1-516-991-4678